Praise for *Sons and Soldiers*

"*Sons and Soldiers* tells the remarkable story of how 2,000 German-born Jews were able to get the crucial intelligence that saved American lives and helped win World War II. . . . The message of their courage and patriotism should not be lost in today's war on terrorism."
—Leon Panetta, former director of the CIA and former secretary of defense

"A gripping tale of how 2,000 Jews who fled Europe during the Nazi reign returned to that war-torn continent, determined to free their homelands from Third Reich tyranny and prevent further atrocities. It is a story of courage and determination, revenge and redemption, grippingly told in a fast-moving narrative. . . . A history with personality. . . . Opens a window into a much-ignored aspect of the war. . . . A magnificent story, one crying out to be told, and one that is told very well."
—*Boston Globe*

"An inspiring story. . . . Fans of Stephen Ambrose and World War II histories will enjoy this look into a little-known aspect of U.S. Army operations."
—*Library Journal*

"In a highly readable, often thrilling narrative, prolific nonfiction author Henderson focuses on the members of this elite, 2,000-man unit who escaped from Europe and by one means or another made it to the United States. . . . A gripping addition to the literature of the period and an overdue tribute to these unique Americans."
—*Kirkus Reviews* (starred review)

"The last great unknown tale of World War II. . . . Harrowing adventures of the Ritchie Boys."
—*New York Post*

"A mesmerizing account of how frightened boys grew into fearless young men . . . to fight Nazi barbarianism. Henderson delicately recalls heartbreaking farewells throughout Germany as unescorted children were sent to America and placed in the homes of distant relatives or foster families in order to escape Nazi persecution. . . . A fascinating look into how German-born Jews, serving as American soldiers, helped defeat an enemy that sought to annihilate their families and their religious ancestry from the face of the earth."
—*San Antonio Express-News*

"Bruce Henderson crafts an irresistable history of the World War II Jewish refugees who returned to Europe to fight the Nazis. . . . *Sons and Soldiers* kicks into high gear with the invasion of Europe, as many Ritchie Boys traveled with the 82nd Airborne and Patton's 3rd Army, questioning POWs in time to use the information for the next day's battle plans. They were in extreme jeopardy—if they were captured and the Germans discovered who they were or where they came from, they risked execution on the spot. Henderson tells their stories with clarity and detail."
—*Newsday*

"A revelatory work about a group of Jewish men whose World War II journeys are so implausible and heroic it's difficult to understand why so few of us knew about them before now. A book of fear, flight, and almost divine retribution."
—Steve Twomey, Pulitzer Prize–winning author of *Countdown to Pearl Harbor*

"Henderson is a wonderful storyteller who has written a never-before-told chapter of the Second World War. *Sons and Soldiers* is a must-read."
—Jewish Book Council

"An inspiring account of a little-known aspect of World War II. . . . Chronicles how, despite great personal risk if their Jewish identity was discovered, these soldiers were on the front lines in Europe, gathering crucial intelligence." —*Booklist*

"Henderson is a skilled storyteller. *Sons and Soldiers* records concrete acts of courage, commitment, compassion . . . and, of course, unspeakable cruelty." —*San Francisco Chronicle*

"A triumph! More than seventy years after World War II ended, historians scramble to unearth a fresh story. With *Sons and Soldiers,* Bruce Henderson has found one. This gripping account of German Jews who fled their nation only to return as members of an elite U.S. Army unit to help defeat the Nazis tugs at every emotion." —John Wukovits, author of *Tin Can Titans*

"Pays homage to [the Ritchie Boys'] achievements. . . . Henderson's narrative achieves a rare intimacy, putting readers in foxholes and interrogation rooms." —*Forward*

"An invaluable, must-read addition to the canon of important World War II books, about the thousands of European-born American soldiers whose own odysseys were ingrained in the twentieth century's two most significant narratives: the Holocaust and the Allied war against their families' oppressors in Nazi Germany."
—Steven Karras, author of *The Enemy I Knew:*
German Jews in the Allied Military in World War II

"Fascinating. . . . Extensively researched." —*Winnipeg Free Press*

"This is an extremely informative book on a little-known subject and is highly recommended." —*Journal of America's Military Past*

SONS AND SOLDIERS

SONS AND SOLDIERS

The Untold Story of the Jews Who Escaped the Nazis
and Returned with the U.S. Army to Fight Hitler

BRUCE HENDERSON

<parsWILLIAM MORROW

An Imprint of HarperCollins*Publishers*

HarperCollins books may be purchased for educational, business, or sales promotional use. For information please e-mail the Special Markets Department at SPsales@harpercollins.com.

A hardcover edition of this book was published in 2017 by William Morrow, an imprint of HarperCollins Publishers.

FIRST WILLIAM MORROW PAPERBACK EDITION PUBLISHED 2018.

Designed by Fritz Metsch

Library of Congress Cataloging-in-Publication Data has been applied for.

ISBN 978-0-06-241910-1

19 20 21 22   RS/LSC   10 9 8 7 6 5 4 3

For them all

Contents

———•———

Introduction

When Hitler came to power in Germany in 1933, he declared war on his country's half million Jewish citizens. They were stripped of their most basic rights. Judaism was defined as a race, not a religion, and Jews were excluded from German citizenship. Restrictive edicts put in place by the Nazis affected Jews of all ages and in all walks of life, and even Jewish children were forced out of public schools. A harsh reality for German Jews was the growing realization that neither they nor their children had a future in the country. This fear culminated in November 1938 with Kristallnacht, known as the "Night of Broken Glass," when Jewish homes, businesses, and synagogues were ransacked by Nazis. Nearly a hundred Jews were killed that night, and up to thirty thousand were arrested and sent to concentration camps, where hundreds of them died within weeks of their arrival. Though by then tens of thousands of German Jews had already immigrated to the United States, this was the final confirmation anyone required that Germany was no longer safe for Jews.

But departing meant leaving behind their ancestral home, relatives, friends, and life savings, and there was no guarantee they would be able to get past restrictive U.S. immigration quotas, and those in other countries, which made it difficult for more Jews to immigrate.

It was often impossible for an entire family to get out of Germany, and many faced an excruciating decision of splitting up, perhaps forever, when parents discovered they could get only one child, under age sixteen, to safety through the efforts of Jewish relief organizations in America and England. Who went and who stayed often meant the difference between life and death. By the time Germany went to war with the United States in 1941, the Nazis' determination to create an Aryan Germany had switched from a policy of forced Jewish emigration to one of mass annihilation of those Jews still in the country and the millions of other Jews trapped in Nazi-occupied territories, solving what Hitler called the "Jewish problem."

Many parents chose to send away their eldest sons so they might carry on the family name. Throughout Germany, there were heart-breaking farewells at railway stations and seaports where mothers and fathers said good-bye to their sons. Those German Jewish boys who arrived in America in the 1930s without their parents or siblings had to adapt to life in a new land on their own. Placed in the homes of distant relatives or foster families, they enrolled in public schools and immersed themselves in a language, culture, and world unfamiliar to them. But with the help of dedicated teachers and new friends, they quickly became Americanized, although still carrying the telltale accents from their homelands.

Yet they were served well by the Old World values instilled in them by their parents, emphasizing education and hard work. By the time the United States entered the war, these beloved sons who had been sent to America by their desperate families were stalwart young men who loved everything about U.S. democracy and freedom. They were also eager to return to Europe with the U.S. military to fight Hitler, not only out of patriotism for their new country, but their own personal vendetta as well. Unlike many other victims of the Nazis, the German Jewish refugees who became American soldiers had a means to help destroy the regime that had persecuted them and their families.

But there was a snag. When Germany declared war on the United States in December 1941, German citizens residing in America were automatically declared "enemy aliens." Even after Congress passed legislation allowing enemy aliens to be inducted into the army, some found themselves assigned to U.S. bases where they were mistrusted and their accents ridiculed by other GIs.

War planners in the Pentagon soon realized that the German Jews already in uniform knew the language, culture, and psychology of the enemy best and had the greatest motivation to defeat Hitler. By mid-1942, the army began molding them into a top secret, decisive force to help win the war in Europe. Over the next three years, thirty-one eight-week sessions were held at Camp Ritchie in Maryland, consisting of extensive classroom work and field training. The largest group of graduates was 1,985 German-born Jews trained to interrogate German POWs. They were fast-tracked for U.S. citizenship and sent overseas with all the frontline units fighting the Germans. The Ritchie Boys, as they came to be known, had no idea what they would find when they returned to Europe. Many still did not know what had happened to their families that had sent them away to safety in America.

Sons and Soldiers follows a group of Ritchie Boys from their boyhoods in Germany, to their escapes to America, to their return to Europe as U.S. soldiers to fight in a war that for them was intensely personal. They parachuted with the airborne forces on D-Day, landed at Omaha Beach, raced with Patton's tanks across occupied France, and fought in the Battle of the Bulge, Hitler's last desperate gamble to win the war. They then crossed into Germany with the Allied armies and were with the forces that entered the Nazi concentration camps, where they saw with their own eyes the horrors of the Holocaust. When the shooting finally ended, it was time for these sons to look for the families they had left behind.

To this day, the exploits and strategic importance of the Ritchie

Boys are little known. They took part in every major battle and campaign of the war in Europe, collecting valuable tactical intelligence about enemy strength, troop movements, and defensive positions as well as enemy morale. In the course of the war, tens of thousands of newly captured Third Reich soldiers were interrogated by teams of these German Jewish soldiers. A classified postwar report by the army found that nearly 60 percent of the credible intelligence gathered in Europe came from Ritchie Boys. Yet there has been no publication of their operations or a complete roster of these men made public. As members of Military Intelligence, they were warned not to reveal their branch of the service or their training or duties during the war, and similar restrictions applied postwar to any documents, reports, or notes they may have retained. They held no reunions and were disinclined to join veterans' organizations, as their German accents made them unwelcome in the usual circles of U.S. veterans. Their story is one of the last great untold sagas of World War II.

I am honored to tell the true story of these little-known heroes.

Bruce Henderson
Menlo Park, California

SONS AND SOLDIERS

Prologue

GERMANY 1938

Loud banging at the front door jolted Martin Selling out of a sound sleep. It was shortly before sunrise, November 10, 1938.

Martin lived in Lehrberg, in southeast Germany; he and his relatives were the only Jews living among the thousand other residents of this tranquil agricultural village. Over the course of the previous day, the Nazis had carried out a series of brutal, coordinated attacks against Jews across Germany. But Martin wasn't aware of that yet.

This widespread campaign of malevolence would forever become known as Kristallnacht, the "Night of Broken Glass," so called because of the mounds of glass shards from broken windows that littered the streets after thousands of synagogues and Jewish-owned homes, businesses, and hospitals were looted and destroyed. The violence began after a teenage boy in Paris fatally shot a German embassy official—an act of retaliation, as his parents had been expelled from Germany, along with thousands of other Polish Jewish immigrants. Using the shooting in Paris as a pretext for a long-planned roundup of Jews, Nazi storm troopers took to the streets on the night of November 9.

Twenty-year-old Martin had recently returned to Lehrberg, his childhood home, from Munich, where he had been working as a tailor. Munich was the city in which Hitler rose to power and the national headquarters of the Nazi Party. Martin had seen Hitler numerous times; when his motorcade sped through the streets, everyone on the sidewalks was expected to stand at attention and snap a stiff right arm in a "Heil Hitler" salute. If Martin heard the Führer's motorcade approaching, or even saw groups of marchers waving Nazi flags, he tried to be as inconspicuous as possible, slipping away or ducking into a side alley.

Earlier that year, Hitler had become aware that his motorcade regularly passed a large synagogue on its way to party headquarters. On the Führer's orders, the congregation was given less than a day to remove its books and valuables; a few days later, the site was a newly paved parking lot. Martin's boss, an older Jew, had finally seen enough. He fled to Italy, leaving Martin jobless and with no choice but to return home to Lehrberg.

The pounding on the front door did not stop but became louder and more menacing. By the time Martin reached the door it was in danger of being kicked in. He opened it to four storm troopers of the Sturmabteilung (SA), in matching brown shirts with red and black swastika armbands, who pushed him aside and rushed in, though at six foot two Martin towered over them.

Without giving a reason, the SA men searched the house—helping themselves to an expensive camera—then took Martin into custody along with his uncle, Julius Laub, who had been managing the family's textile store next door since his sister, Ida—Martin's widowed mother— passed away two years before. She had run the store following the death of Martin's father from a heart attack fifteen years earlier. The SA men also arrested the housekeeper, the only other resident in the house. At the same time, other SA men were picking up Martin's aunt Gitta and her three children, who lived nearby.

They were all driven five miles to an outdoor sports arena in the town of Ansbach, where they joined sixty other Jewish men, women, and children. The terrified group huddled in the bleachers for the rest of the icy night, shivering from fear and the chill of the blustery winds. Conversing softly with the others, Martin learned that the synagogue in Ansbach had been set ablaze, local Jewish homes vandalized, and Jewish men beaten. When Martin and some others asked the SA men what was going to happen next, they didn't seem to know. They had only been ordered to arrest all the local Jews.

The following afternoon, at about 3 P.M., the women and children, as well as men over the age of fifty-five, were released without explanation. Martin, his uncle, and about fifteen other men remained in custody. They were marched to the local prison, an old, primitive structure, and locked up in a single cell. There was no running water or toilet—only a metal "honey bucket"—and the food was primitive and scarce. After two days in these cramped quarters, they were sent to Nuremberg, thirty miles away.

The Nuremberg district prison was filled nearly to capacity. Several hundred Sudeten Germans, ethnic Germans from Czechoslovakia, had also been arrested after raising opposition to Germany's annexation of the Sudetenland, where three million ethnic Germans lived, two months earlier. The local Jews picked up during Kristallnacht—about a hundred in total from Nuremberg—were locked inside the prison gym, which had been furnished only with bare mattresses on the floor. Martin's group joined them.

Most of the guards were older men accustomed to dealing with hardened criminals, not political prisoners, and they seemed overwhelmed by the crowded conditions. They did their duty and nothing more, which meant the prisoners were largely left alone. An inmate crew brought food from the kitchen to distribute among the prisoners, and at one point everyone was allowed to take a shower in a communal washroom, which had a row of multiple showerheads. The prisoners were let out of the locked gym in small groups for an hour a day; they could pace circles in the prison yard only after it had been cleared of Aryan prisoners so they would avoid contact with the Jews.

Within a week, some of the Jewish prisoners were released, Martin's uncle among them. The decisions about who got out and who did not were utterly mysterious to Martin and everyone else. While some of the guards revealed that they had received the release orders from the local Gestapo, none of the feared secret police had shown up at the prison, and no prisoners had been questioned. By December 22—six weeks after Martin's arrest—nine of his original group remained. On that day, guards thundered down the corridor, announcing that they were being moved to the Dachau concentration camp.

Martin, who was now in his own cell, felt as if he had been kicked in the stomach. He knew about the existence of Dachau, as did most Germans, but it was spoken about only in ominous whispers. Opened in an old World War I munitions factory near Munich in March 1933, Dachau was the first concentration camp established by the Nazis after they came to power. Schutzstaffel (SS) leader Heinrich Himmler had announced in the newspapers that Dachau would be utilized to incarcerate those who "threaten the security of the state." During its first year, the camp held nearly five thousand prisoners, primarily German communists, Social Democrats, trade unionists, and other political opponents of the Nazis.

But Martin had a very personal history with Dachau, too. In April 1933, his cousin, a lawyer in Munich, had been arrested and sent there. He died in Dachau three months later. Based on the grim stories he had heard, Martin considered the move to Dachau to be his own death sentence.

The locks on the cells of the Dachau-bound prisoners were rapidly keyed open and the doors swung ajar by guards. Frantic to write a farewell note to his twin brother, Leopold, who lived with an aunt elsewhere in Germany, and to his uncle Julius, Martin scribbled on a scrap of paper. When he stepped into the corridor and passed the cell of a prisoner he had gotten to know, Martin pushed his folded-up note through the bars.

At the Nuremberg train station, Martin and the eight other men brought in from Ansbach were loaded into a modern passenger train car, where they remained under guard for the hundred-mile ride to the Dachau depot. Upon arrival, their car alone was shunted to a sidetrack. The first thing Martin saw was SS troops in black uniforms with red swastikas, carrying rifles with fixed bayonets, surrounding them on all sides.

The SS pushed the prisoners off the train and down the platform, then herded them past some administrative buildings, the guards' barracks, and an outside shooting range, where the SS practiced their marksmanship. Martin would soon learn that it doubled as an execution site. A heavy iron gate opened onto the prisoners' fenced compound, above which was a metal sign that read, ARBEIT MACHT FREI, "Work will make you free."

Electrified barbed wire enclosed the rectangular compound— about three hundred by six hundred yards—on all sides. Tall gun towers rose up at strategic locations. Inside the compound was an infirmary, a laundry, workshops in which inmates produced goods ranging from bread to furniture, and a main yard for roll calls and other assemblies.

The inmates lived in ten single-story barracks made of brick and concrete; each had been built to house 270 prisoners and was subdivided into five rooms designed to hold fifty-four men apiece. The men in each room were referred to, in military fashion, as a platoon. Every room had thin wooden bunks covered with straw and an attached washroom with a few sinks and flush toilets.

When Martin and his group arrived, the guards pushed them into a large room and made them strip off their clothing. After their heads were completely shorn, they were ordered into a cold shower and herded naked into another room, where a camp doctor did a quick examination. They were then given lightweight, blue-and-white-striped uniforms to put on. Some of the men had arrived clutching the small bags they had been allowed to take from home when they were arrested. Now they had to leave the bags, and the only personal items they could take with them were whatever toiletries they could carry.

In prison in Nuremberg, Martin had become friendly with a man named Ernst Dingfelder, who was deeply religious. Now Ernst whispered to Martin that he wanted to keep his *Tallit,* or Jewish prayer shawl. Martin couldn't believe his ears; it struck him as crazy to try to sneak a Jewish prayer shawl into a Nazi concentration camp. He argued back and forth with Ernst, telling him that if the guards found the shawl, they would likely wrap him in it before shooting him. At last, Martin convinced Ernst to leave it behind.

Each prison uniform at Dachau had a number above the right breast. Martin's was 31889. He soon realized that, according to Dachau's numbering system, he was the 31,889th inmate since the camp's opening. What he did not know was that he was also one of more than ten thousand Jews who had entered the concentration camp in the weeks since Kristallnacht.

It was midnight when Martin's group reached block 8, room 4. Crammed into the unheated space were two hundred prisoners, four times more than the space was built to hold. To make room, the built-in bunks had been replaced with two levels of six-foot-deep wooden shelving, one at ground level, the other about four feet off the floor. A thin layer of straw crawling with lice and fleas covered each one. Without room to turn over, the men slept body to body, their heads against the wall. Despite the freezing temperature, many spent the night uncovered, as there weren't enough blankets to go around.

Exhausted after little sleep, at five o'clock the next morning Martin stood for his first roll call. When this was complete, he and the others were led back inside and given watery ersatz coffee and bug-infested porridge. Dachau was a labor camp, but with the rapid influx of so many new prisoners, the officers in charge had not yet been able to schedule them all for forced-labor duties, which consisted of digging in gravel pits, repairing roads, and draining marshes, all under the watchful eyes of the guards. Instead, Martin and the rest of his group spent the day milling around in the main yard, clapping their hands and stamping their feet to keep them from freezing.

That night, dinner was a stew that resembled swill fed to pigs. Whatever meat was in it looked to Martin like chitterlings and other unidentified organs. Every third day, pairs of men shared a small loaf of bread; unfortunately, this wasn't that day. Ernst, Martin's friend, recoiled at the sight of the nonkosher meat and refused to touch the mysterious stew. Thereafter, Martin tried to help him stay kosher by trading his bread for Ernst's stew. In the face of the indignities and deprivation of the Nazi concentration camp, Martin was determined to persevere, and in the process stay true to his principles and commitments. Helping a friend in need was one of them.

Martin saw right away that the prisoners who had been in Dachau longer—months, even years before he arrived—were dulled mentally and weakened physically by the daily grind and the brutal treatment they received at the hands of the guards. Beatings were commonplace, and many prisoners had lingering injuries and bad bruises. Others were feverish and sick. Most were afraid to seek treatment at the infirmary; not only was the medical care deplorable, but anyone reported as being sick was labeled a malingerer and could be subjected to punishment—most commonly solitary confinement for long periods of time or twenty-five strokes across the back with a whip that cut into the flesh. But the list of offenses for which prisoners received savage penalties at Dachau was long. An escape attempt meant death, warned a notice posted in the courtyard, as did "sabotage, mutiny or agitation." Anyone who attacked a guard, "refused obedience," or declined to work at assigned labor was to be "shot dead on the spot as a mutineer or subsequently hanged."

Prisoners particularly dreaded Saturday afternoon inspections. Beforehand, the stubble on the men's heads was trimmed to the skin. Room 4 had two dull hair clippers for two hundred men, with their dull blades, the clippers pulled out clumps of hair. Aluminum food bowls were inspected. The bowls had to be spotless, even though there was no soap and the men were prohibited from scrubbing with anything abrasive. Beatings were given out when guards found specks of food or scratches on the bowls.

When Martin failed one inspection, he had to stand at attention, motionless, while a leather-gloved guard repeatedly slapped his face. Martin had seen others similarly punished. The more they flinched, the longer the beatings lasted. With incredible determination not to show fear, he kept his reflexes under control and did not recoil from the blows. The guard gave up and moved on. It was a test of grit and resolve that Martin did not forget.

The cruelty of the SS was unlike anything Martin had imagined men could be capable of inflicting. He suspected that guard duty at Dachau was not a choice assignment, and that many of them were ordered there to be trained in brutality for duties in other camps and newly conquered territories. Dachau's was a hierarchy of violence: the young soldiers were subject to such harsh treatment by their leaders that they were quick to vent their pent-up anger on the inmates. The process reminded Martin of training attack dogs.

One evening at roll call, the camp commandant announced that a prisoner had escaped. As punishment, all inmates would be held at attention in the main yard until the escapee was caught and returned. The long hours of the night crawled by, and it was bitterly cold under the bright spotlights. When the guard shifts changed, the men standing in the assembly area heard the clicking of machine guns in the gun towers—the loaded weapons were being checked.

Martin stood at the end of one row of prisoners. After midnight, exhausted and nearly frozen, he began to drift off to sleep on his feet. He must have swayed, though he was still standing when a rifle butt struck him in midback with painful force. He struggled to keep his balance and not fall.

In the morning, the assembly area was littered with men who had collapsed during the night—as far as Martin could tell, all were dead.

The other prisoners were taken away briefly for food and water, then returned to the parade ground. The bodies had been removed.

Everyone remained standing until four that afternoon, when the escapee was returned to camp. Whisked out of sight, he was never seen again.

The man's death would not have been easy, Martin knew. A favorite torture technique at Dachau had its roots in the medieval Inquisition: a victim was placed underneath a gallowslike structure, hands shackled behind his back, and pulled into the air by ropes attached to his wrists. Weights were added to the victim as he swung to inflict more intense pain on his arms and shoulders. Martin knew of men who had dangled helplessly for up to an hour as punishment for some real or imagined infraction. Most ended up with dislocated or broken bones and joints; some were permanently crippled.

Despite the horror of the consequences, there continued to be escape attempts by desperate men, but they seldom resulted in freedom. Some inmates chose another type of escape. A man would run toward the fence, attracting a hail of bullets from the gun towers. If he made it all the way, he would throw himself against the wire to be electrocuted. The SS guards usually made the quick kill, but not always. One prisoner, shot before reaching the fence, was left on the ground to writhe. His cries lasted all night.

On nights like that, with moans and shrieks sounding in the air and the constant cold biting at his body, Martin did more thinking than sleeping.

The big question was always: Why? As an avid reader with an interest in history—he had hoped to go to college, but when he turned sixteen in 1934, he was told he had received all the schooling to which a Jew was entitled in Germany—he knew about medieval Europe and the Inquisition. What difference was there between the suffering of men four centuries ago—*ad majorem Dei gloriam* (for the greater glory of God)—and what the Nazis were doing now? Suffering was still suffering. And if there was supposedly only one God, whose was it?

Some inmates at Dachau, like Ernst Dingfelder, were devoutly religious when they arrived. Others became more religious the longer they stayed. And then there were those who found they could no longer believe in God—*any* God—because of what was taking place. Martin identified with this group. He would, he decided, observe and participate in the traditions and ceremonies he had grown up with, out of a desire to acknowledge his Jewish heritage. But for the rest of his life, he knew, he would just be going through the motions. The horrors of Dachau had destroyed his belief in God.

Prisoners were allowed to write one letter a week, though with Nazi censors reading all outgoing mail, there was little they could say. Martin could not describe the effects of the starvation diet and all the weight he had lost, or the painful, open frostbite sores on his feet that made walking a torment. If the inmates failed to say everything was fine, their letters would not be mailed. Since his letters were the only documentation his family had that he was still alive, Martin wrote dutifully each week. Under the sender's name was the line: "Concentration Camp Dachau." The return address included the words *Schutzhaft-Jude,* or "Jew in Protective Custody."

On January 1, 1939, Martin turned twenty-one. As he was now of legal age, Uncle Julius was no longer his guardian or trustee of the home his mother had left Martin. How camp officials discovered these facts he never knew, but shortly after his birthday, Martin was summoned to an administrative office and shown a document mostly covered by a blotter. He was told not to attempt to read the paper—only to sign it.

"Was ist das?" he dared to ask.

"Sie haben drei Sekunden." He had three seconds to sign. *"Sonst."* Or else.

He signed, and the paper was taken away. Only then was he told that he had signed a power of attorney allowing his mother's house to be sold.

Martin Selling knew then that he would not be going home.

PART ONE

———◆———

Give me your tired, your poor,
Your huddled masses yearning to breathe free,
The wretched refuse of your teeming shore.
Send these, the homeless, tempest-tost, to me,
I lift my lamp beside the golden door!

—STATUE OF LIBERTY INSCRIPTION
by nineteenth-century Jewish poet Emma Lazarus

1

SAVING THE CHILDREN

For nearly twelve years, Günther Stern had the best of childhoods.

He spent those idyllic days in Hildesheim, one of the oldest and most picturesque towns in northern Germany, built along the windswept banks of the Innerste River and surrounded by rolling hills dotted with farms, dairies, and grazing livestock. The town's cobblestone streets were lined by centuries-old, spire-topped buildings and churches.

Reaching skyward as it climbed up the sides of the Hildesheim Cathedral's apse was a thirty-five-foot dog rose reputed to be the world's oldest living rosebush. It was nearly the same age as the town, which is how it got its name: Tausendjähriger Rosenstock ("Thousand-Year Rose"). According to local legend, as the pink-blossomed rose flourished, so did the town.

Since its earliest days, Hildesheim had been the seat of a Roman Catholic archbishop, and for centuries the majority of its residents were Catholic. After the Reformation, which had its roots in Germany, many Catholics turned Protestant (mostly Lutheran), and by the 1930s, Hildesheim's sixty-five thousand inhabitants were divided between the two major Christian religions. There were fewer

than a thousand Jews in the town, which mirrored their representa-
tion nationally. A June 1933 census found less than one percent of
Germany's population was Jewish: roughly a half million Jews out
of 67 million people.

When Jews settled in Hildesheim early in the seventeenth century, they built half-timbered houses with ornate wood-carved
façades. The town's Moorish-style synagogue was built on Lappenberg Street in 1849, an area that became one of Hildesheim's most
scenic neighborhoods.

Günther was a bright and inquisitive boy. He had his mother's
sunny disposition, his father's intelligent eyes, and unruly ears that
refused to lay flat. Born in 1922, he made his first visit to synagogue
at age six, when his parents took him for services on a High Holiday.
For once, the boy hadn't complained about being dressed in his best
clothes. His mother had told him how important it was to make a
good first impression on the Lord. They walked with other families to the synagogue, all dressed in their finest. Smiling passersby
stepped aside, nodding to the Jewish procession as it passed, the
men lifting their top hats in greeting, again and again.

Günther, the eldest child of Julius and Hedwig Stern, was four
years older than his brother, Werner, and twelve years older than
his sister, Eleonore. The family was solidly middle class, as were
most of Hildesheim's Jews. The Sterns lived in a rented apartment
abutting Günther's father's small fabric store, which was located on
the third floor of a well-maintained building near a bustling market-
place in the center of town. The apartment had high ceilings and
good light. Fine curtains draped the tall windows. Each room had
a wood-burning stove for heat, and the kitchen was outfitted with a
modern stove.

The two boys shared a room on one side of the apartment. Their
parents' bedroom, where their little sister also slept, was at the other
end. The bedrooms had hardwood floors; the carpeted living room
had a sofa, two upholstered chairs, and Julius's dark wood desk. The
formal dining room, with a pastoral landscape by the Austrian artist

Ferdinand Georg Waldmüller on the wall, was reserved for special occasions. Günther and his brother's favorite part of the house was a tile-floored vestibule that served as an indoor playground, complete with a Ping-Pong table that they put to regular use.

Günther's father was a slight man known for his boundless energy. Julius Stern worked six-and-a-half-day weeks, taking off only Saturday mornings to attend synagogue, where the sermon was in German and the service in Hebrew. He showed fabric samples and took orders in his store and on trips to outlying villages, where he called on customers who made their own clothing. The only ready-to-wear clothes he sold were men's gabardine overcoats. His wife, Hedwig (née Silberberg), did his typing and billing. A raven-haired woman with dark, soulful eyes, Hedwig had a gift for writing witty limericks featuring relatives and friends.

Günther began his education in a one-room Jewish school. His teacher met the challenge of keeping students of varying ages and grade levels interested and engaged throughout the school day. None of it was lost on Günther, and he blossomed as a serious reader and an excellent student. Günther also enjoyed attending a Saturday afternoon youth group conducted by the synagogue's charismatic young cantor, Josef Cysner, who led lively discussions about Jewish books and culture.

As was customary, Günther entered Andreas-Oberrealschule at age ten, in 1932. He was one of three Jews among his incoming class of twenty students. Even before starting school, Günther had had many non-Jewish friends; in Hildesheim at the time, young gentiles and Jews easily assimilated. They visited one another's homes, attended the same parties, bicycled and swam together, and played soccer in the same athletic clubs.

But in 1933, the Nazis came into power, and they immediately started passing restrictive new laws targeting Jews. Hitler pledged to transform the nation: "Give me ten years," he promised prophetically that year, "and you won't recognize Germany."

On April 1, 1933, two months after Hitler became chancellor, the government called for a twenty-four-hour nationwide boycott of Jewish-owned businesses. Storm troopers stood in front of stores, denouncing the proprietors and blocking the entrances. *Jude* was smeared on store windows; stars of David were painted across doorways. Local boycotts of Jewish businesses spread throughout Germany. Nazis marched through the streets, shouting anti-Jewish slurs; oftentimes these processions were accompanied by arrests, beatings, and extensive property damage.

Like many Jewish proprietors, Julius gradually lost most of his non-Jewish customers. They were afraid to be seen coming and going from his store; when he went to call on them at their homes, he was greeted by signs that read: JUDEN IST DER EINTRITT VERBOTEN. (Jews are forbidden entry.)

At the time, Günther, though an inveterate newspaper reader, had only a partial understanding of what was taking place in Germany. But he noticed when his friends became slow to greet him and then stopped speaking to him altogether. He found himself being invited to fewer birthday parties, and he was soon banned—along with the other Jewish youth of Hildesheim—from swimming at the local pool and playing on his soccer team. Even his athletic club eventually kicked him out; though he had accumulated enough participation points to earn a medal, he was not awarded it. These were formative years for Günther, and it hurt him deeply to realize he had become an outcast among his peers. The rupture in his young life was unexpected and wrenching.

At school, many of the teachers were replaced by newer instructors, from Berlin and elsewhere, who wore swastika pins and espoused Nazi propaganda. While a few of the older teachers showed empathy toward their Jewish students, they had to be careful for fear of being reported and losing their jobs.

For a time, Günther had a protector: Heinrich Hennis, a bright boy who was a year older and a head taller. More than once, Heinrich jumped between Günther and his tormentors. But all the non-Jewish boys were required to join a Nazi youth organization, and

Heinrich was no exception. His leader singled him out for special indoctrination, perhaps because word had gotten around that he was protecting Jews. Eventually, Heinrich also stopped speaking to Günther. Soon, Nazi slogans spouted from the lips of this former friend.

Choir had always been one of Günther's favorite classes. A few years earlier, his parents had taken him to the world-famous Hanover opera house for a performance of Wagner's *Lohengrin*. Ever since, he'd enjoyed music and choral singing. But one afternoon after the Nazis came to power, the choir teacher had the students rise to sing *"Deutsche Jugend heraus!"* Written a few years after Germany's defeat in World War I, the song's lyrics were violent and provoking: "German youth, gather! Slay our enemy in his own backyard, down him in earnest encounters." Embraced by Hitler Youth organizations for its rousing nationalism, the song had been included in a 1933 songbook released by a pro-Nazi publisher.

It was Günther's old friend, Heinrich Hennis, who indignantly shouted to the teacher: "How can you let Jews sing a song about German youth?"

The choir teacher stopped and said apologetically, "Our Jewish students will sit this one out." Günther and the two other Jewish students sat down and remained silent as the class sang. Mortified and angered at the same time, Günther realized the Nazis had found a way to take even music from him.

Throughout 1933, Günther watched as German and European history was literally rewritten. One day, his history teacher came into the classroom and passed out single-edge razor blades. "Take out your textbooks," he ordered the class, and he began writing page numbers on the blackboard. The students were to cut out the listed pages from their books and replace them with new pages. "Be sure to leave enough room on the margins," he added helpfully, "so you can paste the new pages into the book."

Excited murmurs rose up at this unusual assignment. When a razor blade reached Günther, he did as instructed. A few pages into the cutting, he began to read the passages, and realized with a jolt that the pages being taken out of the books all dealt with major accomplishments by Jews.

As the non-Jewish students were subjected to more and more anti-Semitic propaganda, at school and at home, they became increasingly hateful and aggressive toward their Jewish classmates. One day after school, Günther was cornered and beaten up by five boys from his school who took turns striking him as the others held him down. He limped home, bruised and battered physically as well as emotionally.

Nor was his family spared such violence. One night, his father worked late, and he took some letters to a mailbox a block away. On his way home in the dark, he was jumped by several men spewing anti-Semitic curses. They hit and kicked him. A sympathetic policeman passing by found Julius crumpled on the ground and took him to a hospital for first aid. When Günther saw his father the next morning, his father's face was covered with cuts and bruises.

As the violence and hatred mounted around them, Julius and Hedwig Stern decided it was time to get the family out of Germany. They began writing to Jewish organizations, seeking information about emigrating to America.

A serious impediment for the Sterns and other Jews wanting to leave Germany was a new law passed by the Nazis, which restricted the transfer of cash, bonds, or other assets out of the country. Previously, Germans had been permitted to take out up to the equivalent of ten thousand dollars, but the Nazis reduced this amount, initially to four thousand dollars. As their campaign to plunder Jewish property and assets expanded, the amount was reduced further still, to ten Reichsmarks, which was then worth about four U.S. dollars. The criminal penalties for exceeding this amount were stiff, including imprisonment and forfeiture of property.

At the same time, the U.S. State Department was diligently following a special order, issued by President Herbert Hoover in 1930, that required visa applicants to show they would not become public charges at any time, even long after their arrival. If they lacked the immediate means to support themselves, an affidavit was required from someone in America guaranteeing they would not end up on the public dole. The public-charge mandate and the various machinations one had to go through to prove financial independence—something not required of earlier immigrants to America's shores—reduced the number of aliens admitted from 241,700 in 1930 to just 35,576 in 1932, and became a major impediment to anyone wanting to immigrate to the United States.

Desperate to escape from the Nazis, the Sterns wrote to Hedwig's older brother, Benno Silberberg, who had moved to America in the 1920s and become a baker in St. Louis. Would he sign an affidavit for the family to come to America? they asked. It was not clear that Benno would be able to help them, but he was their only relative in America.

By spring 1937, school had become so fraught with anguish, anxiety, and actual danger that Günther's mother and father pulled him out of all his classes. Instead, they hired a tutor to improve his English for their planned move to America. Those easy, bright years of Günther's in German schools—from the one-room Jewish school where his curiosity was first awakened to the courses, choir, and sports he enjoyed in the public high school—were over. In their place? The sixty-year-old tutor, a graying, stooped, emaciated-looking gentile named Herr Tittel. Beginnning in the mid-1920s, he'd worked as a teacher at a Brooklyn orphanage. But after eleven years, he grew homesick and returned to his hometown of Hildesheim, where he eked out a living teaching English, mostly to Jews hoping to emigrate.

Günther grew to like Herr Tittel, who told him colorful stories about America during their weekly lessons. While living in the U.S., Herr Tittel had become a fan of professional baseball, and he wove grand narrative descriptions for the young Günther, extolling Grover Cleveland Alexander's masterful pitching and Babe Ruth's epic home runs. Herr Tittel was easygoing and somewhat eccentric, and would frequently start humming popular American tunes in the middle of lessons. Within a few months, Günther had learned more conversational English—albeit in peculiar German-accented Brooklynese—than he had in three years with his high school teacher.

That summer, Günther's parents gave him permission to join three friends from his Jewish youth group on a monthlong bicycle trip to the Rhine, a six-hundred-mile round trip. His parents, certain the family would soon be leaving Germany, thought this might be their older son's last chance to explore the geography of his ancestral country. Once they left Nazi Germany, Hedwig and Julius agreed, none of them would ever want to return.

The boys asked their youth leader to write a letter vouching for their character and wrote to Jewish community leaders in towns along their planned route to find places to spend the night. For most of the trip, families put them up, though in one town the best they could do was sleep on benches in the dressing room of the local Jewish soccer team. All three boys were good bicyclists, and they covered twenty-five to thirty-five miles a day.

In a sleepy river town, they pedaled along the riverside, watching people in canoes and paddleboats enjoying a day on the water. A short distance away, they saw a different scene: a line of docked military boats with heavy guns mounted on their decks. Their steel hulls shone, glinting in the sun; they looked newly built and ominous. Each vessel flew a Nazi battle flag with a swastika. These were unlike any boats the boys had ever seen. It was clear to them now: under Hitler, Germany was getting ready for war.

Günther had been home only a few hours when his parents called him into the formal dining room for a talk. The family never used this room unless they had company, so Günther knew this conversation was serious.

They had heard from Uncle Benno, Julius told his son. He explained to Günther that America was deep in a Depression, which meant that millions of people were out of work. The U.S. government required an affidavit of financial support for immigrants such as themselves, who had to leave their country with no money. But Uncle Benno had lost his full-time job and was picking up only part-time work, which meant he didn't have the resources necessary to sign an affidavit for an immigrating family of five.

Günther's father spread out a serious-looking document, several pages in length, on the table.

All this time, his mother had remained silent. Now at last she spoke up, her voice low and solemn. "Uncle Benno's affidavit has come through for you alone," she said, explaining that Günther would live with Uncle Benno and Aunt Ethel in St. Louis until the rest of the family could join him. "You have an appointment at the American consulate in Hamburg in a few weeks," she added softly.

"*Mutti,* I am going alone to America?" asked a shocked Günther. He could not believe what he was hearing.

"*Ja,* Günther."

Since Uncle Benno had been able to provide an affidavit for only one person, she explained, it had to be Günther. Neither she nor his father would go without the other; at nearly sixteen, Günther was the oldest of the children. They would keep trying to find a sponsor for the rest of the family and hoped to all reunite in America soon.

It was obvious to Günther that his mother was struggling with this decision as much as he was. He had never pictured this day, and she had never fathomed sending her teenage son away to a foreign country alone.

Perhaps once he got settled in the United States, she suggested, Günther could find someone there to help them. She said this was a serious, grown-up assignment to give him, but she and his father believed he was mature enough to handle it. Most important to her and his father, his mother said, was that Günther would be safe in America.

His father, always the practical businessman, began to describe the logistics of Günther's trip to Hamburg, one hundred miles north of Hildesheim. He had already worked out a ride for him with a Jewish family who had an appointment at the consulate the day before Günther's. After what would be the longest automobile ride of his life, Günther would spend the night at a students' pension, then return home the next day with the local family.

Günther's father had contacted a Jewish organization in Hanover, which was helping plan his emigration. An affiliated group based in New York, German Jewish Children's Aid, was taking small groups of Jewish children out of Nazi Germany. Günther would be joining one of these groups. The organization would pay for his ocean passage, provide a chaperon, and make sure he reached his aunt and uncle in St. Louis safely. The group had already sent a social worker to interview Benno and Ethel Silberberg; the social worker, according to her report, had found them to be "kindly, wholesome people" eager to welcome their nephew into their home.

The prospect of leaving without his parents, his brother, and his little sister saddened Günther deeply. Other than visits to his grandparents and his bicycling trip, he had never been away from home for any length of time. Going to America was an opportunity to leave behind the upheaval, suppression, and violence consuming Germany, and visions from Herr Tittel's colorful stories about America—the land of the free, of baseball and Hollywood movies and pizza!—danced in his mind. Yet, even as he began to dream of these things for himself, Günther was apprehensive about leaving the rest of his family behind. How and when would they reunite?

In early October 1937, Günther stood before a U.S. official who, unbeknownst to the youth, held his future if not his life in his bearlike hands. Vice Consul General Malcolm C. Burke, an impressive, barrel-chested man of fifty, had been in charge of administering immigration laws and regulations in Hamburg since 1924. Günther was lucky that his visa application had been assigned to Burke. Many other U.S. consuls, quick to find sworn affidavits inadequate, routinely denied visa requests. For example, in 1933, seventy-four German refugees had applied to the U.S. consulate in Rotterdam, but only sixteen visas were granted. All but one of the fifty-eight refusals were based

primarily on the grounds that the would-be immigrants were likely
to become public charges.

For a long time, Burke had been an outspoken critic of inconsis-
tent interpretations of U.S. immigration law. Beyond that, he was a
strong believer in having the resources of the friends and relatives
who signed the affidavits investigated in the United States, at the
place where their assets were located and their income earned,
rather than by overseas officials making arbitrary judgment calls.
Günther had another advantage in being assigned to Burke: unlike
some of his less compassionate, even anti-Semitic colleagues in the
U.S. State Department at home and abroad, Burke recognized that
Jews were being persecuted by the Nazis and was willing to look for
loopholes in the laws and regulations that would allow them to enter
America.

Burke had in front of him Günther's paperwork, including the
affidavit signed by Benno Silverberg. The bank balance on the document had been swelled by short-term loans from coworkers and
friends, whom Benno had repaid a week after receiving his bank
statement. Burke had enough experience reviewing affidavits and
financial statements to know when they'd been fudged, but if he
harbored any suspicions about the St. Louis baker's sizable bank
balance, he did not raise them officially or voice them to Günther.
He asked the boy, in German, for his full name, date of birth, and
years of schooling. Then, inexplicably, he asked, "What is the sum
of forty-eight plus fifty-two?"

"*Einhundert*," Günther responded.

With that simple bit of mathematics, the consul stamped and
signed Günther's *Jugendausweis* (youth card). Günther Stern had
been accepted by the U.S. State Department for entry into America.

Now that he had an approved visa, things moved quickly. Within
a couple of weeks, the Sterns received word from the Jewish organization that they had a group of children leaving Germany on a ship
to the United States in November, and that Günther could join
them.

In late October, Günther's friends gathered in the Sterns' apartment for a boisterous farewell party. The event added to his growing excitement—and yet, the whispers of fear remained. Not a single non-Jew attended, not even Günther's longtime classmate and one of his few remaining non-Jewish friends, Gerhard Ebeling. This fact did not escape Günther's attention.

Gerhard, a gentile, couldn't openly criticize the mistreatment of his Jewish classmates by pro-Nazi teachers and students. However, he would occasionally say something quietly to Günther about staying strong during these difficult times. Further complicating matters, Gerhard's father was a customs official, the type of government job generally reserved in those days for Nazi Party members.

Customs officer Ebeling did something unusual the week before Günther was to depart, however. At that time, anyone preparing to leave the country had to show up in advance at the customs house to have his or her baggage inspected and sealed. Now Herr Ebeling

Günther Stern's youth travel document, bearing two Third Reich stamps with swastikas, which he used to emigrate to America. *(Family photograph)*

telephoned Julius and offered to come to their apartment, saving the Sterns the labor of bringing in the heavy steamer trunk packed with clothes and family memorabilia Hedwig wanted to get out of Germany. That afternoon, Ebeling placed the official seal on the trunk without looking inside and wished Günther safe travels. In normal times, this would be a small gesture by a friendly official, but these were not normal times.

On October 27, 1937, Günther and his parents—Hedwig and Julius had arranged for someone to stay with the two younger children, both of whom cried brokenheartedly when Günther left—went to the Hildesheim railway station and boarded a northbound train for Bremerhaven. One of Germany's most vital ports, Bremerhaven had become a hub of emigration from Europe.

After a daylong train trip, the Sterns arrived in the late afternoon and checked into a boardinghouse. Early the next morning, Günther and his parents met at a designated spot on the pier with the other children, their parents, and the chaperon from the Jewish organization. Looming above them was the ocean liner that would take the children to America, the SS *Hamburg*, a steamship nearly seven hundred feet long that could make a speedy twenty knots at sea. They could clearly see the large German flag flying high above its bridge.

It was time to say good-bye. Günther's mother was weeping and dabbing her eyes with a hankie. They hugged and kissed. Determined not to feel helpless and hoping to make his mother a little less sad, Günther promised ardently to do everything he could to find someone in America to sponsor them. They *would* be reunited in America, he vowed, no matter what.

Hedwig nodded as she fought back more tears.

Günther turned to his father, who gave him a hug and a firm handshake. Throughout the Nazi years, Julius had hammered home the need for Günther to remain inconspicuous, to keep unwanted attention from being drawn to him. "You have to be like invisible ink," he had cautioned many times. "You will leave traces of your existence when, in better times, the invisible ink becomes visible again."

For several weeks, as his beloved son's date of departure drew closer, his concerned father had imparted such pieces of wisdom and a litany of instructions. Now, as he draped his arm over his son's shoulders and drew him close, he had a final word of advice. Speaking softly, so none of the others could overhear, he reminded his son that he would be on a German flagship. He would not leave Third Reich territory until he set foot in America.

The last words his father spoke to him were familiar ones.

"Remember, Günther, be like invisible ink."

Manfred Steinfeld was born in 1924, between two world wars, in the town of Josbach, located in the very heart of Germany. He would carry with him just two vivid memories of his father, Abraham, both from before he was five years old.

He remembered sitting next to his father, who wore a white robe over his clothes, and watching him as he prayed at synagogue on Yom Kippur.

And he remembered overhearing his father and his uncle Solomon discussing *der Krieg* (the war). At the time, the little boy didn't understand much of what they said. Years later, Manfred learned that they had been talking about World War I, and that the Steinfeld brothers had fought in a far-off place called Macedonia, where Solomon won the Iron Cross for battlefield bravery. And that their younger brother, Isador, had been killed in the Battle of Verdun in France in 1916; growing up, Manfred had often wondered about the uncle he never knew whose name was engraved on the town's stone war memorial.*

A short time later, Manfred lost his father. Abraham died of

---

* One in six German Jews, more than one hundred thousand in total, fought for their country in World War I, and twelve thousand of them died on the fields of battle on the western and eastern fronts.

pneumonia at age forty-four, leaving his wife, Paula, with their three children—Irma, six; Manfred, five; and Herbert, three. She took over her husband's dry goods store, which was the family's only means of support. They were already living in the house of her mother-in-law, Johanna Hanschen Steinfeld, who helped Paula take care of the children.

Josbach was a town of 419 residents, just sixty miles from Frankfurt, one of Germany's largest cities, but a world apart. Most of Josbach's citizens were subsistence farmers, working the land with plows pushed by hand or pulled by cows or oxen; few could afford horses for the task. No one had tractors or other farm machinery, and there was only one automobile in town. The wealth of a German farmer could be measured by the size of his manure pile, which was indicative not only of how much livestock he owned, but also of how much fertilizer he had available to spread on his fields.

There were only six Jewish families in Josbach: three Steinfelds, two Kattens (Paula's kin), and one Fain. Abraham's and Paula's ancestors had settled there in the early 1800s, and by the 1920s, the only retail business not Jewish owned was the tavern. In addition to the Steinfeld store, which sold shoes as well as material and ribbon for home dressmakers, there was a hardware store, a livestock trader, and a confectionery shop. The tradesmen—the town's carpenter, painter, shoemaker, and tailor—were all gentiles. This collection of businesses and trades provided the townsfolk with all of their basic needs.

Manfred's childhood home was located next to the town well, and it was the only house in Josbach with running water, thanks to Abraham's ingenuity: in the 1920s, Manfred's father had run a pipe the short distance from the water pump to their house. The first floor had a living room, kitchen, and two bedrooms, one of which Manfred shared with his grandmother. There was a third bedroom on the second floor. A root cellar was used to store potatoes, turnips, and other vegetables from the garden during the winter months. During the summer harvest, Paula canned fruits and vegetables, stocking the pantry. She went to the community bake house on Friday mornings, which by town tradition were reserved for the Jewish women to make challah and cakes for Shabbat.

For Manfred, the absence of his father was filled by his extended family of aunts, uncles, cousins, and especially his grandmother, with whom he was especially close. She loved helping him with his homework and was overjoyed the day he came home and announced he was the best student in his class and the first to know all his multiplication tables.

"The teacher says I'll probably be a finance minister when I grow up," Manfred reported.

Serious minded and hardworking at an age when many boys were not, Manfred seemed older than his years. He had a classically proportioned face, twice as long as it was wide, and symmetrical features, making him look mature for his age. A willing harvester of apples and plums for his mother's canning, he earned his first money picking and selling blueberries by the basket. He also made deliveries on his bicycle to his mother's customers in surrounding towns.

Education for the children of Josbach took place in a two-room schoolhouse, with grades one through four in one room and five through eight in the adjacent room. Out of seventy students, ten were Jews. There was only one teacher, who went back and forth between the two classrooms. Although Josbach had its own synagogue, they were one Jewish male shy of the minyan required to hold communal worship. Worshippers walked two or three miles to the synagogue in Halsdorf for weekly services instead. Occasionally, arrangements were made for a tenth man to come to Josbach from another town so local services could be held for bar mitzvahs and High Holidays.

When Manfred was nine, his grandmother became ill. After several days, a physician was summoned. Manfred waited anxiously with the rest of the family for the arrival of Dr. Heinrich Hesse from Rauschenberg, eight miles away. It had been snowing all day, and the doctor finally showed up in late afternoon. He examined Johanna and left some medication for her chest congestion. What Manfred would never forget about this day had to do with what the doctor told them as he was putting on his overcoat to leave.

The date was January 30, 1933. With a cheerful lilt in his voice, Dr. Hesse announced, "Something wonderful has happened today. Adolf Hitler has been made the new chancellor!"

The changes wrought by this news came more slowly to isolated hamlets like Josbach—in those days in Germany, there was a little village every few miles. But it was only a matter of time before the quiet, rural town felt the brunt of Nazism. Manfred's family first became aware of the anti-Semitic fervor sweeping the country during the twenty-four-hour boycott of Jewish businesses two months later on April 1, 1933. Even in neighborly Josbach, many customers observed the boycott and stayed away from the stores owned by Jews, although there were none of the demonstrations or outbreaks of violence that were so widespread in cities like Frankfurt and Berlin.

In November 1933, Germany held its first national election since Hitler had taken control of the government. All opposition parties had by then been banned, and voters were presented with a single slate of Nazi Party candidates. The voting was not by secret ballot, and in most locations, voters had to hand their ballots directly to party officials. Setting the tone for future elections during the Nazi era, voter intimidation was commonplace. Citizens were threatened with reprisals if they voted against Hitler, or even if they failed to vote. As a result, voter turnout was 95 percent, and the Nazi Party received nearly 40 million votes, some 92 percent of all those cast.

Manfred's uncle Solomon went to the polls proudly wearing the Iron Cross he had earned fighting for Germany in the last war. Like so many other Jewish war veterans, Solomon, who owned the Josbach hardware store, believed that he would be protected against Nazi persecution because he had fought for the Fatherland. Like most German Jews, Solomon considered himself a German first and a Jew second. This feeling of security and a desire not to be ostracized led Solomon Steinfeld to vote for the Nazi slate. He was not alone; other Jews in Josbach, including Grandma Johanna, voted for the Nazi candidates, if only to avoid being identified as "no" votes.

In Josbach, it was local custom for Jewish families to gather each week—usually on Fridays after dinner or on Saturdays after lunch—to discuss topics of interest to them and their community. Most children would run around and play instead of paying attention to the grown-ups, but Manfred was fascinated by the adult conversations. One discussion he overheard had to do with Hitler and the Nazis. Most of the adults thought there was little future for the Nazis, and that Hitler and his party, for many years the minority, would not last long in power. Many chancellors and cabinets before them had lasted only a short time. Josbach had only one known Nazi in town, a man named Heinrich Haupt, who had joined the party in the 1920s.

A few of the adults were convinced, however, that the Nazis were a growing threat, and to bolster their argument, they pointed to surrounding towns, which were known to have more Nazis and had seen increased reports of persecution against Jews.

It took some time before Manfred sensed any divide between the Jewish and non-Jewish students at his school. But one day they were told that their teacher had retired. His replacement was a younger man from out of the area who preached Nazi doctrine. The appearance of this new teacher signaled a shift for Manfred and the other Jewish children. From that moment on, in the classroom and during recreational activities, the Jews were increasingly ridiculed by the teacher and bullied by their classmates.

The next summer, Manfred spent part of his vacation with his mother's brother, Arthur Katten, and his wife, Lina, in nearby Rauschenberg. After befriending some neighborhood boys, Manfred was invited to attend a local meeting of a national organization, Deutsches Jungvolk, for boys aged ten to fourteen. Manfred was excited to hear that they would be participating in sports, camping, and hiking. However, the group was affiliated with the Hitler Youth movement, and when they learned that Manfred was a Jew, he was promptly excluded as being unfit.

Not long after Manfred returned home, the first of his family members was picked up by the Nazis. To his shock, it was his uncle Arthur. Arrested at home by uniformed storm troopers, his mother's brother was held in "protective custody" for six weeks before he was released without any charges being filed. Arthur had honorably served his country in World War I, but he realized now that this meant nothing under the Nazi regime. He immediately began making plans to try to get himself and his family out of Germany as quickly as possible.

Anti-Semitism grew ever more prevalent in the daily life of Josbach, and the local Jews became convinced that the Nazi regime had entrenched its power, with Hitler in full control as the supreme leader of Germany. In 1935, the Nuremberg Laws were enacted, making Jews second-class citizens and revoking most of their political rights. Only Germans with four non-Jewish German grandparents were deemed "racially acceptable," and Judaism was now defined as a race rather than a religion. It was irrelevant whether people practiced Judaism or were even practicing Christians; by law, if they possessed "Jewish blood," they were Jews.

Guided by Third Reich dogma that encouraged "racially pure" women to bear as many Aryan children as possible, mixed marriages between Jews and persons with "German or related blood" were made a criminal offense. Hitler and his Nazi Party promulgated the notion that an enlarged, racially superior German population was destined to expand and rule by military force. One early step toward that goal—and the global conflict that would soon follow—took place in 1936, when Hitler sent German military forces to occupy the Rhineland, a demilitarized zone in western Germany established under the terms of the Treaty of Versailles.

In that same year, Manfred's teacher, who kept a swastika pinned on the lapel of his jacket, herded all the students outside and lined them up like young military recruits along Josbach's main street, where he told them a "special" motorcade was scheduled to pass through town. Some of the students eagerly pushed their way forward, but Manfred hung back. He had an idea it was going to be some Nazi-inspired demonstration, and he had no desire to be standing in front. Their wait wasn't long. A black, open-roofed car approached at moderate speed. As they had practiced in school, upon the teacher's command nearly all of the children snapped their right arms straight out.

"Sieg heil!" shouted a crescendo of high-pitched children's voices.

Manfred did not raise his arm or his voice. He just stared at the mustachioed man in the backseat. He had seen his picture many times.

As the car passed, Hitler seemed to raise his hand to the side of his head in acknowledgment of the mass salute. Then he let it drop out of sight.

"Sieg heil! Sieg heil!"

The salutes ended only when the car turned a corner and was gone.

Young Manfred sensed that the mustachioed man in the black car meant danger to him, his family, and every Jew in Germany.

The day that two men in Nazi uniforms came to threaten his grandmother with arrest, she and Manfred were home alone. What crime could an old, sickly woman be guilty of? It seemed that Johanna Steinfeld held a first mortgage on a property in another town that these two men owned. But they had never made any payments and were thus greatly in arrears to her. Now they threatened the elderly woman with jail on a trumped-up charge if she didn't agree to cancel the mortgage on the property. She went ashen. Turning to Manfred, she told him to run as fast as he could and bring back the mayor.

In 1930s Germany, a town's *Bürgermeister* held a great deal of authority, even with outside officials. By then, the man who had once been Josbach's first and only member of the Nazi Party, Heinrich Haupt, was serving as mayor. He was well liked by all, and even got together with some Jewish friends on Saturday nights to play Skat, the most popular card game in Germany.

Haupt hurried back to the house with Manfred and immediately asked to see the men's credentials, which they showed him. But when he demanded to see a court-issued arrest warrant, the men admitted they did not have one.

"You have no jurisdiction here," Haupt said sternly. "Mrs. Steinfeld is a citizen of this town, and your attempt to arrest her is totally unfounded."

With that, Mayor Haupt kicked the uniformed men out of town.

For the Jews of Josbach, even their traditional Saturday morning stroll to the synagogue in neighboring Halsdorf had become unsafe. Whenever a flour-mill operator saw them approaching, he released his guard dogs with the command: *"Los, fass die Juden!"* (Go, get the Jews!) After several incidents, the procession of well-dressed men, women, and children started taking the long way around to bypass the mill.

Military convoys rattled through town almost daily. Once, a group of SA brownshirts stopped and began chanting, "When Jewish blood flows from the knife, that time will be so much better!" A pack of Hitler Youth rode through town on bikes, stoning stores with Jewish names and smashing windows. Even longtime customers were afraid to be seen patronizing Josbach's Jewish merchants.

In 1937, Paula Steinfeld decided it was time to get her family out of Germany. Several Kattens had already left, including Arthur and his wife; after Arthur's arrest, they had left to join their married daughter, who had settled in New York in the 1920s. Having come to the realization that Germany held no future for Jews of any age, and no matter their background, other Kattens and Steinfelds, including Uncle Solomon, were taking steps to emigrate.

By then, a backlog of Germans—most of them Jews—seeking entry into the United States had begun to form. Under the Immigration Act of 1924, the U.S. State Department was authorized to issue 150,000 immigrant visas annually, subject to quotas assigned to a country in proportion to its contribution to the U.S. population in 1890. As such, 85 percent of immigrants admitted came from Europe. Quotas were based on birthplace, not citizenship or place of residency. By 1937, when Paula decided to get her family out of the country, Nazi Germany was still open to the idea of Jewish emigration, but the annual quota of 27,270 Germans and Austrians allowed into the United States was filled rapidly.

Given the emigration numbers, Paula was told that the family would go on a waiting list for U.S. visas, but they might not make it to America until 1940 or 1941. There was also the difficulty of finding someone to sign an affidavit of support for a widow with three children. None of the relatives who had made it to America were in a position to accept financial responsibility for the family.

A desperate Paula resolved to get her children to safety, even if it meant doing the unfathomable: sending each one to a different foreign country, alone. In Jewish tradition, her oldest son was expected to carry on the family name, which meant Manfred would leave first. Information about emigration was flowing freely in Jewish communities, and Paula heard about the Hebrew Immigrant Aid Society (HIAS), an organization based in the United States that helped unaccompanied children under sixteen get out of Germany. Due to increased demand, and in the interest of fairness, the group accepted only one child per family. When she signed up Manfred he was just shy of fourteen.

A deluge of paperwork followed: five copies of his visa application; two copies of his birth certificate; a certificate of good conduct from German authorities (which became increasingly difficult for Jews to acquire from Nazi officials and was eventually eliminated from U.S. immigration requirements); proof of good health from a physician; and signed documents from HIAS as well as from Paula's sister, Minna, and her husband, Morris Rosenbusch, who had left Germany in 1936 and were living on Chicago's South Side. They had agreed to take Manfred, who knew little English, into their home.

In June 1938, Manfred's U.S. visa came through, and an early-July departure date was set. He was to take a train to Hamburg, a major port city in northern Germany, which connected to the North Sea by the Elbe River. An HIAS escort would meet him there, and he would join other German Jewish children aboard an ocean liner for the trip across the Atlantic to America.

As part of an agonizing round of farewells, Manfred bicycled fifteen miles to visit his grandmother's brother. Manfred had an idea this would be the last time they would see each other, and his elderly granduncle seemed to share his feelings. As they said goodbye, the old man reached into his pocket and took out a crinkled U.S. ten-dollar bill that he carefully smoothed out and handed to the boy. "To help you start a new life in America," he said.

Paula had been warned that Manfred could bring very little cash with him, so she sewed the bill into the cuff of a pair of his pants. Other Jewish families who had sent loved ones abroad gave her another idea. She purchased two seventy-five-dollar Leica camera lenses and placed each one at the bottom of a talcum-powder can, covering the valuable lenses with talcum. She tucked the cans under some folded linens in Manfred's steamer trunk, which was sent ahead to the ship in Hamburg. She advised her son to sell the lenses in America when he needed money.

Early on the morning of his departure, Manfred said good-bye to his sister and brother and the other relatives who had come to see him off. It was particularly hard leaving his little brother, Herbert, who idolized Manfred in the way younger brothers are inclined to do. They even looked alike; Herbert, although a head shorter, had the same open, pleasant countenance as Manfred.

Herbert always followed his big brother around like a shadow, wanting whatever Manfred had or did; *"ich auch"* (me too) was a common refrain. As a junior partner in work and play, Herbert was always happy to help with the chores and anything else to get his big brother's attention and please him.

Manfred held his grandmother's long, tight hug, understanding that it was likely to be their last. Then he was off, still feeling her teary kisses on his cheeks as he looked back to see her sadly waving good-bye with both hands.

He and his mother bicycled to the rail station in Halsdorf, where they boarded a train for the ten-mile trip to Kirchhain. Once there, Paula bought her eldest son a one-way ticket on the express train to Hamburg. She handed him a folded white handkerchief and ran through some final instructions: keep the handkerchief in his pocket until arriving in Hamburg, then take it out and hold it in his left hand. He would see a lady on the platform with a white handkerchief in her left hand. She would be his escort, and she would take him to where the other children were gathering to board the vessel.

When his mother had no more instructions, she began to cry. She kissed Manfred and hugged him tightly. She had told him that she was very happy and relieved he was getting out of Germany, and that he would soon be safe in America. But even at fourteen, Manfred understood that what his mother was doing was a cruel opposite to her most basic instincts and to the nature and desire of every Jewish mother he knew: to love, protect, and care for her children.

"*Auf Wiedersehen, Mutti,*" he said, bidding farewell with more brightness than he felt. After so many heart-wrenching good-byes, this was the one he dreaded the most. He did not want to reveal to her his worst fear, which had been gnawing at him ever since he learned of his upcoming move to America.

Her last words to him, "Be quiet and do not draw attention to yourself," would stay with him throughout his rail and sea journeys. Stepping into the train compartment, he found a window seat. He and his mother waved to each other as the train pulled out of the station. He could see that she was sobbing now, standing there alone on the platform. His train gained speed, and his mother grew smaller and smaller, until he could no longer make out her figure.

Manfred Steinfeld was deathly afraid he would never see her again.

For Paula Steinfeld, sending her oldest son away, alone, across an ocean to a foreign land to live with others, had been an agonizing decision. Now she prayed this move would save his life and ensure his future, even if she never saw his sweet face again. With a heavy heart, she returned home to Josbach and began to plot how to save her other two children.

Stephan Lewy was seven years old in 1932, when his father, Arthur, a widower for the past year, left him at the Baruch Auerbach Orphanage for Jewish Girls and Boys in Berlin. Stephan's mother, Gertrude, had been an invalid for several years, and for a time after her death, Arthur had been able to care for his son with the help of a woman he hired to run the household.

The boy missed his mother terribly. She had been a soft and gentle presence in his life. When he did something well, it was his mother who hugged, kissed, and praised him, while his father slapped or spanked him for his transgressions. One of Stephan's earliest memories was of his mother saying the blessing over the Shabbat candles on Friday night before the special meal she had prepared. But he had many more memories of her bedridden, due to a weak heart. They both enjoyed her reading to him as he snuggled up next to her, and Stephan liked doing things for his mother that she was unable to do herself.

Three months after Gertrude's death, her younger brother, Ewald, defaulted on a sizable loan that Arthur, a tobacco merchant with his own shop, had guaranteed, against his wife's advice. In satisfying the debt, Arthur lost the family's savings and even their household furniture, which Stephan watched being taken away by movers from his perch on a windowsill.

Arthur could no longer afford the hired woman to care for Stephan while he was at work, and none of Gertrude's relatives were willing or able to help with the little boy. Arthur's parents and seven siblings were all dead by 1902, wiped out by some contagion, leaving him the only surviving member of the family at the age of nine.

Stephan Lewy with his mother, Gertrude, shortly before her death in 1931. *(Family photograph)*

A Jewish organization had brought a frightened Arthur to the Auerbach Orphanage, where he remained until he was eligible to leave
at age sixteen. Drafted into the German army in 1914, Arthur saw
combat on the western front, including the second Battle of Ypres
in Belgium, in which the Germans used mass poison gas attacks for
the first time in history, killing thousands.

After he was discharged following the armistice, Arthur was
invited by an army buddy to a dinner party. There, he sat next
to a charming young woman dressed in pale gray chiffon; as Arthur would later tell friends, he fell in love with Gertrude between
the soup and the apple strudel. They were married several months
later.

While still in her twenties, Gertrude endured a near-fatal bout of rheumatic fever that left her heart damaged. A doctor warned her that the rigors of childbirth would endanger her life, and Gertrude and Arthur agreed not to have children. But within a year she was pregnant. The doctor repeated his dire assessment and offered to terminate the pregnancy.

"I'm going to have this baby," she told the doctor and her worried husband. "And we're both going to survive."

Near the end of her life, Stephan saw his mother growing weaker, but even when she was hospitalized for the last time, he was too young to seriously consider the possibility that she would really die and leave him for good.

He was with his father, packing boxes in the back of the tobacco store, when the hospital telephoned. His father hung up the phone and said heavily, "She's gone, my son. Your mother is dead."

They sat down together on a wooden crate and cried. It was the first time that Stephan saw his stern father show any emotion.

"We are all alone now," Arthur said, weeping. But, he reassured his son, they would be all right, because they had each other.

Then came the loan default, bill collectors, and furniture movers. Arthur lost their two-bedroom apartment in downtown Berlin; he could afford only a sparsely furnished room that came with kitchen privileges and a shared bathroom.

Sitting his son down for a talk, Arthur said in his most serious tone, "Do you remember what I told you about where I grew up?"

Stephan nodded.

"You are a good boy, and I am not doing this to punish you. But for your own good, I have decided to send you to the orphanage."

"But, Papa, you said we'll be all right, because we have each other."

"This is not open for discussion," said his father. He would not be dissuaded by sentiment or emotion. "I am familiar with the place. I feel sure you will receive proper care and supervision."

A few days later, Stephan's father took him to the Auerbach Or-

phanage. The ornate, three-story structure at Schönhauser Allee
162 was topped with a towering spiral; it had been built in the late
1800s as a beer brewery and still had a dank, dark interior. Stephan
waited in a long hallway while his father went into an office.

When his father reappeared, Stephan could tell he wasn't interested in a prolonged good-bye. He said Sundays were visiting days,
bent down for a quick hug, then backed away and shook the boy's
hand.

Stephan, his heart beating rapidly, was left alone in the hallway.

An older boy soon appeared and led him to the boys' dormitory,
where Stephan unpacked his small suitcase. That night, he covered
his face with a pillow so no one would hear him cry. When he woke
the next morning to a clanging bell, his pillow was damp from tears.

One hundred children lived at the orphanage, all of them Jewish.
Most had no parents, though there were some, like Stephan, whose
single parents were unable to raise them for various reasons.

During the week, the children attended a public school, but
other than that, they stayed at the orphanage. There were many
rules, and if they behaved and had local relatives, they could visit
them on Sundays, though they had to be back by 6 P.M. Having been
raised in a home with a strict father aided Stephan's adjustment to
the authoritarian atmosphere.

Spring 1933 arrived; Hitler rose to power, and the orphanage,
like the rest of the country, found itself abuzz with news of all the
political happenings and the new anti-Semitic laws. The Nazis were
banning Jews from holding public office and closing many profes-
sions to them, not only in civil service but in radio, newspapers,
teaching, and theater arts.

"Stephan," one friend said, "there will be nothing left for us
when we grow up."

When he heard about the boycott of Jewish-owned businesses,
Stephan worried about his father. Would he be able to keep his shop?
He knew his father called himself a socialist. Although Stephan

Seven-year-old Stephan Lewy in the yard of the Baruch Auerbach Jewish Orphanage in Berlin, 1932. *(U.S. Holocaust Memorial Museum)*

didn't know what that meant—he was still only eight years old—the older boys who read the newspapers told him that socialists were among the people being rounded up by the Nazis.

Not long after, Stephan was called to the superintendent's office. A grim-faced man behind a desk said, "I am sorry to tell you that you will not be allowed to go home for a Sunday visit until further notice."

"But—what did I do?"

"The request came from your father."

Stephan left the office weeping and confused. What had he done to make his father not want to see him? First his mother had died, and now this. He was alone in the world with no one who loved him. His wounded feelings soon turned to anger at Arthur, who he believed had completely abandoned him.

Months went by. Stephan heard nothing from or about his father. Then the mother of a friend from the orphanage, who had been bringing Stephan home with her son for Sunday visits, told Stephan the truth. The Nazis had arrested his father and were holding him in a concentration camp. The orphanage officials had tried to protect him from this terrible news, but she believed the boy should know why he was unable to see his father.

Arthur Lewy had been sent to Oranienburg concentration camp, one of the first detention facilities established by the Nazis after they came to power. Located in the town of Oranienburg, near Berlin, the camp's initial purpose was to hold Hitler's political opponents from the region, and by 1933, it was crowded with Social Democrats, socialists, and communists, along with others deemed "undesirable." The SS took over the camp in mid-1934 and often marched the prison-uniformed inmates out for the day to perform hard labor.

Arthur was released from Oranienburg in 1935, after suffering a heart attack, and was admitted to a Jewish hospital in Berlin. Shortly after his discharge, he came to the orphanage to see his son. This time, he gave Stephan a big hug and kisses on both cheeks as they were reunited, standing in the same hallway where father and son had parted two years earlier. As overjoyed as Stephan was to see his father, he found his appearance deeply alarming. Arthur was missing most of his teeth, and his once solid build had withered.

A friend had kept the tobacco shop running in his absence, Arthur told Stephan, but the new laws made it difficult for Jews to own businesses, and he was being pressured to sell out for a low price to a non-Jew. "People are taking advantage of the situation," he lamented. Now he was back to living in a rooming house.

As they talked, Stephan could not believe how his father had changed. Not only physically, but he had a warmer, less stern manner about him.

Stephan had changed, too. In the institutional setting of Auerbach, the little boy who had always tried hard to please had become proficiently mischievous. He was rarely caught doing anything wrong, however, even when he carried off pranks like leading boys through airshafts to spy on the girls as they took showers. And for the most part, Stephan obeyed the rules. He also did well in his studies.

As a reward, in early 1938, shortly after his bar mitzvah, he became a shamus, which meant he would be responsible for opening the synagogue, which also served the local Jewish community, on the top floor of the orphanage. Each morning, Stephan reset the Torah scrolls for the day's reading and turned on the electric organ to warm it up. The older boys at the orphanage attended services three times a day. They learned to conduct services, too, and studied Hebrew so that they could read the scriptures. Surrounded by their religion, they lived Judaism at Auerbach Orphanage—in Stephan's case, more fully than he had at home.

The neighborhood school had a mix of Jewish and non-Jewish students, with the boys and girls segregated. One day, a group of adults entered Stephan's classroom: a nurse, a doctor, a policeman, and a Nazi official, all in their respective uniforms. The official announced they would be taking "Aryan measurements," and ordered all the Jews—there were ten or twelve in the class, most from the orphanage—to stand in one corner. The other forty boys formed a wide circle, with the adults in the center. One by one, each stepped forward so the doctor could use a mechanical device to measure the size and shape of his skull. The doctor made other measurements, such as the distance between their ears and the length of the brow and nose, calling out the figures to the nurse, who wrote them down in a book. They used a board filled with color samples to match and document the color of each boy's skin, eyes, and hair.

Off in the corner, Stephan and the other Jews were ignored.

In the fall of 1938, Stephan's father remarried. His new wife was Johanna Arzt, and Stephan had played a role in how the couple met:

Johanna was the sister of the woman who'd brought Stephan home with her son on Sundays while his father was in the concentration camp. After Arthur's release from Oranienburg, father and son attended several Sunday dinners with the Arzts, and it was at these dinners that Arthur and Johanna were introduced.

Stephan, starved for a mother's love, quickly grew close to Johanna, a nurturing and kind Jewish woman like his mother. Soon, he felt close to her and was calling her *Mutter* without reservation.

By then, Arthur had lost his shop. At night, he went out to knock on the doors of old customers, taking tobacco orders. He turned these over to an Aryan tobacconist to fill and received small commissions. Johanna worked as a bookkeeper. They still lived in a tiny rented room, so Stephan stayed at the orphanage.

As he was returning from school one day in early November 1938, Stephan saw a banner headline at a corner newsstand.

JEW KILLS GERMAN ATTACHÉ IN PARIS

Stephan knew immediately that this was big news, and he dug into his pocket for the change to buy a newspaper.

A week earlier, more than twelve thousand Polish-born Jews, who had resided legally in Germany for years, had been expelled from the country. Forced from their homes in a single day, they were taken to the nearest railroad stations and put on trains to the Polish border. Four thousand were allowed into Poland, but the remainder were denied entry and found themselves in limbo, trapped on the desolate frontier between the two countries. They spent a week in the rain and cold, enduring a lack of adequate food and shelter. Then, on November 7, Herschel Grynszpan, a seventeen-year-old boy living in Paris, the son of two Polish Jews who had been rounded up, walked into the Third Reich embassy there and shot the diplomat. He wanted to avenge the Nazis' treatment of Jews, and his family in particular.

At the time, Hitler and Joseph Goebbels, his minister of propaganda, were reveling at the annual celebration of the Beer Hall Putsch in Munich, which commemorated Hitler's first attempt to seize power in 1923. Within hours of hearing the news, they had plotted a response. They viewed the killing—Nazi propaganda called it the "first shot of the Jewish War"—as an opportunity to unleash a long-planned, violent mass action against Jews. Later that day, Goebbels outlined to wildly applauding party leaders the nationwide pogrom that would become known as Kristallnacht.

Beginning at midnight, secret teletype messages from Gestapo headquarters in Berlin went out to military and police units across the country, ordering organized anti-Jewish demonstrations in cities, towns, and villages throughout Germany, encouraging the destruction of synagogues and other Jewish properties, and authorizing the mass arrest and detention of Jews.

In Berlin the next day, angry crowds filled the streets, chanting, "Down with the Jews!" Nazi gangs—many of them SA brownshirts in uniform or Nazis in civilian clothes—armed with guns, knives, crowbars, and bricks, assaulted Jewish men at random, made widespread arrests, and plundered and set fire to synagogues and Jewish homes and businesses. Firemen stood by and watched as the buildings burned.

Early the next morning, a group of uniformed Nazis burst through the doors of the Auerbach Orphanage, taking the staff members, all of them Jewish, into custody. They went into the dormitories on the ground floor of the U-shaped building—one wing for the boys and the other for the girls—and rounded up the children, herding them all upstairs to the synagogue. The coverings on the *bimah*—a raised platform from which the Torah is read—had been ripped away. The holy ark where the Torah scrolls were kept had been torn off the wall, and other symbols were destroyed.

The terrified boys and girls filled the pews and lined up along the walls, waiting to see what horrible things the Nazis had in store for them. But the Nazis simply left the synagogue without saying a word, leaving the frightened children to exchange confused looks.

A few moments later, Stephan heard the jangle of keys and the sound of the door being locked from the outside. Then he smelled the gas. The eternal light (*ner tamid*), located in front of the ark and symbolizing God's enduring presence, had been smashed; the gas line that fed the flame had been cut. A steady stream of gas was flowing through the broken pipe and into the synagogue filled with children. If they did not escape from the confined space—and quickly—they would all die.

Some of the older boys desperately tried to break down the heavy door, but it wouldn't budge. When the children realized they couldn't get out, their fear turned to panic. Many of them, crying and screaming, started coughing and choking from the fumes.

One of the older boys picked up a chair and began smashing it against the beautiful windows. Stephan and some other boys joined in, and working together, they were able to break out several tall panes. The openings allowed fresh air to come in and the fumes to begin to dissipate. The children remained locked inside the synagogue for the rest of the day, until a concerned neighborhood policeman came by and let them out.

Two days later, the orphans were directed by staff members to return to school. Those orphanage staff members who had been released from custody seemed eager to bring some normalcy back to the children's lives. "Pick up your lunches and go to school," they told the orphans. "Life goes on."

The sights Stephan saw on that two-mile walk would stay with him for the rest of his life. Buildings were burnt shells; stores had been looted; Torah scrolls and prayer shawls lay crumpled in the streets. Armed Nazis patrolled corners and rooftops. Jewish men, forced to sweep up in front of their destroyed stores and homes, were beaten and jeered as they worked.

Shortly after Stephan and the other boys from the orphanage reached the school and took their seats in their classroom, a uniformed Nazi came into the room to lecture the children about the "mixing of our pure Aryan race." He announced that Jewish children could no longer attend "Aryan state" elementary schools. "You have to leave this school now," he said.

Puzzled but not daring to ask questions, Stephan and the other Jewish students quietly collected their things and left. Back at the orphanage, the administrators had also just been informed of this new policy. A building on Kaiserstrasse—about a forty-minute walk from the orphanage through downtown Berlin—was soon designated as an all-Jewish school.

By then, the children were all well aware that anti-Semitism surrounded them any time they ventured outside. There was no escaping it in Germany's capital city and no way to prevent the inevitable: it followed them to their new school. On most afternoons, the students were confronted by uniformed Hitler Youth, lined up in rows on either side of the sidewalk for about one hundred feet. Swinging their leather belts overhead, they whipped the students—who were forced to run the gauntlet—with the buckle ends like cattle. Policemen stood by and watched, but did nothing other than stop the Jews from trying to defend themselves.

Thirteen-year-old Stephan understood that his life had changed. This realization was confirmed when he went home the following Sunday and told his father about the night of horror at the orphanage and about the other appalling things he had seen. It wasn't only happening in Berlin, his father told him in hushed, tense whispers, but all across Germany. Although Jewish newspapers and magazines had been ordered to cease publication, he had heard that hundreds of synagogues had been destroyed. Thousands of Jews were being rounded up and sent to concentration camps.

Two Gestapo agents had come to pick him up the other night, Arthur said, when he was out taking tobacco orders from his customers. Jewish men were being arrested in their own homes for no reason, he explained; the Nazis would show up late at night, when they thought people would be in bed. When they came for Arthur, Johanna told the men she didn't know when he would be back. They waited for an hour before leaving. When would they return? Afraid even to be home, Arthur had begun leaving in the early evening and walking the streets most of the night. He and Johanna had worked out a signal. If men were waiting, she would place the parakeet's cage in the window, and Arthur would keep walking. If he didn't see the cage, it was safe to come up.

They had decided it was time to get out of Germany, he told his son. Johanna had a distant cousin living in Boston. Though they had never met, she had written him to see if he would be able to sponsor the three of them for entry into America. Stephan's father explained that they would be submitting visa applications to the U.S. State Department. It was still possible for Jews to leave Germany as long as they didn't take any money or other assets. But the emigration doors could slam shut at any time; America's policy could change as well. Adding to these uncertainties, the German government had recently started civilian rationing of meat, coffee, and butter. Arthur took that as a sign that all-out war was imminent. If they didn't leave soon, he feared that they might never be able to get out.

Part of the visa process involved an appointment at the U.S. consulate for medical exams to ensure the applicants were not carriers of infectious diseases and were otherwise in good health. Johanna and Stephan passed, but Arthur was notified that he had failed because of his high blood pressure. He would go on medication, change his diet, and try again to pass the exam, but it would take time.

Arthur and Johanna broke the news to Stephan during his next Sunday visit. Though he was disappointed to hear that they would not be leaving Germany any time soon, the thought that they would not all be together made Stephan feel even worse. He had thought a lot about what it would be like to be part of a family again, to live at home with parents instead of at the orphanage. Emigration to the United States had offered more than safety—it was a chance to again live under the same roof with his parents at long last.

"You know how concerned we are for your safety?" asked Johanna.

Yes, Stephan did know.

It had become increasingly dangerous for Jews to remain in Germany, Arthur said. He and Johanna had decided to send Stephan out of the country ahead of them. "We are taking advantage of a plan offered through the orphanage," he said.

"What kind of plan?" Stephan asked.

His father explained that European countries like England, Denmark, Holland, and France were admitting unaccompanied Jewish children as refugees. He had learned from Auerbach administrators of arrangements they were making to send some children to Paris, where they would be cared for by a Jewish rescue organization. He had already signed Stephan up. It would be safer for him in France, said his father.

"Leave Germany without you?"

Stephan realized his dream of reuniting with his parents was lost.

His father promised that they would join him as soon as possible in France—or possibly in America. "We'll see. We will write each other."

On July 4, 1939, Arthur and Johanna took Stephan to Berlin's cavernous Anhalter Bahnhof railroad station. There, they found a group of about forty boys and their chaperons off in one corner. Stephan knew about a dozen of the children from the orphanage. As relatives said their good-byes, many of the younger boys were laughing, joking with each other about the great adventure they would soon embark on. Aware of the trip's implications, Stephan stayed silent.

None of the adults present, including Arthur and Johanna, revealed to their children any foreboding that they might not ever see each other again. Of course, as the situation in Germany worsened daily, the grown-ups knew this was a possibility. Arthur had had to sign a conservatorship document assigning the legal responsibility for Stephan's welfare to the rescue organization until he was eighteen. Even without parental permission, the organization would be free to take Stephan to wherever they felt he would be safe.

As the group moved toward the train platform, Stephan heard his father calling out to him: "Be sure to behave."

Stephan went back to the last car as the train pulled out of the station, and looked out a frost-covered window at Berlin, fading into the distance behind him. With his finger, he drew three X's in the condensation on the pane. The triple X was a well-known German sign of displeasure. It would be left, for instance, by a customer on the check at a restaurant after a bad meal, signifying that he would not come back.

Stephan was a German, but he was also a Jew. And after what he had already lived through in his young life, he never wanted to return to Germany.

2

ESCAPING THE NAZIS

B y January 1939, hundreds of the Jews interned at Dachau concentration camp after the Kristallnacht roundups two months earlier had already died, casualties of SS brutality or the vile conditions. After being forced by camp officials to sign over title to his mother's home, Martin Selling didn't think he would leave alive. He had every reason to believe the rumors he heard that the crematories in Munich were working day and night to process the corpses from Dachau, a result of the major influx of Jews into the camp beginning in November 1938.[*]

But some Jewish prisoners were luckier—about half of those brought in after the roundups had been released to ease overcrowding, with priority given to those who could prove they had a way to get out of Germany. The population decrease in the camp meant there were now enough thin blankets to go around; each inmate could have his own during the frigid nights. Martin found some sewing kits and put his tailoring skills to work, repairing the straw mattresses and prison uniforms. He also gathered some of the clean-

---

[*] A crematorium was built at Dachau in 1940, and a second, larger crematorium with a gas chamber was erected in 1942.

ing cloths used to prepare the barracks for inspections and sewed them together into a long-sleeved undershirt. Wearing his new shirt under the lightweight prisoner garb helped cut the chill. When the other prisoners saw what he had done, they asked him to make undershirts for them, too. The guards began to notice the shortage. Word spread that at the next inspection, the guards would be looking for the missing cloths, and anyone found with them would be punished. Martin collected all the undershirts he had made, took out the seams, and folded them so as to hide the alterations. When the guards searched, they found only neat piles of cleaning rags, which had somehow reappeared.

The highlight of each day came after the evening meal, when the guards posted a list of the prisoners who would be processed for release the next day. Every day Martin hoped his name would be on the list, and every day he was disappointed. By the time his name appeared—January 27, 1939—he was the last of the nine men who had come in with him on the transport from Nuremberg still at Dachau. His friend Ernst Dingfelder, who had tried so hard to stay kosher in Dachau, had been let out a few days earlier.

Martin didn't sleep at all that night. Each day had been spent just trying to survive. What lay ahead now? he wondered. As he lay awake, he thought about other inmates, men whose names might never appear on the list.

Another friend he had made at Dachau, Alois Stangl, had been a deckhand on a Danube river barge. He was thirty-five years old, but after five years at Dachau, he looked fifty. Although Stangl was a German Aryan, he had been an outspoken member of the Socialist Party, which meant the Nazis considered him an enemy of the regime. His sister was married to a fervent Nazi official, who had denounced Stangl to the party, leading to his arrest. His release would be an embarrassment to the man who had put him there, he told Martin. Alois Stangl saw no chance of ever getting out of Dachau alive.

The next morning, Martin and the fifty other men being released that day were taken to the communal shower room, where they stripped and showered. Next, they went for a medical examination with a singular purpose: anyone with evidence of maltreatment or injury had to wait until their wounds healed, else they be used to corroborate claims of physical abuse. Martin was pulled aside because of a long scar on his right knee, which he explained to the doctor was an old injury. The SS physician seemed skeptical. Martin had to show he had full range of motion in his knee before he was allowed to continue on.

To the surprise of Martin and the others, the prisoners were handed bags marked with their names; inside were the clothes they had been wearing upon arrival. After they dressed, an SS officer lectured them about the threat of reincarceration if they spoke publicly about Dachau. He also reminded them that they were Jews, not Germans, a refrain that had been drilled into them daily, often while they were being beaten by the guards.

Martin had grown up with Judaism as his religion and German as his nationality. His family celebrated Jewish religious holidays as well as German national holidays. Their ancestral roots in the country went back centuries, and the family included men such as his mother's brothers, Hugo and Julius Laub, who had fought for the German empire in the trenches of World War I and were proud, patriotic Germans. As Manfred Steinfeld's uncles, Solomon and Arthur, had also once believed, Martin's uncles held on to the hope even after Hitler rose to power that their country would not turn on its veterans. But for Germany's Jewish veterans that was not to be. It had been forcefully impressed upon Martin and his uncles, as well as Manfred and his uncles, and thousands like them, in countless insidious ways, that they were no longer Germans.

Calling the prisoners about to be released *verdammte Saujuden* (damn dirty Jews), the SS officer warned, "After you leave Germany, the louder you complain abroad, the less likely will you be believed."

The prisoners boarded the train at the same platform from which they had arrived. A number of armed SS guards boarded with them. Although they were told that they were no longer in custody, but were merely being escorted to Munich, Martin and the others were afraid to show relief or any other emotion. They remained silent. Lulled by the rhythmic sound of the train on the tracks, an exhausted Martin, who had not slept in forty-eight hours, struggled to keep his eyes open. He was about to lose the battle and drift off when a prisoner sitting across from him let out a sharp cry. Martin's bleary eyes darted open. The man was holding his bloodied nose. The SS had to get in a last lick.

"No one falls asleep in my presence!" hollered the guard who had struck the sleeping man with the butt of his rifle. "So you thought you were already rid of us?"

After that, no one dared to close his eyes. Even after the released prisoners had been turned over to the reception committee from the Jewish Community Council at the Munich station, even after the guards had long since departed, Martin kept looking over his shoulder to see if they were being followed by SS or Gestapo goons.

The next day, Martin took a train to Nuremberg, where he was met by his mother's sister, Isa Laub. He learned it was Aunt Isa who had secured his release from Dachau; she had sent to the authorities documentation showing he had been accepted to a large, newly formed Jewish refugee camp in England and could emigrate immediately. She told Martin he would be allowed to remain in England until he was able to secure a visa to the United States.

Shortly after his mother's death in 1936, Martin had applied for a visa to the United States and had begun learning English at a private language institute. The other students were all Jews, who hoped similarly to reach America. With so many wanting to flee Germany, his name was still on a long waiting list for America.

Aunt Isa, who invited Martin to stay with her until he left for England, had some tragic family news. Martin's father's brother, Siegfried Selling, a bachelor in his fifties, had been arrested in Nuremberg on Kristallnacht and kept for two days at Gestapo headquarters. There, he had been questioned about his non-Jewish housekeeper, a violation of one of the Nuremberg Laws, which prohibited Jews from employing non-Jews, and badly beaten. When Uncle Siegfried was released, he returned to his apartment and took his own life by hanging. Aunt Isa had also heard about her late sister's house in Lehrberg being sold. Martin told her about the papers he had been forced to sign in Dachau.

Martin had a picture taken, which showed his telltale concentration camp haircut, and took it to the passport office in Nuremberg. On the visa application form, he wrote his full name, Martin Ignatz Selling, and checked the box for *Jude*. The passport clerk rejected his form, explaining that under the Nuremberg Laws, his middle name must be recognizable as Jewish. The clerk did not think Ignatz qualified. In the absence of such a middle name, he said, all Jewish males must use "Israel," and all females "Sarah."

Martin had not been overly alarmed when the Nuremberg Laws were first enacted in 1935. At the time, he was leading an unobtrusive, simple life working for a Munich tailor, and had no interest in politics. He was terribly wrong, he knew now. These dangerous laws declared Jews and other non-Aryans racially inferior and robbed them of their German citizenship. The laws were designed by the Nazis not only to discriminate against Jews; they were meant to keep the Aryan race pure by outlawing racially mixed marriages between Germans and Jews. Martin had seen the disastrous results of the prejudice and hatred they bred, both in and out of Dachau. He had seen the brutality of the Nazis close up, witnessing innocents being killed for no reason except that they were Jews or other "enemies" whom Hitler and his henchmen considered inferior and undesirable. At Dachau, he had believed he would end up a victim, too. Even though he had been among the lucky ones to make it out of the concentration camp alive, he knew he was still not safe.

The wait to pick up his passport grew nerve-racking as his scheduled departure date inched closer. Less than two weeks before he was to leave, Martin was finally able to pick up his new passport.

His name was listed as "Martin Israel Selling," and there was a big red "J" stamped next to his grim picture. Also stamped on the passport: "*Gut nur für Auswanderung!*" (Good For Emigration Only!) Martin hurried to the foreign consulates to get visas to transit Belgium and enter England.

In late June 1939, Martin joined a group of eighty German Jews assembled in Cologne by an international relief agency. Cologne, Germany's fourth-largest city, spread along both banks of the Rhine less than fifty miles from the border with Belgium. The plan was for the men to travel together in a special passenger rail car attached to an express train, cross into Belgium, and head directly to the coastal city of Ostend, where they would take a ferry across the English Channel to Dover. A bus would then take them to the refugee camp in Kent, England.

But when the train was halted at the border with Belgium, the German authorities ordered that the rail car with the Jews be detached and pushed onto a siding. Soon, it was swarming with Gestapo agents in black leather coats and helmeted SS soldiers, who ordered everyone out. Martin and the other men were taken into a nearby warehouse and subjected to thorough body searches; their luggage was opened and rifled through. While this was happening, the interior of the rail car was checked for hidden contraband.

This went on for close to six hours. At last, they were allowed to reboard, and the rail car was coupled to another train about to depart. Within minutes, they had crossed the border into the lush, rolling countryside of eastern Belgium. Their destination, the port of Ostend, lay three hundred miles to the west.

Only now did Martin allow himself to believe he was out of danger. At the border, he had been dead certain he and the others were about to be taken into custody. Since his arrest on November 10, 1938, he had been trapped in an unending nightmare. His release from Dachau had not relieved the tension and anxiety he felt living in the country he had once thought of as his homeland. But now

that he had finally made it out of Nazi Germany, he was both relieved and exhausted.

Mesmerized by the clickety-clacking of the tracks, his body
went limp. He fell into a stupor, the deepest sleep he had enjoyed in
months. He stayed sprawled across the seat until the conductor gently shook him awake; the man wanted to know, strangely, whether
he was all right.

"I am now," said a groggy Martin, who then went back to sleep.

Growing up in Berlin, Werner Angress often wondered why he was
blond and blue eyed and the other Jewish boys were not. And why
did he do well in athletics but not academics, like so many of them?

Born in 1920, Werner was the oldest of three boys. His brother
Fritz was younger by three years, and Hans by eight. His parents,
Ernst and Henny Angress, were third-generation Berliners whose
forebears had been bourgeois Prussians. They had married rela-
tively late, at thirty-six and twenty-seven, respectively, and were
solidly middle class with little formal education. In other ways, they
were a study in contrasts. Henny was outgoing and fun to be around.
She loved to give parties, dance the polka, and sing Schubert songs
at the grand piano in their apartment. A brunette with dark brown
eyes, she was always well dressed and coiffed. In contrast, Ernst
was balding and rotund, the managing director of a bank. He favored conservative three-piece suits and was a conscientious businessman who espoused Old World virtues and demanded precise
accounting, even of household expenditures. Though he could be
upset by something as small as the cost of dinner ingredients, he
was incapable of denying his attractive wife a new dress or sweater.

At the same time, he managed to teach his sons the value of
money. When Werner was ten years old, he asked what it meant to
be Prussian. His father didn't hesitate. Responsibility, he told his
son. Honor. Thrift.

For young Werner, who wanted so much to please his father by striving for those upstanding qualities, meeting them in his school-work did not come easily. Though he earned high marks in read-ing, writing, and gymnastics—even leading his school squad to a regional championship—he earned Ds and Fs in geometry, algebra, physics, and chemistry. In middle school, he was barely promoted to the next grade, and his parents received a letter warning that he would have to repeat eighth grade if his work didn't improve.

Going to school became even more uncomfortable for Werner af-ter January 30, 1933. On that cold, rainy Monday, he rode his bicycle home past the newsstand at the Botanical Garden train station and saw blaring headlines announcing that Hitler had been appointed chancellor. On the same day, three hundred miles away in the ham-let of Josbach, Manfred Steinfeld was hearing the "wonderful" news from the physician treating his sick grandmother.

When Werner reached the apartment, he was surprised to see his father home early from work. A friend of his father's was visiting, and both men, along with Werner's mother, were in the living room, cracking jokes about Hitler.

"Hitler was running back and forth in the state chancery open-ing all the desk drawers and cabinets," said Werner's father. "When asked what he was looking for, Hitler answered, 'My government program.'"

Ernst added confidently, "He won't last two weeks," expressing a point of view about Hitler that many Germans held at that time.

His mother said she had heard a good one at the fish store. "Know what a Hitler herring is? You take a herring, remove its brain, tear its mouth wide open, and you have a Hitler herring."

This was the last time Werner heard his parents joke about Hitler.

When Werner stepped into the room, his father asked how the kids at school had reacted to the news. Werner said they had not known before school let out. Uninterested in any further discussion of politics, he went to his room.

The next day at school, Werner could feel the tension as soon as he walked into the classroom. His teacher hadn't shown up yet, and in his place at the podium was one of the students in his Hitler Youth uniform. When the boy spotted Werner, he instructed the class to shout in unison, "Wake up, Germany! Death to the Jews!" He received a round of applause.

Werner felt the eyes of his classmates following him as he took his seat, his knees suddenly wobbly, a red-hot blush spreading across his face. With his blond hair and blue eyes, he was accustomed to not being identified as Jewish, and to be singled out was extremely uncomfortable. Like everyone else, he raised his arm to give the obligatory German salute and shout "Heil Hitler!" at the beginning of each class. None of his classmates had ever commented about his doing so; in fact, Werner knew, *not* doing so would make him a spectacle.

When the twenty-four-hour boycott of Jewish-owned businesses was staged two months later, Werner's mother made a point of shopping at a Jewish sewing store for items she didn't really need. She brought Werner with her, and they passed SA brownshirts taking photos of anyone entering the store. Inside, Henny found a packet of needles and Werner picked out a spool of thread. They left, his mother holding her head high, Werner beside her, hoping none of his friends had seen him in a ladies' sewing store.

Later, out of sheer curiosity, Werner went downtown to watch a large Nazi rally. At first, he couldn't see over the crowd—he was a thirteen-year-old boy among adults—but the next thing he knew a helpful bystander had hoisted him up several rungs of a ladder. From his perch, he easily saw to the front of the rally, where uniformed Nazis were waving torches and flags. He heard their amplified voices yelling hateful slogans, each of which was loudly cheered by the enthusiastic crowd.

"A bunch of dirty Jews!"

"Throw them out of our Fatherland!"

"Send them off to Jerusalem, but first cut off their legs so they can't come back!"

Werner climbed down from the ladder and headed home.

On the first Yom Kippur after the Nazis' ascent to power, Werner went with his parents to synagogue, which he had attended since age ten. As the worshippers made their way toward the tall, imposing temple, uniformed storm troopers crowded the sidewalks, shouting catcalls and insults as the Jews walked past. Tucked between his mother and father, Werner was frightened not only by the Nazis but by the fear he saw etched on the faces of his parents and the other Jews who walked with them.

At the synagogue, Werner followed his parents to their seats. Soon he would become a bar mitzvah in this same temple, although he had yet to learn the short prayer he had to recite, let alone the passage he was to read in Hebrew from the Torah.

That night, two Nazis sat behind the congregation to monitor the sermon. The young rabbi, Dr. Manfred Swarsensky, spoke explicitly about the political turmoil taking place across Germany. Condemning the outrages being committed daily by the Nazis, he quoted, in conclusion, the New Testament and the dying words of Christ on the crucifix.

"Lord, forgive them, for they know not what they do."

Nearly everyone in the congregation was weeping. Werner kept a steady gaze on the rabbi, this holy man who had dared to speak up publicly before the Nazis when so many others remained silent. Werner knew he was hearing something special from a very brave man. He watched to see if the young rabbi was arrested by the two Nazis after his sermon, but to the boy's relief he wasn't.

When the 1933–34 school year began, a substitute teacher in Werner's biology class paused the lesson to advocate for the superiority of an Aryan master race. To demonstrate what he meant, he tried to show how different skull shapes dictated various racial characteristics. At one point, he pointed to Werner, who always sat in front of the class because he was nearsighted and didn't want to wear glasses.

"This boy has a typical Aryan skull. Just look at its shape. Exactly the same sort of head as Reichsminister Dr. Goebbels."

Uproarious laughter erupted from the students, who knew that the visiting teacher had picked out the one Jew in the class. Several of the kids came up to Werner after class, not to make fun of him but to ridicule the teacher and the nonsense they were being fed by Nazi teachers.

After Hitler came to power, most Jewish children and teenagers attending German public schools eventually transferred to private Jewish schools. Werner did not. Instead, his education stopped at age sixteen. No one considered Werner too slow witted for higher education, least of all his parents, but he was simply not motivated. He had seldom been challenged; at school, his unimaginative teachers had seemed more concerned with going through the prescribed curriculum than with getting students interested in the material.

Werner told his father he wanted to leave school and learn a trade. Ernst knew that, based on his grades, Werner would not be attending university, and he agreed that there was thus little reason for him to continue in school. He encouraged Werner to look for a field not barred to Jews, which he could enter after he finished the term in spring 1936.

Werner wasn't interested in working in retail, but he liked animals and hit upon the idea of working at a zoo. Perhaps, he thought, with the optimism characteristic of youth, he might one day lead an expedition to darkest Africa and capture exotic creatures.

Rather than dismiss the idea out of hand, his father helped him write a letter to the director of the Berlin zoo, inquiring about an apprenticeship. The director wrote a polite letter in return, thanking Werner for his interest but pointing out that, under the Nuremberg Laws, he was prohibited from hiring non-Aryans to work at the zoo.

"You see," said Ernst, "even the chimpanzees are anti-Semitic now."

One Sunday afternoon, Ernst invited him out on a walk. Werner knew this was how his father liked to have serious talks; out of earshot of the two younger boys—Fritz, thirteen, and Hans, eight—as well as his wife, he could speak more freely.

They strolled down Willdenowstraße, beside the botanical gardens, under old trees, and past the sprawling villa of Reichsminister Walther Darré, a member of Hitler's cabinet. Black-uniformed SS soldiers stood on guard outside. Other well-known Berlin neighbors were Dr. Joseph Goebbels, who had once lived above a delicatessen on Reichskanzlerplatz, and Hermann Goering, whose old apartment was in a nondescript building on the corner of Kaiserdamm, but none had been as interesting to the neighborhood children as boxer Max Schmeling's mother, whom Werner once talked into giving him a signed picture of her famous son.

On their walk, in a voice trembling with emotion, Ernst told his son that he could not stay in Germany. The Nazis, he said, had taken away their rights and honor. He was convinced that the younger generation of Jews to which Werner and his brothers belonged no longer had a future there, and must make a life elsewhere. His own generation, his father said, would likely have to stick it out in Germany; resettling at their age and position in life was difficult. He told Werner to keep looking for a trade he wanted to learn, and promised to help him find some practical training, preferably abroad. Werner loved the sound of going "abroad" and looked forward to having an adventure.

Two weeks later, Werner's father showed him an item in a Jewish newspaper announcing the start of a training farm for prospective Jewish emigrants. Located in western Poland, the farm trained boys and girls over the age of sixteen in agricultural, animal husbandry, and teaching crafts in preparation for emigration to other countries. The sound of working outside and with animals was to Werner's liking, and he applied. On April 1, 1936, days after finishing the school term, he was called in for an interview with Curt Bondy, the forty-two-year-old psychologist and social educator who headed the program.

The only question Werner would remember from the fifteen-minute interview was Bondy asking him how he felt about being Jewish. Since Werner knew nothing about Bondy's own position on the subject, he gave a very cautious answer, attesting mainly to attending temple with his parents on holidays. In truth, he had nothing to worry about; Bondy was Jewish, and had been a university teacher until the Nazis fired him in 1933.

A few days later, Werner got a call telling him he had been accepted. The next month, his mother took him to the train station. Their parting was quick and painless, as Werner had been assured he would be able to come home for regular visits. Henny was pleased that her son had the opportunity to learn a trade that would help him emigrate, and Werner was filled with thoughts of forthcoming travel and adventures.

Gross Breesen was a former knight's manor owned by a Polish Jew who had purchased the property after World War I and was leasing it to Bondy's group. Upon arrival, Werner found himself in the middle of rolling hills, surrounded by groves of fruit trees and cultivated fields. A large manor stood apart from the livestock barns. The setting looked ideal to Werner; here, he could learn farming and work with animals. He joined more than fifty boys and girls, nearly all of them German Jews, living in the stately manor in the middle of nowhere, with modern conveniences like electric lights, central heating, and bathrooms with hot and cold running water.

Unlike in school, Werner found a real purpose in what he learned at Gross Breesen. From his first six-week training assignment in the dairy barn—up at 4 A.M. every day to feed the cows, milk them by hand, separate the cream, churn the butter—to training in carpentry, hoeing out the weeds in the potato and turnip fields, harvesting crops, and driving horse teams, the lessons, labors, and camaraderie with instructors and trainees alike suited him. The long workdays ordinarily lasted until 6 P.M., although at harvest time they kept working well past sunset, picking crops in the moonlight.

The next year and a half went by quickly for Werner. He learned to farm, grew taller and sturdier, and gained new confidence. Then, in October 1937, a few months after his seventeenth birthday, he received an ominous postcard from his father.

*My dear son, I am writing you at this unusual time for a
reason. I must speak to you, and ask you to come to Berlin.
Don't ask questions. We will talk about it when you're here. A
big kiss, Papa.*

It sounded serious, though Werner had no idea what it could
mean. The next Saturday, he took the train to Berlin and went
straight to his family's apartment on Holsteinische Straße. His
mother was there alone; his two brothers were out with friends.
Henny was clearly happy to see him, but she seemed nervous and
distressed. Werner soon found out why.

Papa had decided, Henny told her son, that the entire family had
to get out of Germany. It was no longer safe for them to stay. Almost
breathlessly, she described their escape plan. Werner's head spun,
trying to take it all in. His banker father, always so honorable in his
financial dealings, planned to
smuggle the family's money to
Amsterdam, thereby violating
the strict national currency
laws put in place by the Third
Reich to stop emigrating Jews
from taking their assets with
them. If they were caught, the
consequences would be severe.

Werner's mother said Papa
was in Amsterdam that very
day, making final arrangements, and he would return
to Berlin by Sunday. On the
Friday of the following week,
she and the two younger boys
were to leave Germany, quite
legally, as tourists visiting Amsterdam. They would each

Werner Angress, sixteen, at Gross
Breesen, 1936. *(Family photograph)*

carry only the allowable ten marks. The next day, Werner was to fly with his father from Berlin's Tempelhof Airport to Amsterdam, taking only carry-on baggage, so as not to arouse suspicions. A few days later, a Jewish moving company would empty out the apartment and ship their furnishings to them in Holland.

Werner's first inclination was not to join his family on their desperate journey. He had already discussed with Bondy the possibility of settling elsewhere with friends from Gross Breesen—perhaps even in America, where Bondy was talking about setting up a new agricultural training operation. Werner told his mother he didn't want to wait around for his father to return, that he needed to get back to Gross Breesen. He left soon after for the railroad station, where he caught the next train.

When he arrived back at the farm, Werner told Bondy of his father's audacious escape plan and his own desire to stay at Gross Breesen. Bondy didn't say anything as Werner spoke. When he finished, Bondy explained that he was going to Berlin the next day, and that they would speak upon his return.

Two days later, Bondy called Werner into his office. He had spoken with colleagues in Berlin, and they had all agreed it would not be possible for Werner to stay at Gross Breesen after his parents fled Germany. The authorities would soon learn that his father had taken their money out of the country; they would most likely arrest Werner and hold him until his father returned to face criminal charges. That could put the entire Gross Breesen program in danger.

Bondy's next news sent a jolt of surprise through Werner. He had met with Ernst while in Berlin, Bondy said. He advised the conflicted young man to do what his father expected of him. Ernst understood Werner's feelings about Gross Breesen and promised to consider any future settlement plans. Given all that was happening, Bondy said Werner could hardly expect more generosity from his father. For his part, Bondy promised to include Werner in any plans for a new agricultural settlement in the United States or elsewhere.

Werner realized that Bondy was right. He had reacted like an impetuous teenager. If his father felt so strongly that the family needed to get out of Germany, the danger must be great indeed. In such perilous times, he belonged with his family.

On Friday, October 29, 1937, Werner took an overnight train to Berlin, where he met his father at the station café. They embraced warmly, and over a quick breakfast, his father calmly explained that *Mutti* and the two boys, Fritz and Hans, had left the day before and were now safely out of the country.

What Ernst did not tell his son—for Werner's own good, in the event that he was questioned—was that a young German woman had arrived that morning at their apartment with an empty briefcase. She was there to pick up the currency Ernst had brought home from the bank the night before and hidden under his mattress. Together, they packed a hundred thousand bundled-up Reichmarks (then worth about forty thousand U.S. dollars) into the briefcase.

Ernst had offered the young woman money for a taxi, but she demurred; taxis, she told him, could get into traffic accidents. It would be better if she took a streetcar to the train station. And then she was gone. After turning over his family's entire life savings to a complete stranger, Ernst wasn't sure whether to laugh or cry. But it was done; there was no turning back. The money-smuggling operation, which was based in Amsterdam, would receive 10 percent of whatever currency made it there. True to his upstanding character, Ernst had withdrawn only his own money and left the bank's other deposits untouched.

From the café, Werner and his father took a taxi to Tempelhof Airport in south Berlin. Werner had all his clothes and about a dozen books stuffed into two suitcases, while his father carried a small bag suitable for a short trip. At the airport, which had four or five departure gates, Werner followed his father. At their gate, his father showed their airplane tickets to two men wearing long trench coats and derby hats, which everyone knew was the favorite attire of Gestapo agents, who were now closely monitoring all modes of transportation out of Germany.

Asked the purpose of their trip to Holland—they both had valid passports that bore the red "J"—Ernst said he was taking his son to Amsterdam, where Werner was to enroll in special agricultural training. The Gestapo men searched his bag, then allowed Ernst to pass through. After Werner's bags were searched, he joined his father in the waiting area.

Before they sat down, they heard an announcement over the terminal's loudspeaker: the plane for Amsterdam had been unable to take off from Dresden due to heavy fog. Passengers bound for Amsterdam could either wait until the next day's flight or take the train that night.

Flights were departing from other gates for Copenhagen and Paris. Ernst knew it would look suspicious if they suddenly changed their destination to Denmark or France. They had given the Gestapo agents a specific reason why they were traveling to Holland.

"We'll take the night train to Amsterdam," he told Werner.

Since the train did not leave until midnight and it was now only noontime, they had a long wait. During their time together, Werner learned more about what had finally compelled his father to get the family out of Germany. New restrictions on Jews were being enacted all the time, he said, including the confiscation of their properties and assets. Germany was witnessing the "gradual strangulation of Jewish businesses." Ernst feared that sooner or later there would be no opportunity for carrying on business and no way for him to make a living. Under the Nazis, he feared the family would eventually end up paupers with no place to go.

After sitting in a neighborhood café for a while, his father suggested they go see a movie. Dragging their bags along, they took a taxi to the cinema and settled into seats for a film, which was preceded by a newsreel entitled "Papi's Fortieth Birthday." It turned out that "Papi" was Joseph Goebbels, who had just turned forty. He was shown celebrating with his wife, Magda, and their young children, who presented bouquets of flowers to the beaming Nazi propaganda minister.

It was all too much for Ernst. He whispered to Werner that he should stay and watch the movie; they could meet afterward at the nearby apartment of his good friend Leo Gerson, to whom he wished to say good-bye.

Werner decided it was a good thing his father had left. The movie was about police chasing bank robbers in Amsterdam.

A surprise awaited Werner when he reached Leo Gerson's apartment. Before he'd even had time to take off his jacket, his father told him there'd been a change of plans. Werner was to take a taxi to the train station and board the sleeping car, on which his father had reserved a private compartment. Once there, he would tip the conductor two Reichmarks and tell him that his father had been delayed in Berlin on business and wouldn't be making the trip.

"I am to go to Amsterdam alone? What do you plan to do, Papa?"

"I don't know yet," Ernst answered.

His father said only that they would meet up in Amsterdam, and hurriedly sent Werner on his way with money for expenses. Shortly after Werner left, Ernst went to the same railway station, but to a different platform, and took a train heading in the opposite direction. He had a plan, of course, but had thought it was best for them both if he kept Werner in the dark. Ernst had also decided it was safer for them to travel apart. As he'd expected them to be on that morning's flight to Amsterdam, he had advised his longtime secretary, Else Radinowsky, and the bank's owner, Leo Königsberger, to report the missing funds to police that afternoon, so they wouldn't be suspected as co-conspirators. When the flight to Amsterdam was canceled, Ernst had decided against contacting either his secretary or the bank's owner, for fear of their becoming entangled in his crime. By now, they had likely notified police that the missing Jewish director of the Königsberger and Lichtenhein Bank had withdrawn all of his personal capital and was apparently fleeing the country. If that was the case, the authorities would try anything they could to stop him.

Ernst's fears were justified. By that afternoon, his colleagues had reported the missing money, and the police in turn had notified customs officials, who sent out telegrams to all border crossing stations reading: "Family of five named Angress to be arrested."

As he boarded the midnight train, Werner didn't know any of this. He followed his father's detailed instructions: he tipped the conductor and said his father would not be joining him as originally planned. The conductor asked for his passport, and Werner handed it over. In the sleeping compartment, Werner undressed and lay down on the lower bunk. Exhausted, he fell asleep before the train had even left the station.

A few hours later, the train stopped in the dark at Bentheim-Grenze, the last station in Germany before the Dutch border. Werner was still asleep when the light came on in the compartment; he awakened to three men standing next to his bunk. One was the conductor he had tipped. The other two wore trench coats and derbies—one of them held Werner's passport, which he was studying intently.

Your last name is Angress? he asked in German.

A groggy Werner said yes.

Where is your father?

Without hesitating, Werner coolly lied as his father had instructed him and said he was in Berlin.

After further questioning, the Gestapo left the compartment and went into the corridor for a short conversation. They had been advised to be on the lookout for a family of five, not a teenage boy traveling alone. They handed Werner's passport back to the conductor and left.

The train soon started rolling again. Werner dressed quickly and was given back his passport by the conductor, who said his shift was about to end.

In a few minutes, the train stopped at Oldenzaal, the first station in Holland. Only when the new conductor, speaking German with a Dutch accent, greeted Werner did it register on him that he was out of Germany and traveling in a free country. His mother and brothers were also safe; his one remaining concern was his father. Werner hoped that whatever plan his father had come up with yesterday would also bring him safely to Holland, and that they would find his mother and brothers waiting for them there and be reunited.

In Amsterdam, Werner went directly from the station to the Pension Rosengarten on Beethovenstraat, using directions his father had made him memorize. When he found the address, he saw that it was an old, dark apartment building, filled with newly arrived German Jews who were also waiting to make connections to someplace else. The owner, who was the head of the currency-smuggling ring, had just received a telegram from Ernst, asking if "Werner and Minna" had made it to Amsterdam. "Minna" was code for the briefcase filled with money. The owner was now able to wire Ernst that both Werner and Minna had indeed arrived safely.

It took Ernst another week to reach Amsterdam. To avoid arrest, he followed an agonizingly circuitous route. From Berlin, he had taken the train to Prague. When he arrived at the Czech border, he exited on the wrong side of the train and walked across the tracks, avoiding the German border guards. Entering Czechoslovakia, he identified himself as a Jewish refugee from Germany. He assured the Czech border guards that he was en route to Holland via Austria, Switzerland, and France—a path German refugees called the "Jewish Southern Loop"—and thus avoided being sent back.

In Amsterdam, the family was finally reunited. Yet, for weeks after they had moved into a rented apartment, Ernst struggled to put the ordeal behind him. He had done things in an effort to get his family out of Germany that he had never thought he was capable of doing. He had not only broken the law for the first time in his life, but in doing so, he had subjected his wife and sons to dangers as well. Adding to these deep blows to his self-esteem, Ernst had to reckon with all that the family had left behind in the city and country of their birth. There was their home and all their belongings, which Ernst heard had been seized by the Gestapo, and the respectable reputation he had built in his profession. There were also their extended families and ancestral burial sites, all left behind. No matter how safe they were outside Germany, there were so many things they could not replace or replicate elsewhere.

Werner was nearly inconsolable, too. He'd left all his friends in such a hurry that he hadn't even been able to say good-byes. After the financial crimes his father had committed, he would never be able to return to Gross Breesen or Germany. Like it or not, he was in exile, too. He talked about this with his father, who understood how he felt. He had always been a German patriot, Ernst told his son. When he was in the army in the last war, he had volunteered to go to the front to take part in the fighting, and had been disappointed when he was assigned to military base duty because of a hearing disorder. But now—

"Hitler and the Nazis aren't letting us be Germans anymore," Ernst said bitterly. "They have humiliated and degraded Jews to second-class citizens. For that reason, Werner, Germany is no longer our homeland. I'll take up a gun against those crooks anytime!"

His own heart made heavier by his father's sorrow and deep sense of betrayal, Werner had no idea how soon the day would come when he, rather than his father, would be taking up arms in just that fight.

Stephan Lewy's train ride out of Germany landed him and the other Jewish orphans from Berlin on the outskirts of Quincy-sous-Sénart, a French village of fifteen hundred residents about twenty miles south of Paris. The boys were awestruck as they approached their new home, a majestic old château owned by Count Hubert Conquéré de Monbrison. The count and his wife, Princess Irina Paley, a cousin of the last Russian czar, had for years opened the château to refugee girls from the Russian and Spanish civil wars, and they had recently been asked by a board member of a Paris-based Jewish children's aid society, Oeuvre de Secours aux Enfants (OSE), to take in German Jewish refugee children, whom the group had been rescuing after Kristallnacht.

When the forty boys arrived from Berlin in July 1939, there were

no rooms available in the château; most were already occupied by
Spanish girls. For the first several months, while the girls waited to
be taken in by local families, the boys had to stay in an annex building, along with instructors and other staff, most of whom were also
Jewish refugees.

The boys were enrolled in the village school across the road.
Since Stephan and the others didn't speak French, they were
placed in the first grade. Stephan, who was already fourteen years
old, picked up the language quickly. And given how good he was
at mathematics and geography, he was soon advanced to his grade
level.

One of the things he learned in his French history class was that
France, a country of forty million, had lost two million men in the
last war with Germany. It was a crushing loss, one that still lingered
in recent memory. And yet, in spite of the rise of Hitler and the Nazis, and the rearming of Germany, there existed among the French
a cheerful optimism and a strong sense of safety and security. The
newly constructed Maginot Line, which consisted of miles of concrete walls, obstacles, and fortifications on the French side of the
border with Germany, was believed to be impenetrable. Built to
replicate the static defensive combat of the first war, French military
experts thought it would protect their country from future German
invasions.

From their own experiences with the Nazis, and after the military buildup they had seen in Germany, Stephan and the other
Berlin boys did not share the locals' sense of well-being. Stephan's
father, Arthur, had predicted that Hitler would wage war in the fall,
"after the crops are in the barn," so as to feed his army. This was the
same timing Germany had employed in the last war, his father had
explained to Stephan before he left Germany. Now Stephan worried about what would happen to his parents, still in Germany, and
to himself in France in the event of war.

On September 1, 1939, everyone in the château gathered around
the console radio to hear the BBC bulletins about Germany's inva-

sion of Poland. Columns of horse-mounted Polish cavalry were reported to be charging armored tanks. Two days later, France and England, allies of Poland, declared war on Germany. With the Germans unleashing a new type of modern, highly mobile warfare tactics that became known as *blitzkrieg* (lightning war), the battle in Poland lasted just weeks. Warsaw surrendered on September 27, and a week later the nation of Poland ceased to exist, subjugating thirty-five million Poles, including more than three million Jews, to Nazi rule.

After the fall of Poland, news reports indicated that the warring nations had found themselves in a defensive stalemate, with French and Allied troops manning the Maginot Line and Germans holding the fortified Siegfried Line on their side of the border. In what the British press and politicians labeled the "Phoney War" for its lack of major fighting, for months only minor skirmishes took place. But Stephan was unable to send mail to Berlin or to receive it, and as a result, he lost all contact with his parents after fall 1939.

In May 1940, German troops invaded Belgium and Holland. Deftly bypassing the Maginot Line to the north, the Germans split the French-British-Belgian defensive front and drove Allied forces back to the coast at Dunkirk, where hundreds of small boats ferried more than three hundred thousand evacuees across the English Channel. In the south, German forces broke through the suddenly obsolete Maginot Line, and the *blitzkrieg* steamrolled into France, headed for Paris and the Normandy coast.

Early one morning, Stephan and the other boys were awakened by the sound of several large vehicles pulling up in front of the château. Jumping from their beds, they ran to the windows and looked out. The large courtyard was filling up with French military trucks and artillery pieces. Within an hour, the French soldiers had set up their big guns, pointing in the direction of their country's capital. The soldiers waited, ready to try to halt the anticipated German advance after it rolled through Paris. One played an accordion; others idly smoked cigarettes.

At 10 A.M., a clearly distressed Count Monbrison gathered the boys and their instructors. He told them that the Germans were approaching Paris; and he could not guarantee the refugees' safety. They needed to escape, and he had arranged for two trucks to take them to Limoges, 250 miles to the south. The boys went to their rooms, rolled up their blankets, put a single change of clothes in their backpacks, and went outside to the waiting trucks. They and several instructors piled into the canvas-covered back of the bigger truck; the smaller truck was loaded with their belongings and several bicycles.

Not long after leaving the château, the trucks joined a long line of stalled traffic. The German invasion had set off a mass exodus of civilians in cars, buses, trucks, bicycles, and carts, clogging the highways and secondary roads leading south. After four hours, the two trucks had made it just six miles—to the town of Corbeil, where boats and barges of varying sizes and power were motoring westward on the Seine. One instructor left to find a vessel to take them to the coast, in the hope that the waterways would be less congested than the roads. He returned an hour later and took the boys to a nearby *péniche,* a steel motorized river barge built for moving cargo. The vessel was about a hundred feet long, but just fifteen feet wide; it had limited space above deck for the boys and their instructors. The only available space below deck was a cargo hold half filled with coal. The boys packed into the unlit space atop the coal, and the hatch was closed. The air, thick with coal dust, was nearly unbreathable.

At dawn, the hatch was opened; the boys, blackened with soot from head to toe, came out into daylight. Stephan was surprised to discover that the barge had traveled only a short distance on the river; now it was held up in a line of traffic at a floodgate. It took a few more hours for the barge to pass through. When they finally came to a village, they docked to find food and water.

By about noon, they were back aboard the barge, ready to get underway. Suddenly, gunfire sounded all around them, and they heard people screaming on shore. Stephan had never heard gunfire before, and he had not pictured how loud it would be. The shots sounded very close. The boys had no choice but to rush back down into the darkened cargo hold, and the hatch was slammed shut after them. The barge slowly pulled out into the middle of the river. A short time later, no more than a half hour, they heard shouted orders in German, followed by the sound of the barge's motor shutting down.

The staccato clicking of heavy boots sounded across the deck, and the cargo hold's hatch flew open. The Jewish boys looked up to see German soldiers pointing guns down into the cargo hold.

"*Juden!*"

One soldier spat, *"Ein Haufen schmutziger Juden!"* (A bunch of dirty Jews!)

The soldiers laughed, then slammed down the hatch.

After the soldiers left, the instructors let the terrified boys out and huddled for a tense meeting. They decided to get everyone off the barge. Traffic on the river was moving too slowly, and in any case, the German army had overtaken them. The last thing they wanted to do was wind up near the front lines of a battle between the German and French armies. The instructors told the boys it would be best to return to Quincy, now some twenty miles in the opposite direction.

They found a big wooden pushcart, pulled by two long handles, and loaded their belongings. The trek back was against the flow of vehicular and pedestrian traffic, which still poured forth out of Paris as the mass evacuation of civilians continued southward.

After sunset, far-off fires and explosions turned the sky bloodred, and the boys heard the muffled explosions of distant bombs. In the dark, they walked into a checkpoint manned by French paratroopers. Wary of the group of young Germans, the soldiers questioned them closely. Where had they come from? Where were they going? Had they seen any German soldiers? Finally, they were allowed to pass. They found a barn in which to spend the night, but heard gunshots around midnight—very close. Few of the boys slept, and they were back on the move at sunrise.

As the morning dew settled on the ground, the group found themselves surrounded by an eerie, profound silence. It was difficult to believe they were in the midst of a shooting war. When the boys stopped for lunch, the instructors passed out small chocolate bars, crackers, and three sardines in oil apiece. They ate, watching as a billowing white parachute floated down into a nearby field. As soon as the German paratrooper hit the ground, he was cut down by sniper fire. For most of the boys, Stephan included, it was the first person they had ever seen killed. But there was no time for reflection or discussion. They quickly got back on the road and continued on.

A short time later, a German soldier passed them, speeding by on a motorcycle. The sound of nearby machine gun fire caused the boys and their instructors to scramble for cover. Several planes dove out of the clouds, dropping bombs that landed close enough for the boys to feel the concussive waves from the blasts. The planes had the red, white, and blue circular markings of the French military. Booming antiaircraft guns fired somewhere in the distance, and the boys saw in the sky the trailing dark smoke of a plane that within seconds crashed in a ball of fire.

After a second full day of walking, they reached the château. A sentry halted them in the courtyard; to their alarm, he was not French. The German army had taken over. Two older boys accompanied the instructors inside to speak with the officer in charge. When they returned, they reported that the German colonel had given them two choices: be sent back to Germany, or work at Quincy. They opted to stay. Henceforth, the boys would do the soldiers' laundry, clean vehicles and equipment, serve meals, polish boots, and do anything else required. If anyone refused to work or caused trouble, they were warned, the entire group would be deported.

With more than a hundred soldiers occupying the château as well as the annex building, the boys and instructors moved some cots into the basement. The occupying Germans shared little of the meat, dairy, and produce that was delivered to the château, and the boys were constantly hungry. They sneaked out at night and foraged for fruit and potatoes in nearby fields.

Two weeks after they returned, it was announced on the radio— now tuned to German broadcasts, full of Nazi propaganda—that Germany and France had signed an armistice, resulting in the division of France. The Germans would occupy the north and coastal areas, including Paris and Normandy, while newly appointed French leaders would govern the unoccupied southern part from the new capital of Vichy.

One of Stephan's jobs was to do the soldiers' laundry. He put the dirty clothes into a huge pot of water on the stove, added soap, and boiled everything for an hour. When it cooled down, he carried the pot to the sink, poured out the soapy water, and added water to rinse the clothes before hanging them up outside.

As he did the wash one day, Stephan saw dark specks floating to the surface of the boiling water. They appeared to be food particles. Thinking that they must have been left on the table linens after meals, he began scooping them out of the pot, rinsing, and eating them. He had learned how to share growing up at the orphanage, so he split his bounty with some other hungry boys, and they all agreed that the soggy crumbs tasted delicious. Their snacking ended when one of the instructors caught them in the act, and showed the boys that they were actually eating pieces of army T-shirts that had disintegrated in the boiling water and shredded into tiny pieces.

In early October 1940, their instructors awakened the boys in the middle of the night and told them to quickly pack a few essentials. Quietly, they filed out of the basement into the courtyard. Two covered trucks were waiting, engines idling. They pulled out of the darkened courtyard and drove until midday. At the border between occupied and unoccupied France, the trucks stopped, and everyone got out.

When they realized they would be walking into unoccupied

France, out of reach of Nazi troops, the Jewish boys became very
excited. Their gait increased still more when they saw that the German soldiers guarding the border were not going to stop them. By
the time they were on the other side, where the French gendarmes
(police) stood at the crossing, the boys were running and cheering.
They found their ride waiting nearby: a dilapidated old bus that
didn't have enough seats for everyone, so they took turns standing.

They pulled into the village of Chabannes three hours later. This
was a remote and unspoiled region of central France, 120 miles west
of Vichy, whose residents had a spirit of independence and justice
carried over from the earliest days of the French Republic.

The boys' new home was another rambling château, one that
had passed through many hands. The aristocratic d'Anrémont family acquired the estate in the 1870s, but it was rundown by the time
OSE took it over in 1939 to serve as one of its fourteen children's
homes in unoccupied France. (OSE could not operate in German-
occupied France.)[*]

The director at Chabannes was former journalist Félix Chevrier,
an imposing man of fifty-six who came off as gruff but understood
that many of the children laughed by day and cried by night. Chevrier reminded the dedicated staff, which included cooks, nurses,
janitors, and teachers, that they were to provide the children, all of
whom had known exile and separation, not just shelter and suste-
nance but a sense of normalcy in abnormal times.

At Chabannes, Stephan and the other boys from Berlin joined
more than one hundred other Jewish children—mostly Germans,
along with some Austrian and French refugees—ranging from eight
to eighteen years of age.

Given his age, now fifteen, and the overcrowding at the village school, Stephan started learning the leather trade in a well-

---

[*] By the end of 1944, OSE had rescued more than five thousand Jewish children
from Nazi-occupied Europe, sending them to safety in the United States, England, Switzerland, and Spain.

equipped shop sponsored by the Organization for Rehabilitation through Training (ORT). ORT helped refugees immigrate to other countries as skilled workers. Stephan learned to use all of the machines and cutting tables; soon he was crafting handsome pocketbooks, wallets, and comb holders that were sold in the village, with the proceeds going back to ORT.

Sports and physical education were an important part of each day, and there were spirited regular basketball and soccer games. Georges Loinger, a former engineer who coached gymnastics and track and field, often drove the boys to the point of exhaustion. He told them he wanted them fit in case they ever had to run for their lives. Stephan, fast and athletic, excelled in the sports.

There were enjoyable times for the children at Chabannes, too. Music was played every Saturday night after Shabbat, and young and old alike danced; the lively songs were performed by teenagers, with Jean-Pierre Marcuse on guitar, Armand Chochenbaum on drums, Walter Herzig at the piano, and Marjan Sztrum on banjo. Sztrum, an eighteen-year-old Polish Jew, was also a talented artist;

Château Chabannes, Jewish children's home near Limoges, France, where Stephan Lewy lived for nearly two years, 1941. *(U.S. Holocaust Memorial Museum)*

Sixteen-year-old Stephan Lewy (*right*) working in the kitchen at Chabannes, 1941. *(U.S. Holocaust Memorial Museum)*

he painted a fresco on the dining room wall depicting a farmer on a tractor.

The newfound security the children and their instructors began to feel at Chabannes vanished when they heard that gendarmes were showing up at other OSE homes, arresting the older Jewish boys, and transporting them to concentration camps. Tipped off by sympathetic locals in the village as a contingent of French police approached, Stephan ran with some other boys into the woods, where they spent the night hiding out.

Throughout unoccupied France, it had become clear that the one-party fascist regime headed by Marshal Philippe Pétain was nothing more than a puppet government of Hitler's Germany. The Vichy regime became increasingly brazen in carrying out Nazi-ordered pogroms, and in 1940 it began passing its own anti-Semitic laws, banning French Jews from working in certain fields and forcibly expelling foreign-born Jews. The French government gave lists of Jews to Nazis and assisted in identifying and expropriating the assets of wealthy Jewish families. More and more roundups of Jews swept France, and the gendarmes soon became as feared as Nazi storm troopers.[*]

The year after he arrived at Chabannes, Stephan was summoned to the director's office. Months earlier, he had sought Monsieur Chevrier's help in trying to contact his parents, whom he had never stopped thinking about during his own flights through wartime France. Were they in danger? Or had something terrible already happened to them? So much had transpired since they had parted in Berlin. Now the Nazis were at war with the world, not just the Jews in Germany. Although he was terribly afraid he might get bad news, Stephan had decided that he needed to know one way or another. Were his parents dead or alive?

Mercifully, on this day, Chevrier was not bearing bad news. He explained that he had just received a wire from the Red Cross in Switzerland, reporting that Stephan's parents had been located in America.

Stephan wasn't sure he had heard right. "America?"

"Yes," Chevrier said, smiling. "You can write to them."

Stephan was excited and greatly relieved that his parents had found a way to get to America. Would he be able to join them? He hurriedly wrote a letter that same day. Several weeks passed before he heard back. When a return letter arrived, forwarded via Switzerland, it was written in his stepmother's graceful cursive.

Dearest Stephan,
   We were so excited when your letter came we first stared at the envelope before we dared open it . . .

Back in Germany, Arthur had lost weight, lowered his blood pressure, and passed his follow-up physical with ease. In quick

_____

[*] Between 1939 and 1944, more than 75,000 Jews were rounded up and deported from France to Nazi death camps in Poland, where an estimated 72,500 of them perished in the camps.

order, they had received an affidavit from Johanna's cousin, Bert Klapper, in Massachusetts, and visas for the United States. They had taken what they believed was their last opportunity to escape the Nazis, departing Germany in May 1940. It had been an agonizing decision for them because they did not know where Stephan was or even if he was still alive.

On their third day at sea, aboard a ship that left from Rotterdam, they heard news of the German invasion of Holland and Belgium. By the time they arrived in the U.S., France was at war, and the organizations they contacted were unable to find out anything about Stephan. There was more, much more, in the letter: their excitement at locating him, their love for him, how they were determined to find a way to bring him to America, too. Stephan read the letter again, and then, for the first time in a long time, he cried.

Over the next several months, and after some bureaucratic hitches, the paperwork for Stephan's entry into the United States was finished. Johanna's cousin signed an affidavit for him, as did his parents' employer, a Russian Jew who had immigrated to the U.S. in the 1920s and become very successful in business. Arthur and Johanna Lewy were working as butler and maid at his mansion in Boston, Massachusetts. Their employer even gave them five hundred dollars to pay for their son's ship passage.

In April 1942, Stephan said good-bye to everyone at Chabannes and took the train to Lyon, where he picked up his visa at the U.S. consul's office. He then traveled two hundred miles by rail to Marseille, France's southernmost Mediterranean port, and boarded a French passenger ship. Once on board, the captain gathered everyone together and explained the circuitous route he planned to take.

"If we leave here and head straight out into the Mediterranean toward North Africa," he said, "we'll probably get torpedoed by a German U-boat and no one will ever know what happened to us." Instead, he was going to hug the coastline, slipping in and out of every inlet. "If we get torpedoed, I can at least scuttle the ship near land and maybe save our lives."

They reached Barcelona and took on fifty Spanish refugees. Continuing along the eastern and southern coast of Spain, they crossed the seven-mile-wide Strait of Gibraltar, heading toward North Africa. Not forgetting the captain's dire U-boat warning, everyone on board was relieved to finally arrive in Rabat, Morocco.

Stephan took a bus to Casablanca, where he waited several weeks for the ship that would take him across the Atlantic: the Portuguese steamship *Serpa Pinto,* a six-thousand-ton vessel chartered by the U.S.-based Hebrew Immigrant Aid Society (HIAS) to take seven hundred Jewish refugees to America. Because it flew under the flag of a neutral country, the *Serpa Pinto* was one of the few passenger ships still making transatlantic voyages despite the U-boat menace. It departed Casablanca on June 7, 1942.

As the five-hundred-foot ship sped across the Atlantic at near top speed, Stephan found himself unnerved by the ship's running lights, which were left blazing all night. The ship stood out like a beacon in the inky darkness. One morning, Stephan questioned a ship's officer about all the lights. With all the U-boats, wasn't it dangerous to be so lit up at night?

"We are neutral," said the officer. "That is why we fly an extra-large Portuguese flag so prominently with the lights glowing. Any vessel can see we are a neutral ship."

The flag, clearly visible at the stern and lit by flood lighting at night, was a huge green-and-red wooden one that did not crumple or ruffle in the wind. The officer's explanation seemed plausible to Stephan—up until a few hours later, when the vibration of the engines ceased. He joined the other passengers in a rush to the railings and saw a low-slung submarine with a swastika painted on its conning tower.

Several German sailors from the U-boat climbed into a small, motorized launch, which they took to the ship. When they reached

the *Serpa Pinto,* a rope ladder was thrown over the hull for them
to climb up. On deck, there was no chatter from the refugees, only
deathly silence. Stephan felt sick to his stomach. He knew there was
no place to hide.

For three hours, the armed boarding party searched all the com-
partments on the ship, apparently looking for contraband. When
they found none, they had the crew collect the passengers' passports and went through them one at a time. Nearly all carried the
red "J."

At last, the boarding party left and returned to the submarine.
The passengers remained on deck, watching to see what would
happen next. *"Habt keine Angst,"* said a multilingual ship's officer.
He circled the deck, telling the mostly German-speaking passengers not to be afraid.

But every one of them was scared to death. Would the U-boat
turn toward them, launch a torpedo, and sink them? Hoping he
hadn't come this far only to drown in the middle of the ocean,
Stephan joined the others on deck who were praying in German
and Hebrew; they continued until they could no longer see the submarine in the distance.

On June 25, 1942, the *Serpa Pinto* arrived in New York harbor.
The ship slowed as it passed the Statue of Liberty, allowing the
passengers a good look at the three-hundred-foot sculpture of the
Roman goddess Libertas. She held high the copper torch, lighting
the path to freedom from tyranny and suffering for oppressed immigrants from other shores. Some on the boat were smiling and laughing; others were struck speechless.

Stephan Lewy, who had been an orphan for more than half his
lifetime, knew his father and loving new mother were waiting for
him dockside. He breathed deeply, and his eyes filled with tears.
He had made it.

A Place to Call Home

Günther Stern's father had cautioned him to "be like invisible ink" so as to not draw attention to himself. But soon after they said good-bye at the port of Bremerhaven, where he boarded the SS *Hamburg* in November 1937, Günther joined in with the other emigrant children on the ship, running around playing hide-and-seek and pulling practical jokes on one another. The Jewish youngsters were eager to be free of the restrictive rules under which they had been living in Nazi Germany, which required them to be better than good in public so as to remain inconspicuous. In fact, Günther was still so wrapped up in his new oceangoing adventure that he hadn't yet had time to be homesick.

On deck one sunny day, the children befriended an older American who was traveling alone. When he treated them all to an exotic drink they had never tasted before, called Coca-Cola, they became convinced he must be one of those fabled American millionaires. Near the end of the voyage, he told them he was in fact a mailman who had saved up for years for his first European vacation. The refugee children did not believe him: How could an average American afford such a trip? They decided that their generous millionaire simply wished to remain anonymous.

When they reached New York, a committee representative de-cided that Günther, after all his private lessons from Herr Tittel, was fluent enough in English to travel by himself the rest of the way to St. Louis. He would have to change trains in Chicago, how-ever, so someone would meet him there and help him make his connection.

During his short time in the heart of New York City, Günther was most impressed by the jumble of skyscrapers, the crowded sub-ways, and the curious *Automatenrestaurants,* or automats, at which busy people inserted coins in machines and instantly received sand-wiches and other food items.

He arrived in Chicago on a Sunday and had a three-hour lay-over. The woman who met him decided they had time for a quick tour of the Windy City. The excursion included a stroll through the open-air Maxwell Street Market, which occupied several square blocks. Founded in 1912 by newly arrived Jewish immigrants from eastern Europe, the market featured booths selling a variety of dis-counted items: produce, clothes, tools, and all things in between. To Günther, it was a wild mix of cultures and ethnicities; he saw people of all colors and ages, many of them Jews, intermingling eas-ily, talking and joking with each other.

Günther had never seen anything like this in Germany. If this was what it meant to be in America, the land of the free, his days of trying to disappear in public like invisible ink were over.

After another long train trip, he arrived in St. Louis. His aunt Ethel and cousin Melvin met him at the station. Uncle Benno, his mother's brother, was working the night shift at a bakery, and Günther did not meet him until he came home later that night. His uncle's story was familiar to Günther; as a rebellious youth of four-teen or fifteen, Benno had been exiled by his strict father, who sent him to America in the days when it was easier for immigrants to gain entry. Benno was a short, squat man who had been stymied but not defeated by the Depression. The Silberbergs did not live easy lives, but they had never been threatened with eviction or relegated to standing in a breadline for their next meal. Benno did not apologize for the family's cramped apartment, located in a subdivided mansion on the predominantly Jewish west side, though the accommodations were markedly different from Günther's family's spacious, well-appointed home in Hildesheim. Nor was any explanation offered for Günther having to share a small room and a single bed with another refugee boy, Rudy Solomon, whom his aunt had taken in at the request of the Jewish Aid Society.

Although he quickly began to miss his own family and ache for home, Günther's youthful dreams of adventure in his new country remained intact, no more so than when he enrolled five days later in Soldan High School, a public school reputed to be the finest in St. Louis. At Soldan, students from affluent families sat next to those in threadbare clothes, and all of them were taught and inspired by dedicated teachers and administrators determined to rival the top college-prep schools in the country. It was America at its best.

On his first day, Günther was received personally by the principal, who told him he had been assigned to the homeroom of Mrs. Muller, the German language teacher. When the principal asked if he was interested in any extracurricular activities, Günther quickly answered, "Swimming and the school newspaper."

His first class was geometry, and after being warmly welcomed by the teacher—"our new student from Germany!"—he discovered that the class had just started taking a test. Mrs. Carmody, the geometry teacher, encouraged him to take it, too, in order to "show what you can do." Günther sat down and read through the questions. Approaching the teacher's desk, he asked softly, "Please, what is 'isosceles triangle'?"

She went to the blackboard and drew one.

"Ah, yes," Günther said. *"Ein gleichschenkliges Dreieck."*

He took the test, and received a G for good.

Before long, his natural curiosity led to his becoming a reporter for the school paper, *Scrippage,* whose name was borrowed from Shakespeare's *As You Like It.* Günther got a job in the cafeteria, working for free hot lunches, and in the spring became the number-three breaststroker on the varsity swim team. By then, he had his first girlfriend, Idamae Schwartzberg, an energetic, attractive brunette. They went to free summer musicals, such as the Gershwins' *Of Thee I Sing* and Jerome Kern and Oscar Hammerstein's *Show Boat,* performed outdoors at Forest Park.

Even though she had a rather improbable name of her own, Idamae had little patience for Günther's name, which she termed a "German tongue twister." She decided he should retain the first two letters and add a "y." Happy to assimilate, Günther became Guy. It caught on; everyone agreed that the name suited his upbeat personality well.

And his transformation was not in name only. The past several years in Germany, during which he had been required to be endlessly unobtrusive, had led to an inevitable loss of confidence, even feelings of worthlessness. Guy's climb back to self-assurance and self-worth in his country of refuge came faster than anyone, even he, would have thought possible. His kind heart, winning smile, and playful sense of humor won him a legion of new friends.

Guy's two biggest stories for the school paper, which earned him the nickname "Scoop," were interviews with bandleader Benny Goodman backstage at the Fox Theater in midtown St. Louis—they discussed jazz and swing for half an hour—and the German novelist Thomas Mann, winner of the Nobel Prize in Literature (1929), who came to town for a lecture at the Young Men's Hebrew Association.

Mann, who wrote in German, was accompanied by his daughter, Erika, an actress and writer who translated his books and speeches into English. With a heavy German accent, he read his speech, "The Coming Victory of Democracy," in precise but at times uncertain English, to a capacity crowd of three thousand. He damned the Munich Agreement of 1938 as a "betrayal" by England and France for permitting Germany to annex the Sudetenland portions of Czechoslovakia, which Hitler proclaimed as German territory.

He criticized British prime minister Neville Chamberlain's efforts to appease Hitler and warned that Hitler's thirst to expand Germany's borders at the expense of other nations could not be quenched.

Afterward, some twenty chairs were set up in another room for a press conference. Mann arrived before his daughter, who had earlier interpreted some questions from the audience for her father. Mann would answer in German, and she would report: "My father believes . . ." Now, rather than await Mann's interpreter, a *Time* correspondent asked a convoluted question in English, which stumped the novelist. Guy piped up, repeating the query in German and then translating Mann's answer into English.

With Mann looking directly at him, Guy summoned the courage to ask his own question—also in German. Even in such august company, Guy's inquiry revealed his own sharp intellect and grasp of current events. Did Mann, a well-known anti-Nazi advocate since his exile from Germany after Hitler came to power, think that the German dictator and Stalin could find common cause? Mann vigorously denied the possibility. "Dictators can never be appeased," Mann told Guy, "because they will never be satisfied with their territorial gains."

In what amounted to an exclusive interview for Guy, the German novelist went on to discuss his advocacy for national health insurance in the United States in his native tongue. Guy took notes in shorthand, which he had learned in school in Germany, as Mann explained that a democracy is only strong if every citizen is guaranteed his own social well-being, which must include affordable medical treatment, a chance for an education, and a pension.

Erika Mann's arrival at the podium ended Guy's exclusive. But before taking questions from the other reporters, Mann looked squarely at Guy and said in German, "I wish for young people like you to have a tuition-free college education." The next edition of the school newspaper raved: "Believe it or not, a *Scrippage* reporter scooped a *Time* magazine interviewer!"

Guy made his mark elsewhere. His Latin teacher, Rose Kaufman, who was well connected in the local Jewish community, took an interest in him, and in Guy's senior year, she recommended him for part-time work at the historic Chase Hotel downtown. Hired on as a busboy, Guy took pride in being self-supporting and being able to start paying some rent to his aunt and uncle.

As he made his way in his new country, Guy did not forget the promise he had made to his parents: to try to find someone who could sign the affidavit required for the whole family to come to America. Unfortunately, he hadn't yet come across anyone who could help. America was still in the Depression, and most people were out of work or barely getting by. Guy had never dreamed it would take this long. It had been a year since he and his parents had parted at the dock in Germany, and at the time he had believed that they would be reunited in the United States by now. They had kept up their correspondence through twice-monthly letters, but while Guy wrote freely of his life in America, his parents were constrained about conditions inside Germany. These subdued missives did little to soothe Guy's growing urgency as to how and when his family would get out of Germany.

He never stopped trying to obtain the critical affidavit needed for the State Department to allow his family into the United States. To save bus fare, Guy regularly hitchhiked to his hotel job. One afternoon in the fall of 1938, a well-dressed Jewish man driving a luxury sedan picked him up. Guy told his now well-rehearsed story of his immigration to America: how he had arrived the previous year; how his parents and two younger siblings were still stuck in Germany. The man listened, nodding sympathetically at times. Then, as if on cue, he asked, "What's involved in getting them over here?"

Guy said he had to find someone with the financial means to sign a government document guaranteeing that his family members would not become public charges.

"Well, I could do that," the man said breezily.

It was all Guy could do to keep from reaching over and wildly shaking his benefactor's hand as they drove through traffic along Delmar Boulevard.

"But I'm not sure the government will accept me," the man went on. "I'm a gambler. That's how I make my money."

Guy didn't think that posed a problem. Money was money.

"Are you willing to try?" Guy asked.

"Sure. After all," the man added, smiling, "life's a gamble."

It took Guy a full week to get an appointment with a lawyer, whom the Jewish Aid Society had recruited to do pro bono work for refugees. The three of them finally met at the lawyer's office, and the attorney went through a sheaf of forms with Guy and his benefactor, asking a series of routine questions. The process halted abruptly after the lawyer asked the man's occupation.

"*Gambler?!*" the lawyer croaked. "You're a professional *gambler?*" He pushed aside the papers he'd been filling out. "We needn't go any further. The signer of an affidavit for the United States State Department must be a stable citizen with an assured income."

"But, sir," Guy said, "can't you just put down 'businessman'?"

The lawyer shot Guy a withering look. "Circumvent the law to deceive the U.S. government? No, I will not!"

With that, the gambler cursed the lawyer and stormed out.

Guy froze, momentarily unable to breathe, as if he had been punched in the stomach. He could not believe what had just happened. A lawyer designated to provide legal assistance to refugees was more concerned with being a stickler on a government form than with the plight of a Jewish family trying to get out of Nazi Germany? That was the last time Guy saw the gambler, and he never again came so close to getting an affidavit signed for his family.

A few weeks later, Guy had left his aunt and uncle's to walk to school when he passed a corner newsboy hawking the *St. Louis Star Times.*

"Synagogues burning in Germany! Read all about it!"

It was early November 1938, and the news was about Kristallnacht.

The family he tried to save: Guy Stern's parents,
brother, and sister in Hildesheim, Germany, circa 1938.
(Family photograph)

When Guy read about the nationwide anti-Semitic campaign in
Germany that destroyed hundreds of synagogues and other Jewish properties, he was shocked and outraged. The century-old
Hildesheim synagogue he had first attended at age six rose up in his
mind; it had not only been a house of worship, but the center of the
town's Jewish community. Now he pictured it in cinders. He remembered the Saturday morning processions down Lappenberg Street,
the finely dressed families walking to temple. Guy had begun his
education in the one-room school adjacent to the synagogue. Was it
destroyed, too? Was it gone? All of it?

And what of his family? The worst part for Guy was not knowing if they were all right. He had to wait until he received their next letter for news that they were okay, and to have confirmed what he had feared: the town's synagogue was no more. In their correspondence, his parents, worried about censors, had developed a kind of code, which Guy could now easily decipher. When they wrote, "If one way doesn't turn out, try always a new way of proceeding," or "Hope you can realize all your plans," he knew it meant "Keep trying to secure the papers for our immigration."

Guy graduated from high school in June 1939 and worked full-time for a year to save money for his college tuition. In fall 1940, he enrolled at Saint Louis University, a Jesuit university known for its high academic standards. Guy found a part-time job at a hotel restaurant only a block from school. It was so convenient, he often dashed back and forth from work to classes still dressed in his waiter uniform.

In the summer of 1942, he received a short, ominous letter from his mother that bore a Warsaw postmark. It read, in part:

Eighteen-year-old Guy Stern (*right*), busboy at the Melbourne Hotel, St. Louis, spring 1940. *(Family photograph)*

We have a room here in the ghetto and we are managing. We hope for better days. As we told you when you left, do the best you can.

Guy knew her words, again, had been chosen more for the censors than for him. The envelope had clearly been opened; the flap had been resealed with an official Nazi stamp bearing a swastika. His mother obviously couldn't divulge their full situation. Had they been forcibly moved from their home? They would never have chosen to leave Hildesheim, and she had never mentioned that possibility in previous letters. And why Warsaw? Guy knew his European geography: Warsaw was five hundred miles east of Hildesheim.

Nonetheless, the meaning of "do the best you can" was clear; though she knew he was still looking for someone, anyone, who could help them get to America, she was absolving him of blame if he failed to do so. Guy held his mother's note in trembling hands, his mind tumbling with terrible thoughts of her and his family's despair. And there was that strange postmark—

Why were the Nazis sending Jewish families to Poland?

Manfred Steinfeld left his sobbing mother on the railroad platform in July 1938. When his train arrived in Hamburg, 250 miles away, an HIAS representative was waiting for him at the station and she took him home for the night. The next morning, with a dozen other Jewish refugee children, he boarded the SS *New York*, owned by the Hamburg-America Line, Germany's oldest and largest steamship company.

Traveling third class, in what was commonly known as steerage, Manfred and another boy his age shared a small cabin with an upper and lower bunk. The communal bathroom was down the corridor; meals were served in the third-class dining room. Heeding his mother's warning to keep quiet and not draw attention to himself, Manfred refrained from speaking to other passengers or crew members, nearly all of whom were Germans. He spent most of his time in his bunk and only came out at mealtimes. For the entire trip he was inundated by fear and anxiety at the prospect of never seeing his family again. Having never traveled far from home before, he also worried about what his life would be like in America.

After eleven long, tedious days at sea, several of them stormy, the ship entered New York Harbor at 5 A.M. and slid past the fog-draped Statue of Liberty. Manfred, who had gone up on deck for their arrival, stood at the railing. The sight was both inspiring and comforting. He didn't move for the hour it took the ship to reach the dock. He began to think that everything would be all right. In fact, he felt safer than he had since leaving home. Another representative of HIAS met the children at the dock and placed identification tags around their necks. Manfred and another boy were the only ones heading to Chicago; the rest were destined for other parts of the country. The two boys were taken to Grand Central Terminal, handed box lunches, and put aboard the overnight train.

Manfred was met the next evening at Chicago's Union Station by

SS *New York,* which took fourteen-year-old Manfred Steinfeld away from Nazi Germany to America in 1938. *(Family photograph)*

Aunt Minna, his mother's sister. He was elated to see someone he recognized, but his relief faded as they stepped outside the station into bustling city streets filled with pedestrians and automobiles. For a boy from rural Josbach, population four hundred, the harshness of big-city sights and sounds was a bit overwhelming.

His aunt was warm and welcoming, but Manfred could tell that his uncle was not as happy to have him there. Like many of Chicago's German Jews, Morris Rosenbusch worked in the stockyards, earning about fifteen dollars a week. The family of eight (now nine) lived in a cramped three-bedroom apartment with one bathroom at 5409 South University Avenue. The twenty-five dollars a month the Jewish Charities of Chicago paid them for taking in their nephew was much needed. Nonetheless, due to the lack of space, there was no bed available for Manfred, and he would sleep on the living room sofa for the next four years.

Held back because he knew only a few words of English, Manfred attended grammar school for several months before entering Hyde Park High School in January 1939. A fast learner, he made strides in the language, relying in part on his circle of new friends in the heavily Jewish Hyde Park neighborhood. These same friends quickly Americanized his name. Manfred Steinfeld of Josbach, Germany, became Manny Steinfeld of Chicago, U.S.A.

As no one gave him an allowance, Manny had to work to earn his own money. He soon picked up a paper route, which paid him $1.50 a week. He had to wake up at 5 A.M. to deliver the *Chicago Tribune* before going to school; in the afternoon, he delivered the *Herald-American* and *Daily News*. He also got a second job at a local drugstore, where he delivered prescriptions and worked the soda fountain. In time, he was able to buy a secondhand bicycle and occasionally spend a dime to go to cowboy movies, which he loved. He also saved up to buy cocoa and coffee, luxuries in Josbach, which he mailed to his mother in Germany.

Mother and son wrote one another often, and through her letters, he learned that shortly after he had left, she had sent his brother,

Herbert, to a kibbutz training center in Frankfurt. In November 1938, twelve-year-old Herbert was one of thirty-five students selected to emigrate to Palestine, where they settled in a children's village near Pardes Hanna, outside of Tel Aviv. Soon after arriving, Herbert began writing regularly to his brother in Chicago and sending snapshots. Herbert adopted his Hebrew name, Naftali, and his long letters—he was a much better letter writer than Manny— were filled with colorful stories about life in Palestine. Manny was elated with each new letter, attesting to his lit-

Manny Steinfeld's sister, Irma, and his mother, Paula. *(Family photograph)*

tle brother's safety now that he was out of the reach of the Nazis.

With two of her three children safely out of Germany, Paula Steinfeld focused on her daughter, Irma. In the summer of 1939, with the help of a Jewish rescue organization, Paula succeeded in securing a visa for Irma to emigrate to England. But two days before Irma's ship was scheduled to depart, Germany invaded Poland. England immediately declared war on Germany, and all commercial ship traffic between the countries was suspended. Irma had no choice but to return to Josbach.

Manny learned all this from his mother's letters. She also wrote that Jewish properties were being confiscated, and that she had been forced to sell the family home to a gentile family. For the time being, the new owners were allowing Paula and Irma to stay in the upstairs bedroom above the store, but Paula continued to explore their escape options. For a while, the most promising route seemed to be through the Soviet Union, but in June 1941, Germany invaded that country, and that option closed as well.

Several months later, his mother wrote about a new batch of disturbing rumors, which were circulating hotly. It seemed Josbach's Jewish families were to be moved out of Germany, although they had no idea where they would end up or why they were being moved.

Alarmed, Manny wrote right back. He did not receive a reply.

Born to Russian-Jewish émigré parents in 1923, Victor Brombert spent the first ten days of his life in Berlin, where his mother was the patient of a famous gynecologist who had helped her conceive and attended the delivery. Victor's parents returned with their new baby to their home in Leipzig, in eastern Germany.

Jacob and Vera Brombert had met while attending law school in Russia. Both came from families that had attained the level of social and financial standing one needed to be able to live in Moscow and St. Petersburg, places in which few Jews were then able to afford. It was also not a common occurrence in those days for a woman, particularly a Jewess, to be admitted to a Russian law school, but it was not so unusual in well-to-do and socially prominent families.

Jacob was soft-spoken and studious, and he possessed an innate sense of order and fair play. He came from a family of prosperous merchants, which for several generations had traded in raw skins for the luxury fur market. His father had paid for Jacob to attain two law degrees—first in Paris, then in Russia—with the understanding that he would eventually inherit and manage the family business.

That day came sooner than Jacob could have imagined. He was in his thirties when his father died, propelling him overnight into the business. Jacob rapidly learned the intricacies of the fur trade: attending wholesale auctions throughout Europe, then grading, shipping, and selling skins to furriers in Italy, France, England, and America, who made coats and stoles for the retail market.

Jacob and Vera were on their honeymoon in Denmark in 1917

when they learned about the start of the Russian Revolution. They decided against returning to their homeland, where private property ownership was being restricted and factories turned over to workers. After a few months in London, whose cold, foggy weather Vera did not like, they settled in Leipzig, which was a center of the European fur trade. The young couple became stateless, eventually receiving Nansen passports, which were issued by the League of Nations, starting in 1922, to Russian exiles who could not obtain travel documents from their government.

Some of Victor's early memories were of trips with his parents to Marienbad, a popular spa in Czechoslovakia. His parents believed strongly in the curative benefits of Marienbad's spa treatments, including its natural carbon dioxide springs, as did celebrities such as Thomas Edison and Mark Twain and European rulers like Edward VII of the United Kingdom and Czar Nicholas II of Russia, all of whom regularly traveled to Marienbad to be rejuvenated. Vera, who had visited France often and spoke the language fluently, was on the French championship bridge team that competed at the resort.

During one such trip, in the early 1930s, the Bromberts' train stopped at the border before leaving Germany. Given their status as stateless refugees, Jacob and Vera were always anxious at border crossings. This time, men with swastika armbands roughly dragged an older couple who had been seated nearby off the train.

Fellow passengers whispered among themselves. A word—*Devisenschieber*—was audible. "What is *Devisenschieber*?" Victor asked.

His parents hushed him.

After the train started again, his father told Victor that *Devisenschieber* had to do with trying to sneak currency out of Germany, which was illegal.

By this time, Victor was an only child. His younger sister, Nora, an attractive, dark-haired, and loving little girl, had died during surgery in 1930, at age five, as German doctors operated on a brain tumor. For Victor, then seven, it was his first brush with mortality. He had

sobbed alongside his mother when she told him the news. As he
grew older, Victor came to understand how much his sister's death
had affected his parents, who were torn between self-pity and a feeling of guilt they never completely overcame.

After experiencing the effects of one revolution, Jacob and Vera
watched Hitler's rise to power in 1933 with great alarm. It was clear
to them early on—with the street demonstrations and violence, the
mass arrests, the pogroms—that the rise of Nazi nationalism was an
ominous development. Unlike some German-born Jews who held
on to hope for their homeland and waited too long to leave, or others who wanted out but were trapped by their circumstances, the
Russian émigré couple wasted no time in departing. Thanks to the
international nature of the fur trade, Jacob had valuable inventory,
bank deposits, and accounts receivable outside the country, making
their speedy emigration possible.

Their move meant another memorable train trip for Victor, from
Leipzig to neutral Switzerland, where they had arranged to stay
on Lake Geneva while awaiting visas for permanent residency in
France. His parents had their own sleeping compartment on the
overnight train, as did Victor and his faithful German nanny, Marianne. When the train stopped in the dark at the German-Swiss border, Victor awoke to loud voices in the corridor. He heard *"Juden"*
repeated several times, and hard knocks, followed by doors sliding
open and shut. Fear gripped him, but he stayed still; he had been
warned by his father not to unlock the door to his compartment
unless ordered to do so.

After the train started rolling, his mother rapped softly and Victor let her inside. She wanted to know if he and Marianne were all
right. They had crossed safely into Switzerland, she told them.

When they finally arrived in France, they spent their first days
in Paris at the apartment of Jacob's sister, Anya Adler, a longtime
widow. She took young Victor to his first street market, where he
was bedazzled by the displays of flowers, fruits, vegetables, meats,
and especially the fish stands offering plump pink shrimp and live

crabs. That day, Aunt Anya also introduced Victor to a strange new vegetable, the artichoke, which he was initially wary of but liked once she showed him how to pull off its thorny leaves and which parts of it to eat. Aunt Anya had lost her fireman husband years earlier in Russia, and in Paris she had settled into an independent life that she praised as *une vie facile* (an easy life), which she lived thanks to her brother Jacob's generosity.

After staying at Anya's for a few days, the family rented an apartment decorated with delicate eighteenth-century furniture in the affluent Sixteenth Arrondissement, which was home to a colony of fellow anti-Bolshevik émigrés, most of them well-heeled. Years earlier, Jacob and Vera had managed to bring their own surviving parents out of Russia to Germany. In addition to Russian, Victor's maternal grandmother, Anna, spoke French to him, as his mother often did, and by the time they moved to Paris he was already fluent. At home, his parents also spoke Russian, and for his first nine years in Leipzig, Victor spoke German in and out of school, a language he continued to use in Paris with his nanny, who remained with the family for two years before returning to Germany. So Victor was stumped whenever he was asked his native tongue. He dreamed in German, French, and Russian, and when counting repetitions in calisthenics, he switched from one to another without thought.

In time, France, where Victor would spend more than eight of his most formative years, came to feel like his true home, and French became his preferred language, culture, and identity. Were it not for the Russian Revolution, he would have been Russian; were it not for Hitler, he would have grown up German; because of them both, he became a proud Frenchman.

Victor attended Lycée Janson de Sailly, one of the most prestigious schools in Paris. He was a poor student in mathematics but received top grades in French literature and history. His first contact with English came from a teacher who believed the key to fluency was to translate and recite from memory English poets such as William Wordsworth. For his part, Victor learned more English from movies starring Fred Astaire, Ginger Rogers, Loretta Young, Tyrone Power, and Bing Crosby.

Having attended synagogue only for High Holidays, Victor grew up with little religious instruction. In fact, his father pointedly taught him the meaning of the word "agnostic," and both parents warned him against the dangers of doctrines and dogmas espoused by church or state. Nevertheless, Victor was bar mitzvahed when he turned thirteen, in 1936. To prepare, he was taught the rudiments of Hebrew while he and his mother summered at Marienbad, studying in a hotel room with a local rabbi who had been hired as his tutor.

The ceremony was held in a small, modern synagogue on the rue de Montevideo, a quiet street near the Bromberts' apartment. Victor was nervous but not particularly moved by the event; his favorite part was giving the chanted prayer an operatic intonation, as he harbored the fantasy of one day becoming a famous opera singer. For his parents, the ceremony seemed a formality, albeit a joyful rite of passage for their son. It also meant they could throw a lavish party, which turned out not so different from their other parties, with vodka and caviar served to guests, most of whom were also Russian émigrés.

Victor, who intended to become a naturalized French citizen when he came of age, was certain he would one day do his compulsory service in the French army. He looked forward to that day in spite of his pacifist parents' concerns; they insisted he read antiwar novels like *All Quiet on the Western Front,* but this did not always have the expected results. Victor spent hours fantasizing about a life of adventure and days filled with heroic acts of courage.

The summer of 1939, spent with his parents at Deauville, a beach resort in Normandy, was much more than a family holiday for Victor. He had to study for an exam in the fall that would determine—due to his poor grades in mathematics—whether he would repeat the previous year of school. His mother reminded him daily of this looming event and set Victor up with a tutor. There were also afternoons spent with friends, playing volleyball and tennis, and when it was cold outside, a new board game called Monopoly. Still, there was time for the sixteen-year-old to fall in love for the first time.

Her name was Danielle Wolf, and Victor became so infatuated that he thought of little else. Dany was two years older, short and well proportioned, with curly brown hair brushed back, dancing eyes, and full lips. Victor spent all the time he could with her, even if it meant failing to show up for his tutorials. Once, he incurred the anger of his usually composed mother by spending his tutor's fee on treats for Dany as they strolled on the beach boardwalk. At night, they lay on the sand, fingers entwined, gazing skyward and counting shooting stars. Hours after parting, he remained consumed by her; he could still taste her lips and smell the intoxicating scent of her hair.

Victor's near-magical summer came to an abrupt end on September 1, 1939. As he and his parents were preparing to return to Paris, they heard the BBC radio bulletins about Germany's invasion of Poland. Two days later, when France and England, Poland's allies, declared war on Germany, rumors circulated that the powerful armies of the Third Reich would now turn against France. Jacob, who for years had not shared the level of complacency or safety felt by so many Frenchmen, decided that the family should not return to their Paris home after all. Suspecting the capital would be a major target, he found a villa in Deauville to rent.

With the war as yet distant and unreal, Victor was at first delighted by the change of plans. He would miss the big exam, and there would surely be no school in the foreseeable future. On that last point, he was mistaken. Many other vacationing families extended their stay in Normandy—to Victor's utter disappointment, Dany's was not among them—and a school was organized in a local hotel. Either Victor got lucky or the standards were lower than those in Paris; he was admitted into the top class of the secondary education cycle leading to the *baccalauréat*.

And yet, he had begun to wonder: With France at war, what was the point of preparing for university? What did a degree or career

Victor Brombert with Dany Wolf on the boardwalk of Trouville, Normandy, summer 1939. *(Family photograph)*

matter? When he turned eighteen, he decided, he would go in the army to fight for France. Period.

Despite the lack of major fighting during the so-called Phoney War, there were very real casualties. That winter of 1939, the war drew uncomfortably close for Victor and the other students, who gathered together to help evacuate a trainload of wounded French soldiers to a local hospital. The students waited at the Deauville station for hours; when the troop train arrived late at night, they carried stretchers bearing the injured to waiting ambulances.

That winter, Victor accompanied his father on a brief business trip to Paris. After Dany had left at the end of the summer, she and Victor wrote to one another. His letters were hopelessly romantic, with passages drawn from the great poets. Dany's replies from Paris were tender if noncommittal; her French Jewish parents favored an older, more appropriate suitor for their eighteen-year-old daughter. But Dany and Victor arranged a rendezvous on the Avenue des Champs-Élysées. When they met, so far removed from the sands of Normandy, they were nearly strangers. Victor had hoped for much more, even a rekindling of what they had once felt, but it was not to be. It was his first hard lesson in the ways of love, although it would not keep him from trying again.

A few months after that trip to Paris, in May 1940, German troops pushed through the Ardennes into France within days of their invasion of Holland and Belgium. Across the bay from Deauville, Luftwaffe bombers hit the oil refineries at Le Havre. Victor and his parents, with gas masks close at hand in case of a poison gas attack, watched from the other side of the bay as fiery-red explosions ripped across the night sky and the earth trembled. They packed quickly and left the rented villa the next morning, determined to make their way to a safer region in southern France.

By the time they reached Paris, the collective exodus to the south was well under way. With roads out of Paris jammed by all forms of foot and vehicular traffic, they decided to take a train to Bordeaux, four hundred miles to the south, despite warnings that not all trains were reaching their destination due to aerial attacks.

They made it safely, arriving in Bordeaux on a mild spring day, and settled in a small hotel. Jacob decided to go to the Portuguese consulate, in the hope of obtaining visas for the family to enter that neutral country, and he invited Victor along. As they rode in a horse-drawn carriage along the city's broad avenues, his father explained how important it was in such times to make contact with proper officials and slip into their palms or place on their desks an envelope with a few banknotes at the right moment. Jacob wanted Victor to understand that he considered such inducements not only illegal but also morally reprehensible; in normal times, they would not be necessary. The world being what it was, however, bribes were sometimes necessary. Money could save lives. Victor waited outside the consulate, but when his father rejoined him, he still had the envelope of money—and no visas.

By June, the French army had been crushed by the Germans at a cost of nearly one hundred thousand dead, and a million and a half French soldiers interned in prisoner-of-war camps. German forces arrived in an undefended Paris on June 14. Within days, Germany dictated the terms of the armistice, dividing France into occupied and unoccupied zones and setting up the new pro-Nazi government in Vichy, which agreed to deport any political refugees who had sought asylum in France.

When Jacob heard that Jews who had settled in France faced arrest and extradition, he chose Spain as the family's next sanctuary. He thought it unlikely Hitler would invade that country, as it was ruled by the fascist dictator Francisco Franco. Jacob hired a car and driver and bought gasoline at black-market prices. With their suitcases strapped onto the roof, the family fled to Biarritz, a town on France's Basque coast, twenty miles from the border with Spain. After two days, they had made no progress in acquiring visas, and news reports indicated that France's entire west coast would soon be occupied by German forces. Desperate to keep his family from being caught by the Nazis, Jacob hired an old ambulance to take them inland to Pau, where they found themselves facing the great wall of the Pyrenees, a centuries-old natural barrier between the two countries. His vague plan—to find a place somewhere along the frontier to sneak across, on foot, if necessary—now seemed both unrealistic and unsafe.

Instead, they made their way more than three hundred miles up the coast to Nice, situated in Vichy-controlled southeastern France. Seemingly safe for the time being, they rented an apartment, and Jacob set his sights on getting the family to America. He made regular trips to Marseille, also in the Vichy zone, where there was an American consulate, carrying with him the family's passports as well as letters and affidavits provided by Vera's brother, a successful businessman who had settled in New York years earlier. Jacob worked tirelessly through the official channels, and by summer of 1941 had pulled together the litany of required documentation: U.S. immigration visas, French exit visas, Spanish transit visas, and expensive boat tickets.

They were to meet their ship in southern Spain, at Seville, the country's only commercial river port, which was some fifty miles from the entrance to the Atlantic. Getting there required several days of train travel. At the Spanish border, men in unfamiliar uniforms questioned Jacob at length as they examined the family's travel documents. Victor sat sweating in the train's stifling compartment, scared that some unforeseen technicality would stop them, that a new regulation would invalidate their permits and all his father's efforts to acquire them would be for naught. But his fears were unfounded. Their papers were at last approved and stamped, allowing them to transit through Spain.

The vessel that awaited in Seville was owned by a Spanish shipping company, and had recently been chartered by Portuguese entrepreneurs looking to cash in on the willingness of desperate people to pay large sums of money to put an ocean between them and the Nazis. The SS *Navemar*, listing slightly, was four hundred feet long, with a high hull, bulky, massive, not a passenger ship but a freighter. It had cabin accommodations for only twenty-eight passengers, and other than those spaces it had no facilities, not even toilets. Tickets for the few cabins went at exorbitant prices. The captain even gave up his own cabin and charged two thousand dollars each to as many people as could fit themselves into the small space. Jacob told his son he had paid one thousand dollars apiece for the least expensive tickets. Though it was a price they could afford, he was critical of the charter company for engaging in scandalous exploitation of people in danger, many of whom could not afford such an expense. The cargo hold was filled not with bananas or coal but with 1,120 refugees, most of them Jews from Germany, Austria, and Czechoslovakia.

The ocean crossing, made on a zigzag course to avoid German U-boats, took six weeks, and included ports of call in Lisbon,

Havana, and Bermuda, although the refugees were not allowed off
the ship at any stop. Food was in short supply aboard ship, with the
main staple being potatoes.

Victor and his parents spent most days topside on a meager
deck that they shared with a few live oxen, which, one by one, were
slaughtered for meat along the way. They slept on deck or in one
of the lifeboats, rather than below, where tiers of primitive bunks
had been fitted into dark, airless holds. The space was soon thick
with the stench of vomit and excrement. Many people fell sick with
typhus and dysentery; six died during the crossing and were buried
at sea.

Early one morning, as
he lay wrapped in a blanket
on deck, half asleep, Victor heard a commotion. He
joined other passengers at the
crowded railing to watch as
the ship entered the waters of
New York Harbor. Visible off
in the distance were the skyscrapers of Manhattan, and
he could also make out the
Statue of Liberty. He knew
the statue from the smaller
replica, which stood on a
little island where the Seine
wound its way through Paris.
He had learned in school that
the statue in New York's harbor was a gift from France,
commemorating the Ameri-
can and French revolutions
and symbolizing the friendship between the two nations.

Victor Brombert's father, Jacob, aboard
the freighter *Navemar*, overloaded with
more than a thousand refugees, most of
them Jews escaping the Nazis, September 1941. *(Family photograph)*

The famous, copper-robed *mademoiselle* holding the torch lighting the way to freedom made Victor feel at home.

After the ship docked in Brooklyn on September 12, 1941, Victor and his parents stood in a long line to disembark, waiting while immigration and health officials processed the departing passengers. Victor, Jacob, and Vera were told that the local newspapers had referred to the *Navemar* as a "floating concentration camp," bringing Jews out of Nazi-occupied Europe. Its long-awaited arrival was greeted by officials, photographers, reporters, and joyous relatives.*

His parents found a tenth-floor apartment to rent on West 72nd Street, near Riverside Drive. They quickly wearied of complete strangers congratulating them on their good fortune in being allowed to enter the United States. They were also confronted with endless questions about what had happened in France in the summer of 1940. "Why didn't the French fight the Germans better?" they were asked again and again.

And they faced an even tougher question, too: "How did you get out when others can't?" It was a question Victor thought about himself, often. He knew a degree of luck had played a role, but only to a point. In all the adventure stories he had read—*The Three Musketeers* was a favorite—the heroes fit a certain mold: dashing looks, skill with weaponry, superhuman strength. His father had none of those qualities, yet he was the real hero in their story. Time and again, he had invented escape routes. When one didn't pan out, he found another. His tenacity, courage, and intelligence had saved them. Jacob was a meek man, but he was not weak. His heroic perseverance got his family out of Nazi-occupied Europe under the most difficult and dangerous circumstances.

---

* Four months later, on January 23, 1942, the *Navemar* was torpedoed and sunk in the Strait of Gibraltar by the Italian submarine *Barbarigo,* which the following year disappeared with all fifty-eight officers and crewmen while transporting war materiel from Germany to Japan.

Although the fall semester had already started, Victor received late acceptance to Harrisburg Academy, an elite boarding school in the heart of Pennsylvania, on the banks of the Susquehanna River. It was his first time living away from home. Much to his surprise, academic success came easily. The French educational system had prepared him well. He was soon made captain of the tennis team, and enjoyed excursions and cookouts with other students in the nearby pinewoods. As a Jewish refugee who had escaped from Nazi Europe, Victor became a minor celebrity among the teachers and students. He stood out; this was a campus that held Christmas assemblies at which students sang "Jingle Bells" and began each regular daily assembly with a prayer. Widely traveled, handsome, erudite, and with a charming French accent, he became popular on campus.

Victor was soon invited to be a special guest at a Republican women's club luncheon. When he entered the banquet room, he saw that all the ladies looked alike. They wore white gloves and small hats, which partially concealed the bluish tint of their hair. Their faces were wrinkled but smiling broadly at him. The star attraction at his table, Victor answered many questions. It became apparent that, while the ladies remained polite, they did not believe his descriptions of the war in Europe. He told them about the Nazis, their policies of hatred, the concentration camps like Dachau, their planes machine-gunning fleeing civilians on the highways of France, the disgrace of the armistice and of the pro-Nazi Vichy government, the zeal of the French police in rounding up Jews, and the shameful deportations.

The ladies' smiles began to fade.

When the club president introduced Victor and asked him to come up front and say a few words to the group, he began by saying how grateful he was to be safe with his family in America. He saw only big smiles now: this was exactly what those assembled wanted to hear. Then he added, "I very much hope this country will get in the war and help defeat Hitler."

The smiles, even the polite ones, vanished.

By the time Victor sat down, he had the uneasy feeling that he had committed a social faux pas. While they had been professing interest in world affairs, these educated ladies clearly did not want to face the realities of the war that had overtaken Europe and threatened millions of its people. They acted as if Victor, given his youth, was misinformed or exaggerating. For the first time, Victor began to understand the power of the American "isolationism" he had read about. Whether it was a matter of having their heads stuck in the sand, these ladies and many other Americans had no desire for the U.S. to intervene in the war in Europe. The lukewarm reception he received did not alter Victor's thinking or change the opinions that he expressed in and out of school. He had seen too much to stay silent.

Japan's surprise attack on Pearl Harbor on December 7, 1941, was the most exciting event to occur during Victor's year at Harrisburg Academy. As word of the attack spread through the corridors, dormitories, and classrooms, he found himself wondering how the outbreak of war in the Pacific would impact Europe. When Germany declared war on the United States a few days later, Victor found reason for renewed hope. With U.S. military involvement, he was certain that Nazi Germany would eventually be defeated and his beloved France would be liberated, along with the rest of occupied Europe.

Victor graduated a few months later with the highest standing in his class and delivered the valedictorian speech. He covered much of what he had said at the ladies' lunch, speaking of the need to defeat Hitler, crush Nazism, and liberate Europe, but instead of being dismissed as a warmonger, the crowd of students, parents, and instructors hung on his every word. Rousing applause stopped him more than once. He realized later that he had hardly said anything about Japan and its surprise attack on the U.S. fleet. The Pacific wasn't Victor's war.

America's war with Hitler and Nazi Germany was his own, and he very much wanted to be part of it.

PART TWO

We were fighting an American war, and we were also fighting an intensely personal war. We were in it with every fiber of our being. We worked harder than anyone could have driven us. We were crusaders. This was our war.

—GÜNTHER "GUY" STERN

4

Camp Ritchie

Former Dachau inmate Martin Selling, still waiting for a visa to get into America, had been at the refugee camp in Kent, England, for only two months before Europe went to war.

The United Kingdom declared war on Germany in the wake of Hitler's invasion of Poland on September 1, 1939. Immediately, Martin and the thousand other German Jews at the camp were classified as "enemy aliens." This was a common practice among nations at war, carried out because the refugees had been born within an enemy country in which they still held citizenship. Most in the camp, like Martin, were single men who had been released from Nazi concentration camps on the proviso that they immediately leave Germany.

What surprised Martin was not Germany's armed aggression, but the sense of security the British maintained in the insular environment of their island nation. Most Britons seemed shocked by the outbreak of war. Only a year had passed since British prime minister Neville Chamberlain signed an agreement allowing Germany to annex parts of Czechoslovakia—a nation sacrificed in a vain attempt to satisfy Hitler—returned from Munich, and declared "peace in our time." Martin could have told anyone who thought such appeasements would keep Hitler at bay that he or she was badly mistaken. He had seen the streets of Germany filled with tanks, military hardware, and goose-stepping parades; he had witnessed the fierce determination with which Hitler marched his country toward war; and he knew firsthand the Nazis' determination to impose their will.

The Kitchener Refugee Camp was situated on a former army base on England's southeastern tip. After the war started, security tightened. The refugees who were now enemy aliens were required to reside at the camp until they emigrated elsewhere. They could move freely only within five miles of Kitchener, and had to return each night. Traveling greater distances required the permission of local police, which was often withheld.

After Britain entered the war, Martin noticed, refugees stopped arriving at the camp. He understood what this meant: that countless more Jews would now be trapped in Nazi-occupied Europe, unable to get out even if they had visas to other countries. If his own departure from Germany had been delayed by even two more months, he would have been among them. It was a sobering thought.

No heating had been installed in Kitchener's old barracks, each of which was divided into two rooms with twelve double bunk beds and little else, not even chairs. Every bunk had a mattress, a pillow, and a wool army blanket, surplus from World War I. Refugees were allowed one suitcase; the rest of their belongings were kept in a warehouse. Sanitary facilities were primitive, and there was no hot water in the washrooms. Many men complained about the food, but after Dachau, Martin considered the meals a vast improvement.

Their conversations in German always turned heads, and some locals made it clear that they were not welcome in nearby towns. But soon, the British military decided to put their native language skills to use for the war effort. The Nazis were believed to be using commercial radio stations on the continent to send messages to U-boats offshore and to spies in England. A British army unit came into camp and set up twenty large radio receivers in one of the barracks, connecting them to a bank of Dictaphones, which could be switched on to record suspicious talk. Teams of refugees monitored the receivers, each of which was set to a different German-language radio station.

Though Martin was eager to help out and immediately volunteered, it didn't take him long to see that the operation had some major shortcomings. First, the volunteers weren't told what they should be listening for and recording. The British suspected that the enemy was using some type of code, but the refugees weren't given any help in figuring out what it might be. A verse from a song or a poem, or a string of numbers? More importantly, they weren't allowed to raise antennas any higher than the tops of the low barracks, which severely limited their range.

A British army lieutenant oversaw the listening detail. Billeted at a hotel in town, the officer, who had learned some German in school, had a receiver installed in his room. Since it had a much higher antenna, set atop the peaked roof of the hotel, he got better reception and received stations the refugees could not pick up in camp. It wasn't long before he became frustrated by the refugees' lack of results; when they pointed out the problems caused by the lack of antenna height, their concerns were dismissed. Despite the best efforts of Martin and the other volunteers, the situation turned acrimonious. It was clear that they were not trusted because they were Germans, and the operation was closed down.

Before departing Germany, while he could still pay in Reichmarks, Martin had bought an open-ended Cunard–White Star Line ticket from England to New York. It was a purchase he would have been unable to make after emigrating, given the laws against taking money out of Germany. In the refugee camp, he had very little cash, but it almost didn't matter: the steamship ticket to America was much more valuable.

Early in the new year, after long, agonizing years of waiting, Martin's immigration quota number finally came up, and he went to the U.S. consulate in London to get his visa. On January 30, 1940, the British shipping company honored his ticket, and he boarded

the MV *Georgic* at Liverpool. This was one of the ship's last Atlantic crossings carrying civilians; it was soon requisitioned by the
military for troopship duties.

Martin arrived in New York ten days later. His twin brother,
Leopold, and his uncle, Julius Laub, with whom he had been arrested during Kristallnacht, met him dockside. Both had made it to
America a few months earlier and were living in a rooming house in
Newark, New Jersey. Julius had been unable to find a job, but Leopold, who had been born with a clubfoot, worked in a bakery for a
dollar a day and all the stale doughnuts he could carry home, which
was often the men's main meal. Martin found a job in a dry cleaning
store, then got a better-paying job in a machine shop for forty cents
an hour.

Martin was pleased to have the job and relieved that he did not
have to work as a tailor, a trade he had hated in Germany. Nevertheless, at times he felt forlorn and disoriented, especially when
he became lost in the bewildering maze of the New York subway
system. With limited English, he struggled with signage and directions. His knowledge of the United States, its people, its culture,
and its geography was rudimentary, and he was perplexed by the
differences between the Old and New Worlds. Going into a bank
to cash his paycheck or to the post office to mail a letter required
that he ask for instructions, which were often unintelligible to him.
Self-serve stores were a brand-new experience, and he was certain
if he picked up an item off a shelf, he would be arrested for shoplift-
ing. He was stymied whenever he tried to use a phone booth. The
nickel kept plopping back into the coin receptacle without his call
going through, and as he tried to figure things out there was usually
someone banging loudly on the door for him to finish up.

One day, Martin overheard another worker talking about night
school. He expressed interest, and the man told him about Newark
Technical School, a college that would later become part of Rut-
gers University. Martin went to find out about enrolling. He had ten
years of schooling, which in Germany was the equivalent of a U.S.

high school education. The registrar was patient with Martin's halting explanations in his poor English and allowed him to enroll. For the next two years, Martin attended classes four evenings a week while working full-time. He had to put in many hours of studying to improve his English, but he sailed through his science and math courses with ease.

After the Japanese bombed Pearl Harbor on December 7, 1941, and Germany declared war on the United States four days later, bringing America, which had been neutral, into the European conflict, Martin became an enemy alien for the second time. Still, he did not view the widening war or his own situation with any sense of dread. He had hoped for several years that America would involve itself militarily in Europe, believing it the only way to stop Hitler and the Nazis. And filled with a vengeance since those dark days of his captivity at Dachau, Martin was more than ready to join the fight.

He was now twenty-two and eligible for the draft as a noncitizen resident, but he did not wait to get a letter from Selective Service. Instead, Martin went to the Army Air Corps recruiting office in Newark. Unlike most of the eager young men crowded into the room, when he reached the front of the line he told the recruiters that he did not want to be a pilot.

"I want to be a bombardier," Martin explained, "so I can drop bombs on German targets." Suspicious of his German accent, the recruiters treated it as a big joke when they found out he was an enemy alien.

Four months later, Martin received a notice to appear before his draft board. He was the first at work to be called up, and his coworkers were so convinced he would be leaving right away that they gave him a farewell party and some small gifts. But the next day, he was back at work, embarrassed and disappointed, having been rejected again: this time, his immigration papers were not in order.

Three months later, Martin was notified that all his papers had been located, and he was ordered to come in for a physical examination. Asked by the doctor whether he had suffered any recent illnesses or injuries, Martin described his months of maltreatment at Dachau. After completing the physical, the doctor patted him on the shoulder.

"Considering what you went through," he said, "you are in fine shape."

The draftees who passed their physical exams were told they could take a week to get their personal affairs in order before reporting for duty. Martin stepped forward and asked if he could waive the waiting period. After the embarrassment of his previous call-up, he didn't want to return to the machine shop and face his coworkers. That day, he shipped out to Fort Dix, New Jersey.

Martin's main accomplishments on his first day at Fort Dix were finding where the meals were served—called the "chow hall"—and claiming an empty bunk for the night. In the morning, the new arrivals were issued ill-fitting fatigues and given a battery of tests. The next day, they were assigned to different branches for their training—infantry, armored, etc. Martin scored well on the tests and asked for the air corps, still hoping to drop bombs on Germany. This was impossible, he was told; his enemy-alien status rendered him unfit for any type of weapons training. Assigned to the medical corps, he was sent to Camp Pickett, Virginia, for twelve weeks of basic training.

Martin was furious and disgusted, even humiliated, at the idea of being excluded from fighting in the war. He hadn't joined the U.S. Army during a time of global warfare against Hitler and the Nazis only to serve as a noncombatant.

On his first day at Camp Pickett, he and the other recruits were screened for any experiences or special qualifications related to the medical field. Martin, still seething, told the army doctor who interviewed him that he was in the medical corps only because he had been born in Germany and the army didn't trust him with a gun. He was a Jew who had been interned at Dachau, he added with a sharp edge. He wanted to face the Nazis on the battlefield.

The doctor responded sympathetically and said he appreciated how Martin must feel, but his advice was to "take it easy, son.
Things will turn out all right." Martin would be serving as a hospital orderly, the doctor explained; it was an important job, and he
wished Martin luck.

The first weeks of medical basic training were filled with marching drills, exercises, barracks cleaning, lectures on sanitation and
the treatment of wounds, and endless hours on KP duty, scrubbing
pots and pans.

Then, in February 1943, after only six weeks at Camp Pickett,
Martin was summoned to battalion headquarters. The clearly baf-
fled sergeant had a train ticket and a set of orders for him. Martin
was also surprised and confused by this state of affairs. A recruit
was never transferred when he was only half finished with basic
training, the sergeant said. On top of that, Martin was being sent to
a top secret base the sergeant knew nothing about.

"What crime have you committed?" the sergeant asked.

Martin had no idea, but after all he had been through, being imprisoned as an enemy alien seemed as likely as any other scenario.

Wearing fatigues and carrying his duffel bag, Martin boarded
a train early the next morning. He traveled all day by train and
bus to a small army camp tucked into a wide valley between two
mountains in rural Maryland. The main entrance had tall, rock tur-
rets befitting a Norman castle. The only signage in front of a set of
wrought-iron gates read STOP.

Stepping up to the guard booth, which was manned by a tall
military policeman (MP), Martin handed over his orders. To his
disbelief, the MP addressed him in German.

When he had first read the orders directing him to report to the
Military Intelligence Training Center (MITC) at Camp Ritchie,
Maryland, Martin had wondered what he could possibly know or
do that would be of any value to U.S. Army Intelligence. Now, conversing in his native German with the MP, he had his first inkling of
why he had been transferred here. The next one came soon after he

Camp Ritchie's front gate when the only sign read STOP. *(U.S. Army Signal Corps)*

walked into the top secret Camp Ritchie. A platoon of soldiers was marching smartly down a street. In full-dress Wehrmacht uniforms, a sergeant was counting cadence in German:

"Links, zwei, drei, vier."

Soon after Werner Angress's close call in October 1938, when the Gestapo agents boarded the night train out of Germany as he fled to Holland, he signed up for a farming collective. With his parents and younger brothers settled in Amsterdam, where his ex-banker father, Ernst, had bought and was managing a women's lingerie shop, Werner moved to Wieringen, on Holland's north coast. As at Gross Breesen, he thrived on the farm, rising with the sun and the roosters each morning and working outdoors all day long.

Early in 1939, plans jelled for the Gross Breesen people to start an agricultural training operation in Virginia. Program director Curt Bondy remembered his promise and offered Werner the opportunity to join them. He told Werner it would likely be possible for him to emigrate to America on an agricultural quota, and Werner, now nineteen, signed on.

After Germany invaded Poland in September, Werner's pending emigration became as important to his parents as it was to him.

"Sooner or later," his father warned, Hitler would attack neutral Holland. "It's important for *Mutti* and me to know you are safe." If things looked bad in Holland, Ernst added, he would try to get the family out of Europe, and perhaps join Werner in America.

Through Bondy's connections, the American Jewish Joint Distribution Committee in New York found Werner a sponsor: Lewis L. Strauss, co-owner of the New York investment bank Kuhn, Loeb & Co. Werner's father was in awe; when he saw Strauss's affidavit, he exclaimed, "He is a senior partner of one of the biggest banks in America!"*

In late September 1939, Werner was summoned to appear at the U.S. consulate in Amsterdam. The official asked him a series of questions, most of which called for only one-word answers: Had he ever been a member of the Communist Party? Did he want to murder the president of the United States?

A week later, Werner returned to the consulate to take a physical examination, which he passed, completing the last step toward obtaining his visa. Farewells with his family were short but emotional. None of the Angresses knew when—or if—they would see each other again. His mother, Henny, tried hard to smile as she kissed and hugged him. His youngest brother, Hans, now eleven years old, cried uncontrollably. Werner's last glimpse of his father was almost

---

* Lewis L. Strauss (1896–1974) was a Jewish American businessman and philanthropist. A leader in Jewish causes and a member of the American Jewish Committee, he was committed to helping relieve the plight of Jewish refugees. During World War II, he worked in the U.S. Navy Bureau of Ordnance and later as a troubleshooter for Navy Secretary Frank Knox. In 1947, Strauss was appointed to the newly formed Atomic Energy Commission, and he became a major figure in the development of nuclear power in the United States.

a still-life of Ernst, wearing a three-piece suit and looking like the respected banker he had once been, standing by the car, faintly waving. Werner struggled to hold back his own tears as he walked away from them with a pounding heart. He boarded a train for Antwerp; there, he would board the SS *Veendam* of the Holland America Line for the voyage to America.

The Dutch ship was overcrowded with Jewish refugees, and there were often at least four people staying in cabins meant for two. Most of the twelve-day crossing of the North Atlantic was stormy, and many people spent all day in their bunks. Werner was among the few who did not get seasick, and with so many not eating because of their upset stomachs, he enjoyed double and triple portions in the nearly deserted dining room.

The SS *Veendam* arrived in New York on November 11, 1939, and with a Breesen friend who met him in the city, Werner did a little sightseeing, including a stroll through Central Park. The boulevards and skyscrapers were impressive, but also overwhelming. The "city that never sleeps" seemed too big and too crowded, with masses of people every which way Werner turned. After a couple of days—and nights spent in a youth hostel crammed with other foreigners—he was more than ready to find his way back to a quiet life on the farm. But before he did, he wished to personally thank his sponsor. He went to the Manhattan offices of Kuhn, Loeb & Co., but was told by a secretary that her boss had "no time for that." Still, Werner later wrote Lewis Strauss a thank-you letter.

Werner had gotten off the boat with fifty dollars his father had given him, and he still had most of it when he boarded a Greyhound bus headed to Virginia, where his destination was the sixteen-hundred-acre Hyde Farmlands, located not far from Richmond. Two Jewish American businessmen, cousins Morton and William Thalhimer, owned the property, and they supported Bondy's mission of teaching Jewish refugees to farm and become self-sufficient.

The main house was a white-columned antebellum mansion surrounded by picturesque lawns dotted with mature Virginia willows. About a hundred yards away was the former slave house, used in recent years to store livestock feed. Werner and two old friends from Gross Breesen cleaned it out, and the three of them moved in. They were soon busy planting two hundred cherry trees and fifteen fig trees, and making concrete cinder blocks for chicken coops.

The next six months passed quickly for Werner. He found the labor in the fields hard but rewarding, and in his free time he fell in love with his new surroundings. He enjoyed walking through virgin woods, showering under a waterfall, riding horseback on a moonlit night—they all reminded him of his youthful cowboy dreams from reading the adventure books of Karl May.

Then, on May 10, 1940, came the news that Hitler's armies had invaded Holland, just as Werner's father had predicted. The fighting lasted only a few days before Dutch forces surrendered, and within a week, German troops occupied Holland, Belgium, and Luxembourg.

Everyone at Hyde Farmlands, all Jews from Germany or other Nazi-occupied countries in Europe, talked of little else but war and what was happening in their homelands. Werner was sick with worry about his family, and desperate for contact and news. Had they gotten out? Holland had fallen so quickly; they'd had only a little time. He thought of his mother struggling to smile as she kissed him farewell and of his little brother Hans, who couldn't stop crying. And of his brother Fritz, who at sixteen had stood tall when they shook hands good-bye and kept his emotions in check like a big boy. Werner believed in his father, who had not only orchestrated their escape from Germany, but had smuggled their savings out of the country under the noses of the Nazis. Had he been able to pull off another miraculous escape for them?

In late June, Werner finally got a letter from his parents. There had been no desperate flight; they were still in occupied Amsterdam, "for the time being doing well under the circumstances," they wrote. Their lives continued mostly as before, Papa working at his store, and Fritz and Hans going to school. Werner's spirits soared, but as delighted as he was with their news, he wondered just how long such normalcy could last with the Nazis occupying Holland.

On the evening of December 29, Werner joined a group seated around the wood-cabinet radio in the mansion's clubbish library and listened to President Franklin Roosevelt's fireside chat about defense.

"My friends: This is not a fireside chat on war. It is a talk on national security, because the whole purpose . . . is to keep you now and your children later and your grandchildren much later out of a last-ditch war for the preservation of American independence and all of the things that American independence means to you and to me and to ours."

The American president's deliberate, calm cadence filled the room, and Werner found himself unable to look away from the radio. Roosevelt called for a national effort to provide "as much as possible," to give economic and military aid to keep England "as strong as possible" against the Axis powers. He wanted his listeners to understand that "the Nazi masters of Germany have made it clear that they intend not only to dominate all life and thought in their own country, but also to enslave the whole of Europe, and then to use the resources of Europe to dominate the world."

Though at this time Roosevelt was still maintaining that the U.S. would not enter the war, he concluded his forty-minute speech with a rousing call to arms. "We must be the great arsenal of democracy. For us, this is an emergency as serious as war itself."

After the speech, everyone seemed too deeply lost in his or her own thoughts for much discussion. Werner went to his room and wrote in his diary, "great speech, clear, simple and honest." The next morning, he saw Bondy, and they talked about the radio speech. Bondy shared his sobering assessment with Werner: "We will soon be facing totally new conditions," he said. "Probably no more people will be able to leave the occupied countries."

Like a shot, Werner's thoughts again went to his family—in truth, they were never far from his mind. Were they now trapped in occupied Europe? His diary entry from that night revealed his anxiety and concern: "I am so damned tired, in body as well as mentally. Damned, what is going to happen now?"

Two months later, the owners of Hyde Farmlands informed Bondy that their philanthropic endeavor had become financially untenable, and they had decided to sell the property. The thirty residents, most of them young men and a handful of women, discussed the future. For the men, Bondy suggested the army, and many—Werner among them—agreed that the military was preferable to bouncing around local farms looking for work. If America was drawn into the war, as they all hoped would soon happen, they would have a jump on the wave of new recruits and be able to do their part that much sooner.

Werner volunteered for service, and was inducted into the U.S. Army on May 7, 1941. That day, he took the train with the other recruits to Maryland's Fort Meade, home of the 29th Virginia National Guard Division, to begin training. The day before he left, he gave the diary he had been keeping for the past five years—starting with his arrival at Gross Breesen and ending with his last day at Hyde Farmlands—to a friend for safekeeping in the event that "anything should happen to me, and that is not unlikely." His final entry read:

May 6, 1941: Tomorrow my time as a soldier begins. During these five years I have learned agriculture, left Germany, seen western Europe, and immigrated to the U.S. Most of it was full of excitement, restlessness, wildness. The world is at war and maybe I will perish in this war. Maybe it will be true some day that Germany will be there again for me. If I were to end up over there, my life would make sense. Next month I will be 21 years old. What will become of me I don't know. I only know one thing: there is no laying flat for me, there is no time without fighting and without longing.

Werner was assigned as an infantryman to B Company, 116th Regiment of the 29th Infantry Division. Many of its members were from Lynchburg, Virginia, in the foothills of the Blue Ridge Mountains, but they readily accepted the foreigner with the strange accent and regaled him with stories of their hometown, located on the tree-studded banks of the James River. Eighty years after the Civil War, pride was obvious in their voices when they explained that Lynchburg was the only major city in Virginia not captured by the Union Army.

For Werner, the long practice marches were the most difficult part of the training. During maneuvers around Fort Meade, and in other parts of the South, the recruits could go twenty miles or more in the blazing summer heat and humidity, all the while loaded down with packs, rifles, ammunition, bayonets, and other gear. Werner credited his ability to meet the physical challenges of the infantry entirely to his strenuous work on the farm.

In the army, he quickly made a new friend: John G. Barnes, a civil engineer from Newport News, Virginia. A tall man in his mid-thirties, Barnes had a face that Werner, at first sight, thought was so ugly as to be distinctive. But there was nothing off-putting about his personality and his genuine concern for others. Upon hearing Werner's fractured English, Barnes asked if he would like a tutor, and Werner accepted the offer. Barnes began by reading to Werner from the political section of the *New York Times;* he would then have Werner read back an article and explain it. Within a few months, Werner was reading and speaking proficiently and had no trouble understanding others, even the down-home twang of southern drill sergeants.

Although Werner still had a definite German accent, no one in the division seemed bothered by it or by his German heritage. Until December 1941, he was able to keep up a regular correspondence with his mother, and among the things she told him was that, earlier in 1941, officials from a German agency that enforced laws against currency transfers abroad had come to the house and arrested his father. A short time later, Werner received a brief note from Ernst, written from an Amsterdam jail cell. In his mother's most recent letter, she told him that Papa had been moved to Berlin, tried for smuggling money out of the country, and sentenced to Brandenburg Penitentiary, one of the most secure prisons in Europe. Its inmates were doomed to lengthy sentences of hard labor.

This heartbreaking letter, which arrived shortly before the U.S. entered the war, was the last one Werner received from his mother. After that, nothing came—from her, his brothers, or his imprisoned father. A desperate Werner wrote letters to Holland but received no replies. He began to fear the worst.

In June 1942, the 29th moved to Camp Blanding, near Jacksonville, Florida, and went on alert and was ordered to prepare to sail for Northern Ireland. Werner was excited by the news, and his disappointment when he was told that he would not be going overseas with them was profound. His U.S. citizenship was not yet final, even though a new law had been passed to expedite the process for those in the military.* Because Werner had joined the army during peacetime, no restrictions had previously been placed on his training or assignments, but after Germany declared war on the U.S. in December 1941, and given that he still held German citizenship, he automatically became an enemy alien.

Saying farewell to his friend John Barnes, whom he would never see again, Werner was transferred to the 79th Infantry Division, which also trained at Camp Blanding. After more months of maneuvers, he was notified that he would be joining the other soldiers who hadn't yet received their citizenship papers in a new creation called an "alien

---

* The Second War Powers Act of March 27, 1942, provided for the "expeditious naturalization" of persons in the armed forces of the United States. Under this legislation, immigrants (including enemy aliens) who had served honorably in the armed forces for at least three months were eligible for naturalization. Previously, all immigrants, even those in the military, were required to be residents of the United States for five years before they could obtain naturalized citizenship.

detachment." There were twenty men in the division, most German-born Jews, and a few non-Jews of German descent from the Chicago area. They were ordered to turn in their weapons and dress uniforms, and were refused weekend passes to go into town. They were not quartered in barracks, like the other soldiers, but were relegated to small tents in the middle of a field. For the next six months, they did menial chores like cleaning windows, raking leaves, and scrubbing latrines. At night, drunken soldiers coming back from town would curse loudly at them, calling them "Nazi pigs" and worse.

How had he ended up in such a situation? Werner wondered. After all, he had been an enemy alien for his last six months in the 29th Division, and nobody had said anything about his German heritage or lack of U.S. citizenship. No other divisions were known to have alien detachments. At length, he heard that the unit was the brainchild of a "nearly senile" colonel and his sergeant from Brooklyn. The sergeant had persuaded the colonel, who was the division's intelligence officer, that the enemy aliens, even those claiming to be Jewish, might be Nazi spies.

After almost a year, to the surprise of the men in the alien detachment, they were given their uniforms back and granted ten days' leave in the summer of 1943. No explanation was given, and they all quickly left the base on the same day before the higher-ups could change their minds. Werner went to Richmond, Virginia, where Bondy had moved after the Hyde Farmlands closed.

Coincidentally, Werner arrived just as an army officer was interviewing Bondy—part of the investigation into Werner's work history for his naturalization application. Asked by the officer how his army service was going, Werner took a deep breath, decided what the hell, and told him all about the alien detachment, holding back no details. The shocked officer said such a detachment was in violation of regulations and promised to report it.

By the time Werner returned to Camp Blanding, the tents in the field were gone and the alien detachment had been disbanded. Werner and the others were given back their weapons and assigned to regular units and duties on the base. But it was not so easy for Werner and the others to forget the treatment they had been subjected to for nearly a year.

A few weeks later, Werner saw a notice on a barracks bulletin board calling for any soldiers who spoke a foreign language to apply at the Military Intelligence Training Center to become translators, interpreters, and prisoner-of-war interrogators. Realizing this could be his ticket out of the division he had come to loathe, he immediately applied and was accepted. He was soon on his way to Camp Ritchie.

Located at the foot of the Blue Ridge Mountains in western Maryland, not far from the Civil War battlefield at Gettysburg, Camp Ritchie was surrounded by woods and lakes. On rainy days, of which there were many, the surroundings could be bleak, isolated, and forlorn. But when the sky cleared and the forest and waterways shimmered with streaks of sunlight, it was easy to understand why at the turn of the nineteenth century the region had attracted the well-heeled of Baltimore, Philadelphia, and Washington, D.C., to lake resorts to escape the summer heat.

In 1926, the Maryland National Guard had selected the site for its summer encampment, purchasing 638 acres with two lakes. The camp was named in honor of the state governor, Albert C. Ritchie, and over the next decade buildings were constructed using local fieldstone. On either side of a headquarters building, two block-long kitchen facilities were built. A parade field, pistol range, and machine gun range were also completed.

In 1940, the year before the U.S. entered the war, General George C. Marshall, U.S. Army Chief of Staff, became concerned about the poor state of intelligence training in the army. In spring 1941, he sent a group of officers to England to study military intelligence training and operations in the British army. As a result of their report, the recommendation was made to create a centralized location for the training of interrogators, interpreters, and translators, all of whom the U.S. Army would need in event of war.

The matter remained under consideration through the second half of 1941, as divergent views were exchanged at the highest levels. Secretary of War Henry Stimson had shut down the U.S. State Department's cryptanalytic office years earlier, when he was Secretary of State, saying, "Gentlemen don't read each other's mail." A Pentagon conference on military intelligence was scheduled for December 8, but the meeting was canceled when Pearl Harbor was attacked on December 7. Once the country was at war in the Pacific and in Europe, it was no longer a question of whether centralized intelligence training was necessary, but rather how quickly it could begin. On January 22, 1942, Stimson, who had rapidly reversed his opinion about intelligence gathering, wrote a directive stating that "demands have disclosed a crying need for the enlargement of training in combat intelligence."

On June 19, 1942, the U.S. Army leased Camp Ritchie from the state of Maryland for a dollar a year, to open the first facility for centralized intelligence training in the history of the U.S. military. Eighteen miles from the nearest city—Hagerstown, Maryland, population 32,500—and seventy miles from Washington, D.C., Camp Ritchie's remote setting made it ideal for the type of secret training that would take place here, yet still easy to reach from the Pentagon. The army spent five million dollars completely redoing the facilities, building two-story barracks, classrooms, a hospital and clinic, a new headquarters, and administrative buildings.

A camp theater was constructed for propaganda training sessions, which would one day include mock Nazi rallies with a Hitler look-alike, Harry Kahn, a German Jewish immigrant with a fake toothbrush mustache who became a professional mime after the war. For instruction in conducting raids and house searches while avoiding enemy booby traps, an authentic-looking German village was built; its façades resembled the back lot of a Hollywood movie studio. This was all done even before the first students arrived, with

Camp Ritchie barracks, winter 1944. *(NARA)*

a level of security second only to that given to the development of the atomic bomb at the Manhattan Project, which started that same summer in Oak Ridge, Tennessee.

The importance the army placed on Camp Ritchie's mission was exemplified by the choice of its first commanding officer: Colonel Charles Y. Banfill of the Army Air Corps. Banfill, who had been serving as assistant chief of staff for the Military Intelligence Corps in Washington, D.C., was the brother-in-law of his boss: Major General George V. Strong, chief of Military Intelligence. Owing to his support in Washington, Banfill had the authority to transfer to Camp Ritchie any army personnel possessing knowledge of a foreign language. The search for such persons was assisted by Pentagon keypunch operators, who inputted data and sorted through tens of thousands of punch cards to find soldiers whose records indicated foreign language fluency, a process that led to certain qualified men receiving orders to report to Camp Ritchie.

A training demonstration of Nazi hysteria. *(U.S. Army Signal Corps)*

The first eight-week class at Camp Ritchie graduated twenty-three German-speaking students in September 1942 from a course called Interrogation of Prisoners of War (IPW). Thereafter, the classes became much larger, and a new one started each month. The thirty-four classes that followed graduated on average five hundred students per month.

Some graduates from the early classes were rushed overseas to participate in the British-American invasion of North Africa in late 1942. In an August 1943 letter to the Camp Ritchie commandant, Major General Terry Allen, commander of the First Infantry Division, described the "particularly outstanding" work by the IPW teams assigned to his units in the North Africa campaign. Through their interrogation of German prisoners, Allen said, "new antitank intelligence" had been developed that helped defeat Rommel's Afrika Korps. The IPW teams had furnished infantry commanders with "overlays which showed them practical routes that might not have otherwise been ascertained. . . . All of this was done on a scale which had never before been attempted."

On August 25, 1943, Werner joined the Eleventh Class at Camp Ritchie as a member of a course designated IPW-Ge (Interrogation of Prisoners of War–German). The Eleventh Class also had students enrolled in courses for Italian interrogators (IPW-It), photo interpreters (PI), and terrain intelligence (TI). There was no foreign language requirement for the latter two courses, whose graduates learned to interpret aerial photographs and terrain maps, rather than conduct prisoner interrogations.

Some students, especially those who had been out of school for a while, found the studies arduous. Unexcused absences and tardiness were not allowed. The washout rate varied from class to class, but at times was as high as 40 percent. Those who failed to make the grade were sent back without fanfare to their original units.

Throughout the camp and in areas like the chow halls and PX, a cacophony of foreign languages filled the air: French, Italian, Norwegian, Spanish, Japanese, Greek, Dutch, and others identifiable only to native speakers. It wasn't uncommon to find persons conversant in several languages. One such student was Sergeant Hugh Nibley, a thirty-three-year-old native of Portland, Oregon, who had been a Mormon missionary and had served as a professor of ancient history at Pomona College; he spoke sixteen languages and claimed a familiarity with twice as many.

The training center became a foreign enclave, complete with intellectuals, writers, artists, filmmakers, teachers, and students. Many of these unlikely soldiers were older than the typical GI about to be sent to war. Some of them clearly despised military drills, but they made up for it by being motivated, intelligent, and creative. The barracks and chow halls were alive with discussions of politics, history, and the arts, discourse more typical of a university campus than an army camp. Even the food served to the students was atypical. The camp's head cook had been the chef at New York's Waldorf-Astoria, and he oversaw the preparation of what Werner and the other veteran soldiers declared to be the finest chow in the army.

Werner was assigned to a large barracks full of predominantly German Jewish immigrant soldiers, which felt like a homecoming. They had much in common, including close calls escaping from the Nazis and leaving loved ones behind in occupied Europe. Now they were U.S. soldiers being trained in special skills so they could go back and do their part to defeat Hitler. To a man, they couldn't wait for that opportunity.

His large IPW class formed into groups of thirty or so for classroom instruction—all of it in German. In the field, they broke into smaller teams. They went to class seven days straight, with every eighth day off. Evenings were often filled with hours of study and practice.

The IPW students and their instructors were not the only ones who spoke German. So did a company of support troops, who, for the sake of authenticity, often wore uniforms from captured German prisoners in North Africa. These troops put on demonstrations at the firing ranges using enemy rifles, pistols, mortars, hand grenades, artillery, and machine guns, so the students would become familiar with the sound, range, and effect of German gunfire.

One exam tested the students' immersion in the details of the German military. Each student was given a clipboard with the numbers 1 to 50 preprinted on a sheet beside corresponding descriptions, such as #4, Technische Nothilfe badge (Technical Emergency Corps), and #9, AT rifle scope. They had to find and identify the items in a field over which hundreds of parts of uniforms, weapons, and other German army items had been scattered about.

Werner, who in Berlin had grown so bored with school that he quit after the eighth grade, found himself once again listening to teachers lecturing in German. But this time around, he paid rapt attention.

Everyone agreed that the most challenging course was Order of Battle (OB), which covered the structure of the German army. By definition, "order of battle" was meant to include "all known information of the enemy." The course did not cover the German navy

(Kriegsmarine) or air force (Luftwaffe), because IPW teams were trained to interrogate only enemy soldiers captured during ground operations. For all the divisions and other units likely to be encountered in Europe, the students had to learn unit designations, terms and abbreviations, their arsenal of weapons, the nature of their supply system, and their chain of command.

The army had conducted a wide search to bring qualified individuals to teach at Camp Ritchie. Given the uniqueness of the training, recent graduates who excelled in the course work were often assigned to the faculty. Werner's OB instructor was one of them. Captain Herbert Cohn, a 1929 graduate of the University of Heidelberg and a German Jewish immigrant, had graduated in the Second Class. Having become an expert on the German army, he lectured about units ranging in size from armies (one hundred thousand men) to divisions (fifteen thousand) to regiments (five thousand), their makeup and hierarchy, and the quality of their soldiers and leaders.

The primer for the OB course was *German Order of Battle,* a classified study of the German army prepared by the Military Intelligence Division of the War Department. Much of the information in the courses, however, had to be committed to memory, as most of the materials, including classroom notes, could not be taken with them in case they were captured. Overseas, the leader of each IPW team was given a numbered copy of the OB book, nicknamed "The Red Book," which had on its title page a stern warning: "This document must not fall into enemy hands."

Living with Hitler's military organization by day, Werner sometimes found himself dreaming of it at night, which was far better than awakening in the middle of the night bathed in sweat after a nightmare about his family, whom he had still not heard any more from, in mortal danger. During his waking hours, his head was crammed with names, dates, ranks, insignias, units—all nature of information about the German army from top to bottom.

German Order of Battle excerpts:

2. Armed Forces High Command (OKW).
HITLER is the Supreme Commander of the Armed Forces
(*Oberster Befehlshaber der Wehrmacht*). His deputy as such is
Generalfeldmarschall Wilhelm KEITEL, Chief of the Armed
Forces High Command. KEITEL is responsible for the
smooth functioning of the High Command and sees to it that
HITLER'S orders are carried out, but he has comparatively
little to do with major decisions or policy.

3. Army High Command (OKH).
   a. *Field headquarters*—Since December 1941, when von
      BRAUCHITSCH was dismissed as Commander in Chief
      of the Army (*Oberbefehlshaber des Heeres*) and HITLER
      took direct control of the Army, the field headquarters of
      the OKH has been virtually merged with that of the OKW.
      The functions of the two, however, have remained distinct,
      and there has been no personal union except at the top.

214TH INFANTRY DIVISION

Commander: Genlt. Max HORN (age 56)
Composition: Two infantry regiments (355th; 367th), one artil-
      lery regiment (214th), one mobile battalion, one engineer-
      ing battalion, one signal battalion.
Homestation: Hanau (Ge).
Formed in the summer of 1939 with a high proportion of
      Landwehr personnel (older militia or home guard) later
      largely replaced by younger draftees. On the Saar front
      until December 1939. In southern Norway from May 1940.
      Since December 1941, one of its infantry regiments has
      been detached for service in northern Finland.

Such detailed information about German army units was useful
not only for improving the questions they would be able to ask pris-

oners, Captain Cohn explained. It could also be used as a show of knowledge to impress prisoners; what the Americans already knew might prove unnerving. For instance, casually dropping the name of someone's commanding officer could have a profound psychological effect on a prisoner being interrogated. If the Americans already knew this much, the prisoner might think, it wouldn't hurt to answer a few questions more for a cigarette or a chocolate bar. This in turn could lead to the German giving away valuable tactical intel that might save American lives.

For these reasons, Cohn added, once they were in the field it would be their duty as interrogators to keep up to date on all the available information about the enemy.

As the days turned into weeks, Werner began to understand that he and the other German-born soldiers weren't at Camp Ritchie just because they spoke the language. They also knew the culture and psyche of Germans better than anyone else—a deep, intimate knowledge born from the small details of their lives growing up in Germany. As children, they had gone to school and played sports with boys who were now soldiers in the German army. And as interrogators of German prisoners of war, they would be familiar with the workings of German minds, the habits of German life, and the influences of Nazi doctrine upon German soldiers and civilians alike. Their innate understanding of the enemy could not be taught to someone born in the U.S. and could make all the difference when it came to acquiring valuable tactical information from captured German soldiers.

During the course called German Army Organization, students studied wooden mock-ups of German armored tanks and vehicles. They learned the uniforms worn by German soldiers until they could take a quick look at someone who dashed in and out of the room and correctly identify the branch, rank, medals, ribbons, piping on a cap, any special training, and their participation in battles and campaigns.

In the Documents course, everyone was expected to be able to read German documents, including those in Gothic print or in the handwritten script called Sütterlin. At times, Werner found this course could be fun—as when the instructors handed out captured documents taken from actual German prisoners for students to read aloud. Occasionally, there was a letter to a wife or sweetheart at home evoking past moments of intimacy. These were delivered amid many guffaws and jokes. Students already proficient in German shorthand were singled out for a class in advanced reading of shorthand, just in case they came across such documents in the field.

In Terrain and Aerial Intelligence, the students learned how to draw a topographical map indicating distances and elevation. They also interpreted aerial photographs taken by the Army Air Corps and identified the features that were displayed in the photos. In a special room equipped with practice keys and headphones, they became proficient in sending and receiving Morse code transmissions. At the end of the course, every student was tested by transcribing messages sent by an instructor and answering them back.

Major Rex Applegate, a recognized authority on close combat with or without weapons, taught a course that he designed called Close Combat. He had written his own instructional manual, *Kill or Be Killed,* and the students paid careful attention to his lectures and demonstrations, knowing that his techniques—including the best method for garroting a sentry—might someday save their lives. Students also had to qualify on the firing range with their issued weapons, which meant several different models of rifles—first the M1, later the M1 carbine and M3—as well as a .45-caliber pistol, which all commissioned officers and enlisted interrogators carried as a sidearm. Instructions in shooting a tommy gun were also given to some classes.

On the morning of October 5, 1943, Werner was scheduled to begin a two-day field maneuver. Now a staff sergeant, thanks to his more than two years in the army, he had been assigned to lead a squad through the woods and over the 2,150-foot summit of nearby

South Mountain using a compass and map. However, just as they were to leave, Werner was ordered into a truck with some other students for a ride into nearby Hagerstown to be sworn in as naturalized U.S. citizens. It was a short distance, but on a bumpy road in an army truck, it took an hour. In Hagerstown, they waited in the lobby of city hall for their names to be called.

When it was Werner's turn, he entered an office and stepped up to a desk. An army clerk with a stack of documents sat before him. After verifying Werner's identity, the clerk said all his papers seemed in order. He handed Werner a card containing a printed statement and told him to read it loud and clear. Though he had awaited this day for so long, Werner realized it was going to entail no more ceremony than his matter-of-fact swearing-in to the army.

"I hereby declare under oath that I absolutely and entirely renounce all allegiance and fidelity to any foreign state or sovereignty of which I have heretofore been a citizen. That I will support and defend the Constitution and laws of the United States of America against all enemies, foreign and domestic. That I will bear true faith and allegiance to the same. That I will bear arms on behalf of the United States . . ."

When he finished, the clerk stamped an official paper and handed it to Werner. He was now a naturalized citizen of the United States of America. Werner's first thought was of how pleased his parents would be—but then, of course, he remembered. He had no way of telling them: not his mother or brothers, with whom he had lost contact, or his father, imprisoned in Berlin.

Still, Werner felt a huge sense of relief, as did the other new Americans on the ride back to camp. For weeks, there had been much speculation as to what might happen if those graduates who were born in Germany were rushed overseas after graduation before their U.S. citizenship went through. If they were captured, would they still have protection as POWs under the Geneva Conventions? Or would they be executed by the Nazis as traitors or because they were German Jews in the U.S. Army?

It was early afternoon when they arrived back at camp. The ten men he was to lead on the exercise had waited for him, and they were impatient to get started. The other teams had left long ago. Werner and his men were loaded into the back of a truck, with a canvas cover dropped over the back so they couldn't see where they were being taken. The truck left them at the edge of a forest with a map, a compass, and nothing else. Werner didn't recognize any of the names on the map, because they were all located in France—the idea being that it would be more difficult to ask locals for directions. Only by following the map's topographical contour lines would they get to their destinations.

Their assignment was to hit all the checkpoints, solve intelligence problems at each one, and get back to camp in no more than forty-eight hours. Anyone showing up after that would have to repeat the exercise. As they were starting off six hours behind everyone else, Werner drove the men hard. At each checkpoint, an examiner handed them an envelope with tasks to complete. Some involved a test; others required interrogating mock prisoners in German uniforms, who might be carrying documents that had to be interpreted.

On the second night, they stumbled across the countryside in the pitch dark. The only way Werner could check the map was to kneel on the ground, cover himself with a ground cloth so no light would leak out, spread out the map, and turn on the flashlight. Support troops were out in the woods, too, and if they spotted lights or heard noises, they "shot" the offenders with blanks that were as loud as live ammunition. The exercise was meant to mimic a combat patrol whose only geographical markers were terrain features. As they progressed, Werner discovered that the best method was to seek out distinctive markers—railroad tracks, a river, or a lake. Using such points of reference, he got his team to all their checkpoints without getting lost for long.

At one point, they found themselves facing a barbed-wire fence. Behind it, a nasty-looking bull stood, eyeing them warily. They had been instructed not to stop for fences, but as exhausted as the men were, they decided to take the long way around. They had also been warned that they might be mistaken for prowlers, and farmers with real bullets in their guns might shoot at them. In such cases, they were to shout: "U.S. soldiers on patrol!"

In the early days of Camp Ritchie, locals had called the police in alarming numbers to report a "German invasion" after farmers plowing their fields had looked up to see heavy trucks marked with swastikas barreling past, filled with German infantry and field artillery guns. But by now the rural residents of western Maryland had largely gotten used to the men with heavy German accents running around, some of them in German uniforms and steel helmets and others in U.S. Army uniforms. Eventually, locals began to offer a standard refrain to one another about these curious activities: "It's just the Ritchie boys."

Werner's group finished the field exercise slightly past the deadline, but because they had made up most of the six hours they'd lost, they passed the test and were even commended by their instructors.

For the final exam in the interrogations course, a student had to show he knew how to extract tactical information from someone acting as a German prisoner. Instructors as well as other students (past and present) played the role of prisoners, and were briefed as to how to respond to various methods, from subtle questioning to browbeating, and when to reveal (or not reveal) the desired information.[*] If the interrogator proved inept, the prisoner was told to clam up. The interrogation was observed and graded by an examiner based on how well the student extracted the "essential elements of information," or the most critical information regarding the enemy— strength, location, etc.—that could assist a U.S. commander in "reaching a logical decision." Tactical intelligence was described as the current location of mortars and machine guns, whereas the

---

[*] Some IPW students were able to interrogate real German POWs captured in North Africa and shipped to Camp Ritchie.

Local residents were at first alarmed by the "German invasion" in the countryside around Camp Ritchie. *(U.S. Army Signal Corps and NARA, top to bottom)*

location of the factory that manufactured them was considered strategic intelligence. Given that tactical information could be old and of little use after days or even hours in a fast-moving battle, interrogations were to take place as soon as possible after an enemy soldier became a prisoner; not only would the information be more current, but this was the time when a new prisoner was most frightened and felt most vulnerable. It was also for this reason that IPW teams were assigned to frontline combat units.

When it was time for his test, Werner got unlucky: he drew an examiner he had hoped to avoid. The man was a second lieutenant who had interrogated Germans in North Africa, but suffered shell shock during that campaign. After recuperating in the States, he had been assigned to Camp Ritchie. The day before the testing started, the lieutenant had given the entire class an overview of what the examiners would be expecting. The students were to find out which military unit the prisoner belonged to, its strength, where it was located, and other tactical information. The lieutenant had definite ideas as to how a prisoner should be treated. He must be forced to stand at attention in front of the seated interrogator, heels together and hands along the trouser seams. Under no circumstances could he sit down or be offered water or a cigarette. As prisoners stood at attention, they were to be yelled at nonstop.

"This is the way to do it," said the lieutenant. "It is the way I did it, and why I had such great success in North Africa. It's how you will do it."

Although he had yet to conduct a single wartime interrogation, Werner considered the lieutenant's methods pigheaded. Despite the officer's claims, Werner had a hard time imagining this boastful banty rooster having had much success yelling at the tough vets of Rommel's Afrika Korps. In any case, Werner had no intention of becoming a screaming interrogator. He believed, from the outset, that there were better and more humane ways to extract information from another human being, even if he was the enemy. Although he was stuck with the lieutenant for the final exam, Werner, given his

German-language prisoner interrogation practice at Camp Ritchie. *(NARA)*

time in the army and his sergeant rank, was not cowed by the brash
junior officer. That, added to his innate stubborn streak, made
Werner try an approach he thought would be more effective when
the day came for him to interrogate actual German prisoners on the
battlefield.

When Werner walked into the examining room, he saw the lieutenant already sitting in a chair in the far corner. Making every effort
to ignore him, Werner turned his own chair around so his back was
to the officer.

Werner had brought a bottle of water and a pack of cigarettes,
which he placed on the table. When the mock prisoner entered the
room, Werner addressed him in German, telling him to grab a chair
and join him. He then offered him water and a cigarette, which he
took. Werner asked in a normal tone of voice a series of harmless
questions, such as his name, rank, and serial number, all of which
prisoners could answer under the Geneva Conventions.

After about ten minutes of smoking and responding to numerous harmless questions from Werner, the pretend prisoner seemed to tire of the charade and started volunteering information, as if to get it over with. He freely detailed his unit, its location and strength, and similar pieces of information. With that, the interrogation was over; the lieutenant and Werner were left alone in the room. Werner turned around and looked at the lieutenant, who was staring at him in shocked disbelief.

Though Werner had extracted the information he was supposed to get, that didn't stop the lieutenant from giving him the sort of dressing-down he hadn't experienced since childhood. The lieutenant said Werner was "incapable of interrogating" and lacked the "necessary military bearing" to be taken seriously by captured Germans. He said he would not be giving Werner a passing grade in interrogations.

When Werner graduated with 184 IPW-Ge classmates on October 23, 1943, his lowest grade was in interrogations, although it was still a solid 85. Combined with his other grades, all in the mid to high 90s, he earned a final course grade of 91. His language skills were rated E for excellent. The combined evaluations by his instructors did show the one blemish on his record:

> An extremely conscientious worker, intelligent and eager, who makes a favorable and soldierly impression. Possesses fine control of both languages and handles them most efficiently, however, because of somewhat slow psychological reactions, not quite an interrogator.

Werner's Eleventh Class, which graduated 427 students, also trained 74 Italian-language interrogators, who would soon participate in the Allied campaign in Italy, 136 photo interpreters, and 33 terrain intelligence specialists. In the interests of security, all were warned not to tell anyone—even family members—that they would be working in Military Intelligence.

After graduation, the members of Werner's class heard that they would be sent away to another base for additional maneuvers. The thought of more training exasperated Werner. That was all he had done in the army—train, train, and train some more! Sick and tired of drills, he was ready for action. He was more than ready to get into the war and do his part. He found the colonel in command of Camp Ritchie, who was willing to hear him out.

"Sir," Werner said, after finishing a sharp salute and remaining at attention, "I would like to volunteer for the next transport overseas."

It must have been an unusual request. The colonel looked at Werner with raised eyebrows. "You really want to go, Sergeant?"

"Yes, sir."

"Fine, you'll be on the next one."

The colonel kept his word, and a few weeks later, Werner joined a contingent of other Camp Ritchie graduates boarding a ship in New York headed for England, where Allied forces were massing in preparation for the invasion of occupied France.

Four years had passed since Werner Angress crossed the same ocean as a German Jewish immigrant fleeing Hitler and the Nazis. Now he was going back as a Ritchie Boy to fight against them.

5

GOING BACK

Victor Brombert and Werner Angress did not know each other, but after graduating from Camp Ritchie they sailed with a contingent of nearly two hundred other Ritchie Boys across a storm-tossed Atlantic aboard the RMS *Rangitata,* a New Zealand–built passenger liner–cum–troopship. They left on January 28, 1944, from a Brooklyn pier that was near the spot where Victor and his parents had arrived on the freighter *Navemar* overloaded with Jewish refugees three years earlier. As Victor stood at the rail of the *Rangitata* and watched the Statue of Liberty fade in the distance, he was struck by a kind of symmetry between his arrival as an immigrant and now this departure as an American soldier.

Victor had spoken often to his friends and family about how much he wanted to be involved in the fight to free France from the Nazis' tyranny. But he also knew that this worried his parents, who had already lost one child—his sister, Nora, at age five. They would be devastated if they lost him, too. After his speech at Harrisburg Academy in which he spoke to the urgency of defeating Hitler, he had enrolled in dental school, but in winter 1942, a summons from the draft board arrived, and the decision was no longer his to make. Victor was soon on his way to basic training at Fort Dix, New Jersey.

His fellow recruits called him "Frenchy," and he made it through close-order drill even though he had some difficulty understanding the Alabama drill sergeant. He enjoyed learning how to disassemble, clean, oil, reassemble, and shoot all the weapons. Field training was less agreeable: running the obstacle course; climbing, jumping, and crawling under simulated or live fire; endless push-ups and sit-ups; thrusting bayonets into sagging dummies; and instruction in hand-to-hand combat. But by the time he finished the training, Victor felt like a real soldier. So he was terribly disappointed when he was transferred to the medical corps because he wasn't a U.S. citizen. While his parents were happy when they heard he would be serving as a noncombatant and not an infantryman, Victor was delighted when his training as a litter bearer was interrupted by orders to report to Camp Ritchie.

After he completed the IPW course, Victor, who like many other foreign-born students at Camp Ritchie became a naturalized U.S. citizen in Hagerstown, was kept an extra three weeks at Camp Ritchie. Given his fluency in French, he was among twenty-two students selected for a special graduate course to learn how to interrogate French civilians. They were taught the nature and locations of the various French Resistance groups, the typical structures of their local cells and how to best contact and work with them, what they should try to achieve during these interrogations of civilians, as well as an understanding of how French cities and rural towns were run. After taking the IPW course in German, for which he received a final grade of 89 (his highest grades were in Organization and Tactics), Victor was delighted to be speaking and reading French again. He put his best efforts into the course, hoping to secure his participation in the upcoming Allied landings that everyone knew were being planned for the coast of France.

Enlisted men who graduated from an IPW course were usually promoted to one of four sergeant ranks. But at the completion of his two courses, Victor went from private, the army's lowest rank, to its highest noncommissioned rank: master sergeant, a promotion usually attained by career soldiers after years in the army. It had to do with the "needs of the service" rather than his soldiering, as sergeants and junior officers were needed to lead small teams of interrogators, and many such rapid promotions took place for this reason after graduation at Camp Ritchie. After five short months in the army, Victor went from having no stripes to wearing a stack of six chevrons on his sleeves. Not yet twenty years old, he was surely one of the youngest master sergeants in the U.S. Army.

The *Rangitata* took more than two weeks to cross the Atlantic in a convoy that could only move as fast as its slowest ship. They were tightly grouped together and protected by warships due to the threat from German U-boats. The destroyers and torpedo boats guarding the convoy detected submerged enemy submarines on several occasions and detonated rounds of depth charges.

Victor had a completely different journey across the Atlantic than his first. This time, he slept on a clean bunk in a well-aired space that was neat and orderly, and he and his fellow soldiers played poker to pass the time. He befriended a fellow master sergeant, an Alsatian who had also been through the training at Camp Ritchie. The two of them spoke to each other in their native French. The other soldier was a few years older than Victor, and he had left a wife behind in the U.S.

One bitterly cold day, as the two of them stood on deck watching the undulating seas, Victor was talking excitedly and at some length about the nobility of fighting and liberating Europe and taking heroic action. The older man listened, then finally shook his head. *"Tu as le virus,"* he said, his sarcasm evident as he described Victor as having the "bug" for war. He prophesied that Victor would lose it soon enough.

They arrived in Liverpool in mild weather to a dockside crowd holding WELCOME YANKS signs. Victor's first meal at an army mess in England caused a stir. As he walked past a table of older U.S. Army sergeants, they stopped eating with forks in midair to stare at him. Victor, who was years younger than any of them but outranked them all, offered a greeting. When they heard his French accent, they looked even more astonished. How could a Frenchman be a master sergeant in the U.S. Army?

Victor would experience many such double takes, as would other Ritchie Boys, due to their foreign accents and senior rankings. However, within Military Intelligence, they were not outcasts. Once the Camp Ritchie graduates were assigned to small teams attached to a division or regiment, they largely operated independently of regular army units and commanders, and were free to move about on their own.

Victor was assigned to a six-man team—officially designated Military Intelligence Interpreters–French—whose main mission was to interrogate French civilians and acquire information from members of the French Resistance, which would entail reconnaissance work behind enemy lines. The team's two officers were both lieutenants; as the only master sergeant, Victor was the ranking enlisted man. Officially, the officers and Victor were the chief interrogators, with a staff sergeant serving as a documents examiner and two technical sergeants to handle translations and the typing of reports as well as drive the two jeeps the team had at its disposal. But this table of organization—the same for every IPW team—turned out to be theoretical, as everyone shared the various tasks. All were Camp Ritchie graduates who spoke French, although Victor alone spoke it like a true Frenchman. He and another team member, Staff Sergeant Willi Joseph—at thirty-five the team's old man—were the only ones fluent in German as well.

In February 1944, the team was sent to southern England, not far from prehistoric Stonehenge, to join the 2nd Armored Division. Known as "Hell on Wheels," this was a battle-tested outfit, formerly commanded by George S. Patton Jr., which had seen action in North Africa and Sicily. Rumor had it that this seasoned division, with two regiments that each had more than one hundred tanks, along with a regiment of infantry and support battalions of armored engineers, signal corps, and reconnaissance, would be one of the first U.S. armored divisions to land in France.

For now, the 2nd Armored was conducting nearly nonstop pre-invasion maneuvers that included long marches, special drills, and war games on the grassy, rolling hills of Salisbury Plain, good ground for practicing tank tactics. During this period, Victor taught himself how to drive using one of the team's jeeps. And although none of the Ritchie Boys were expected to handle a tank, Victor was given a demonstration ride in one. For the entire time, he was gripped by intense claustrophobia as he imagined being trapped inside a burning tank during battle.

In early May 1944, Victor was tapped to speak to a group of more than one hundred 2nd Armored officers about what they might find in France as they moved inland after the invasion. He decided to draw them a verbal picture of a typical French town, centering around vivid descriptions of characters they might meet—the town mayor, pharmacist, doctor, priest, banker, schoolmaster—as well as familiar places like the church, boulangerie, town square, and town hall.

Victor spoke at a dais with a pointing stick before a large map of the French coastal region. He was not familiar with the area around Calais, where the distance across the English Channel was the narrowest, and which many—including Hitler and his army generals—thought was the most likely place for the Allied landings. So Victor chose a region he knew well for the location of his mythical town: Normandy. He gave colorful descriptions of the place where he had spent a summer falling in love with a girl named Dany, which seemed like a lifetime ago.

Weeks later, when they learned where the men and tanks of Hell on Wheels would be landing on the coast of France on D-Day, some of the officers present that day—as well as his own team—refused to believe Victor had not been secretly briefed by someone on high at Supreme Headquarters Allied Expeditionary Force (SHAEF) in London. But he hadn't been. It was just chance that Victor had pointed on the map that day to the spot that would soon be known as Omaha Beach.

Guy Stern ended up a Ritchie Boy only because the U.S. Navy rejected him.

A couple of months after America entered the war, Guy, in his second year at Saint Louis University, took seriously the military posters that went up in the school hallways, especially one that said to all with special skills like a foreign language: NAVAL INTELLIGENCE WANTS YOU! He went to the navy recruiting office in downtown St. Louis. When he reached the front of the line of young men eager to enlist, he told the recruiter he had seen the Naval Intelligence poster and wanted to sign up.

"I speak German," Guy said.

"I hear an accent. Were you born in this country?"

"No, I was born in Germany."

"Can't use you. Naval Intel is only taking native-born Americans."

Guy was crestfallen, and he worried that he would be unable to do his part in the war. But four months later, he received his draft notice.

Guy wanted to get into the war because he had become convinced that defeating the Nazis was the only way he would ever reunite with his family. In just a short time, he had made America—the country that had taken him in and given him a new life—his home, and he had developed his own patriotism for the U.S. But he also retained strong feelings for the land of his birth, and felt a strong sense of duty to go back and help rid his homeland of Hitler and the Nazis.

Along with a dozen other recruits from St. Louis, he was sent to the U.S. Army Induction Center at Fort Leavenworth, Kansas. After two weeks of mostly sitting around until the army decided what to do with them, they were sent to Camp Barkeley, the basic training center for medical administration outside of Abilene,

Texas. There, the recruits endured long hikes under the broiling sun carrying a full field pack, then took classroom instruction from local high school teachers who taught the fundamentals of the paperwork involved with medical treatment and hospitalization.

On the first day of May 1943, while still in training, Guy and a group of other foreign-born recruits took a bus into Abilene, where they went before a federal magistrate for a mass citizenship ceremony. They were told that the court could change their Germanic or Jewish-sounding names if they wished. A number of soldiers, not wanting to go overseas with their birth names on their dog tags in case of capture, opted to do so. That day, Günther Stern of Hildesheim legally became Guy Stern of St. Louis.

Guy expected that once his basic training was complete, he would be assigned to a military hospital or medical support unit. But before he finished at Camp Barkeley, he was called into headquarters, where a sergeant informed him he was being transferred that day to another camp.

"Where to, Sergeant?"

"Can't tell you. Your orders are sealed."

He was ordered to board a train heading eastward with two other German Jewish soldiers. Three hours into what seemed like an endless trip across the grasslands of east Texas, they opened their orders as instructed. They were to change trains in Baltimore for a local to Martinsburg, West Virginia, where a jeep would await them. The mystery continued until a day later when they arrived at the front gate of a Maryland army camp surrounded by lush greenery with a lake in the center. The MP carefully checked their orders, then greeted them in German.

"Willkommen im Camp Ritchie."

Guy found the training at Camp Ritchie much different than in Texas but equally demanding. He was soon joining other students on nighttime exercises that consisted of being dropped off deep in the woods with only a map in some unfamiliar language and a small compass. An assembly point was marked on the map, but if

they weren't there by 11 P.M., they would miss their ride and have
to hike twenty-five miles back to camp. For Guy's first exercise, his
group had with them a colonel, who handled the map and compass. After hours of groping around, he admitted he had been looking at the map upside down. Exhausted, they worked their way
back in the dark, arriving in camp just in time for the first class the
next morning.

On Guy's next nighttime exercise, the map made no sense to him
or his companions; one of them guessed it was in Icelandic. They
made a beeline for the first farmhouse, where they received a hearty
hello from its owner. Clearly, they were not his first wayward foreign travelers from Camp Ritchie.

"Hi, fellows. What kind of map do you Ritchie Boys have tonight?
Let me have a look." The farmer studied the familiar geographical
features on the map. "Okay, that building in the center, that's a school
about two miles north of here. Then comes a crossroad that's really
no more than a path. You take the fork to the left, follow it for five
miles and you'll be where the truck is waiting for you. Hurry along,
you'll make it."

Although they were not supposed to ask locals for directions,
lots of students did so when they became lost. Guy guessed that
their instructors knew this and secretly wanted the future Military
Intelligence graduates to develop their wiles and find ways to solve
such problems in the field.

Guy found that the fieldwork at Camp Ritchie was rivaled by the
intellectual demands of the classwork. There were few aspects of
the most current intelligence about the enemy that were not covered.
From memorizing whole passages from *German Order of Battle* to
analyzing aerial maps to identifying the piping on a Wehrmacht cap
and medals on an SS uniform, it all went toward the goal of preparing them to quickly extract vital information from prisoners.

In learning how to conduct interrogations, Guy was taught four
basic techniques. The first, "superior knowledge," called for overwhelming the prisoner with details about enemy units that the inter-

rogator already knew. "Form of bribery" entailed eating a chocolate bar or lighting up a cigarette in front of the prisoner, and when they asked for something to eat or a smoke they were told they could have it only if they cooperated. "Find common interests" played on a prisoner's likes and inclinations. If he was a soccer fan, the interrogator would talk soccer until the prisoner forgot that the interrogator wore a different uniform. Last was "use of fear," in which the interrogator learned a prisoner's anxieties and fears, and made him think they would become a reality if he failed to cooperate.

In case any of the students got the idea there were no legal or moral boundaries when it came to prisoner interrogations, a lawyerly major from the Judge Advocate General's Corps went over the rules and regulations. "First and foremost, and remember this if you recall nothing else I tell you: *Never touch a prisoner.* That is a clear violation of the General Convention on Warfare."

Guy was among 130 graduates of the IPW-Ge course in Camp Ritchie's Eighth Class. He received his highest grades in Signal Communications (96), Staff Duties (89), and Counter Intelligence (90). His evaluation by instructors: "Quiet, unassuming, theatrical, quite intelligent. Good German. Good documents man. Good stenographer and typist." Upon graduation, he was promoted to staff sergeant.

Private Guy Stern, 1943. *(Family photograph)*

After two months of still more training and maneuvers at Fort Polk, Louisiana, among copious snakes, alligators, and feral pigs in the swamps, Guy was thrilled to at last be going back to Europe when he joined two hundred other Ritchie Boys—including Werner Angress and Victor Brombert—in January 1944 aboard the *Rangitata,* headed for England.

Upon their arrival they took

the train to the headquarters for Military Intelligence teams in England, which were located in the small, quaint town of Broadway in the heart of the Cotswolds, northwest of Oxford. Largely unchanged since Shakespeare's time, the town's name was derived from the wide, grass-fringed main street lined with red chestnut trees and honey-colored limestone buildings, many dating back to the sixteenth century. Most of the Ritchie Boys were billeted with local families, who invited their guests to join them for meals, outings, and other social occasions. In turn, the GIs shared their special rations, such as hard-to-get chocolates and cigarettes.

Here the Ritchie Boys' training continued, occasionally enlivened by guest lectures from seasoned British intelligence officers. Many hours of practice interrogations took place at a holding camp north of town, where two hundred German POWs from North Africa were being held. Referred to as "the cage," it was a place to practice interrogation methods on actual Third Reich soldiers, although after being questioned many times and knowing the war was over for them, the POWs had become immune to most interrogation techniques.

At war with a powerful enemy entrenched just across the Channel, all of England had become an armed camp, which made the Ritchie Boys nervous whenever they had to don German uniforms and visit camps bristling with U.S. troops to teach them a thing or two about the enemy. They were most concerned about the British Home Guard, many of them older men armed with ancient rifles and pistols, taking potshots at "invading Krauts." Guy always ended his presentations with what he thought would be a very practical German phrase for the GIs to know. He would soon have an entire barracks of beaming soldiers yelling resoundingly, choral-style: *"Hände hoch oder ich schieße!"* (Hands up or I will shoot!)

Guy was a member of a six-man IPW team attached to the headquarters of the massive U.S. First Army, then made up of six infantry and airborne divisions totaling some one hundred thousand men. The First Army had recently been activated under the

A demonstration of German uniforms and equipment to GIs in England shortly before D-Day. *(U.S. Army Signal Corps)*

command of Lieutenant General Omar Bradley, who had been designated by his former West Point classmate General Dwight Eisenhower, Supreme Allied Commander, to serve as commander of all U.S. ground forces in Operation Overlord, the invasion of Nazi-occupied France.[*]

Guy soon discovered that the vast majority of the twenty-four officers and enlisted men in the four IPW teams assigned to First Army headquarters (other IPW teams were attached to its divisions and their various regiments) were German Jewish refugees who, like him, had been deprived of their homeland and cut off from loved ones. To a man, these Jewish exiles were willing to leave their American asylum and return to Europe to fight the Nazis. Sharing a missionary zeal, they all considered themselves crusaders against evil.

One of the team's preinvasion assignments was to select future

---

[*] U.S. Military Academy class of 1915: known as "the class the stars fell on" because 59 of the 164 graduates—some 36 percent—attained the rank of general, a record that will likely never be surpassed.

sites for large POW cages in France beyond the initial beachheads; close, but not too close, to First Army headquarters. The sites had to be accessible to highways for quick evacuation of prisoners, close to where the interrogators would bivouac so they would have easy access to the prisoners, and have ample space for what was hoped would be a large number of Germans, who would have to be fed and guarded by ancillary units. They put together the list of future POW cages, and then, like the hundreds of thousands of other Allied troops who had massed in England for the invasion, they waited for D-Day.

Guy's team had been briefed: when the alert came, they would convoy from First Army headquarters in Bristol, a city of nearly a half million people in southwestern England, some one hundred miles on roads cleared of other traffic to Southampton, a seaport on England's southeastern tip that had been selected as a major embarkation point for hundreds of ships and landing craft carrying invasion forces.

With stormy weather over the Channel, the wait continued.

To kill the boredom one afternoon, Guy wandered into the large, darkened tent where movies were shown in the evening. Usually there were no matinees, but today a new Hollywood film was playing to help relieve tensions. The movie was *Shine on Harvest Moon,* starring Ann Sheridan, a popular wartime "pin-up girl" who reportedly received 250 marriage proposals a week, many from soldiers. About twenty minutes into the film and shortly after Sheridan belted out the hit tune "Time Waits for No One," the lights in the tent went on. A voice came over the loudspeaker: "All personnel report to quarters! Be ready to move out in convoy in half an hour!" Guy and the other GIs rushed out of the theater.

The invasion was on, and Guy Stern's fervent wish to go back and fight the Nazis who had taken his family away was about to come true.

Werner Angress had never planned to jump out of an airplane.

Before he went to Camp Ritchie, he had turned down the chance to take parachute training. Being an infantryman in the war, he thought, would be risky enough. Upon arriving in England, he had again been asked if he would like to volunteer for the paratroopers, and he had again said firmly, "No, thank you." Yet, to his great surprise, after a few weeks at Broadway, he was assigned to an IPW team attached to the 82nd Airborne Division, which had fought in North Africa, Sicily, and mainland Italy. It had recently arrived in England and had been strengthened with replacements and new equipment in anticipation of D-Day. Now at full strength (approximately eighty-five hundred men), the 82nd comprised three parachute infantry regiments (PIR): the 505th, 507th, and 508th. One IPW team was assigned to each regiment and one to division headquarters.

Werner's team was assigned to the 508th. When he was interviewed by a regimental officer, who asked under what circumstances he had left Germany, Werner gave him a short version of his family's flight.

"So you're Jewish? You don't look it. Are you jump qualified?"

Werner stared blankly. After a hesitation, he said, "Not yet."

His response hadn't been for effect, although he had been wondering what it would mean to be in an airborne unit and not be a parachutist. After two years in the army, serving in the infantry, reaching the rank of staff sergeant and graduating from Camp Ritchie, Werner was determined to be a good soldier and not shirk his duties.

The officer seemed pleased with Werner's answer. He explained that most of the men in the airborne unit had gone to jump school at Fort Bragg, North Carolina, but some late arrivals had been trained in England. He promised that Werner and the other newbies would get parachute training prior to the invasion. The officer admitted their training would not equal six weeks of jump school instruction, but it would at least include the five practice jumps required to qualify as a paratrooper.

Werner's IPW team included three other German Jews who had

Werner Angress in England after joining the
82nd Airborne Division. *(Family photograph)*

immigrated to the United States after the Nazis came to power.
They had all received infantry training before arriving at Camp
Ritchie. They knew that D-Day—which they anticipated with a
mixture of excitement and resolve—was fast approaching, and they
discussed how they should conduct themselves with actual prisoners of war. They rejected any kind of force during interrogations
and felt strongly that as American soldiers, they had a responsibility
to act in a civilized manner, in a way that they felt would distin-
guish them from the Nazis. They all knew, of course, that not every
German soldier was a Nazi, and expressed empathy for "those poor
bastards" who had been cajoled by Hitler and his party but would
be needed when the war was over to help create a new Germany.

Captain John Breen, head of the regiment's intelligence section
(known as S-2), kept trying to arrange the practice jumps for Werner.

Breen, in civilian life an investigator for the U.S. Treasury, was pleasant and likable; he was the only officer in the regiment who would join the men at a nearby pub, in violation of the rules against officers fraternizing with the enlisted ranks. But weeks passed when the weather was too bad to fly or there were no planes or pilots available.

In late May, the 82nd was placed on alert. Everyone was ordered to pack their clothing and equipment and wait to be transported to an airfield. They all knew this meant that the invasion was close at hand.

As he was packing, Werner was approached by a regimental officer who told him that he would be staying behind with the other "nonjumpers," who were to be delivered by landing craft to the coast of France several days after D-Day, once the invasion beaches were secured.

Werner was furious. After all his army training before and after war began—and his fruitless wait for parachute practice that never happened—he was going to be left behind when his airborne division parachuted into Nazi-occupied France on D-Day? He was going to be delivered later on a boat like a sack of potatoes? He voiced his vehement objections to the officer to no avail. But Werner, as usual, was not one to be cowed by the army's chain of command; he decided to go straight to the top.

He rushed from the barracks and ran to division headquarters, where he arrived out of breath. Panting from his sprint, he told the duty sergeant that he was there to see the commanding general.

"The general is busy," the sergeant said. "What do you want?"

Werner told the sergeant, who directed him to the office of the assistant division commander, General James Gavin, who within a few months would become the 82nd's commanding general. He was known as "Jumpin' Jim" for his practice of taking part in combat jumps with his paratroopers.

The tall general turned from where he was standing at a wall map.

Werner stood at attention, saluted, and said, "Staff Sergeant Angress reporting."

"Okay, Sergeant. Shoot."

"Sir, I have been assigned to the division as an interrogator with the understanding that I'd be given jump training. For reasons mostly having to do with the weather, I did not get that training. But I request permission to jump with the division."

By the time Werner finished, the general was looking at him with a trace of a smile. "Well, my chauffeur has never jumped in his life. Besides, he's overweight. But I need him in France, so he'll jump. If he can go, so can you. Tell your superior officer you have my permission."

Werner snapped a smart salute and raced back to the barracks. He told the surprised regimental officer how well his meeting with the general had gone, and soon was on a bus headed to the airfield.

Typical of the army's hurry-up-and-wait policy, Werner's regiment spent the next several days in a giant hangar at Royal Air Force Station Saltby in Leicestershire, ninety miles north of London. Four U.S. troop carrier squadrons had flown in from Sicily, and their C-47 Skytrain transports, which would soon be taking them over France, were parked outside on the tarmac. Hundreds of folding cots had been set up in the hangar for the paratroopers, who played cards and dice with new invasion currency they valued like Monopoly money. A military band played every afternoon and a movie was shown each evening.

Werner read much of the time, a favorite being his slim, well-read volume of Kipling's *Barrack-Room Ballads,* especially "Gunga Din" and the other army poems about the Boer War. He wrote letters to his Gross Breesen friends, several of whom were also in the service, and to Curt Bondy in Virginia. He would have liked to update his parents, but he had been out of contact with them since his mother's letter two years ago telling of his father's imprisonment in Berlin. All the letters he had written since had gone unanswered. He did not know if his mother and brothers were still in Nazi-occupied Holland or if they had been taken elsewhere.

Werner kept himself busy cleaning and oiling his weapons,

over and over again. He had been issued an M1 carbine, which was favored by many paratroopers because it was lightweight and easy to carry, but the tradeoff was that it didn't have much stopping power in a firefight. He had bought from a British officer a German Luger pistol, which U.S. soldiers weren't authorized to carry, but Werner decided to take it with him for D-Day, thinking it might come in handy.

On the morning of June 4, they again went on alert, and rumor had it that D-Day would be the next morning. They packed their extra gear in duffel bags that would be delivered to them after the invasion. That afternoon, they learned their destination: the Cotentin Peninsula in Normandy. The division's paratroopers were to land between the Douve and Merderet rivers hours before the assault forces hit the beaches and capture the key town of Sainte-Mère-Église, eight miles inland.

Werner was assigned to a C-47 with a group of thirty troopers, called a "stick." Their jumpmaster was a sergeant and veteran of many parachute jumps. When he heard Werner had not gone to jump school, he began calling him "Chicken." He decided Werner needed some training in the hangar. He showed Werner how to push his steel helmet back on his head before he jumped so he would be able to look up to see if his twenty-eight-foot canopy had been deployed by the static line attached to the cover on the pack holding the parachute. He explained that the fifteen-foot line was designed to pull open the parachute pack, then break free and remain attached to the aircraft. If Werner's chute hadn't opened automatically within three seconds or if any panels had been ripped out of the silk canopy, which would dangerously increase the speed of his fall, he was to pull the handle on the smaller reserve chute, which he wore in a chest pack. The jumpmaster also showed Werner how to keep his legs slightly apart when he hit the ground so he wouldn't break a leg. Pulling on two of the risers connecting the main parachute to his harness would reduce his midair oscillation so he could land securely on his feet. For a finale, the jumpmaster had Werner scramble atop a large wooden crate and jump as if he were leaping from a plane. He landed nimbly on the balls of his feet and in the correct position. That "jump" and those fifteen minutes were the extent of Werner's parachute training.

The invasion set for the next day was called off due to bad weather over the English Channel. The following morning, the paratroopers awoke to clear skies and knew nothing would stop the invasion now.

In the afternoon, they sat on the ground outside the hangar, dressed in their olive-green fatigues and polished jump boots, as General Gavin addressed them. He gave them an overview of the area where they were to be dropped and their mission. The general did not sugarcoat things. They were being dropped ten miles behind enemy lines to soften up German defenses and to secure targets that included bridges, towns, and road crossings. They would be at the far western flank of the invasion beaches and were to stop any counterattacks from that direction against the seaborne forces as they waded ashore. If the sea assault failed to secure a foothold and the invasion forces withdrew to England, there would be no rescue for the paratroopers. Gavin instructed the men to not take any German prisoners initially, as under the circumstances they would be an unmanageable burden. He closed with a cheery, "Good luck and good hunting!"

Werner was alarmed by what he heard. *Take no prisoners?* Wasn't that a violation of the Geneva Conventions? Turning to the Ritchie Boys seated next to him, Werner asked why the hell any of them were going if they weren't interrogating prisoners? One of them speculated that this was only temporary, and typical for the early hours of an airborne operation, which required speed and stealth behind enemy lines. They couldn't very well take the time to build and guard prisoner cages.

Army cooks had set up a mobile kitchen outside the hangar. At the end of the long chow lines stood the officers, a rule of General Gavin's: officers in the 82nd Airborne always ate after their men.

The night before, the cooks had served steak, what they thought was a fitting final send-off for the men. Now, because of the weather delay, they had to prepare a second final dinner on short notice. They produced a watery macaroni and cheese, which all agreed did not taste like the Last Supper. Afterward, the soldiers used the grease and ashes from the portable stoves to blacken their faces so they wouldn't shine in the moonlight. Werner thought they all looked like something out of a costume ball.

About midnight, they moved slowly out to the parked planes, each man loaded down with fifty to seventy pounds of equipment. Werner sweated under his load. Two parachutes, one on his back and the other on his chest. A gas mask was tied to one leg, a small hoe for digging foxholes tied to the other. Clipped to his chest harness above the reserve chute were two fragmentation hand grenades. He wore a web belt from which hung a canteen of water, a bayonet, a first-aid kit, extra ammo, and a trench knife. Strapped under the chest chute was his musette bag, containing a phosphorus grenade, a compass, chewing gum, bouillon cubes, water purification tablets, Hershey bars, a shaving kit, extra underwear and socks, and his volume of Kipling.

As his stick lined up at the bottom of the ramp to their plane, Werner noticed a name painted boldly on the side of the fuselage: SON OF THE BEACH.

Above it was a cartoon drawing of Donald Duck in swim trunks.

There was a lot of chatter back and forth between buddies in other sticks as they waved, wisecracked, and in one way or another said their good-byes to one another.

"Chicken, stop!"

Werner stepped out of the line already starting up the ramp.

"You board last," said the jumpmaster.

"Last?" Werner couldn't imagine the reason. "Why?"

"You're going out the door first."

6

NORMANDY

By the time Werner Angress boarded the plane, most of the paratroopers, wearing steel helmets and burdened like pack-horses, had plopped into metal seats set in facing rows along either side of the cabin. Near the door were equipment bags containing a machine gun, a mortar, ammunition, and food rations. They were strapped together and attached to a parachute pack with a static line that would connect to a wire cable running along the cabin's ceiling.

By then, all the razzing had ceased. With the interior of the aircraft lit by red lights so as to preserve their night vision, it was as if the men had entered another world. Their darkened faces now looked a ghostly blue.

The silence was broken by the pilot's voice on the intercom reading a D-Day message from General Eisenhower to all Allied forces.

"You are about to embark upon the Great Crusade, toward which we have striven these many months. The eyes of the world are upon you. The hopes and prayers of liberty-loving people everywhere march with you. In company with our brave Allies and brothers-in-arms on other fronts, you will bring about the destruction of the German war machine, the elimination of Nazi tyranny over oppressed peoples of Europe, and security for ourselves in a free world. Your task will not be an easy one. Your enemy is well trained, well equipped and battle-hardened . . . We will accept nothing less than full victory. Good luck! And let us all beseech the blessing of Almighty God upon this great and noble undertaking."

The sound of the plane's engines starting up soon went from backfiring and sputtering into a reassuring drone. They taxied in single file with other C-47s loaded with 82nd Airborne paratroopers to the takeoff runway. When it was their turn, the heavily laden aircraft rolled down the runway, rattling and shaking as it gained speed until it lifted off the ground, clawing for altitude.

This was Werner's first time flying, and it struck him that he was about to experience several others. First parachute jump. First night jump. First combat jump. At the moment, he wasn't thinking about what he might face in Normandy, although it occurred to him that as the first man out of the plane he would be a choice target for any Germans waiting on the ground to shoot U.S. paratroopers floating down under their parachute canopies. He hoped he didn't freeze up when it was time to jump, that his chute would open, and that he'd land in one piece.

They flew circles over the blacked-out English countryside as the aerial armada formed up. Werner saw other planes joining them, their red and green wingtip lights sparkling against the night sky. When they straightened out, they proceeded in formation over the Channel toward the French coast. To avoid overflying the Normandy invasion fleet of hundreds of ships and chance being shot at by jittery ship gunners, the planes circled wide over the German-occupied Channel Islands, thirty miles off the coast of France. They flew at low altitude to evade enemy antiaircraft guns set to shoot at high-flying bombers and passed over the islands without a shot being fired. Within thirty minutes they reached the French coast and climbed to the jump altitude of one thousand feet.

"Stand up and hook up!" roared the jumpmaster.

The men rose and formed a single line facing rearward. They all snapped the ring-end of their static line into the overhead cable.

"Equipment check!"

Everyone checked the static line of the man in front of him to be sure it was securely attached to the cable and not looped under an arm or fouled in a strap or webbing, which could prevent the parachute from opening properly.

They came under enemy fire as they crossed the Cotentin Peninsula.

Looking out the wide-open exit door, Werner saw rising in the sky countless orange tracer rounds from antiaircraft fire, which helped gunners on the ground adjust their aim. At first, the fireworks display looked almost beautiful. Then the plane next to them took a direct hit and burst into flames. Horrified, Werner watched as it cartwheeled out of sight without a single parachute emerging.

Suddenly everyone on Werner's plane heard a sickening thud and felt a lurch, which were their first indications that their own plane had been hit. Werner saw the red light next to the exit door go out. The pilot was supposed to illuminate an adjacent green one when they were over the jump zone, but the strike had caused an electrical failure in the cabin.

The jumpmaster cursed. With the lights not working, he would have to go up to the cockpit to get the jump order from the pilot, and he began squeezing past the men in the aisle to make his way there.

The plane twisted and turned as the pilot tried to evade the antiaircraft fire that pockmarked the sky with fiery, red explosions, and the men swayed with the wild gyrations, struggling to stay upright.

"Whaddaya expect?" said the guy next to Werner. "SNAFU as usual."

When the jumpmaster came back from the cockpit, he yelled for Werner to help him push the equipment bags out the door, and as soon as that was done, he turned to Werner again and yelled, "Here we go! Jump, Chicken!"

Werner pushed the metal ring along the cable that connected his parachute to the static line above him as he moved to the doorway, then stepped out without a moment's hesitation.

The time was 2:15 A.M. The date was June 6, 1944.

Werner had been told to count aloud "one-thousand-one, one-thousand-two, one-thousand-three," then to look up to see if his main parachute had opened. If it hadn't, he was to yank the handle on his chest pack to manually deploy the reserve. He got as far as one-thousand-two when he felt the painful jerk of the harness against his groin and shoulders. Looking up, he was relieved to see all the silk panels intact. Spinning round and round, he pulled the risers to reduce the oscillation. There was no sensation of falling, only floating.

The moon was bright but ducking in and out of clouds. He wondered why he didn't see any other canopies in the sky. Neither were there lights on the ground nor any indication of people shooting at him. It was so quiet he even heard a horse neighing in a pasture below.

He saw he was going to land in an orchard. As the ground rushed toward him, he yanked on the risers and altered his direction enough to miss hitting a tree. But even so his parachute got caught high in the branches, abruptly halting his descent a foot short of the ground. He unhooked himself and dropped down the rest of the way.

He quickly checked his surroundings and didn't see anyone nearby. He looked at his compass and set off to the east, the direction they had been told to go to reach their planned assembly point. All around him were apple trees, separated every hundred yards or so by rows of tall, thick hedges rather than fences.

Werner arrived at a set of railroad tracks and cautiously crawled over them. A nearby highway ran parallel to the tracks, and as he hid in some bushes, he watched the light traffic, mostly motorcycles, pass by. He could tell from the shape of the drivers' helmets that they were German soldiers. He had known he'd be facing enemy troops in Normandy, but he never thought he would be alone when he did, and it now seemed unreal.

Werner waited for a break in the traffic, then crossed the road and took a narrow path into a forest. After walking for ten minutes, he came to a moonlit clearing. As soon as he entered it he saw on the other side, about thirty yards away, the silhouettes of three German soldiers standing in a dugout with a mounted machine gun pointed into the center of the clearing.

Werner kept moving very quietly, hoping to pass without being seen, but one of the Germans yelled out for him to identify himself.

"*Unteroffizier auf Patrouille!*" Werner answered.

As soon as the words left his mouth, Werner knew he had made a mistake. Although he had spoken perfect German with his slight Berlin accent, he had claimed to be a corporal on patrol duty. But he knew from one of his Camp Ritchie courses that Wehrmacht corporals didn't generally go on patrol alone. One of the enemy soldiers ordered Werner to come closer.

His M1 was slung over his shoulder, and by the time he swung it around, they would have plenty of time to cut him down. In any case, his carbine peashooter was no match for a machine gun. It was too late for him to turn back, so Werner strolled into the clearing in front of the pillbox, unhooked a grenade, pulled out the safety ring, heaved it in their direction, and, without breaking stride, turned and ran like hell, which wasn't at all fast because of all the equipment he was lugging.

In sports, throwing had never been his strong suit. As he ran, he heard the surprised Germans yelling just before the explosion. Werner looked back, and that was another mistake. The grenade had bounced along the ground and exploded in front of the pillbox. And one German had already climbed out of the dugout and was aiming a pistol at him.

Certain he was about to be shot in the back, Werner leapt into the brush at the edge of the clearing, desperate to disappear in the foliage.

At the single crack of the German's gun, a bullet struck Werner's helmet with a reverberating clang. He dove to the ground with his carbine at the ready and waited. Panting heavily and his heart pounding in his ears, he lay perfectly still. He heard more yelling and cursing; he could make out that one of the machine gunners had been wounded by the blast. To Werner's surprise, no one came after him, and he crawled away deeper into the woods. After he put a distance of perhaps a quarter mile between him and the Germans, he decided against further thrashing about in the dark, and settled in to await sunrise.

Inspecting his helmet, he saw that the bullet had torn though the camouflage net and made a small dent in the back of the helmet. If it had pierced the steel, the bullet would have struck him square in the back of his head. *That fellow could shoot!* Werner knew he was damn lucky to have survived his first combat. He told himself he would have to do better next time. He needed to be more care-ful, quicker on his feet, and more agile, so he started lightening his load. He buried things he didn't consider essential, like his gas mask, hand hoe, the parachute harness he was still wearing, and the white phosphorus grenade—nicknamed "Willie Pete"—he had been issued that he had no intention of using on another human being, even an enemy. Unlike his one remaining fragmentation gre-nade, which caused an explosive blast when it went off, the Willie Pete was an incendiary weapon that burned fiercely and ignited cloth, fuel, and ammunition and could burn a man alive.

When the sun came up, he studied his map and checked his com-pass. None of the terrain around him corresponded with what was on the map, and he knew he was lost. But he decided to keep head-ing east, as they had been instructed. After his encounter with the German soldiers, he stayed in the woods when possible, although he had to cross a few roads. Whenever he did, he saw only German military traffic, and waited for it to pass.

Later that afternoon, he heard voices coming down a path, so he moved over into a thicket and waited. As they drew closer, he saw it was an old lady and a young girl carrying armloads of firewood.

He stepped out in front of them, forgetting his face was still covered with soot and grease.

They took one look at him and shrieked.

"*Je suis parachutiste américain,*" he said in his schoolboy French.

Although they seemed delighted to hear he was a U.S. soldier, the old lady still trembled as she answered his questions. She said the next village was Videcosville, about a quarter mile away, and that Werner should be careful because Germans were stationed on the other side of town.

After they left, he found Videcosville on his map and saw it was twelve miles *north* of Sainte-Mère-Église. Their drop zone was supposed to be a few miles *south* of Sainte-Mère-Église. He had been dropped more than fifteen miles off target! Recalling the pilot's wild, evasive flying after the plane was hit, he now wondered if the entire stick had jumped in the wrong place. In their prejump briefing, they had been told that the pilots were under orders not to deviate from their assigned course for that reason. What about the rest of his regiment? And the division? If there had been other similar mis-drops, there could be stragglers all over Normandy.

After lying awake all that night, he walked most of the next day without seeing anyone. Late in the afternoon, he came across a farmer who was milking his cows in a barn. The Frenchman didn't seem at all surprised to see an American soldier. He gave Werner a cup of warm milk fresh from one of the cows, followed by a glass of amber liquid. Werner thought it was apple juice, but it was actually calvados, a Norman apple brandy. The liquor hit his empty stomach like a punch. Werner realized how exhausted he was and knew he needed to sleep before continuing. The farmer led him to another barn, where Werner collapsed in a haystack.

Around midnight, he was awakened by a teenage boy who said there were two U.S. soldiers nearby. They had been briefed to expect assistance from French civilians eager for their liberation, but they were warned that others could be collaborating with the Germans, and would gladly turn them in for a reward. Holding his

Luger at the ready in case it was a trap, Werner cautiously followed the boy to a hollow in a field surrounded by a dense hedge. Sure enough, hiding there in the bush were two lost paratroopers with the "Screaming Eagle" shoulder patch of the 101st Airborne. Happy to no longer be alone, Werner greeted them enthusiastically, and suddenly found himself looking into the business end of their carbines.

Realizing that his German accent had alarmed them, he rapidly explained that he was an American GI just like them, even though he was of German descent, and that he had escaped from the Nazis some years ago and was now serving as a prisoner interrogator for the 82nd. But they also spotted his Luger pistol—the favored sidearm of German officers—and Werner had to do some additional explaining. Luckily, though, one of the men, a Jew from Brooklyn, finally believed him and helped Werner convince his buddy, an Irish redhead from Boston, that Werner was a fellow U.S. paratrooper.

Once Werner had convinced them that they were on the same side, the two privates pointed out that since he was a sergeant, Werner was in charge. His first order was that they should each take turns standing two-hour watches at night while the other two slept.

Over the next several days, the teenager brought to their hiding place other American stragglers he found. By June 10, the group numbered more than two dozen paratroopers from both the 101st and 82nd who had been scattered over the countryside and had not been able to find their own units. The senior officer was a captain, and he decided they should strike out in an effort to reach their divisions and catch up with the war.

They could hear the sounds of artillery and bombs in the distance, and they headed toward the fighting, moving only by night to lessen the chance of being spotted. They heard German troops, trucks, and armor hurrying northwest, away from the invasion beaches and toward the German-held port of Cherbourg. They took it as a sign that the D-Day landings had gone well and the Allied troops were pushing inland.

Werner was the only one who spoke French, so he took on the responsibility of getting food from the local farmers. And he had to approach them cautiously and be sure they weren't collaborators. Some of the farmers gladly donated the food they could spare to their liberators, but in most cases, he purchased it with invasion currency printed up by the Allied command. The French had never seen this kind of money and only begrudgingly accepted it because they weren't able to spend it while under German occupation; the currency would only be good in the event the Allies were victorious. With a diet of mostly milk and bread, and never in ample quantities, hunger was a constant for the lost paratroopers.

On June 15, Werner found a farmer who agreed to use his horse-drawn wagon to deliver cans of milk and loaves of bread for which Werner paid him in advance. The farmer had said he would bring them at 10 P.M. to the edge of the woods where they were encamped. But he never showed up; instead, he reported their position to the Germans.

Not long after the appointed hour, a large number of German troops began firing from a wooded hillside toward the paratroopers' hidden positions, and a fusillade of bullets whizzed overhead. One enemy machine gun had pinned Werner down at the edge of a field, and he thought the hissing of its bullets only inches above his head was the nastiest sound he had ever heard. He rolled onto his back and lobbed a grenade in the direction of the gun. The firing stopped long enough for him to crawl back into the trees. As the paratroopers returned fire—they had no machine guns, mortars, or other heavy weapons—the Germans paused only briefly before opening up again.

Soon came the distinctive *ack-ack* of a 20 mm antiaircraft weapon, which had been brought up and leveled to fire at the tree-tops above the paratroopers, who were showered with hot shrapnel and splinters.

When the tree above him exploded, Werner went momentarily blind and deaf. He knew he was still alive when he felt a sharp pain from a shrapnel wound in his upper left thigh and the warmth of flowing blood, both of which he found oddly reassuring.

Even with his ears ringing, Werner could hear orders being barked in German.

"What are they saying, Sergeant?" asked the captain.

"They're going to feed us shrapnel for as long as it takes," Werner replied.

The booming, earth-shaking shelling continued.

The captain decided—rightly so, Werner thought—that their situation was futile. They were low on ammo and surrounded behind enemy lines by a larger force with greater firepower. Fighting back would only result in a senseless slaughter.

Werner Angress asked for a new set of dog tags before going overseas, replacing the "H" for Hebrew with a "P" for Protestant (lower right corner). *(Courtesy Holocaust Memorial Center, Farmington Hills, Michigan)*

"You speak the lingo, Sergeant," said the captain. "Tell those sons of bitches we surrender."

Werner told the officer that if the Germans heard him speak their language they would know he had grown up in Germany. What he left unsaid was that their captors would likely think that *any* German fighting for the Americans was Jewish. Many of the Ritchie Boys had requested and received new dog tags before going overseas, removing or altering the single letter on their ID tags that designated a religious preference. Werner had changed his from "H" for Hebrew to "P" for Protestant.

"Well, goddammit," the captain hissed. "How do I go about it?"

Werner told the captain to yell *"Kamerad, Kamerad,"* which he did, and after a moment the firing stopped.

The twenty-eight American paratroopers dropped their helmets and weapons to the ground, clasped their hands behind their heads, and walked from the woods into captivity.

After all the training the U.S. Army had put into making Werner Angress a prisoner interrogator, he was now a prisoner of the German army.

Victor Brombert returned to his beloved France two days after D-Day with Hell on Wheels, the first U.S. armored division to land at Normandy.

The bulk of the 2nd Armored had loaded onto LSTs (Landing Ships for Tanks) at the docks in Southampton, England, on June 7 and started across the Channel. They arrived off Normandy late that afternoon and spent the night onboard, many crews remaining inside their tanks. In the darkness, one of the four-hundred-foot-long LSTs struck a mine, setting off such a powerful explosion that it rocked nearby ships. It sank quickly, taking with it seven men along with thirty tanks, trucks, and half-tracks.

When daylight broke, the LSTs were beached, their bow doors opened, and their ramps lowered. The men of the 2nd drove their tanks and other vehicles onto Omaha Beach, a seven-mile-long stretch of curved shoreline bookended by rocky cliffs. Although they arrived at Easy Red sector forty-eight hours after the first assault waves hit the beach, they could see the horrific evidence of D-Day still strewn across the sand.

Victor drove a jeep down the LST ramp onto wooden planks stretched across the beach so vehicles wouldn't get stuck, past overturned landing craft, demolished vehicles, abandoned equipment and ammunition belts, and what remained of the German defenses: broken poles that had supported mines, and V-shaped antitank ditches pointing their teeth toward the sea. Dead soldiers lay in shallow trenches dug in the sandy ground, temporarily shrouded in cotton mattress covers. The gently sloping tidal flat, which had offered no cover for the attacking troops, extended three hundred yards from the low-water mark to a masonry seawall, where wounded GIs, evacuation tags tied to their buttonholes, leaned. One had his head swathed in bandages with only narrow slits left open for the eyes.

From exhausted engineers working to open winding beach exits through the barren and forbidding dunes for the troops, vehicles, and supplies pouring off ships, Victor heard eyewitness accounts of the chaos of Omaha Beach on D-Day. How many of the soldiers who stepped from landing crafts were blown apart by mortar rounds or mowed down by machine guns firing from strategically placed concrete pillboxes. How the wounded were pulled under by the turbulent surf. How the engineers had been unable to clear all the booby traps and obstacles in the water near the beach because infantrymen under heavy fire used them to take cover. How body parts washed up everywhere and the sea turned red with blood. How many assault troops, pinned down and paralyzed by panic and confusion, refused to budge from the beach.

Victor drove tensely along a steep, pebbly path up a two-hundred-foot bluff to a brush-covered plateau where his team of French interpreters assembled. One of their jeeps pulled a two-wheel trailer covered with a tarp and filled with their duffel bags and Military

Intelligence documents, including a bound copy of *German Order of Battle*. They headed into the village of Saint-Laurent-sur-Mer to start questioning the nearly two hundred residents and find out what they knew of German troop strength and defenses inland.

His first night on French soil in nearly three years, Victor, too exhausted to dig a foxhole, wrapped himself in a blanket and stretched out at the edge of an open field. A few hours later, he was jolted awake by the shriek of a low-flying German plane plunging earthward under the bright light of an aerial flare. A line of rapid-fire bullets tore across the field as Victor hugged the damp earth. With no place to hide and unable to summon a prayer, he made two promises. If he survived, he would consider life a precious gift and would never complain about anything. And he would never sleep outside a foxhole in this war again.

Victor and the other interrogators soon discovered how challenging it would be to get accurate information from the farmers and peasants in this area. Some were openly uncooperative, while others were overly zealous in trying to please the French-speaking Americans by telling them what they thought they wanted to hear. When one of the interrogators asked a French gentleman, "Where did the Germans lay mines?" he emphatically pointed to the left side of a road while saying, "Off that road to the right." Even eyewitness accounts could be unreliable, with descriptions varying widely. Victor and his team would learn that the key was to speak to as many people as possible, and compare their answers to filter out inaccuracies and exaggerations.

Victor was surprised that not everyone in Normandy was delighted by the Allies' arrival. On the surface, there was enthusiasm for *libération*, but there was also a current of resentment among some locals because the invasion had caused the deaths of innocent French civilians as well as the hated Germans, *les Boches*, and the indiscriminate Allied bombing had damaged their homes, churches, and stores. Also, the Calvados region exported dairy products, cider, apple brandy, and cattle, and its prosperity had not suffered under German occupation. Due to shortages elsewhere, the local black market had flourished, which was why Normandy had been less fertile ground for the Resistance.

The Normandy landscape, with its endless hedgerows, posed special problems for military operations, particularly the armored units. It was the one type of terrain the tank drivers of the 2nd Armored had not trained for during maneuvers in England. (To have done so would have revealed to any watchful spies that Normandy was to be the location of the landings.) A countryside dotted with small fields surrounded by thick hedgerows, sunken roads, and many intersections was excellent defensive ground but placed added burdens on an attacking force. It was perfect terrain for German snipers and hidden machine gun nests that could wait until infantry and armor were within one hundred yards before firing. After losing scores of tanks when their underbellies, not protected by armor, were exposed to antitank guns as they climbed over the hedgerows, the division tried without success to use satchel charges to blow holes in the dense vegetation. Then someone thought to mount a set of bulldozer blades on the front of a tank to cut through the hedges. That worked so well that special blades were fashioned and attached to scores of tanks, which became known as Rhinoceroses.

The men of the 2nd Armored quickly learned other ways to adapt to fighting in the hedgerows. When the Germans stayed hidden in the hedges and allowed the lead tanks to cut their way through, then open fire on the foot soldiers following, the tankers came up with a new, deadly trick. They loaded their main guns with canister shot, an antipersonnel ammunition consisting of lead or iron balls, and pointed them to their flanks. As the tanks crashed through, they fired parallel to the hedges, annihilating anyone who might be waiting in ambush. This strategy earned the grudging respect of the Germans, who nicknamed the division "Roosevelt's Butchers," a moniker the men of the 2nd gladly accepted.

Victor's team customized their jeeps after they heard reports about drivers being decapitated by wire strung across narrow roads. Since they were supposed to drive with the front windshield folded down to prevent the sun's reflection from attracting snipers, they installed vertical wire-cutters with sharp teeth placed several feet above the front bumpers.

In Normandy, Victor was disabused of the notion that war was heroic or noble. As his Alsatian friend had prophesized aboard the *Rangitata,* he had quickly lost the "bug" for war. On their first night in the field, he had discovered that heroism was fine in literature, but it meant little when the lead was flying. The big picture carried far less importance than he could have imagined. Rather, the focus had to be on What was happening *now*? Then, What was going to happen *next*?

As he made his way through Normandy, questioning the residents of newly liberated towns for any valuable information about the German defenses, any booby traps the Germans had left behind, and their troop movements, Victor seldom passed an orchard or pasture or crossing free of dead soldiers and lifeless animals. Germans were easily identifiable in spite of the condition of the corpses, if only by their hobnailed boots. One sight that seared into his memory was of a young German lying under an apple tree with his mouth agape in apparent agony, as if echoing Edvard Munch's *The Scream*. The number of dead livestock in the region was also staggering: cows bloated in grotesque positions, usually on their back with legs stiff in the air, their rotting heft often serving as cover for soldiers.

Victor was particularly horrified by the corpses of 2nd Armored crews with their tanks; the tank commanders, their bodies folded over the turret, or the drivers, gunners, and mechanics trapped inside who had tried to crawl out the escape hatch of their burning tank but did not make it and were scorched beyond recognition. Victor thought the demolished tanks tipped onto their sides or overturned looked like mutilated prehistoric beasts with gutted bellies. And then there was the stench: spilled fuel and cordite from spent ammunition, mixed with burnt human flesh.

While he kept in mind the greater cause—the fight against Hitler and the Nazis—these awful scenes were tough to bear. A poem he wrote in Normandy and sent home to a cousin began:

> *The wounded tanks, men pierced with holes,*
> *Images of the war nobody wanted . . .*

A week after the 2nd Armored arrived, it was given the task of rooting out enemy defenders in Cerisy Forest, a woodland in Calvados. With its abundant growth of beech, oak, and Scotch pine, the forest seemed to Victor like a fine place for walks and picnics in normal times. But the overhead canopy turned deadly when struck by bursts from enemy shells that exploded upon contact with treetops and showered shrapnel. Even slit trenches did not provide protection when the assault came from overhead. There was a common chorus, day and night, as shrapnel fell from airburst shells: loud explosions and sharp crackles from disintegrating trees followed by shrieks of "Oh God! I'm hit!"

During the fighting in Cerisy, Victor was pulled into a mad and dangerous scheme by his division's intelligence officer (G-2), a West Point graduate who had commanded a tank battalion under Patton in Sicily. The colonel decided that the enemy troops facing them might be convinced to surrender if they only had some encouragement. He wanted Victor's team to address the enemy troops in German over loudspeakers aimed at their outposts. When he was told that only two members of the French team were fluent in German, he called them both—Victor and Willi Joseph—to headquarters and briefed them on his harebrained idea. They were to broadcast three times a day to the Germans about the "wonderful opportunity" they had to surrender. He believed the German commanders had brought up young and inexperienced replacements who might be convinced to give up.

Victor knew there were mobile Psychological Warfare Units that had special trucks equipped for just such work. These teams had been trained at Camp Ritchie, and they were now drafting propaganda leaflets that were air-dropped over enemy positions and were trained to broadcast propaganda messages while playing popular German music over loudspeakers. But their large trucks could not easily get up to the front lines and, in any case, the colonel decided that Victor and Willi were the men for the mission.

"Get yourselves out there," he barked, "and do your job."

So that Victor's and Willi's voices could be amplified to reach the enemy soldiers, signal company technicians were ordered to install a public address system close to German lines. One of them climbing up a tree to install a speaker was shot and killed by a German sniper.

After locating the infantry company nearest the front, Victor and Willi set out toward enemy lines. They had been told they would find an American platoon dug in past a sunken road one thousand yards from the Germans. When they cleared the trees and reached the sunken road, they crawled the rest of the way, past bullet-ridden corpses and steel helmets.

When they reached the public address system set up for them, Victor began delivering a cajoling message. He had given some thought to what he would say. No threats. Above all, he wanted to express a shared feeling of complicity. *War is horrible. We dislike it. You dislike it. Peace is wonderful. We have come to liberate Europe. You will be treated well when you come over.*

The enemy's answer soon came in a barrage of mortar fire.

Yet the two Ritchie Boys still crawled up to the front lines three times a day for two successive days and delivered their message over the loudspeakers. Each time, the response was a mortar shelling.

Not a single German surrendered.

Guy Stern tried to control his fears as the landing craft he was on pushed through the heavy surf toward Omaha Beach three days after D-Day. He was pressed shoulder to shoulder with other GIs, all of whom he was certain had their own apprehensions. No one in his right mind approaching Omaha Beach by sea in early June 1944 was free of them.

One worry had lingered with Guy since his training at Camp Ritchie. What would happen should he be captured by the Germans and they identified him as a German Jewish "traitor" who was now working for U.S. Army intelligence? Captured traitors and spies were usually shot.

That wasn't his only fear. He was also concerned about his lifelong squeamishness at the sight of blood. Since boyhood, if someone even cut their finger in his presence, he would run out of the room. How would he fare amid war's carnage? And would he be able to perform, dispassionately and professionally, the tasks for which he was trained? The Nazis had been responsible for his parents sending him away when he was fifteen, and they had taken his family from their home in Hildesheim and shipped them off to the Warsaw ghetto and an unknown fate. Given the hatred he carried for Hitler and his henchmen, could he control his emotions enough to do his job?

On the beach, Guy's jeep passed a line of wounded soldiers heading in the opposite direction toward the landing craft. They were the walking wounded, able to carry themselves off the beach. To a man they looked not only bloodied, but shattered and dazed. Farther up the beach they drove past bodies being processed by graves registration personnel. The dead apparently did not have priority for evacuation. Guy surprised himself by being able to see the grotesque display of corpses with a kind of detachment. Somehow, his lifelong squeamishness had left him.

"Get the hell over here! We've got too many prisoners!" yelled the team's leading noncom, Master Sergeant Kurt Jasen, a German Jew in his mid-thirties who fled Berlin with his family after the Nazis came to power. He had changed his name from Jacobowitz when he became a naturalized U.S. citizen, and graduated in Camp Ritchie's Eighth Class with Guy.

Guy's six-man IPW team had been split up before the invasion, with three of them arriving the day after D-Day and the other three today. Sergeant Jasen had come in with the earlier group, and they had been overwhelmed by the number of prisoners taken. Awaiting the arrival of the rest of the team, he now directed them to the path up to the plateau above the beach to start interrogating prisoners.

Driving to the top of the overlook, they came to a barbed-wire holding pen where hundreds of captured Germans were guarded by eagle-eyed MPs until they could be loaded onto empty LSTs heading back to England, bound for POW camps. The interrogators were to get as much information about coastal defenses as possible before the prisoners left.

In an open field, Guy set up an improvised desk using overturned crates. The first prisoner he came face-to-face with was a tough-looking German whose uniform had a red collar insignia, which Guy knew from his Camp Ritchie training was worn by artillerymen. The prisoner's artillery rank, *Wachtmeister*, was equivalent to sergeant, and his age, rank, and grizzled looks suggested he had experienced his share of battles and campaigns in the war. To Guy's initial questions, the German responded with only his name and rank. No matter what tack he took, the prisoner didn't budge, and Guy dreaded failing in his first wartime interrogation.

Just then, an artillery shell whistled overhead, landing nearby, and both men hit the muddy ground.

Guy bounced up right after the explosion, not realizing that one incoming artillery round was almost always followed by others. The *Wachtmeister* knew better and stayed flat on the ground, anticipating a barrage from his own howitzers.

"Krieg deinen verdammten Arsch hoch und antworte auf meine Fragen, du Feigling!" hollered Guy, ordering the prisoner to get his "damned ass up and answer my questions."

The German rose cautiously. He seemed incredulous at Guy's foolish action, somehow assuming it was due to bravery, not just inexperience. He now began answering Guy's questions. Luckily, that single artillery shell was not followed by more, as the *Wacht-*

meister had expected, but the one that did land had changed the dynamic of the interrogation and put Guy in charge. He may not have fully understood the reasons why, but he knew he had taken control of his first wartime interrogation, which gave him fresh confidence that he could do his job after all.

Within a week, Guy's IPW team had moved four miles inland to a large POW camp outside the town of Foucarville. A few days later, the officer in charge of the team, Captain Melvin Rust, a Texan who had learned his German in Brownsville, pulled Guy aside and told him they had three Spaniards who had escaped from German captivity on the Channel Islands off the coast of France. "You have Spanish in your record," Rust said, "so I'm assigning them to you."

When Guy joined the army, he had noted on a form that he had taken two years of Spanish at Saint Louis University. But his interrogation of the Spaniards got off to a rocky start as they began talking all at once at a much faster clip than he could decipher. Guy was eventually able to get them to speak slower, one at a time, and he learned they were veterans of the Spanish Civil War who had escaped to France, where they were captured by the Germans. All were engineers, and they had been shipped to the Channel Islands—British Crown dependencies in the Channel near the coast of Normandy—after the Germans occupied them in June 1940. They had been forced into labor by the Germans to help fortify the islands' defenses. But beyond that, much of what they were trying to tell Guy he didn't understand. His Spanish vocabulary in college had not included military terms.

The Spaniards wanted to help, and they asked for pencils and paper. Guy left them in a tent, and when he returned they had drawn sheets of detailed schematics of where every antiaircraft weapon, artillery gun, machine gun, and other military installation was located on the Channel Islands.

When Guy took the drawings to his captain, he was awestruck. "Quite an interrogation, Stern," Rust said in his slow Texas drawl.

Guy didn't tell Rust he hadn't been able to speak to the Spaniards in great detail about the military defenses or that it had been the engineers' idea to make the drawings. But he had succeeded in getting a complete picture of German defenses that would be critical should the Allies attempt to retake the islands, the only part of Britain to be occupied by the Germans during the war.

As a result of Guy's "brilliant work" with the Spaniards, Rust decided he had another job for Guy. They were getting questionnaires from headquarters, Rust explained, asking about strategic tactics. What was the best way to estimate the morale of German troops? And what were the most and least effective U.S. propaganda leaflets?

"I need a survey section to conduct and review interrogations and prepare detailed answers to these types of questions," Rust said. "I'll reassign some interrogators to Survey. You'll be in charge, Sergeant."

In high school and college, Guy had enjoyed researching and writing term papers. From the sound of it, his new job would essentially be no different, except he would be gathering data not from books but from captured German soldiers.

One of the few female war correspondents on the continent arrived at Foucarville the following month to do a story. Guy recognized the thirtyish brunette in fatigues and helmet as soon as she walked into the IPW tent. She was Virginia Irwin, a reporter for the *St. Louis Post-Dispatch,* and he had served her lunch many times at the café where he waited tables to pay his way through college.

"You look a lot different in those GI pants and that tin hat," Guy said, smiling, "but I remember you, Miss Irwin. You always wore a black dress even in summer and had your hair fixed up way high in the front."

She laughed and said she remembered him, too, but they had never been properly introduced. She wrote down his name and address, and the names of his aunt and uncle, all of which she later included in her article for their hometown newspaper.

She arranged for Guy to serve as her interpreter for a tour of the camp. One German, self-conscious of his unshaven face and dirty clothing in front of the woman reporter, said he was sure the war was hopelessly lost for Germany. He also said he wasn't surprised by the news of the July 20 attempt to assassinate Hitler, adding that he believed Germany's only salvation would be to establish a new democratic government that would favor the working class.

When Irwin stopped to speak to another prisoner, he told the reporter through Guy that when he was captured and taken through the American lines and saw all the equipment moving forward that he knew "we were no match for that."

Before she left, Irwin asked Guy what he thought of the morale of German fighting men. He told her he thought 90 percent of them "believe the war is hopeless but that only 75 percent will admit it." The discrepancy, he told her, could be chalked up to a combination of German pride and Nazi fanaticism.

ONLY PRISON CAMPS ARE LIGHTED
Stand Out in Normandy Darkness Like Hollywood Premier
By Virginia Irwin, a War Correspondent of the *Post-Dispatch*

SOMEWHERE IN NORMANDY, July 24—In the absolute blackout that is enforced here in Normandy it is a strange and eerie sight at night to see prisoner of war cages lighted up like a Hollywood theatre marquee for an opening night of "Gone With the Wind."

These prison cages are the only places on the peninsula where even a glimmer of light is to be seen after dark. Jeeps and trucks crawl along roads without lights of any kind so as not to provide targets for military planes; it is a military offense to smoke cigarettes outside after 10 P.M. and flashlights can be flicked on only in case of absolute emergency.

But inside the prison cages, Germans move about their

barbed-wire enclosures in the white glare of tremendous floodlights—a glare heightened by the pitch-black of the surrounding countryside.

Today I visited a prisoner camp. Thousands of Germans have been evacuated to England through this one enclosure alone, 4000 to 5000 passing through every 24 hours in the days following the fall of Cherbourg in late June.

Through an interpreter, who turned out to be Staff Sgt. Guy Stern of 1116A Maple Place, St. Louis, I talked with several Germans who had been captured in the early stages of fighting for Saint-Lô. . . .

Not long after the reporter's visit, Guy was in a jeep driven by Paul Rabinek, an Austrian Jew he had met at Camp Ritchie. They were returning from First Army Headquarters, now inland, heading back toward the beach. Rabinek knew a shortcut, but soon they became lost. All of a sudden, they heard German voices. Somehow, they had slipped behind enemy lines. As Rabinek turned the jeep around, it lurched to a stop, out of gas. There was a canister in the rear of the jeep for extra gas, but Rabinek admitted he had traded the fuel for the local apple brandy known as Calvados. Improvising, they poured the potent liquor into the jeep, and were safely on their way. Thereafter, Rabinek's nickname was "Shortcut."

Back at Foucarville, Guy soon received word of a newly captured German who had been a concentration camp guard. As there was neither the time nor the manpower to interrogate all of the thousands of prisoners pouring into the POW cage, it was the responsibility of trained IPW screeners—after asking one or two preliminary questions—to identify prisoners likely to have valuable information and give their names to the interrogation teams for close questioning.

Guy had the former guard brought to him, and he turned out to be a fresh-faced enlisted man who had worked at Sachsenhausen-Oranienburg concentration camp, twenty miles north of Berlin.

He told Guy about the conditions at the camp, which he said held several thousand inmates, many of them Jews but also communists, criminals, and homosexuals. Inmates were forced to work in SS workshops manufacturing aircraft parts and other war-related materiel. Camp punishments were harsh; one common tactic, the former guard explained, involved suspending inmates in the air by ropes tied to their wrists, which were cinched tightly behind them. Those caught trying to escape were publicly hanged. Other executions were carried out by firing squads.

"I frequently volunteered for the execution squad," the young man added with no discernible emotion.

"Why did you volunteer?" asked Guy, keeping an even tone.

He shrugged. "If I hadn't, someone else would have."

The former guard explained there was a bonus for volunteering. "I would get a pass to go into Berlin. The great concert halls were still open. I love concerts, especially Beethoven and Mozart."

Guy pushed a paper and a pen in front of him and told him to write out a statement, which he did and then signed as a confession.

He then had the man taken out of his sight, back to the cage.

Guy was shaken by the prisoner's admissions, and especially by his matter-of-fact demeanor—so conversational, with little prodding, and no apparent guilt. So imbued with Nazi ethics, the German was unable to recognize the enormity of his own actions. What he said was nearly beyond belief, but Guy believed every word.

After Guy finished his report on the interrogation, he sent it to First Army headquarters and other commands. He expected to hear something back, but he never did. As yet, there was no mandate to document war crimes or identify war criminals. It was still too early in the war. The most valuable intelligence was actionable, tactical information that would save American lives and help the Allies win the next battle. Guy never found out what became of the prisoner who found it so easy to confess to executing innocent people so he could attend his favorite symphonies.

Guy made a practice of sifting through stacks of German army

pay books taken from new prisoners to see whom he might want
to interrogate. Unlike U.S. identification papers, which gave away
nothing, German pay books—called *Soldbücher*—contained all
kinds of useful information, such as unit number, previous assignments, and date and location of the last leave taken by a soldier.
When Guy came to the pay book of Günther Halm, he recognized
the name. Now a Wehrmacht *Oberleutnant,* Halm had been in the
same youth sports club in Hildesheim that Guy had belonged to
until all the Jews were kicked out. Companions growing up, they
had often competed in athletics. Here was someone who might have
information about his family, from whom Guy had still not heard
anything more since their last letter in summer 1942. Halm's pay
book showed he had gone home to Hildesheim on leave. Perhaps he
would have some information?

Guy waited until midnight to have the prisoner brought to him.
In the darkness of the tent, with only a torchlight shining on Halm's
drowsy face, Guy started the interrogation by commenting that because of Halm's athletic appearance, he surmised that he had been
an excellent athlete. Guy knew Halm had been a star in every sport.
That got Halm talking about sports. Guy next asked him about
their hometown to test his veracity. The prisoner was meticulously
precise in his descriptions of Hildesheim.

The youth Guy remembered as being rather quiet and passive
had turned into a warrior; he wore on his tunic the coveted Knight's
Cross, which he had won for bravery while serving with Rommel's Afrika Korps. Guy would later learn that Günther Halm of
Hildesheim was, in fact, the youngest Africa Korps soldier to be
awarded the Knight's Cross.

Guy next asked about what type of training Halm had received,
and the German went on in some detail and with obvious pride
about the excellent training he had received in antitank weaponry.

Guy asked if Halm had had any contact with French civilians
before his capture, adding that he had probably studied French in
"Realschule."

As soon as he said it, Guy knew he had slipped up. There was only one *Realschule*, a high school that offered a more modern curriculum—such as modern languages rather than ancient ones—in Hildesheim. Guy and Halm had both attended the school.

Puzzled by how the American interrogator could have such information about him, Halm tried to shade his eyes from the light to get a better look at the face in shadows across from him.

"Why do you know so much about me?" he asked suspiciously.

"*Oberleutnant,* you are a highly decorated officer, and we keep exact information on highly decorated enemy officers."

Guy did not know if Halm believed him. Realizing he risked being recognized, Guy halted the interrogation and had Halm returned to the cage.

The next morning, Guy had the prisoner from Hildesheim taken to another POW camp so they would not see each other in the light of day. He did so without ever asking the question: *What happened to my family?*

It had been stressed to the German-born interrogators at Camp Ritchie that identifying themselves as such was not only dangerous for their own safety should they fall into enemy hands, but it could jeopardize any family members they had in Germany or occupied territories. But there was another reason Guy had not asked the one question uppermost on his mind.

He feared the answer.

The German soldiers took Werner Angress and the other captured U.S. paratroopers into a field. They ordered them to strip—including removing their watches and rings—and lie on their stomachs. Their clothes were searched for hidden weapons before being returned, with most of their personal items gone.

One of the other paratroopers turned toward Werner. "Sergeant, tell the Heinie I want to keep my wedding ring!" A German was admiring the gold band.

Werner looked up, horrified to be given away as German.

"I can't," Werner told the GI under his breath. "Sorry."

The paratrooper understood, nodded, and lost his wedding ring.

After that, no one came close to revealing what they knew about Werner. They were trucked from the field to a barn, where they spent the night without food or medical care for their wounds. The next morning they were searched again, then taken in small groups to a farmhouse that served as a command post for the unit that had captured them.

Werner was interrogated by an older warrant officer. He got the impression that this bespectacled, middle-aged *Sonderführer* had been a teacher in civilian life because he spoke typical school English, heavily accented. This worried Werner, because he thought the warrant officer might pick up on his own German-accented English. Werner was limping noticeably from the shrapnel wound, and his interrogator had promised him he would be taken to a hospital to have his wound treated as soon as they were finished.

"What unit do you belong to, Sergeant?" asked the interrogator.

Werner pointed to his 82nd Airborne shoulder patch.

"Yes, but what regiment?"

As two 82nd regiments had jumped on D-Day and one had been held in reserve in England—and might or might not have yet arrived in Normandy—such information could prove helpful to the enemy.

"I can't tell you," Werner said, "and you wouldn't if you were in my shoes. Under the Geneva Conventions, all I have to say is my name, rank, and serial number."

"Your first name is Werner. Are you of German descent? Perhaps you were named after your grandfather?"

Werner realized the interrogator had given him a plausible answer.

"You are correct," said Werner. "I was named after my grandfather Werner." *Why stop now?* "Grandfather and other members of the family immigrated to the United States in the nineteenth century."

"Where were you born?"

Werner, the native Berliner, picked Lynchburg, Virginia, a town he had never visited but knew of because it was home to most of the men from his first army unit—Company B, 116th regiment, 29th Infantry Division.

"Lynchburg!" crowed the interrogator. "I have been there!"

Werner tried not to show his distress. What were the chances that a German interrogator in Normandy would have been to Lynchburg, Virginia? Rather than wait for a question that he might be unable to answer because he didn't know Lynchburg from Timbuktu, Werner went on the offensive. "When were you last there?" he asked warily.

"In 1926," said the interrogator. "I was a very young man traveling for a German textiles firm. They sent me there for three weeks."

Werner asked if he had been back since, and the man said no. Relieved, Werner said, "Well, Lynchburg has changed tremendously since then."

The German seemed almost wistful. "Oh, I have no doubt it has."

Werner knew it was time to change the subject. "Is it possible to get something to eat?"

"Yes, as soon as we are finished, we'll give you some food. Now, when and where did you parachute jump?"

Werner felt back in control. "You know I can't tell you that." His training at Camp Ritchie was paying off now that he had found himself, quite unexpectedly, on the opposite side of a prisoner interrogation. He knew what he could say and what he wasn't compelled to say under the Geneva Conventions, and also, more subtly, how to keep up a friendly and reasonable dialogue during an interrogation without giving anything away.

A few minutes later, a tall Wehrmacht lieutenant, who had been conducting an interrogation in another room, walked in. He asked the older interrogator in German what he had found out. *Nichts,* Werner's interrogator responded. The lieutenant said he hadn't learned anything either.

Werner and the other wounded soldiers were transported to Cherbourg and deposited at the Louis Pasteur Hospital, where there were more than one hundred GI patients, many badly wounded. Some had had limbs amputated. Werner's leg wound was treated with sulfur powder to avoid infection and dressed. Since he could still walk, he was assigned to assist the German and French orderlies with feeding the Americans.

Werner's job allowed him complete access to the hospital, and his ability to understand both languages proved useful. Starting that first night, he would tell the patients shortly before lights went out what war news he had picked up from overhearing the Germans talking. That was how they all learned with certainty that the Normandy landings had been successful and that U.S. troops were advancing on Cherbourg and its vital port. The Germans were already blowing up docks and other harbor facilities they did not want to leave for the Allies.

Three days later, Werner and other wounded who could walk joined U.S. prisoners being held a short distance outside of Cherbourg in an old barn that had bunk beds teeming with fleas. Werner preferred sleeping on the ground and spent a wakeful night listening to explosions several miles away. Early the next morning, the war came much closer when artillery shells landed three hundred yards from the barn. Several of the guards ran away, but those who remained decided to move the prisoners to a large tunnel complex at the edge of the city. When they arrived, the tunnel, which led into a hill, was serving as the headquarters of the German 709th Static Infantry Division, a coastal defense force that had sustained four thousand casualties since D-Day.

The next morning, Werner was trucked back to the hospital with a dozen other prisoners to help load beds and mattresses to bring back to the overcrowded tunnel. The ring around Cherbourg was growing tighter, and as they rode through town, artillery shells were dropping everywhere.

When they arrived at the hospital, Werner saw that manned antiaircraft guns had been posted around the building. Several German combat soldiers stood in the entrance of the hospital, and they looked daggers at the American POWs. As they passed by, Werner heard the Germans talking of killing the *"amerikanischen Bastarde."* Once inside the building, Werner told the others what he had overheard, but added, "They probably won't, but don't wander off. Stick with me." Werner now felt like a mother hen, with everyone staying close to him as they carried the mattresses out of the hospital and loaded them into the truck. One 101st paratrooper named Sigmund "Sig" Stajkowski, with whom Werner had become friends during their days trying to evade capture, was still loading the truck with some other prisoners as the rest of the group went back inside. At that moment, an artillery shell landed right in front of the hospital. The concussion of the blast knocked down Werner and everyone else in the corridor, which suddenly went dark. Werner heard yelling and screaming outside, the Germans cursing American artillery for shooting at a hospital even as their own anti-aircraft batteries next to it blazed away.

Outside, several German soldiers were dead, five American prisoners wounded, and Sig's dead body lay next to the truck. He had been a sergeant who just before D-Day had been busted to private because he had returned from a weekend leave several days late. Werner knew Sig as a stand-up guy and one hell of a soldier; he had always been willing to help Werner in the often-delicate dealings with French farmers to secure food. Twenty-five-year-old Sig had been a farmer himself, having worked in his family's dairy in Wisconsin prior to enlisting in the army in 1940. Werner knelt down and tenderly placed his hand on Sig's shoulder. He was glad his buddy had taken those extra days of unauthorized leave in England and hoped he'd had a swell time. He removed one of Sig's two dog tags from the chain around his neck—the other one stayed with the body for identification purposes—and helped load his broken body into another truck that carried him away, together with the German corpses, all stacked like a cord of firewood.

The next day, June 24, as American forces were reported to be on the outskirts of the city, the Germans transported the prisoners to the harbor area and led them into an underground shelter.

While some German troops outside continued to blow up the docks, others trickled into the shelter for safety. Werner was amazed to see the bespectacled warrant officer who had interrogated him show up. He greeted Werner like an old friend. Soon, he and Werner were playing chess. Every few minutes the interrogator looked up worriedly at the ceiling, which shook each time there was an artillery strike or bomb blast, and asked if Werner thought it would hold up.

"Probably," Werner said, "unless we take a direct hit."

"Why don't your people stop it?"

"Why don't your guys surrender?"

"This whole war is insane," said the interrogator.

The more they talked, always in English, the more Werner liked him. An older draftee with a paunch, he was not the stereotypical Nazi soldier, physically or politically. He was definitely not someone Hitler would have been proud of. Unlike some American-born GIs, Werner knew, of course, that not all Germans were bad Germans.

As the hours went by, the other German soldiers in the shelter, interested in self-preservation and seeing that the fall of Cherbourg to the Allied forces was only a matter of time, turned decidedly friendlier. They gave the prisoners cigars and champagne left by a general and inquired about conditions in U.S. POW camps. Werner overheard them talking worriedly among themselves. *Tomorrow, we shall be their prisoners,* one said, to which the others agreed. They spoke about wanting to be sent to America, not England, as if signing up for a sightseeing tour.

Werner asked for paper and pencil. By the light of a flickering candle, he began a record of some of his experiences since D-Day. It had been a long three weeks, half spent in captivity. His last entry for June 26: "Tomorrow is my 24th birthday, and I want to be a free man again."

His birthday wish came true the next day, at exactly noon, when the German general charged with the defense of Cherbourg surrendered under a white flag to officers from the U.S. 9th Infantry Division. As they had predicted, the Germans who had been guarding them lined up outside to be taken away under armed guard.

Some of the freed Americans suggested Werner go over to the middle-aged *Sonderführer* who had interrogated him and tell him, in fluent German, that he had been outsmarted by a fellow interrogator. Werner declined. "He treated us with decency from beginning to end," he explained. "The last thing I want to do is humiliate him now that he's a prisoner."

Werner walked over to him. In English, he said, "I hope that we treat you with the same courtesy as you treated us."

They shook hands.

Werner rejoined his regiment later that evening near the village of Vindefontaine, a little south of Sainte-Mère-Église, which he learned had been the first town liberated in the early hours of D-Day by elements of the 82nd, not far from where he was supposed to have been dropped. He was warmly welcomed by his buddies, all of whom had been convinced he was dead. A medical officer checked his leg wound, which was healing. At Werner's pleading, the doctor reluctantly gave him permission to stay with the regiment instead of being sent back to England to convalesce.

Not long after his return, Werner interrogated a prisoner who said he knew of a group of Germans who wanted to surrender but were afraid of being shot by the Americans. Werner had him pinpoint their location on a map. Taking a few troopers with him, Werner walked toward the spot, at the edge of a small wood at the bottom of a hill. When they reached the hill, Werner decided to walk down it alone. Reaching the bottom, he shouted in German to the hidden enemy soldiers that their war was over now, and it was time for them to surrender. He assured them they would be well treated.

Two dozen Germans emerged from the brush with their hands behind their heads, led by their ranking noncommissioned officer, a corporal. Werner told the corporal to stay with him and directed the others up the hill.

From the corporal, Werner soon knew the number of his regiment, where the remaining men of his badly shattered unit were hiding, and other bits of information. The corporal came from Berlin, he told Werner, and was a shoemaker in civilian life. He and his men were fed up with the war and had decided Why get killed now?

Just then, one of the paratroopers up the hill hollered to Werner that an American lieutenant they didn't know had arrived on the scene and wanted to shoot their prisoners.

Directing the corporal to follow, Werner hurried up the hill, where he found the lieutenant pointing a rifle at the group of prisoners. Werner's men had spread out protectively in front of the Germans, telling the officer they were the prisoners of Sergeant Angress and that he should stand back. The lieutenant refused, ordering them several times to step aside, but the troopers stood firm.

"Get out of the way now!" ordered the young lieutenant.

What Werner immediately suspected about the lieutenant was soon verified: he had just arrived at Normandy by boat and was keen to bag his first German and be a war hero.

"Lieutenant," Werner said firmly, "I am under orders from regiment to bring in these prisoners for interrogation. This is not your business. I will turn you in to my captain if you don't leave."

Werner's men raised their weapons in the lieutenant's direction. He reluctantly lowered his rifle, gave Werner an angry look, then stomped away. Werner and his men escorted their prisoners off the field of battle to a POW cage to be interrogated. The eager lieutenant, Werner later heard, was killed in action a few days later.

Plans were being made to "celebrate" the Fourth of July holiday with an assault against the German lines. Captain Breen, Werner's regimental intelligence officer, told him to focus his interrogations on where the enemy units facing them had laid mines. The day before the attack, Werner interrogated a German sergeant who said little but in whose dispatch case he found a map with an overlay of every mine in the area. Recognizing the map as a major find, he rushed it to Breen.

"This is marvelous," Breen gushed. "We have to get maps to our battalions and the other regiments before the attack."

Knowing the precise location of the buried explosives would allow disposal units to dig up and defuse them so Americans troops did not have to walk across live minefields. The information Werner had gained was so important, Breen announced that he would personally deliver a copy of the map to every unit in the division early in the morning before the attack began at noon.

"Would you like to drive me?" Breen asked.

"Yes, I'd like to very much," Werner answered.

Their exchange was not typical of one between an officer and enlisted man, but then neither was their relationship. About ten years older than Werner and married with three children, Breen treated his young sergeant in a friendly, almost fatherly manner. In turn, Werner was quick to volunteer for whatever job Breen needed done and even helped the kindly officer remember the times of staff meetings and other such details that had a way of slipping Breen's mind.

Werner worked late that night marking the location of every mine on more than a dozen copies of military maps. He finally got to sleep shortly before sunrise. By the time he awakened a short time later, the captain had left. Werner was told that Breen had decided not to wake him up, since he had worked all night, and had found someone else to drive.

Around 9:00 A.M., a trooper approached Werner and asked, "You know Captain Breen is dead?"

Werner was stunned. "No! What happened?"

"Jeep hit a land mine."

Getting directions to where the accident had happened, Werner jumped in a jeep and found the spot where the captain's dismembered body still lay in a ditch next to his crumpled vehicle. He was told the driver had been taken to a field hospital with major injuries. Werner fought back tears over the death of the man he considered a friend. It hurt doubly when Breen's effects were delivered to the regiment. Included were the copies of the map he had been distributing, on which Werner had clearly marked the buried road mine that had killed him. The captain's well-known absentmindedness had been his undoing. He had died on July 4.

Werner could not shake his feelings of loss and guilt. If he had driven the captain, he would still be alive. Werner had drawn the mine locations onto the maps and would have taken care not to drive over the mine, information the substitute driver did not possess. Instead, the captain had let him sleep and now the captain was dead. It was the second time in the war, coming after Sig's death, that Werner had felt such personal loss.

And then, word reached Werner of still another loss. His friend and tutor from the 116th Regiment, 29th Infantry Division, Staff Sergeant John G. Barnes, who had helped him learn English by reading aloud the *New York Times* with him, had been killed on D-Day at Omaha Beach in the first three minutes of the invasion. He never made it up from the surf line and died twelve days short of his thirty-eighth birthday. Werner had written Barnes a letter, which he received the day before D-Day, and Barnes had hurriedly written back to Werner that same day. Werner was grateful for their final exchange, in which he had been able to thank John for his friendship. Werner was deeply saddened by the death of a man he would always remember for being a wonderful friend and human being.

A little more than a week later, the 82nd Airborne was relieved after thirty-three days of combat since D-Day. The men were taken by trucks to Omaha Beach to board troopships back to England.

Along the beach, Werner passed large barbed-wire cages, behind which hundreds of German prisoners were waiting for their own boat rides out of Normandy. He thought of his German guards during his final days of captivity in Cherbourg, recalling how they had hoped, as POWs, that they would be sent to America. Werner knew there was a good chance some of them would get there before he made it back.

It had only been one month, and already he had jumped on D-Day, been captured and interrogated by the Germans, been liberated after nineteen days as a POW, captured and interrogated German prisoners, and lost three friends. As he left Normandy, Werner wondered if the whole war was going to be like this, and if it was, how would he possibly get through it?

7

THE BREAKOUT

Martin Selling made it back across the Atlantic in early June 1944. It had been a long time coming for him—from the night he was dragged from his home and taken to Dachau, to his time as a refugee in England, and then to America, where he had been designated an enemy alien when the U.S. entered the war.

By the time he returned to Europe with the U.S. Army, he was an American citizen. A few days after his transfer to Camp Ritchie in February 1943, Martin and thirty other immigrant soldiers had been trucked to the Hagerstown courthouse, where they went before an octogenarian judge recalled from retirement to help officiate the great number of naturalization ceremonies for the foreigners from the army camp. From the bench, he peered at the GIs. "Are you prepared to take up arms in defense of your country?"

"No!" piped up a joker in the back, to much laughter.

The judge slammed his gavel to stop the frivolity in his courtroom. "Shut up, wise guys! Everyone raise your right hand and repeat after me the Pledge of Allegiance." When the group was finished, he banged his gavel again. "You are now all citizens of the United States."

Martin's final field exercise at Camp Ritchie in spring 1943 had gone badly. His group missed finding its assigned destination in the countryside in the middle of the night, and tramped on aimlessly through rocky and hilly forest until they came to a steep canyon. Without a flashlight, all they could do was wait for dawn. Martin's team would have to repeat the exercise. Despite this setback, Martin, who received a grade of 99 in Order of Battle and 95 in Interrogation, graduated in the IPW Fifth Class in April 1943.

Martin had hoped to make it to Europe to take part in the D-Day landings. But two lengthy assignments to participate in maneuvers and war games in Louisiana caused delays, and he was not officially

Former Dachau prisoner Martin Selling, who became a Ritchie Boy and served in the 35th Infantry Division. *(Family photograph)*

released from Camp Ritchie until a year after graduation. Two
weeks later, Martin, by then a staff sergeant, finally set sail across
the Atlantic aboard the British liner *Andes*.

Once he reached England, Martin's IPW team was assigned to
the 35th Infantry Division, attached to the U.S. Third Army, which
had recently changed from a training command to a combat-ready
army with the arrival of its new commander, Lieutenant General
George S. Patton Jr. Rumor had it that Patton's army would be held
out of the D-Day invasion to save them for an all-out push of infantry and armor across occupied France.

The evening before D-Day, as Martin looked into the skies above
southern England at the unending formations of bombers crossing
the Channel, he couldn't help but feel he was missing out on the
main event. Ever since America's first days in the war, when he tried
to join the U.S. Army Air Corps to become a bombardier, he had
wanted to be in one of those planes, delivering deadly payloads to
help win the war. So he was doubly frustrated when he was sent
to London for a two-week course on document analysis, where he
heard little that he didn't already know from his courses at Camp
Ritchie.

On June 13, his classes were interrupted when the first German
V-1 rocket bomb struck about a mile away, and everyone was evacuated to an underground shelter. Although the Allied high command
had suspected their existence, when more than one hundred bombs
hit London over the next hour, civilians and military personnel
alike were shocked. The V-1s were soon nicknamed "buzz bombs"
because of the distinct sound made by the pulse-jet engines pow-
ering the bombs, which, with wings and a tail, resembled a small
aircraft.*

---

* The "V" came from the German word *Vergeltungswaffen*, meaning "weapons of reprisal." They were developed by German scientists at the Peenemünde
research facility on the Baltic Sea. Over the next eighty days, more than eight
thousand V-1s were launched against England, killing thousands of people.

Martin, glad to leave London and the buzz bombs behind him, departed on July 6 with his IPW team. They crossed the Channel and landed on Omaha Beach, which was now protected from air strikes by hundreds of tethered barrage balloons floating overhead. Even after a month, he could see the evidence of June 6 on Omaha Beach: wrecked ships and landing craft, and a new American cemetery on the windswept plateau above the shore.

The 35th Division was deployed twenty miles inland, just north of Saint-Lô, where the IPW team was split up, with three men each going to two different regiments. Martin's half team was dispatched to the 320th Infantry Regiment, a unit that was seeing combat for the first time. Surprised by the interrogators' heavy accents and fearful of having spies in their midst, the regimental officers debated aloud whether to disarm them and assign them to permanent KP duty. But Martin, as the senior noncom, spoke up, explaining that he and his team were specially trained and showing their official orders assigning them to the regiment.

"We'll be useful," Martin promised, "when you want intel from German prisoners."

He persuaded the regimental staff to let the team do its job.

Martin was fortunate with two of his early interrogations. Both prisoners were privates, glad to be out of the war and willing to answer his questions. The first described in detail what was going on behind the nearby hedgerows where his company of about one hundred infantrymen were dug in. Two days later, an even more useful prize arrived: a captured German medic who provided details of the Germans' strength and casualties. He had been moving around the Saint-Lô sector treating the wounded, and as a result he knew more about the terrain and defensive positions than most infantrymen. He worked with Martin to draft a map of all the German positions. It was tedious going, and the map they drew had unusual geographical markers that the medic remembered: a fallen beech tree here, a stinking cow cadaver there. When they were finished, Martin gave the map to a sergeant with the reconnaissance platoon who had viewed the area through field glasses for several days, and he recognized the terrain. The sergeant took the hand-drawn map to regimental headquarters, then to the division's artillery company, where they carefully marked the enemy's positions on a military map that had quadrants used for calling in artillery and air strikes.

The final ground attack on Saint-Lô kicked off the next morning after a massive aerial bombardment. The 320th broke through the area mapped by Martin and his prisoner. Afterward, the reconnaissance sergeant told him that by using his map to select their targets, their howitzers had been deadly accurate and destroyed everything from enemy machine gun nests to their command post. The regiment's commander recommended Martin for a battlefield commission, and from then on, the colonel and his staff were champions of their German-speaking interrogators.

Martin became a student of the art of interrogation. Not every interrogation was successful, as not every prisoner could be convinced to answer every question. Martin decided that the elements of interrogation could be taught, but they had to be practiced under field conditions with real prisoners to be perfected. What had worked in the classroom didn't always work out here. Special-trained interrogation teams were a new element of modern warfare, first used by the British and U.S. in North Africa in late 1942. So everyone was learning on the fly, sometimes under fire.

Most German prisoners were infantrymen captured at the front. The goal was to interrogate them soon after their capture to find out what they knew that could be used against the enemy, and convey it as clearly and speedily as possible to the proper places. This was usually done by messengers, or interrogators reporting their information directly to a command post, as radios were short ranged and unreliable, and field phones required hard wiring, which wasn't always possible to string between frontline units because they moved often.

Tactical information could be outdated within days, if not hours. So it was important to interrogate prisoners before they were processed and moved farther back to large POW cages. These first interrogations became the focus for IPW teams like Martin's that were assigned to regiments, which traditionally were closer to the front—where prisoners were captured—than division or army headquarters. Also, newly captured prisoners were often frightened and confused, which made them more likely to talk. That was what Martin and the other interrogators had been taught at Camp Ritchie, and they were finding it to be true in combat.

It didn't take Martin long to decide that the native German speakers on the IPW teams—mostly German Jews but also a sprinkling of Austrians—were far superior interrogators than Americans who had learned the language in school or had been raised in a German American family. The native Germans' mastery of the language, including vocabulary and jargon, was part of their advantage, but they also understood the culture and psychology of the men they were interrogating. They knew the country, the people, the history. When Martin started a new interrogation, many prisoners looked up at him in surprise, not expecting an American soldier to sound like them. Sometimes, he even resorted to some choice Bavarian invectives to make his point. The use of appropriate colloquialism was effective because it conveyed his familiarity with German customs as well as linguistic competence.

In time, Martin developed his own unique interrogation style. He found that starting out with the standard questions of name, rank, and serial number was not the best approach because it reminded a prisoner that under the Geneva Conventions he did not have to say anything else. Instead, Martin began by asking the prisoner how he had been captured, which got most of them talking. It felt more like a conversation, and nearly all of them answered instinctively and in detail, pleased that someone was interested in them. The response to Martin's opener allowed him to size up the prisoner and, once they were talking, to follow with more specific questions. He always gave them easy ones first to get them talking, saving the difficult ones for later. Convinced that the single most important thing an interrogator could do was develop a rapport with the prisoner, he always avoided asking a question that they wouldn't know how to answer—for instance, asking an infantryman a technical question about an artillery gun or asking an artillerist about the operations of a Panzer tank. That could end a conversation or, even worse, cause a prisoner to spin a fanciful yarn, which was a waste of Martin's time and could result in bad information being passed on.

Whenever Martin sensed he was being given incorrect or misleading information, he asked a question to which he already knew the answer. If the prisoner lied again, Martin's demeanor and tone shifted abruptly, leaving no doubt he could get nasty if necessary. Usually, he only had to raise his voice and most would snap to attention, as they had been taught to do in Hitler's army. As Churchill said in his 1943 speech to Congress, "The Hun is always either at your throat or at your feet." Martin, who had experienced both, preferred the latter.

Martin Selling questions German prisoners near the front in France, 1944. *(U.S. Army Signal Corps)*

Ever since Dachau, Martin had carried with him a smoldering hatred of the Nazis. He had been elated by the assignment to Camp Ritchie, and dreamed of returning to the continent as an army interrogator to wreak revenge—physical and emotional—on the captured soldiers of Hitler's Third Reich. He sometimes fantasized about repaying all the sufferings and degradations he and other Jews had experienced. Of course, he didn't mention this to anyone at Camp Ritchie for fear of being thrown out of the training program, but that motivation had secretly driven him every step of the way.

Now that he finally had his chance to exact revenge, he made a surprising discovery: He was really a softy at heart. He could not work himself up to become mean and angry at individual Germans without provocation, and only an arrogant few provoked him. As for the temptation to use physical force on a prisoner, he considered brutality a waste of time. At Dachau, he had seen it used by the cruelest against the most helpless, and it had accomplished nothing. Furthermore, any intelligence obtained during torture was suspect because most people would say just about anything to stop their pain and suffering. Now that he was in the field interrogating enemy prisoners, Martin wanted only to do his job well and complete it in a manner that allowed him to retain his own humanity.

That said, there were a few times when he did slap a prisoner. Usually, he respected someone's right to be silent, and would quickly have him taken away by MPs and another prisoner brought in for questioning. However, Martin did not tolerate any back talk or lectures from staunch Nazis, particularly those in the SS. Occasionally, when he was interrogating an especially difficult prisoner, Martin would imagine aloud what would have happened to him if he had confronted an SS guard at Dachau with such audacity. "At Dachau, we were slapped around or worse for much less, or even for no reason at all, Jews and non-Jews alike." Whenever Martin let drop his having been at Dachau, most prisoners answered his questions without further hesitation. One obstinate prisoner asked in an accusatory tone just where exactly Martin had learned to speak

German so flawlessly. "In Germany," Martin said curtly, "where I also saw how the SS interrogate prisoners while I was in Dachau." The realization that he was facing a former inmate from a Nazi concentration camp was such a terrible shock to the German that he lost control of his bowels right then and there.

Martin learned to rely on the prisoners' innate fears, unquestioning obedience, and instant reaction to sharp commands. Most of them had lived a brutal life during the war, and they had been mistreated by superiors and subjected to severe punishments for the smallest indiscretions. They had watched their own countrymen behave deplorably in conquered territories, carrying out executions of military, civilian, and political opponents. In some cases they, too, had doubtless participated. So when they were captured, they often expected equally grim treatment from the U.S. Army, which Martin tried to play to his advantage. Time and again, Martin saw how shocked they were when he spoke in a calm voice and their willingness to keep answering his questions if it meant he would maintain this civilized approach.

The day after the fall of Saint-Lô, a young German soldier was brought to Martin to interrogate. During his interrogation, he told Martin that before his capture he had taken part in laying a minefield in their sector. Martin casually asked if he would show where the mines had been buried. The prisoner agreed to do so. With Martin accompanying him, they strolled through the entrenched hedgerows toward the battle-scarred front lines. They were repeatedly stopped by exhausted and wary U.S. soldiers who wanted to know what the hell they were doing walking around in no-man's-land. With the German in his Wehrmacht uniform and with Martin's heavy accent, they had wisely brought along an American-born MP, whom Martin let do the talking.

It was the first time Martin had seen an actual battle zone so soon after the fighting ended. It had been recently bombed by aircraft and bombarded by artillery and little had been cleared away. Dead

German soldiers were lying in the trenches next to disabled German tanks. Warned about booby traps as well as mines, they trod cautiously.

Martin, armed with a .45 pistol, walked a distance behind the prisoner, and was careful to step into the impressions left by the German's hobnail boots. The MP was behind them both with his rifle at the ready. If this was a bogus story, that was one thing. Martin would simply take the prisoner back and return him to the cage. But if this was a ploy to kill a couple of U.S. soldiers by leading them into a minefield, Martin wanted to be sure the prisoner stepped on the first explosive.

They came to a road running through an open field where U.S. Army engineers from a bomb disposal unit were carefully probing for live German mines; those they found were set aside for controlled detonation.

The prisoner sauntered over to the engineers and, with Martin following and translating, showed them the general pattern that had been used in laying the minefield. Then he went over to the excavated mines and nonchalantly dismantled a dozen of them. The engineers watched how he did it, then joined in. By the time they finished, the German had made fast friends; the GIs gave him chocolate and cigarettes and shook his hand.

For Martin, the scene at the minefield made an indelible impression: The best interrogations were not only about collecting intelligence so as to kill the enemy. They were about saving lives.

Twenty-four hours after the D-Day landings and two years to the day since he left Nazi-occupied Europe as a refugee on a ship that was stopped in midocean by a German U-boat, Stephan Lewy left New York Harbor aboard the *Queen Mary* to return to Europe as a Ritchie Boy. His three-man Order of Battle (OB) team was assigned to the 6th Armored Division, about to see its first combat with Patton's Third Army.

It had been a long road for the boy who spent his first thirteen years in Berlin, the last half of them at the Baruch Auerbach Orphanage. After surviving a terrifying night locked in the orphanage synagogue by uniformed Nazis during Kristallnacht, Stephan had been sent by his father from Germany to France: first to Quincy-sous-Sénart, a village twenty miles from Paris; then, when the Germans marched on that city, to the château farther south in Chabannes. It was nearly two years before Stephan, with the help of the Red Cross, was able to reestablish contact with his father and stepmother, Arthur and Johanna, who had since fled Germany for the United States. They helped him get the documents he needed in order to join them, which he finally did in June 1942 in Boston, where they worked as household domestics.

Arriving in America speaking no English, Stephan signed up for night school and within a year was fluent. He registered for the draft in March 1943, on his eighteenth birthday, and was inducted into the U.S. Army five months later. He was first sent to basic training in the medical corps before being transferred to Camp Ritchie, where he found himself in a sea of German Jewish refugees. *My God,* he thought. *I feel like I'm back in Berlin.* After Stephan and a group of other soldiers went before a federal magistrate to be sworn in as American citizens, he wrote his parents: "I am no longer stateless."

The week of his nineteenth birthday Stephan graduated as a French interpreter in Camp Ritchie's Fifteenth Class, then was chosen to complete a four-week Order of Battle course focusing on the structure of the German army. Stephan was able to spend his final few days before heading overseas with his parents, who were still awaiting their U.S. citizenship. Before their final good-byes, his father pulled him aside. Arthur had earned a medal for his service in the German army in World War I, two decades before the Nazis sent him to Oranienburg concentration camp along with other "undesirables." He told Stephan how proud he was of him, but also included a note of caution. "It's not going to be a picnic," he warned. "You better try to be very, very careful."

The night before the *Queen Mary* left port, Stephan was among a capacity crowd of GIs in a dockside building serving as a temporary theater. The movie, *Lassie Come Home,* was no doubt meant as an entertaining diversion. But two hours later, moved by the long, dangerous journey of the loyal collie seeking to reunite with its family, hundreds of soldiers about to go to war emerged from the movie with tears streaming down long faces.

The *Queen Mary* had once been a stately passenger liner; now it was an overcrowded troopship. The Ritchie Boys occupied an adjacent block of bunks. Like Stephan, most of them had been promoted upon graduation to staff or master sergeant, and had so many stripes on their arms that other GIs called them the Zebra Battalion. The Allies had lost numerous ships in the Atlantic to German U-boats, so everyone was alarmed when they learned they would make the crossing unescorted. They were told the *Queen* was so fast it could outrun any enemy submarines they might encounter. Indeed, the big ship, with twelve thousand soldiers and a crew of more than one thousand, made the 3,195-mile crossing in six days flat.

After Stephan's team joined the 6th Armored, nicknamed the "Super Sixth" for its spirit while in training stateside, maneuvers were held in the English countryside. Then came the day when they were taken to another port and boarded ships for still another crossing, this one much shorter than the ocean: the English Channel. On July 19, 1944, they arrived at Utah Beach. Six weeks after D-Day, pontoon docks jutted out from the beachheads, and men and tanks came ashore without even getting wet.

Once all its units had landed, the 6th swung southwest into the Brittany peninsula. On July 29, its first day of combat, the division crossed the Sienne River at Pont de La Roque and its armored tanks advanced twenty-six miles in twenty-four hours. Over the next few days, the 6th liberated several cities against stubborn enemy resistance, capturing eight hundred prisoners in the process. En route, Stephan's team searched houses and offices once held by the enemy, looking for maps and documents that contained actionable intelligence. Then, on August 1, Patton directed the armored division to drive up the center of the peninsula to the westernmost tip of France and capture the port city of Brest, where the Germans maintained a large U-boat base.

As the division's lone Order of Battle team, Stephan and his two teammates operated out of division headquarters, where Patton was a regular visitor. The flamboyant general visited his commanders in the field in a converted 2.5-ton truck with a fire-engine siren that cleared tanks, trucks, men, and anything else in his path. Patton traveled with an entourage of adjuncts and orderlies, and

Staff Sergeant Stephan Lewy. *(Family photograph)*

usually also with his bull terrier, Willie (short for "William the Conqueror"). The general was a vision in highly polished helmet and boots, and matching .45 revolvers with ivory handles swinging gunslinger-style from a wide cowboy belt. It was said he had carried two guns ever since he ran out of ammunition during a 1914 shoot-out in Mexico while hunting down the outlaw Pancho Villa. His legend had evolved from that tale and others, such as his refusing to take cover and blazing away at a diving Luftwaffe plane as it strafed his encampment in North Africa in 1943.

Stephan was present for some of the briefings that Patton was given by the division staff. Whenever Patton was presented with various contingencies of a proposed plan of attack, his first question was always the same: "Which will give me the fewest casualties?"

Stephan's team learned early on not to bother to unload the trailer they pulled behind their jeep. Unpacking was a waste of time because Patton's army didn't stay in any one place for long. His refrain to his commanders was constant: "You gotta get your mileage in for the day!" Stephan thought a lot about what made Patton a good general, and to him it boiled down to two primary factors: his concern for his troops and an aggressive philosophy that held it was better to attack first than to be attacked.

While Stephan conducted some interrogations—he was the only native German speaker on his OB team—his team's primary job was to use the information obtained by the interrogators of the division's IPW teams to identify which enemy units they were facing and determine their fighting capabilities. Their extensive knowledge of the German army was soon put to the test.

Brittany, like Normandy, was hedgerow country, and the hedges in the vicinity of Brest were particularly formidable. Earth embankments, often higher than six feet, were surrounded by trees and scrubs. In the final days of its drive on Brest, the 6th met a fierce and determined enemy. An estimated twenty thousand enemy troops were dug in to defend the port city. As the 6th positioned itself for the final assault, the staff car of a Nazi general decked out in a full-length leather coat drove headlong into the 6th's field artillery battalion. The irate general tore open his tunic to bare his chest and said he would rather be shot than suffer the humiliation of being captured, but the Americans still took him prisoner. Though he refused to talk when he was interrogated, he was identified as Lieutenant General Karl Spang, the commander of Germany's 266th Infantry Division.

From their OB book and more recent intelligence gathered from interrogations, Stephan's team knew that the 266th had formed a year ago in Stuttgart, and had been stationed along the northern coast of Brittany. Some of its units fought in late June as the Allies broke out of their Normandy beachheads. Stephan and his team further determined from documents the captured general was carrying that the division was headed to Brest to help defend the port to the last man.

Based on this key piece of intelligence that a German division was to his rear, the 6th's commander, Major General Robert Grow, changed his plan and canceled the attack on Brest. While keeping a light screen of forces facing Brest, he wheeled the rest of the division in an about-face, moved north in three combat columns, and struck the in-transit German division the next morning. The battle that followed was a complete success due to outflanking the surprised enemy with tanks and infantry led by hedge-cutting bulldozers plowing through the Brittany hedgerows.

The 266th German Infantry was wiped out as a fighting force, and without firing a shot, Stephan's team of Ritchie Boys had played a crucial role.

A month after landing at Omaha Beach, Victor Brombert was ordered to temporary duty with the 82nd Reconnaissance Battalion— known as the "eyes and ears" of the 2nd Armored Division—for the looming battle to capture the German stronghold of Saint-Lô.

Victor considered himself unlucky to have been selected. The recon unit was charged with racing ahead of the main body of troops and tanks to roam behind enemy lines. Having a French-speaking interrogator, like Victor, with the unit would assist them in gathering information from the locals, and if they took any prisoners, Victor could immediately question them in German. It was like having two interrogators in one.

Saint-Lô, twenty-five miles inland from the invasion beaches, was a strategic crossroads with paved roads and railroad tracks that sprouted in all directions. If it weren't taken, the men and equipment of the U.S. First Army would be stalled indefinitely by the hedgerows and orchards, now crammed with fresh troops that had unloaded from transports arriving at the invasion beaches, but had nowhere to go. Taking Saint-Lô would relieve the bottleneck. The Germans knew this, too, and had infantry and Panzer tank divisions ready to defend the town and block the roads.

Riding in the back of a reconnaissance half-track—a lightly armored open vehicle propelled by caterpillar treads in the rear and truck wheels in the front—Victor felt exposed as they proceeded forth on their scouting mission. He wasn't sure how successful he was in hiding his anxiety from the other guys in the unit, who acted as if this were an ordinary assignment, which it was for them.

Before long, they were ordered to halt and await new instructions. They pulled off at the edge of a wood a few miles from Saint-Lô. Something big—code named Operation Cobra—was about to happen, but before it could be launched the weather turned nasty, which grounded Allied air power. For Victor and the men of the recon unit, the suspense grew during the long wait. On the third morning, the skies finally cleared. Soon, a tremendous rumble shook the ground, and they looked up to a sight none of them could have imagined. From horizon to horizon, the sky filled with the silhouettes of American and British heavy and medium-sized bombers—not hundreds but thousands of them, Victor estimated. They watched as the planes disgorged their loads over Saint-Lô, the long strings of bombs spiraling earthward and exploding in a sustained crescendo.

The recon team took cover in the heavy forest, but Victor felt as if his head would implode from the pressure of concussive waves from the bombs dropping nearby. He knew the theory of carpet bombing but had never experienced it firsthand; indiscriminate and imprecise, its intent was to clear a wide corridor through fixed enemy positions even if it meant destroying everything and everyone around them. In a flash, he thought of what it must be like for the poor civilians who hadn't made it out of Saint-Lô.

As the bombing continued, visibility decreased due to the volume of smoke and dust in the air. After the sky emptied of the last squadron of bombers and the blasts ceased, there was an eerie silence.

Finally, the recon team got the signal to move forward. Their half-track crawled across stretches of moonlike landscape, devoid of life and pockmarked with blast craters. Roads and other landmarks were unrecognizable. They passed animals and Germans slaughtered by the same bombs. Some of the soldiers had fallen over one another and were locked forever in embrace. Others had been frozen in ordinary activities at the instant of sudden death, reminding Victor of the pictures he had seen of ancient human figures mummified by volcanic lava. Most ghastly were those corpses left in contorted, lively poses—one young soldier had an arm raised as though cursing the sky that had rained such devastation.

Pulling into Saint-Lô, they found a city in shambles, with buildings turned into burning or smoldering heaps. Although there were isolated snipers and pockets of stubborn German resistance, they continued on, past gutted homes with black smoke bellowing out of empty window frames and collapsed walls of masonry dwellings whose furnishings had been blown out into streets also littered with corpses and destroyed vehicles. Most of the enemy troops and tanks in the area that had survived the bombardment were sent fleeing, at last giving the U.S. Army the breakout of Normandy it so desperately sought. The turning point of the entire Normandy campaign, the taking of Saint-Lô opened the way into the Cotentin Peninsula to the northwest and Caen and Paris to the east.

Victor rejoined his IPW team in Saint-Lô. The 2nd Armored spent the next few weeks on the move, spearheading the Allied thrust. The nature and pace of the war had changed; no longer slowed down by the hedgerows, which were like the trenches of an earlier generation's war, the Allies now turned to a more modern, mobile brand of warfare.

In mid-August, a vast Allied pincer movement forced more than a dozen German army divisions into a fifteen-mile gap between the towns of Falaise and Argentan, south of Caen. In what became known as the Falaise Pocket, the German army suffered a defeat of epic proportions, with as many as ten thousand Third Reich soldiers killed, although at least twenty thousand more escaped through the gap minus their heavy equipment and would be reorganized and rearmed to fight another day.

The 2nd Armored, now attached to Patton's Third Army, had a new objective: to cross the Seine River, which connects Paris to the English Channel at Le Havre. Patton's tank columns forged ahead so fast, rolling over any opposition in their path, that the detailed military maps the tank crews used were frequently no longer relevant because they only showed territory that they had left behind. Lead armored tanks often had to stop at gas stations to pick up local road maps. Some days, they went more than a dozen miles. Many of the IPW team's waking hours were spent riding in their jeeps trying to keep up with the armored columns. The road-weary interrogators agreed they would have a limited appetite for auto sightseeing after the war. Finally, the 2nd came to a grinding halt at Mantes-Gassicourt, so they could do maintenance on the tanks and allow fuel and supply trucks to catch up before crossing the Seine.

On the lightning-quick drive out of Normandy, Victor had been a bit disoriented, losing some sense of time and place. Now, when he realized that he was looking at the banks of the familiar Seine, he knew they were only thirty miles from Paris.

There was another reason the Americans had stopped where they did. Word had come down from the top that U.S. troops were not to enter the city. Out of respect for French pride, the Free French Forces under General Philippe Leclerc were being allowed to liberate their own capital.

But Victor could not bear to be so close to Paris, where he had spent some of his happiest days, and not be present for the liberation celebration. He heard that the 2nd would remain bivouacked where it was near the Seine for a couple of days. Finding a co-conspirator on his team, the two men grabbed their M1 carbines, took one of the jeeps, and drove off into the night for Paris. Although the IPW teams operated with significant latitude and independence—often requisitioning homes and farms to use for interrogations as well as their own private quarters—the two interrogators left without permission.

En route, they picked up a young Frenchman who was hitching a ride a few miles down the road. He carried a rifle, wore an armband with the French national tricolors, and claimed to be a member of the Resistance. He kept mooching their American cigarettes, and as he chain-smoked he told colorful tales of blowing up railroad tracks, derailing German troop trains, and rescuing Allied paratroopers. Victor had his doubts, having already met an endless number of Frenchmen who claimed to have fought for the Resistance. The way the young man handled his rifle made it seem more like a stage prop than a weapon.

Nearly every French person Victor had spoken to claimed to have engaged in some form or other of resistance against the Germans. Entire villages claimed to have been part of the French Forces of the Interior, the underground Resistance group known as FFI. Such claims, he knew, were wildly exaggerated. There had long been a sizable portion of the population—not just the pro-Nazi Vichy government and their gendarmes complicit in mass roundups and deportations of Jews—who had collaborated with the German occupiers for their own gain. An epidemic of collaboration had been followed by an epidemic of denunciations after the Allied landings:

neighbors denouncing neighbors, merchants denouncing other merchants, all accusing one another of being pro-Nazi collaborators. Victor was saddened to see that the end of the occupation had not diminished France's internal strife. The cleansing and purging taking place all over France, by the French themselves, was leading to summary executions without legal proceedings. Women were exposed to public scorn, and at times even brutalized, for having cavorted with or fallen in love with German soldiers. Although there were plenty of French patriots, Victor concluded that France was sick with a bad conscience, not only about how quickly its large army had been defeated, but about how badly many of its leaders and citizens had acted during the occupation.

They reached Paris early in the morning, entering the city through the Sixteenth Arrondissement, Victor's home turf from age nine until he and his parents fled the advancing Germans in 1940. There were very few vehicles on the road, so they were able to get around quickly, and the city unfolded before Victor as if out of a dream. He drove past his old elementary school, where as a boy he had played marbles on the sidewalk, sped down the Champs-Élysées, past the circle of the Rond-Point, onto the boulevards where his mother took him to the movies, and up the boulevard Poissonnière, near where his father had his office. He went by his aunt Anya's apartment building, where he and his parents had spent their first few days in Paris after emigrating from Germany in 1933. He knew from his parents that his aunt, who had taken him to his first street market, had fled occupied Paris for Nice, where she was eventually caught up in a Vichy roundup of foreign Jews; no one had heard from her in more than two years. The quick auto tour revealed that the streets, plazas, squares, and parks that gave Paris its charm were largely undamaged after four years of German occupation. Europe's most enchanted city had been spared the ruin of Saint-Lô.

Driving on Place de la République, Victor had a sudden vision of Dany Wolf, her dancing eyes, full lips, and brushed-back brown curls. This was her neighborhood. Although he had never visited her here, he still remembered the address to which he had written her so many letters from Deauville following the summer of their love. Pulling over abruptly, he asked his team member to wait in the jeep.

Victor knew that Dany and her parents had moved from Paris, as had his own family, to the relative safety of the unoccupied zone. After his family had relocated to Nice for a year, he had learned from a mutual acquaintance that the Wolf family was in Lyon, and that Dany was married and had a child, news that was not shocking but was still bittersweet. That was the last he had heard. He knew that Lyon, the scene of mass arrests even before the Germans occupied all of France in late 1942, had become a dangerous place for Jews.

He walked the short distance to her address on boulevard Voltaire and rushed up the stairs to her family's old apartment. He rang the bell and a gray-haired woman opened the door. Behind her, an even older woman wrapped in a black shawl looked up from an armchair. She looked like a familiar member of Dany's family from the summer in Normandy: a more shriveled-up version of Dany's grandmother.

He told the *grand-mère* his name, then asked, *"Où est Dany?"*

"Déportée," said the old lady in a hollow voice. Dany had been taken away to a camp with her child, the grandmother added, in words that lacked emotion, as if it had all been wrung out.

Victor knew what that meant. He had long understood what the white-gloved ladies of the Republican women's club in Harrisburg did not want to acknowledge when he told them of the roundups and deportations of Jews, and of Nazi concentration camps. But hearing about Dany was not something he could accept or fully take in—especially not today, with the liberation of their city finally at hand after years of occupation.

Left numb and speechless, he turned from Dany's grandmother without another word and fled from the building.

Back behind the wheel of the jeep, he drove frantically to the center of Paris, desperate to lose himself in the celebrations of the youthful quarter. He went down the boulevard Saint-Michel and stopped at the Jardin du Luxembourg, which he knew was a favorite meeting place for students of all ages. He knew this because he had once been one of them. When he arrived, a large crowd had already gathered, and to the joyous cries of *Vive la France! Vive de Gaulle! Vive les Américains! Vive la victoire!,* Victor was handed an opened bottle of wine and received many kisses.

He was told that the exiled leader of the Free French, Charles de Gaulle, had entered Paris the day before and led a triumphant parade down the Champs-Élysées all the way to the Cathedral of Notre-Dame even as some Nazi holdouts scattered sniper fire on them from the rooftops.

Soon, Victor, drunk on wine and the joys of liberation, was standing on the hood of the jeep, holding forth with a speech, the theme of which he would never recall. Some in the crowd were confused. *Is he French? Or American? He wears an American uniform but speaks as a Frenchman.* He stopped long enough only to take another swig of wine.

The next thing he remembered was lying on a leather bench in a café with his head in the lap of a woman stroking his hair. Even before he opened his eyes, he had smelled the strong scent of her perfume.

Hours later, Victor and his buddy left Paris nursing the start of sizable hangovers. When they reached the division's bivouac, it was empty, with only a few soldiers still packing up. They said the 2nd Armored had hurriedly crossed the Seine in pursuit of Germans.

Victor and his buddy looked at each other, and without saying a word understood their dire situation. Although interrogation teams operated on their own, their situation was highly irregular in that not even the officer in charge of their team knew their whereabouts. As they had no authorization to be gone and had been given explicit orders to stay out of Paris, they were technically AWOL. Now that the division was back on the move, that could mean serious trouble if they were reported as missing.

Victor gunned the jeep down the bumpy road after Patton's hard-charging Hell on Wheels to catch up with a war that had left him behind.

8

HOLLAND

anny Steinfeld, the serious-minded boy from the hamlet of Josbach, Germany, was listening to a Chicago Bears game on the radio as he did his homework one Sunday when the broadcast was interrupted with news that Pearl Harbor had been attacked.

When Germany declared war on America a few days later, Manny's first thought was of his mother, Paula, and his sister, Irma, who was now eighteen. How would they get out of Nazi-occupied Europe? He had heard nothing from them in the months since his mother's letter that said they might be deported to the Lodz ghetto, and the lack of further news made him fear the worst. He was sure the best chance to save them was defeating Hitler and the Nazis. The more Manny thought about it, the more he realized the best thing *he* could do for them now was to join the U.S. Army as soon as possible and help his adopted country defeat his homeland.

Manny had been living with his aunt and uncle in Chicago for a little more than three years. He had excelled in school, more because of a photographic memory and an ability to speed-read than any great study habits. When he graduated from Hyde Park High School in June 1942 and discovered that as an "enemy alien" he would have to wait to be drafted rather than enlisting, he thought that going to college was the next logical choice. He enrolled that fall at the University of Illinois, intending to remain in school until his draft number came up. He moved out of his aunt and uncle's crowded apartment, where he still slept on the couch, and found a room near the school and a roommate, another student, to split the fourteen-dollar-a-month rent with him. Manny held down two part-time jobs to support himself; he worked behind the counter at a drugstore during the week, and on weekends, he was a busboy at a Greek restaurant where he earned thirty-five cents an hour and all he could eat. In spite of his newfound independence, the nineteen-year-old was not contented; every day he thought about being in uniform and doing his part in the war in Europe. Finally, in early 1943, he got his wish when he was drafted into the U.S. Army.

His basic training was at Camp Roberts in California, and he did well enough on the intelligence and aptitude tests to be selected for the Army Specialized Training Program (ASTP), which was offered at hundreds of universities around the country and provided training in fields such as engineering, foreign languages, and medicine to meet the wartime mandate for officers and soldiers with technical skills. Considered more demanding than West Point or the Naval Academy, these programs expected students to complete a four-year degree program in eighteen months. In July 1943, Manny was sent to the City College of New York, where his courses included a new language for him, Russian. While he was there, he became what he already was at heart: an American. On November 15, 1943, he was sworn in as a U.S. citizen, something he had coveted since he first sailed past the Statue of Liberty as an immigrant boy of fourteen.

At its peak in December 1943, ASTP had 150,000 soldiers enrolled in school. But criticism mounted that the program was keeping too many young men with leadership potential in school and out of combat. As Lieutenant General Lesley J. McNair put it, "With 300,000 men short [in combat units], we are sending men to college?" So ASTP began to trim enrollment. In February 1944, more than one hundred thousand student-soldiers were notified that they would be transferred to regular units. Manny was one of them.

While most of these men were sent to join conventional fighting forces, Manny's fluency in German triggered a different set of orders. From the campus he went directly to Camp Ritchie, where in April 1944 he graduated in the Seventeenth Class with 150 other German-language interrogators. Receiving his highest grade in Enemy Armies and laudable evaluations from his instructors, he was selected to join thirty other students for a special four-week, postgraduate Order of Battle course that covered the organization of the German army and its war strategy. Once again, his retentive memory served him well. Upon his second Camp Ritchie graduation, he was promoted to staff sergeant, and was soon aboard a troopship crossing the Atlantic on D-Day.

In London, he was assigned as an OB specialist to the headquarters of Allied Intelligence, located at 40 Hyde Park Gate, where he collated and analyzed intelligence gathered by the French Resistance on the movements of German troops in occupied France. His job was to identify every German unit fighting in western France: its structure, commanders, armament, equipment, and fighting capability.

One month after D-Day, Allied Intelligence issued an urgent call for German-speaking GIs with any specialized knowledge of the German army to volunteer for the airborne divisions. Although these were skills that Manny possessed, he had never even been in an airplane, and he couldn't imagine jumping out of one in flight. Yet, believing he should go wherever he was most needed, he answered the call. On his first practice parachute jump over rural England, he was at the front of the line and boarded the plane first, which meant he would jump last. They took off, and Manny was plenty nervous already when the jumpmaster, who would remain on the plane after the trainees jumped, came down the line and stopped in front of him.

"Steinfeld, give me your watch."

Manny took off his watch and handed it over.

"Give me your wallet."

Manny gave him his wallet, too, then asked why.

"There's a chance your parachute won't open," said the jump-master. "One in every hundred thousand chutes has a malfunction. If that happens to you, I want to have your watch and your wallet."

Manny was trembling too much at that moment to bother asking the jumpmaster if he planned to keep them for himself. By the time the jumpmaster gave him a strong shove out the exit door, he was shaking with fright. He was unable to breathe until he felt the reassuring jerk of the harness and saw the canopy open safely above him. He got terrible skin burns from the tight harness straps but was so relieved to be alive, he didn't complain. There were four more practice jumps to come. Manny was just as scared for each one and struggled to control his anxiety. Stepping out of a plane in midair never became routine for him. Somehow, it seemed even worse to Manny than the prospect of being shot at by Germans. He wondered if the other jumpers were as frightened. He knew when he gave up his cushy job at headquarters he had gone against the popular refrain throughout the ranks: Never volunteer for anything. But he had not joined the U.S. Army to sit out the war behind a desk.

He made all his required practice jumps, got his wallet and watch back, and received his Parachutist Badge, commonly known as Jump Wings. Now a fully qualified paratrooper, he was assigned to the 82nd Airborne, which he was told would soon be returning to England from Normandy. When it did, rumors swirled that the all-American division—so called because its predecessor in World War I, the 82nd Infantry Division, comprised soldiers from every state in the union—would take part in other airborne operations over Nazi-occupied Europe.

Unlike other Ritchie Boys he knew, Manny had not changed his name when he became a U.S. citizen, and he hadn't requested new dog tags before going overseas. "H" for Hebrew was stamped on the metal ID tags attached to a long chain around his neck.

Ich bin ein deutscher Jude.

Manfred Steinfeld would live or die in this war as a German Jew.

Werner Angress shipped back across the Channel from France to England with the 82nd Airborne in mid-July. In its thirty-three days of combat since D-Day and without relief or replacements, the 82nd had engaged five German infantry divisions and was credited with destroying two of them as fighting forces. But these victories had come at a terrible cost. By parachute, glider, and landing craft, 11,770 men of the 82nd had gone to Normandy. Fewer than six thousand were on the return trip to England.*

After surviving combat, his capture, and his time as a POW, Werner was thankful to be among those returning. Soon after arriving at the division's encampment in Nottingham, he was awarded the Purple Heart, for the leg wound he received in action, and a Bronze Star. The latter citation read (in part):

> For meritorious service from 6 June to 12 July 1944, in NOR-MANDY, FRANCE. At all times, Sergeant ANGRESS carried out his work in a superior manner and was highly aggressive, showing a high degree of initiative in gaining information from prisoners of war that proved to be valuable to tactical operations. Many times, Sergeant ANGRESS went forward into the front lines to secure prisoners to expedite the receipt of valuable information. On one occasion, when a prisoner surrendered and told Sergeant ANGRESS that others were waiting to surrender near our front lines, but were afraid of being shot by our men, Sergeant ANGRESS took

---

* The 82nd Airborne Division casualties in Normandy included 5,245 killed, wounded, or missing. The division's 508th Parachute Infantry Regiment, to which Werner Angress was assigned, dropped 2,056 troopers into Normandy on D-Day, many in the wrong locations. Of that total, 307 were killed and 754 wounded, a 50 percent casualty rate.

four men to the designated spot without regard to his own personal safety and caused 24 men of the enemy to surrender.

After Normandy, England felt like a glorious homecoming, and the men of the 82nd enjoyed the break. Half the division was given five days' leave right away, and when they returned, the other half took off.

On his first day of leave, Werner took a train to Broadway in the Cotswolds, where more newly arriving Military Intelligence teams were gathering before receiving their unit assignments. He was greeted with a hero's welcome, as the first interrogator and first paratrooper who had returned from Normandy, and also the first to come back after being taken prisoner by the Germans. This gave Werner a measure of authority and notoriety. He was asked to give a lecture to the newcomers from the States about D-Day, the fighting in France, his experiences as a POW, and his own work as an interrogator, which he did to a rapt audience, many of them recent Camp Ritchie graduates.

When his leave ended, Werner was sent on his next assignment:

Werner Angress, paratrooper. *(Family photograph)*

a week at a POW camp in northern England to gather information from captured Germans about the Normandy campaign that might be useful in planning future operations. As soon as he announced himself at the gate, the MPs shot him suspicious looks because of his accent. Next, just inside the camp, he ran into the German corporal who had surrendered his men to Werner in Normandy and then saw them nearly shot by the U.S. lieutenant until Werner intervened. Werner and the prisoner shook hands like old friends and chatted in German, resulting in more dirty looks from the MPs.

Werner told the corporal he was there to speak to the prisoners about their experiences in Normandy, and the corporal offered to round up volunteers. Soon, it seemed every German soldier in the camp wanted to be interviewed, and the long line of prisoners willing to talk kept Werner busy for the entire week.

One German paratrooper, after describing a new antitank weapon first used in Normandy, told Werner that when the war was over, he thought that "paratroopers on both sides should pressure the International Olympic Committee to include parachute jumping in the next Olympic Games."

By the time Werner returned to Nottingham, the 82nd Airborne had received some new equipment and replacement troops to fill their depleted ranks. This mandated more training, and to his extreme frustration, Werner found himself participating in maneuvers dressed in a German army uniform. The IPW teams took turns portraying the good guys and the bad guys in war games. Those in Wehrmacht uniforms were instructed to speak German exclusively after they were "captured" by their American comrades. The Ritchie Boys all hated masquerading around the countryside dressed as Third Reich soldiers. They thought it was particularly appalling that they, as Jews, were made to wear the swastika-adorned uniforms of Hitler's legions for *any* reason, and it was a dangerous act as well. The omnipresent British Home Guard was more determined than ever to keep the hated Krauts from setting foot on their home island or die trying, which made the dangers of being outfitted like the enemy quite real.

On a hot and humid day in August, Werner took part in a parade to honor General Eisenhower at a military airfield thirty miles away in Leicester. In his speech, Ike thanked the assembled troops from the 82nd and 101st Airborne for what they had accomplished in Normandy, and he said that very soon they would be needed for further airborne missions in Europe.

"Like you," Ike told the troops, "I'd rather be home going fishing. One of these days when we have beaten the Nazis, that's what we can do. But in the meantime, I will have more work for you. And it won't be long."

Werner's excitement at the promise for new action was heightened later that month when the 82nd got a new commander, James "Jumpin' Jim" Gavin, the same general (and former assistant division commander) who had given Werner permission to jump on D-Day even though he wasn't a qualified parachutist. Werner's respect for Gavin had only grown since then. Unlike many generals, he treated his subordinates well, doubtless a result of having been a seventeen-year-old army private before attending West Point, from which he graduated in 1929. Any man who dealt with Jim Gavin could be sure of receiving his full consideration. As a result, he was very popular with the troops. At thirty-six, after being a general officer for less than a year, he became the youngest U.S. two-star general to command a division since the Civil War.

As the paratroopers nervously awaited their next call to arms, Werner used the short lull to type an overdue letter to his longtime mentor, Curt Bondy, in Virginia. He knew that Bondy had been told when Werner was missing in action at Normandy and that he hadn't heard until weeks later that he was alive.

> Dear Bo:
> I told you, didn't I, that missing in action does not necessarily mean death? I am sorry that you worried. . . . The news looks very good and I hope that the Stars and Stripes will wave over Berlin very soon. I sure hope I can be there to see it.

Keep your fingers crossed that I can. . . . I still hope to find my parents and brothers in this European mess.

The alert came a few days later for the 82nd Airborne, 101st Airborne, and British 1st Airborne. British ground forces under the command of Field Marshal Bernard Montgomery had already reached the northern Belgian border, and a plan was quickly dashed together to drop the three airborne divisions ahead of them into Nazi-occupied Holland, to prevent the Germans from blowing up the many Dutch bridges, including the long spans over the Waal River and the lower Rhine River, which in Holland was called the Nederrijn. Wholesale destruction of the bridges would delay the Allied push into Germany's northern industrial heartland. Nearly thirty-five thousand paratroopers were to be dropped—most by parachute but others by gliders—along a narrow fifty-mile corridor to secure the only north-south highway through Holland. Their orders called for the U.S. airborne divisions, equipped with only light artillery weapons that could be dropped by parachute, to "seize and hold" their objectives deep behind enemy lines until the British infantry, armored tanks, and heavy artillery could link up with them. Then the ground forces would continue racing northward through Holland and reach Arnhem in four days.

At least, that was the plan, called Operation Market Garden. Werner learned its details at his regiment's intelligence briefing on September 16. In the south, the 101st would drop at Eindhoven, near the Belgian border, and seize bridgeheads required for the pass-through of ground forces. Smack in the geographic middle of the ambitious operation, the 82nd was given a crucial assignment: to drop over Nijmegen, secure the bridges across the Waal River and a nine-span bridge across the Maas River, and capture the highest ground in Holland, located between Nijmegen and Groesbeek. Nine thousand British paratroopers were to drop the farthest north, at Arnhem, and seize the span across the Nederrijn, the Dutch part of the Rhine, which, once taken, would allow ground forces to advance into Germany. Defenses around Arnhem were thought to be fairly weak, only a few thousand Germans. But if Arnhem turned into more of a battle and the U.S. airborne units failed to open up the road northward, the British airborne division would be cut off, with no avenue open to resupplying or reinforcing them.

Werner knew Holland well. Nijmegen was near that country's eastern border with Germany and just seventy miles from Amsterdam, where he had left his family five years earlier. He had not heard anything from them since his mother's last letter—shortly before Germany and the United States went to war—reporting that his father had been imprisoned in Berlin for taking the family's money out of the country. Werner emerged from the regimental briefing excited about their destination. *Holland! My God! I might be able to see my family!* He also hoped to get some better news about his father. Perhaps by now he had served his prison sentence and been released and was even back with the family in Amsterdam.

Compared to the fiasco of parachutists scattered in the dark all over Normandy on D-Day, the daylight jump on Nijmegen on September 17 was every paratrooper's dream. All but two of the 482 planes filled with seventy-three hundred troopers of the 82nd reached their target zones. One of the division's few jump casualties was Gavin, who, as always, jumped first out of the lead plane. He fractured two vertebrae in a hard landing, but with barely a grimace, he unhooked his chute, picked up his M1 rifle, and was soon giving orders in his calm and cool manner. Even with a broken back, he regularly showed up, rifle in hand, at the front where the fighting was taking place.*

Werner's regiment was dropped, as planned, a mile east of Nijmegen, to occupy a range of hills on the division's flank closest to

---

* Gavin's chief of staff, Colonel Robert Wienecke, told visiting journalist Martha Gellhorn rather plaintively: "We have a wonderful system worked out. I stay home with the telephones and my general goes out and fights with the troops."

the German border. Werner had still not received any parachute training, but took his second combat jump like a true veteran, making a soft landing in a potato field, surrounded by the familiar faces of his comrades. While descending in his chute, Werner had noticed a nearby German antiaircraft gun with its long barrels pointed skyward. Its five crewmen, upon seeing the sky fill with hundreds of aircraft and thousands of green, orange, blue, and red canopies of U.S. paratroopers, had lined up next to their big gun without firing a single shot at the planes.

"Hände hoch!" Werner yelled as soon as he hit the ground, and the German artillerymen, happy to surrender to such overwhelming forces rather than fight and die, raised their hands in the air.

For the first few days, Werner's IPW team stayed in a Dutch monastery about a mile from where they landed. When they first entered the building, which had served as a German headquarters, they found an empty dining hall with rows of tables that still held plates of warm food and steins of beer. It had clearly just been abandoned, and in a hurry.

That first night, Werner went up to the monastery's roof garden with several other Ritchie Boys. They looked down at Nijmegen, one of Holland's oldest cities, which was now without power and completely in the dark. A battalion of the 508th regiment was fighting Germans in its winding streets, trying desperately to reach the Waal bridge. The gunshots and red glow of fires raging throughout the city were close enough, yet strangely far off. Werner turned pensive. A poem from World War I came to mind, and he recited the only lines he could remember:

> *But I've a rendezvous with Death,*
> *At midnight in some flaming town.**

---

* From "I Have a Rendezvous with Death" by Alan Seeger, an American killed in action on July 4, 1916, at the Battle of the Somme, while serving with the French Foreign Legion before the U.S. entered the war.

The men with him were amused with Werner's spontaneous rec-
itation but quickly changed the subject to something less morbid,
and Werner didn't mind at all. He had done it partly to impress
them with his literary recall, but he realized that a poem about
death in the middle of a shooting war was not the best subject for
young soldiers.

The next morning, as captured German troops were brought
in to the monastery for interrogation, the IPW team learned something surprising. The enemy commanders were so certain they
could hold the massive, 650-yard-long, steel-girdered highway
bridge across the Waal at Nijmegen that orders had not been issued
to blow it up, which the Germans often did before retreating. But
the bridge, built in 1936, with a steel superstructure that rose nearly
as high as a twenty-story building, had been wired with explosive
charges. For now, the Germans, reinforced by heavy artillery, were
succeeding in holding both the northern and southern approaches
to the bridge along a nearly mile-wide sector.

The taking of the Waal bridge was so important that the Market Garden plan called for it to be captured intact on the first day,
but that objective lapsed into the third day as the 82nd fought off
six major counterattacks. The 82nd was operating under British
Corps commander General Brian Horrocks, who met face-to-face
with Gavin and told him that the bridge must be taken or the entire
Market Garden operation could fail. Gavin knew that the lives of
the British 1st Airborne in Arnhem depended on the British ground
forces reaching them without further delay, which meant the span
had to be taken by his men immediately.

Horrocks and Gavin decided the only way to end the stalemate
was to outflank the defenders by sending a regiment across the
fast-flowing river in flat-bottomed assault boats. At midday on September 20, Gavin ordered his 504th regiment to do just that, under
withering enemy fire from 88 mm cannons, 20 mm cannons, mortars, and machine guns. Each of the boats had only a pair of oars,
so the troopers used the butts of their rifles to row faster and their

helmets to bail out water pouring in from bullet holes in the flimsy boats. In the first wave of the attack, just thirteen of the twenty-six boats reached the other side.

The Waal crossing would cost more than two hundred American lives. The paratroopers who made it ashore assaulted a high bank on top of which were entrenched Germans, and, using grenades and bayonets, they attacked them fiercely in their foxholes and fought their way to the northern approach of the bridge. There, they fought in the steel girders of the bridge itself, where dynamite and detonators had been lashed to catwalks, picking off Germans before they could blow the bridge sky high.

Once the bridge was secured, Werner's regiment crossed the Waal and occupied Bemmel, a village just north of Nijmegen. The paratroopers dug slit trenches and foxholes, and prepared to hold their positions against an anticipated counterattack. But the German assault never came, and things remained quiet over the next few days, during which the Americans took a number of prisoners, including deserters from a regiment of Volksgrenadier directly across from them. From his interrogations, Werner learned this regiment comprised reserve troops—some drawn from the German navy and Luftwaffe—who had little infantry training. They had been sent here as an occupational force when Holland was a backwater affair. Now that there was real fighting, the prisoners said, there were many others like them ready to desert.

A patrol of twenty-five paratroopers was organized to reach the Volksgrenadier lines and bring back as many disenchanted Germans as possible. Of course, they needed a German speaker with them, and the officer in charge asked for Werner.

They left shortly after sundown, and within ten minutes, they realized something was not right. There was a great deal of activity on the German side. As they were crossing a meadow, the Germans sent up an aerial flare, bathing the area in white light. When caught in the open by a flare, they knew the best way to not be seen was to freeze. This went against every human instinct to dive for cover, but a man standing perfectly still could pass in the shadows for a tree or other inanimate object, so Werner and the others froze like statues until the flare died out.

Then they crept forward until they came to a wide ditch, both ends of which disappeared into thick shrubbery. Checking it carefully, the officer said the ditch had been mined. At that instant, another flare went up. They were close enough for the Germans to spot them and to open up on them with machine guns. This time, everyone dove for the ground and whatever cover they could find. When the enemy fire tapered off, the officer in charge of the patrol ordered them all to turn around and head back to their own lines. It was too dangerous to proceed.

They made it back, having accomplished nothing other than not losing anyone on the patrol. The men considered the mission a failure until a couple of days later, when Werner found out from some new prisoners that the Volksgrenadier regiment had been relieved a week earlier.

They had been replaced on the front lines by an elite SS division.

Shortly after Manny Steinfeld finished his jump training, the 82nd Airborne returned to England from Normandy. He was assigned to the division's lone Order of Battle team. His teammates were First Lieutenant Leonard Abel, a Camp Ritchie–trained photo interpreter, and Staff Sergeant Edward Wynne, who had been in Manny's IPW class as well as his postgraduate OB course. Attached to Gavin's headquarters under the division's intelligence officer (G-2), Lieutenant Colonel Walter Winston, they were the 82nd's only OB team and as such were the division's experts on the makeup and fighting capabilities of hundreds of different German army units.

After what Manny had gone through to qualify as a parachutist, he saw the irony in being assigned to ride into Holland—his first airborne operation—aboard a silent, engineless glider rather than by parachute. Nicknamed Flying Coffins, these craft were built for just one flight and a violent end once they were released by their tow plane a mile or so from their drop zone. The most widely used glider—the Waco CG-4A—was forty-eight feet long with an eighty-foot wingspan, constructed of steel tubing and canvas skin. Flown by two trained glider pilots, the Waco had sufficient load capacity to carry thirteen combat-equipped troopers, a jeep, or a field artillery piece and small crew to operate it. The gliders could deliver troops and equipment to more precise locations than parachutes could, but they were even more dangerous. More casualties had occurred during glider landings than parachute jumps in Normandy, where the Germans had planted interlocking ten-foot poles—some wired with explosives—in open fields where gliders were likely to land. Many gliders were impaled or had their wings sheared or blown off as they came in. Even without such manmade obstacles, the two-ton gliders dropped like runaway garbage trucks, slamming into trees or rocks or the ground so hard that they often split open, spilling soldiers and materiel.

Still, Manny was relieved that he wouldn't have to leap out of a plane for Operation Market Garden. He was responsible for the OB team's jeep, and he cautiously backed it up a ramp into one of the gliders that would carry the 82nd Airborne to Holland. He then put blocks under the wheels and helped secure the jeep so it wouldn't shift in flight.

The planes towing the gliders started taking off after the transports carrying the paratroopers had gone. In an airborne operation, the gliders were always timed to arrive last because it was too dangerous for them and their tow planes to fly through a sky filled with paratroopers descending in their chutes. Given that the element of surprise was lost by the time the gliders swooped in, they often had to fly through intense flak. Several gliders carrying 82nd troops came unhooked from the tow planes over the Channel and crashed in the frigid waters, taking to the bottom their pilots and the heavily laden paratroopers. Others were lost when they or their towing planes were struck by enemy fire and went down.

Aboard a glider being towed three hundred feet behind a C-47,

Manny Steinfeld, 82nd Airborne. *(Family photograph)*

Manny was seated in the driver's seat of the jeep. In the passenger seat next to him was Captain George Wood, a thirty-three-year-old regimental chaplain known as Chappie. An Episcopalian minister who conducted nondenominational services and attended to soldiers' spiritual needs regardless of religious affiliation, Chappie was a veteran of three combat jumps with the 82nd Airborne, in Sicily, Italy, and Normandy. Men of all faiths loved him. Not only did he expose himself to great danger—unarmed and wearing a Red Cross armband—to care and pray for the wounded and dying, but he was appreciated for his soaring sermons and powerful words as well. He was famous in airborne circles for having written "A Paratrooper's Prayer" on the eve of D-Day.

Almighty God, Our Heavenly Father . . . Drive from the minds of our paratroops any fear of the space in which Thou art ever present. Give them confidence in the strength of Thine Ever-lasting arms to uphold them. Endue them with clear minds and pure hearts that they may participate worthily in the victory which this nation must achieve in Thy name through Thy will. Make them hardy soldiers of our country. . . .

On the glider, Manny was seated next to Chappie, and he took that as a sign that they would make it to Holland without mishap.

Early that Sunday afternoon, in Holland's fifth year of German occupation, the streets in Dutch towns and villages throughout the country were crowded with young people on bicycles and families strolling along myriad canals and streams. Suddenly there was a roar of several hundred Allied bombers. Instead of continuing on, as they usually did, to bomb cities and factories in Germany, they dropped their high-explosive payloads all over Holland on German positions and antiaircraft batteries. Barely had the bombers left when coming in from the west were waves of transport planes carrying American and British paratroopers who bailed out from low altitudes in order to get on the ground quickly and lessen the chance of being shot as they floated down under their chutes. After the sky emptied of their billowing canopies, the big gliders, cut loose by their tow planes at about two thousand feet, silently swooped down like birds of prey.

As a first-time passenger on a glider, Manny didn't know how it should feel after the tow plane cut them loose. But as they came closer to the ground, he sensed they were coming in much too fast. When he looked over and saw Chappie vigorously praying, he knew something was wrong. Before Manny could start his own prayer, the glider belly-flopped at more than 100 mph and slid amid loud grinding and screeching noises before flipping over. The glider was totally demolished, its sides split open, and Manny was thrown clear, landing some distance away, unconscious. He awakened groggily in a first aid station with bandages on his arms and back. He asked about Chappie, who was said to be a little banged up but already out ministering to his flock. Scratch one OB team jeep, however.

Manny rested on an army cot the remainder of the day. The reprieve allowed ample time for contemplation, and he slept fitfully that night. By the time he joined his team in the morning, he had decided that jumping out of an airplane with a parachute was not so bad after all.

Manny went right to work with the OB team. His job was to translate the information gained from interrogations, quickly and accurately. He would receive the interrogation reports filed by the division's four IPW teams and then determine the identification, strength, and capabilities of the enemy units facing them, and post the results on a situation map at Gavin's headquarters. The most vital information made its way into daily briefings the team prepared for the G-2, Lieutenant Colonel Winston, and Gavin's chief of staff, Colonel Robert Wienecke.

For one ten-day period, Manny and Sergeant Wynne were assigned to an observation post in a dense forest on the border between Holland and Germany. Reconnaissance squads were making nighttime forays into the German lines specifically to bring back prisoners for interrogations, which Manny and Wynne conducted on the spot, then rapidly passed along by messenger anything they knew about the makeup of the German units in front of them. On a daily basis, the two Ritchie Boys exchanged small-arms fire with German forward positions. On the gun range at Camp Ritchie, Manny had qualified as an expert, which had shocked him because he had never fired a gun before joining the army. But in the dense forest, he discovered that shooting at a concealed enemy who was shooting back was much different from hitting a bull's-eye on a range, and after ten days and dozens of rounds he had no idea if he had hit anyone or not.

When the two Ritchie Boys returned to division headquarters, they found it had moved into a grove of trees at the south end of Nijmegen, off St. Anne Street. Although there were structures in town available to house the staff, Gavin believed the accommodations for his headquarters personnel should be no more comfortable than what was available to the men on the front lines. He set the example by sleeping in a tent, which meant everyone else did, too. Manny and Wynne dug a six-by-six foot hole, pitched a tent over it to keep the rain out, placed sandbags around the perimeter, and called it home for the rest of their time in Holland.

The threat of snipers and artillery shelling was constant. On September 30, Technician Fifth Grade Eric Nathan, a twenty-nine-year-old German Jew who had immigrated in the 1930s to Pittsburgh, Pennsylvania, and was attached to the headquarters staff of the 82nd Airborne, was walking down the street in Nijmegen when a German shell landed nearby. He was struck by shrapnel and killed.

And the next week, the Germans threw a new weapon into the fight. Manny happened to be outside in a long chow line at the time. Hearing an unfamiliar buzz-saw sound, everyone looked up. A strange-looking pair of Luftwaffe fighter-bombers without propellers streaked past, raking the ground with machine gun fire. Before anyone could react, the fast-moving aircraft were gone, as quickly as they had arrived.

Manny Steinfeld didn't know it at the time, but he had just seen his first jet planes.

Werner Angress soon saw how different Holland was going to be from Normandy, where the Allies had stayed on the move as the aggressors. Operation Market Garden quickly turned defensive, with brief attacks and counterattacks but no major changes in battle lines.

All the while, German artillery, fired from five to ten miles away, took a toll. Werner, in fact, came close to being killed by enemy artillery shelling on three consecutive days in October 1944. It began on Friday the 13th, with a close artillery strike in front of the jeep in which he and another team member were riding. They disappeared into a plume of dirt and rocks. As they did, the jeep dropped heavily into the shell's crater. Werner never knew how they emerged unscathed on the other side, without a broken axle or even a dented fender.

The next night, Werner and another interrogator dug an extra-deep slit trench in which to sleep outside the regimental headquarters tent. But sometime in the middle of the night, German artillery opened up, and the men listened as the explosions crept closer and closer to their position. Werner realized with alarm that enemy observers must have identified the headquarters tent. *How stupid of us to dig a trench right next to it!* he thought. Now there was nothing they could do but press themselves against the dirt at the bottom of their trench and hope not to take a direct hit as the ground shook and the concussive explosions of artillery rounds threatened to burst their eardrums. Finally, after ten minutes that seemed like ten hours, the shelling stopped. They stayed planted at the bottom of the trench the rest of the night, cracking unfunny jokes and sharing each other's misery. At sunrise, Werner climbed out of the trench to stretch his legs. A few yards away, a thirty-pound German 105 mm artillery shell was sticking half in and half out of the ground. A dud, it had failed to explode, thereby sparing their lives.

Werner spent the next day at the command post of one of the regiment's three battalions, which he took turns visiting because the battalions—each numbering about five hundred men—were closer to the fighting than regimental headquarters and thus had newly captured prisoners to interrogate. Werner got to shooting the breeze with a sergeant he hadn't met before. Toward evening, the sergeant invited Werner to join him in his large slit trench for more conversation and some whiskey from a bottle the sergeant had liberated from a cellar. It was a tempting offer, but Werner was tired.

He declined and retired to his own foxhole for the night. Foxholes were less comfortable than elongated slit trenches because one slept half squatting in them rather than lying down, but they were considered safer because their narrow opening made less of a target for an artillery or mortar shell to drop into —and foxholes were usually deeper, too. During the night, there was again enemy artillery fire but it was less heavy than the night before, and Werner, hunkered down in his foxhole, slept soundly. In the morning, his new friend was dead, the victim of an artillery shell that had made a direct hit on his slit trench.

By now, Werner had seen enough of war to realize there was only one possible explanation for his run of luck. It hadn't been his time to die.

In the meantime, Operation Market Garden was not going as planned. At Arnhem, the British paratroopers were facing much more resistance than anticipated. Six thousand veteran soldiers of the German 9th and 10th SS Panzer divisions were bivouacked in the area when the paratroopers landed, a surprise to Allied planners. What was believed to be a lightly defended target that would make for the quick capture of the most important bridge of the entire operation—the span across the Nederrijn that would open the way into northern Germany—had become a street-to-street fight.

The British ground forces in the south that were supposed to reinforce the paratroopers in Arnhem still weren't close to reaching them. In fact, they were barely moving at all. The terrain was filled with bridges, dikes, and drainage ditches, many of them hard to pass, and the ground on either side of the narrow road was often too soft to support vehicles, so that trucks carrying troops and pulling heavy artillery pieces were forced to crawl northward in single file. And they were frequently under attack, forced to halt and fight a series of battles along the only direct route that led from Belgium up to Nijmegen. It took the lead units three days just to get halfway to Arnhem, and then the combination of the terrain and the Germans halted them altogether. Thousands of soldiers and countless tanks and vehicles were parked bumper to bumper on the road and backed up for miles. The British ground forces finally arrived in Nijmegen, still twenty miles from Arnhem, a full two weeks after the 82nd had jumped on the city. But they never did reach Arnhem.

After seven days on its own, the British 1st Airborne in Arnhem was cut off and outnumbered by enemy forces, and its commander finally had to order a withdrawal to avoid losing the entire division. The statistics were ghastly: of the nine thousand British paratroopers who jumped at Arnhem, nearly six thousand were captured or missing, more than one thousand killed, and a little fewer than two thousand were able to withdraw safely. After losing nearly three-quarters of its strength, the British 1st Airborne would not see combat again. With Arnhem and the bridges over the Nederrijn still held by the Germans, the Allies could not advance any farther.

The two American airborne divisions had largely succeeded in their missions, however, and their new assignment was to stay in Holland to hold the bridges and ground they had conquered. For the 82nd, which had already suffered nearly eight hundred killed, that meant staying in and around Nijmegen, which was still being shelled from a distance by the Germans off and on, day and night, and wrecked block by block. Civilian hospitals overflowed with casualties of all ages.

In October, Werner settled down in a deserted hothouse full of grapevines to write a letter to Curt Bondy, who was trying to keep track of his former charges now serving in the U.S. military.

Heavy rain fell outside, as it had for days, and it dripped through the shattered windows of the hothouse. Smashed glass and grapes covered the ground. The few houses Werner could see from where he sat were torn to pieces, nothing more than rubble and debris.

Rounds of the U.S. artillery were whistling down into German lines a few miles away, and the muffled explosions he heard were satisfying. But Werner was sorry that war had come to Holland for a second time: first, the German invasion in 1940, and now, four years later, the Allied invasion to kick out the Germans. Holland had been the first real harbor of safety for him and his family after they escaped from Germany. He had liked its simplicity and cleanliness, and the hospitality of its people. It was a good country, and once beautiful, but now it was torn and battered.

"The longer this war lasts," he wrote, "the more ugly sights I see and the more I get to know what death looks like, the more I am convinced that it will be our first duty after this war to prevent a second one. I don't know yet whether this will be possible, but at least we should do our best to try."

He told Bondy that he had not yet been able to inquire about his family in Amsterdam, and said he hoped that the military situation would make that possible very soon. He shared with Bondy a kind of moral dilemma he had been pondering often these days.

"The question of what to do with the future generation of Germans? This is the first part of their education. Shells, bullets, retreat, the fact that the Führer is wrong and that there is no master race. It will show what dying and despair mean. It will show them that it does not pay to start wars. Later on, it will take years and years of methodical teaching by handpicked teachers of German and American stock to reeducate the German youth."

At the time he wrote to Bondy, Werner believed that his mother and brothers were still in Amsterdam, and he hoped his father was now there as well. The city was less than a hundred miles away, but it might as well have been a thousand. The mission of the 82nd, and Operation Market Garden, did not include a campaign to liberate western Holland.

He spoke Dutch reasonably well, and whenever he encountered a Dutch civilian, he asked them what they knew about the situation in Amsterdam. But most of them hadn't been there since the occupation, and he learned little.

On November 11, the 82nd was relieved by Canadian troops.

Their campaign in Holland was over. They piled into trucks and rode south to a military camp in France for rest and recuperation.

As they left Holland behind, Werner Angress had a dreadful feeling that he had just lost his best chance to find out what had happened to his family.

9

THE FORESTS

After their unauthorized jaunt into liberated Paris, Victor Brombert and his fellow Ritchie Boy caught up with Hell on Wheels, the 2nd Armored Division, sixty miles down the road. Luckily for them, the leader of their IPW team had covered for them in their absence, and there were no consequences for their wild ride through the City of Light.

As the armored division continued its rapid advance into France's northern plains, nothing stopped them for long. Town after town fell. With the Germans now in a disorderly retreat, victory seemed within sight. A giddy optimism spread through the ranks as well as the Allied chain of command, leading to bold talk of the war being over by Christmas and everyone going home soon.

Victor was one of the first U.S. soldiers to enter Bapaume, a town of a few thousand residents not far from the Belgian border. Nearly devastated during World War I and reeling from years of another German military occupation, the locals went all out to welcome their American liberators. On the public square, a town official rushed up to Victor's jeep and thrust an official proclamation at him, declaring him an honorary citizen. Then, with a flourish, he pinned a Cross of Lorraine on Victor's field jacket. The cross, consisting of one vertical and two horizontal bars, dated back to the Byzantine empire and had been adopted as the emblem of de Gaulle's Free French forces. Although it caused some people to be confused about which army Victor was fighting with, particularly given his French accent, he wore it for months until a U.S. colonel ordered him to remove it.

Leading the way, the division's recon battalion—the same unit Victor had briefly joined during the Saint-Lô offensive—crossed into Belgium in early September, with the armored tanks and Victor's team in their jeeps not far behind. A week later, after traversing the hundred-mile breadth of Belgium nearly unopposed, the 2nd Armored Division approached the outskirts of Hasselt, a coal-mining town in the northeastern corner of the country. Here they were slowed by a series of booby-trapped obstacles, such as felled trees wired with high explosives, left on the roads by recently retreating Germans.

The townsfolk of Hasselt greeted the Americans with open arms and steins of beer in smoky pubs filled with jubilant customers singing Belgian drinking songs. In one of the bars, Victor, who a lifetime ago had dreamed of being an opera singer, belted out a pitch-perfect rendition of the French national anthem, "La Marseillaise." The room was stilled by the line, *Aux armes, citoyens!* (To arms, citizens!), and he drew rousing applause when he finished.

Unfortunately, not all the scenes of liberation were celebratory. The next morning, a rowdy mob dragged through the streets several young women accused of sleeping with German soldiers. The women were kicked and slapped, their heads shaved and swastikas painted on their bare scalps.

In mid-September, the 2nd Armored rolled into southern Holland. But when they reached Maastricht, a few miles from the German border, Victor's French team was abruptly recalled to Paris. Since the division was now well beyond French-speaking territory, they were told that their language skills were no longer needed. A jubilant Victor concluded that the war was over for him, and he envisioned spending the remainder of it in Paris. He imagined a future for himself filled with wine, women, and song in the city he loved.

At first, it appeared Victor might have his wish granted. When the French team reported to Army Intelligence—located on avenue Marceau in an office devoid of furnishings except for utilitarian desks, lamps, and metal chairs—they were officially disbanded. With no new duties for any of them, they were assigned lodgings close to headquarters and told to check in daily.

The neighborhood where they settled, in the center of Paris, was close to where Victor and his parents had stayed in a small hotel before finding an apartment. For Victor, it felt like a homecoming. He strolled through the leafy parks and meandering streets he knew so well. Eager to settle in and get his own place, he checked out of his assigned room within a couple of days and rented a furnished studio on rue des Vignes, a few streets from where he and other boys used to watch the girls come out of school at Lycée Molière. After moving into his new place with his duffel bag and M1 carbine, he went to the corner bar for a drink. There, sipping an espresso and chatting with the bartender, was a petite, dark-haired woman. Seeing Victor's uniform, she smiled, and assuming he was American asked in English if he had been at Normandy. She was astonished when he responded in flawless French.

Her name was Yvette. Her sad eyes below heavy lids and her plucked eyebrows reminded him of Edith Piaf. Later, they went outside and sat on a bench in a park, holding hands. From comments she made, Victor gathered that there had been someone in her life—a husband or a lover—but that it was over now. Victor chose not to ask any questions. Although they did not kiss before parting, they made a date for the next day. She was soon his first guest in his tiny flat, with its crimson walls and soft lights. Yvette liked to pull the top sheet over their bodies to shut out the rest of the world, making it all the easier for Victor to keep at bay any lingering thoughts of war.

But Victor had to check in daily at headquarters, and one day when he did, he was sent to meet with a British colonel who was looking for someone who spoke multiple languages. The colonel needed someone to travel weekly between Paris and London, carrying to Allied Intelligence headquarters in Hyde Park top secret reports identifying German industrial targets that would be used to assign bombing missions to British and U.S. long-range bombers. Just about anyone in the army would covet a cushy assignment like this, safely away from combat, but Victor didn't see it that way because he couldn't think of anything other than the nights he would be away from Yvette. So he did his best to sabotage the interview. He told the colonel he hated "drab office work," and purposefully failed to mention he spoke Russian, which would have added to his impressive list of foreign languages. The colonel, who had initially been interested in Victor, finally gave up on him.

Victor was certain that by flubbing the interview he had guaranteed his stay in Paris for the duration, and he rushed to tell Yvette the good news. But just a few days later, his Camp Ritchie training caught up with him when someone at headquarters saw in his personnel file that he spoke German as well as French, and that he had been trained to interrogate German POWs. The next thing he knew he was a member of a German-language IPW team, which was ordered to report immediately to the 28th Infantry Division, then taking part in a major offensive near the German border.

Victor was furious with himself. He had thrown away the opportunity to be assigned to the choice job in Paris, which, even with the weekly travel to England, would have allowed him to spend several nights a week with lovely Yvette. He could also imagine the stern disapproval of his parents, who were already afraid he would be killed or captured by the Nazis, for failing to play it safe and get a job far removed from the front lines. But the hardest part was saying good-bye to Yvette. His team departed in such a rush that he had to break the news to her over the phone, leaving her heartbroken and both of them doubting that they would ever see each other again.

His new team was an impressive group of Ritchie Boys. Between the five of them—two Germans, one of them a rabbi's son who sang

A portrait Victor Brombert had taken in liberated Paris for Yvette shortly before his transfer to the 28th Infantry Division fighting in the Hürtgen Forest. *(Family photograph)*

old Jewish songs in his cantorial tenor; an Austrian; a Hungarian; and Victor, who was soon being called "Frenchy" again—they spoke fifteen languages, including Yiddish. As for Victor's German, it was impeccable if uncultivated. Because he had left Germany when he was only nine years old, he had a schoolboy's vocabulary. He couldn't discuss eighteenth-century German philosophers but didn't need to in order to interrogate prisoners of war.

When his team caught up with the 28th Infantry Division three hundred miles from Paris, they found it just outside Roetgen, the first Germany city captured by the U.S. Army. A placid town of row houses, Roetgen gave no hint of the horrendous fight under way a few miles away in the Hürtgen Forest.

The plan to push into the densely wooded terrain east of the Belgian-German border had evolved from Eisenhower's September directive to his forces to breach the German frontier and strike deeply into Germany. The initial goal was to pin down a large German force in the Hürtgen Forest, at some fifty square miles one of the largest wooded tracts in Germany, to keep them from hurrying north twenty miles to reinforce Aachen, which was the first major German city about to fall to the Allies. The second phase of the operation was to cross through the forest to drive into the heart of Germany's Ruhr industrial region.

In the dense forest, some of the fir trees had grown as tall as telephone poles, and the terrain was treacherous: steep ridges as well as deep gorges, all wrapped in a cold, shaded dampness. It was some of the most rugged country in western Europe.

To fight off invasions from the west, the Germans had turned the center of the forest into a labyrinth of well-camouflaged defenses, part of the four-hundred-mile West Wall, better known to the Allies as their Siegfried Line—with concrete bunkers, rows of barbed wire, minefields, machine guns, and steel-walled artillery positions. Then there was the simple fact of the landscape. The boggy forest floor, which sun rays seldom reached due to the dense canopy, was not ideal for tanks or other vehicles, and the wintry low overcast and foggy conditions grounded most Allied airpower, which limited air support for the ground troops.

The 28th Division, a unit of the Pennsylvania National Guard that had fought in the Civil War and was declared the "First Defenders" by Abraham Lincoln for racing to defend the threatened capital in response to an urgent plea from Congress, launched its attack with three infantry regiments on the cold, foggy morning of

November 2, 1944. At 8 A.M., thousands of soldiers left their foxholes and moved into the dark woods. Carrying out an attack plan that relied on extensive tank, aircraft, and artillery support—little of which materialized—each of the division's regiments was sent off in a different direction, in violation of a basic principle of war to concentrate combat power at a decisive place.

At first, their worst enemies were the forest and the weather. The GIs, lacking proper winter clothes, were exposed to rain, sleet, and freezing temperatures. Then they encountered the Germans, veterans of winter fighting, bundled in snow-white cold-weather gear, who waited behind trees and inside bunkers to fire point-blank at approaching U.S. soldiers. Even when the Americans spotted them first, the tree growth was so thick in places that they couldn't always make accurate rifle shots. Instead they had to use grenades, but that meant getting close enough to a target to throw them accurately.

None of the 28th's regiments reached their first-day objectives. Some units lost half their men in the opening hours. One regiment was pushed back by German artillery to its original start position, and the others, caught between minefields and barrages, were pinned down. Inexplicably, neither the division commander, Major General Norman Cota, nor his staff had ordered reconnaissance patrols into the forest beforehand. Such probing could have determined the location of the defenses they faced, the minefields, pillboxes, and other obstacles, and, equally important, would have revealed the Germans' true strength in the forest. In addition to the two German divisions they had been told to expect, the 28th also faced a third division that had unexpectedly moved into their sector. Another tactical blunder was designating a narrow, muddy trail through the Kall Valley to serve as the division's main supply route. Almost as soon as the battle began, it became a struggle to keep open this lifeline to the men in the forest.

In the days that followed, Victor's IPW team stayed close to the action, interrogating newly captured German prisoners, several hundred of whom were captured in the first week alone. The Germans had a renewed resolve to defend their homeland from invasion, and Victor soon came to the conclusion that the morale and determination of the German army had been grossly underestimated.

Victor was shocked by what he saw at the front lines: U.S. infantrymen attacking steep, well-defended ridges and bunkers, resulting in atrocious losses. Radios were unreliable in the dense woods, and, absent firsthand accounts, Victor realized that the 28th Division headquarters had little grasp of the disaster unfolding. So he and his team took it upon themselves to question GIs about battle conditions and personally relay that information back to the division command post in the hope that the brass would come to their senses. A new strategy or plan was needed to stop the slaughter.

Victor would always remember the carnage he saw in the forest: the horror of mortar and artillery barrages; unrelenting shell bursts exploding in treetops, against which lying prone on the ground was no protection; torn and bloody clothing and body parts blown into the air and left hanging in tree limbs like Satan's laundry; armored tanks mired in thick mud and unable to move; soldiers too tired or too scared to leave their foxholes, even to relieve themselves. Men were cracking up, one combat medic told him. Some desperate soldiers were inflicting wounds on themselves, shooting their feet, toes, or fingers so as to get a medical evacuation.

Victor had experienced the terror of Normandy and Saint-Lô, but they did not compare with the bloodbath in the woods southeast of Aachen. Hürtgen Forest would stretch into the longest single battle the U.S. Army ever fought—nearly five months. Eventually, American soldiers did cross through the forest into Germany's Ruhr region, but only after months of costly defeats and the reduction of numerous divisions, some of which took as many as five thousand casualties in a matter of days. The total American casualties in the Hürtgen Forest exceeded thirty thousand. Newly arrived soldiers were rushed up from replacement depots and thrown into the fight with such frequency that there was soon a manpower shortage at the depots. Demoralized troops and their commanders, as well as the army's top generals, now knew what Victor had already decided: the determination and ability of the Germans to defend their homeland had been badly misjudged. No longer was there any talk of wrapping up the war in Europe by the holidays.

In late November, the 28th Division, after failing to achieve many of its objectives in the Hürtgen Forest and reeling from nearly 40 percent casualties and the loss of much of its equipment, was pulled off the line and sent to a quiet area in Luxembourg along

Victor Brombert in Roetgen, a German border town near Aachen, and the first German town to be taken by Allied forces, October 1944. *(Family photograph)*

the Our River, which flowed through the Ardennes Forest.* The region's tree-studded hills, quiet valleys, and quaint villages seemed the ideal rest area, and here the division was to be refitted with new vehicles and equipment, issued winter clothing, and its depleted ranks filled with replacements. While this process was under way, however, the 28th was charged with holding a twenty-five-mile front, too great a distance for a single division to cover, even a fully manned, heavily equipped one in top shape. They would be spread thin, but no one gave it much thought. After Hürtgen Forest this felt like a wintry paradise, a true vacation. Division headquarters was set up in Wiltz, Luxembourg, a brewing and tanning town with a two-hundred-year-old castle, twenty miles southeast of Bastogne, Belgium.

The men were exhausted, and a comprehensive program for rest and rehabilitation was put into effect, including two-day passes to Paris and longer stays at rest centers in Luxembourg. Given a three-day pass, Victor took the opportunity to surprise Yvette with a visit, and even the daylong 250-mile ride to Paris on bumpy roads in the back of a truck did not diminish his anticipation of their reunion. When they met, she asked no questions, and he did not speak of the war, so there was little for them to discuss. She seemed to know better than he that their story had no future and that even the present was fleeting. She was correct. That one night of bliss was to be their last together.

Victor returned to Wiltz, where his IPW team had settled in a vacant house in town. They were soon conducting interrogations of captured members of German patrols that had been sent west of the Our River to probe U.S. lines. These interrogations confirmed

---

* The 28th Infantry Division entered the Hürtgen Forest campaign with a battle strength of 13,932 men. According to Headquarters Unit Report No. 6 (12/44), during nineteen days of fighting—from November 1 until it moved to the Ardennes Forest on November 19—the 28th suffered more than six thousand casualties, which included killed in action, wounded, missing, and captured.

the presence of the 26th and 352nd Volksgrenadier divisions oppo-site them. The 352nd had fought at Normandy, with one of its reg-iments defending Omaha Beach on D-Day. The division had also seen heavy fighting near Saint-Lô and was believed to number at least fifteen thousand men. Little was known about the 26th, which had been formed a couple of months earlier and had not yet fought.

From December 12 on, division outposts reported sounds of motors and much vehicular movement behind enemy lines, espe-cially at night. These accounts dovetailed with claims by locals who were sure an enemy buildup was taking place to the east. To try to get corroboration of these disturbing reports, Victor's team split in half, with each taking one of their jeeps to cover greater distances and speak to more people.

Victor and two other interrogators arrived at a village inn along the Our River, and they set out to find anyone with firsthand in-formation about the enemy buildup across the river. One German peasant woman who had recently crossed the border said she had seen large concentrations of German troops across the Belgian bor-der beyond Sinspelt, thirty miles inside Germany. She said there were masses of men and equipment, including many armored tanks, trucks hauling barrels of fuel, bridge-building materials, and river-crossing boats.

Victor and his team spoke with other locals and gathered sim-ilar eyewitness accounts. They were so detailed, and so alarming, that the interrogators drove that night to VIII Corps headquarters in Bastogne to personally report that large numbers of German troops, tanks, and materiel were massing just over the border, with the capability of attacking U.S. lines through the Ardennes.

VIII Corps, under the command of Major General Troy Middle-ton, comprised two battle-weary infantry divisions, the 28th and 4th, both having been refitted after their Hürtgen Forest losses, and the newly arrived 106th Infantry Division, which had no combat experience. These three divisions, filled with soldiers either ex-hausted or green, were stretched across a front that ran parallel to

the German frontier in Belgium and Luxembourg. All that separated them from the Germans was the winding Our River, in many
places no more than forty feet wide and easily fordable.

Victor and his IPW team arrived in Bastogne late on Friday
evening, December 15, and they were surprised by how unim-
pressed the colonel at corps headquarters was with their latest intelligence. He said they had received similar warnings about the
Germans massing troops and equipment, and anyway, there was
little anyone could do about it now.

"Our lines are thin," the officer admitted. "Too thin. We'll just
have to sit and wait. Anyhow, it's probably a diversionary action.
Forget it."

Shown the way out, Victor and his team members returned to
the village inn, where they each had their own room. Although the
night was uncannily silent, Victor's sleep was troubled. He kept
turning the day's events over in his mind. Tactical intelligence
learned from prisoner interrogations was routinely acted upon to
save American lives, but here was a possible coup of strategic intelligence, suggesting that a massive surprise attack could be imminent.
And to be told to *forget it*? The hours inched forward, with Victor
falling in and out of a restless sleep. Then, at around 5:30 A.M., he
awoke with a start, to what he thought was thunder accompanied by
flashes of lightning. When the building began to shake, he realized
it wasn't a thunderstorm after all but an artillery barrage.

Victor had never dressed quicker. Grabbing his few belongings, he raced outside and found the other guys, nervous and half-
dressed, already by the jeep in the courtyard waiting for him. In
addition to artillery bombardment, mortar shells were now landing
nearby. He knew German 88 mm artillery had a range of ten miles,
but the maximum firing range of mortars was under two miles. That
meant that the Germans had crossed the river and were already well
inside American lines.

They jumped into the jeep, and Victor drove as fast as possible through thick ground fog the ten miles back to headquarters in

Wiltz, where they learned that the heavy artillery and mortar barrages, lasting for forty-five minutes, had immediately been followed by tank and infantry attacks along the division's entire front. Orders and counterorders were flying out to the regiments and battalions that suddenly found themselves under attack; the very attack, Victor knew, that they had been gathering intelligence about for days and had tried to warn the colonel about in Bastogne. *Had they been forceful enough? Was there anything else they could have done with the information they had? Should they have acted sooner?*

There were heroic stands by the men of the 28th against two Panzer tank divisions, three German infantry divisions, and a parachute division. The 28th had been brought back with replacements to a battle strength of 14,254 men (although many of the new men were still undergoing training), but the division would suffer nearly as many casualties in the Ardennes as it had at Hürtgen Forest: a total of 4,930, or a 35 percent casualty rate. One of its regiments, the 110th, was virtually destroyed, with most of its officers and men killed, wounded, or captured in a valiant attempt to slow the German advance toward Bastogne.

At division headquarters, the whereabouts of many units was unknown, as was their viability. Some had dispersed or outright disappeared under enemy pressure. General Cota was barking urgent commands over the radio to his units in the field: "Hold at all costs." "No retreat." "Nobody comes back." When radio and phone contact was lost, messengers were sent out to try to reach units that had been cut off, but heavy snowdrifts and icy roads caused collisions and snarled traffic. Low visibility grounded reconnaissance and air-support flights.

By the second day, Wiltz was under attack and in danger of falling, forcing Cota to move his command post out of Luxembourg and across the Belgian border several miles southwest of Bastogne. By the time the IPW team heard the "fall back" order, there was extreme confusion in and around Wiltz.

Fall back to where? was Victor's first thought when he heard the order. Given reports that numerous roads and bridges had already fallen to the enemy, he had no idea which way they should go or whether they would be heading into enemy positions whichever way they went.

The last defenders of Wiltz were a ragtag group of army engineers, sawmill operators, and clerks who fought a rearguard action until the town was overrun by whistle-blowing German paratroopers of the elite 5th Parachute Division firing machine pistols and supported by tanks.

By then, Victor and the IPW team were a few miles west of Wiltz. Victor, driving the lead jeep, stopped at a roadblock where armed MPs demanded the day's password. The MPs were not from the 28th Division and did not know the IPW team. There had been reports over the past two days of English-speaking German soldiers in U.S. Army uniforms creating havoc behind American lines, ambushing GIs, and seizing bridges and crossroads. Some had already been captured in American jeeps or in German tanks disguised to look like U.S. Shermans. Everyone was on heightened alert, and word had gone out that any Germans caught in U.S. uniforms would be executed as spies. Some had been shot on the spot.

Victor and his team, in their mad dash to leave Wiltz, had not learned the day's password. One of the IPW members explained as much, in his German accent. A score of guns were leveled at them. Another interrogator spoke up, but he was a native German as well. Victor, who at least had the advantage of a French accent, asked the MPs if there was some other way for them to prove they were U.S. soldiers.

"What's the Windy City?" asked one MP warily.

Victor had no idea, and neither did anyone else.

"Look, we're all newly naturalized U.S. citizens," Victor said, pleading their case. "Give us another chance."

"Who won this year's World Series?"

None of the foreign-born GIs followed American baseball.

Victor had a grim feeling they were facing some itchy trigger fingers. Protesting their innocence, he demanded the MPs take them to their superior officer. With arms raised and hands behind their heads, they were escorted like captured POWs to a command post, where Victor did some fast talking, explaining that they were a special military intelligence team of German-language interrogators. He and his men all showed their dog tags. Finally their story was believed, and they were sent on their way with the day's password and a warning to "not speak Kraut." Victor knew it had been a close shave at the roadblock. To have come this far in the war only to be shot by their own men was not something Victor or anyone else on his IPW team wanted to think about.

Not long after they crossed into Belgium, they were driving through a village when it came under heavy mortar attack. Pulling up in front of a house, they jumped from the jeep and rushed into a cellar. Inside, they found a group of terrified villagers, waiting out the attack. The wails of the children and loud prayers of the adults could barely be heard over the screaming incoming mortar shells that shook the earth and the foundation above them. Victor had slashed a knee jumping down the cellar steps, and blood was streaming down his leg. When the shelling stopped, bursts of tommy guns and small-arms fire could be heard outside along with shouted commands in German. The village was being stormed and houses searched—and their U.S. Army jeeps were sitting out front!

The Ritchie Boys had to make a fast decision. Stay where they were and risk getting caught by the Germans or take a chance and run for the jeeps? For Victor, being cornered and captured was worse than taking a risk. The others agreed, and up the stairs they bounded and dashed to their jeeps, which miraculously were still untouched and parked where they had left them. They sped out of town without any shots fired.

Victor did not forget the cries and prayers of the frightened villagers and often wondered what became of them. One German potato-masher grenade thrown down the stairs into the cellar was all it would have taken to kill them all. What was certain, and had been since Normandy, was that he no longer harbored any heroic illusions about war, as he once had. He had seen too much violent and senseless death.

Early the next morning, Victor and his team were approaching a wood shrouded in fog and snow southwest of Bastogne when a German armored column bore down on them. Abandoning their jeeps, they ran into the forest, where they found a couple of hundred stragglers from the 28th Division, mostly cooks, typists, and clerks. Suddenly, General Cota appeared and began to address them. Cota was angry and determined, a pistol in one hand and a crazy plan in the other. This was tough "Dutch" Cota, known for helping to rally the troops off Omaha Beach in the early hours of the invasion and saving that bloodied assault force from being pushed back into the sea. Cota spotted Victor's chevrons and stripes, and concluded that as a master sergeant he must be a veteran warrior.

"Sergeant, take your men and dig in," he ordered. "Let the tanks pass and take care of the following infantry."

My men? Dig in the frozen ground? Take care of the infantry? Victor's thoughts raced. They all could now hear the ominous rumble and clatter of enemy tanks. This was the last day of his life, he was sure. Victor thought of his parents getting the news at their apartment on West 72nd Street, and how stupid he had been to not take the cushy job with the colonel in Paris. Regular trips to London? *Wonderful. Sign me up.*

"I'll shoot any bastard who runs," growled the general.

Cota, as if reading Victor's doubts, looked right at him.

They rushed to take up positions on the icy ground just as a tank appeared at the edge of a tree line one hundred feet away. Victor saw it was a much-feared German heavy tank known as a Tiger. He recognized it from the long barrel of its main 88 mm gun even though it was painted in camouflage colors. He had never actually seen a real German tank—just the wooden mockups used for identification courses at Camp Ritchie.

The tank pivoted its obscenely long barrel directly at them and fired a single shot. The ammunition truck parked on the road behind them exploded in a booming fireball that sent fragments flying.

Victor lay dazed on the ground. When he looked up, he was alone. Even the crazy general was gone. At first, he could not find the jeep and thought someone had driven off with it. He staggered around until he found his team members waiting for him with the engine running. They skidded away on the dirt road with other soldiers hanging onto the back.

When his head cleared, Victor checked the map. His teammates called him "a wizard" for his map-reading skill and his reliable sense of direction; time and again he had found the best escape route whenever they were in tight situations just as his father had done years earlier to save the family. Victor now decided to bypass their original destination, Bastogne, and veer northward on rural roads for Aywaille, which he thought would be secure because it was the headquarters of the XVIII Airborne Corps. Once again his instincts saved the day, as a column of tanks from the 2nd Panzer Division, which had crossed the Our River fifteen miles east of Wiltz over a portable bridge, was at that moment on the road to Bastogne, which was about to be encircled.

As a Brombert, Victor had been making good on escapes all his life.

The snow-covered Ardennes was deemed not only an ideal location for rest and reorganization of veteran combat units like the 28th Division after its mauling in the Hürtgen Forest, but was also a training site for new and untested infantry units, like the 106th Infantry Division, fresh off the *Queen Mary* from America.

U.S. Army brass regarded the Ardennes as a comparatively safe section of the European front. Even though one of the opening battles of World War I had been fought here, it had yet to see combat in World War II, as its rugged hills and few east-west roads made it an unlikely setting for large-scale troop and armored movements. Furthermore, Allied Intelligence believed that the enemy units opposite the Belgian-German border consisted of only a couple of Volksgrenadier divisions filled out with jobless naval and aviation personnel from the ever-shrinking Kriegsmarine and Luftwaffe, wounded soldiers returning to duty from hospitals, and others considered too young or old or unfit for frontline units. GIs referred to this backwater sector as the Kindergarten Front or the Old Men Front. Judged by intelligence estimates to be two-thirds the strength of regular Wehrmacht infantry divisions and to have received minimal training, the Volksgrenadier divisions were not regarded as a serious offensive threat. Allied planners did not believe the German army, reeling from losses across France and at Hürtgen Forest, had the strength to attack in force through the Ardennes or anywhere else.

They were wrong. More than twenty-five German infantry and armored divisions—nearly a half million men and six hundred tanks—had massed in western Germany for Hitler's last-ditch offensive. At a December 11 briefing at his new headquarters, a hundred miles away in Adlerhorst, Hitler had set the date for the attack for December 16 and ordered his commanders to break through the Ardennes and capture Antwerp in a week. As far back as August, Hitler had been planning a surprise, all-out offensive to isolate and destroy large numbers of American and British forces and weaken the resolve of the Allies. If his roll of the dice in the Ardennes worked, Hitler confidently predicted the Allies would never recover from the massive surprise attack and would seek a negotiated peace to end the war in Europe. "This battle is to decide whether we shall live or die," lectured the Führer. "I want all my soldiers to fight hard and without pity. The battle must be fought with brutality and all resistance must be broken in a wave of terror."

In early December, the 106th Infantry Division arrived in the Ardennes, its soldiers drenched and miserable after the cold, rainy journey across France and Belgium in open trucks. The 106th was the newest Allied division on any front in the war. It was not only the greenest U.S. division in the Ardennes, it was the first to go into combat with a substantial number of eighteen-year-old draftees, which made it the youngest division in all of Europe. They arrived to relieve the 2nd Infantry Division, which had fought at Omaha Beach and the Saint-Lô breakthrough, then raced to Brest to capture that heavily defended fortress. After a period of rest and refitting in the Ardennes, the battle-wise soldiers of the 2nd were pulling out for a new assignment: to spearhead an attack to seize the Roer River dams in northern Germany.

"Man by man and gun by gun," as its orders read, the 106th took over the positions the 2nd had been holding for two months at the southern shoulder of VIII Corps. Assigned to an area three times greater than an infantry division would normally cover, the young soldiers of the 106th were dispersed along a twenty-seven-mile front. Customarily the 106th would have held one of its three infantry regiments in reserve several miles back, to be in position to counterattack an enemy thrust anywhere along its front. But they were left with no other option than to stretch thin all three regiments—about six thousand men in total—along the front.

The men of the 423rd regiment, commanded by Colonel Charles Cavender, moved into their positions at the center of the 106th's line on December 11, with sister regiments to the north (422nd) and the south (424th). Cavender's regiment was responsible for an eight-mile-wide sector several miles inside Germany. Typically, an infantry regiment would be asked to hold only a front of perhaps two miles in such challenging territory.

With Christmas only days away, the soldiers manned roadblocks, sentry outposts, and foxholes already dug into the snow-covered terrain, all while hoping that their mail and packages from home would find them. "It has been very quiet here and your men will learn the easy way," Cavender, a forty-seven-year-old Texan, was assured by his 2nd Division counterpart upon that division's departure.

The next morning, Cavender inspected his regiment's positions along the front. His southern flank started in the coal-mining town of Bleialf, situated at a key east-west access point, and extended northward around the southern nose of a two-thousand-foot ridge-line amid forested peaks known as the Schnee Eifel (Snowy Mountains). Just north of the Schnee Eifel lay a long, narrow valley that served as a natural corridor between Germany and Belgium. Called the Losheim Gap, it had been the gateway used by attacking Germans in 1870 during the Franco-Prussian War, and again in 1914 and 1940 when they invaded Belgium and France.

Cavender, who began his army career as a private in 1917 before graduating from West Point in 1923, was aware of what a precarious situation his regiment was in. The next day, December 13, Major General Alan Jones, division commander of the 106th, met Cavender at his command post in Buchet, a farming village in the center of his regimental front. Cavender pointed out the corridor at his northern flank and asked, "Where is the help in case [we are] attacked up here? Where is the armor? Where is the help?"

Jones told Cavender that he had asked the VIII Corps commander the same questions and was told: "'There is no help. There is no armor in case of an attack in force through Schnee Eifel. You will have to stay and slug it out.'"

Like it or not, Jones told Cavender, that was the situation.

With that, Jones was on his way back across the Belgian border to Saint Vith, fifteen miles away, to his division command post.

The 423rd was one of two 106th regiments—along with the 422nd—positioned across the German border facing the enemy with their backs to the Our River. They were so far out in front that they represented the farthest eastward penetration of Allied forces into Germany. It was as if the two rookie regiments were being dangled enticingly in front of the enemy. But the quaint villages and towns scattered in valleys ringed by snowy, wooded hills were very quiet. For the troops, the only ominous note so far was a road sign their trucks had passed entering Germany:

YOU ARE ENTERING

GERMANY

AN ENEMY COUNTRY

KEEP ON THE ALERT

The 106th Division had its own Ritchie Boys. An IPW team made up of six graduates of Camp Ritchie was assigned to the division in early December, with three men each sent to the 422nd and 423rd regiments.

The interrogators who arrived at the 423rd command post in Buchet were Second Lieutenant John Seale, twenty-eight, an American who had learned passable German in school; Sergeant Kurt Jacobs, stocky, and at thirty-four considered the team's old man; and its youngest member, Technician Fifth Grade Murray Zappler, twenty, who with his dark hair and swarthy good looks could have passed for a Spaniard. Jacobs and Zappler were German Jews who had become naturalized U.S. citizens prior to shipping overseas.

Jacobs had received a law degree in Berlin in 1932, and he had fled Germany after Hitler came to power—first for Paris, then to Buffalo, New York. He spoke English with a robust German accent. Zappler, whose family had left Germany when he was six years old, had gone to a German grammar school in Belgium before emigrating to the United States, where he graduated high school in New York City. Zappler spoke German fluently—he had also studied the language for a year at the University of Pennsylvania in the ASTP program—and his English bore not a hint of his ancestry but rather carried the accent of his adopted home: the Bronx. Zappler and Seale both graduated from Camp Ritchie's Nineteenth Class in July 1944, and Jacobs from the next class a month later. While they had all done well in their course work, Jacobs, the Berlin lawyer, had received the highest grades. But when the three Ritchie Boys arrived in Buchet, none of them had ever interrogated an actual German prisoner.

When the surprise German attack commenced at 5:30 A.M. on

December 16, with artillery and mortar fire along the entire Ardennes front, Cavender alerted his units to prepare for an all-out enemy ground assault. German artillery quickly zeroed in on the regimental supply yard, destroying a number of vehicles and much of the 423rd's extra ammunition.

As the enemy barrage began to lift shortly after 6 A.M., German infantrymen attacked Bleialf from three directions. Located in the Alf River valley, Bleialf was a village of about a hundred houses clustered around an eleventh-century church. By now, most residents had evacuated. At the southern end of town was a railway station and tunnel that the Germans had used as an underground factory facility. About a mile away, atop a hill to the southeast, was the town of Brandscheid, from which Germans observed U.S. positions.

The attackers seemed to emerge from nowhere, clad in snow-white camouflage and ghostlike in the reflective glow of searchlights bouncing off the clouds. Before the 423rd knew what was happening, the Germans were upon them, firing their weapons at point-blank range and exploding grenades in yards and alleyways. Soldiers on both sides died in the streets and in houses, some shot, some blown up, and others stabbed with bayonets or clubbed to death with rifle butts. The Americans fought hard, but the numbers favored the Germans, and by 8 A.M. the enemy held most of the town, with GIs resisting in isolated groups.

From his command post two miles away, Cavender ordered reinforcements to Bleialf. He sent a company of combat engineers and another of service personnel such as clerks and cooks, for a total of about 170 men. Although few of them had handled a rifle since basic training, this motley force counterattacked with the support of an effective barrage by the regiment's artillery unit, fired from the heights northeast of town. In bitter house-to-house and hand-to-hand fighting, the Americans rallied and cleared the enemy out by 3 P.M. The Germans were left holding only a few houses down the road toward the train station.

During the fighting, thirty Germans were taken prisoner. Jacobs and Zappler hurried into Bleialf to conduct interrogations, and spent the rest of that day and night questioning the prisoners in a requisitioned house. They learned that the units that had attacked Bleialf and the southern flank of the regiment were from the 18th Volksgrenadier Division, which had been formed in Denmark three months earlier by redesignating an older Volksgrenadier unit and absorbing elements of a Luftwaffe field division. They had moved into the area days earlier to take part in what the Germans called the Rundstedt Offensive, named for their commander in chief in the west, Field Marshal Gerd von Rundstedt.

A vital piece of information was revealed by one prisoner during his interrogation: another attack on Bleialf was planned for the next morning by the 293rd Regiment of the 18th Volksgrenadier. He said the assault would be preceded by an artillery barrage and rockets fired from launchers in the surrounding hills. Cavender considered the intelligence so important, he ordered the interrogators to send their report directly to division headquarters, while he also urgently requested reinforcements.

Patrols reported German armor, followed by infantry, moving into position outside of Bleialf by 3 A.M. At the same time, the enemy began firing artillery and rockets from nearby hills, and they were landing in and around the town. This prelude to a large attack corroborated the new intelligence, and as if right on cue, the second leg of the assault began at 6 A.M. on December 17. Waves of enemy troops and tanks pushed down the deserted streets, overrunning pockets of U.S. defenders and driving them back. With the key crossroads back in their control, the enemy rolled infantry and tank columns through Bleialf, pushing up the Schönberg road toward Saint Vith, sealing off any escape to the west. As they did, German troops poured through the Losheim Gap and dropped down from the Schnee Eifel ridge directly into the northern flank of the 423rd.

With both his flanks smashed and having lost contact with his artillery battalion, Cavender now found his center under attack.

His own regimental defense platoon of thirty men, along with clerks and staff, was desperately defending his command post in Buchet. At 10:51 A.M., Cavender radioed division: "Will hold our perimeter. [Air] Drop ammunition, food and medical supplies until route open. We have no artillery."

Cavender had no choice but to await the airdrop and armored column that division said was on the way to reinforce his regiment, but neither ever arrived. Adverse weather prevented the planes from flying, and the relief column got caught in its own fight en route. Meanwhile the situation for his men turned dire. Blocked on all sides, without sleep or food, low on ammunition, and running out of medical supplies to treat the wounded, they fought on until the Germans, satisfied with having achieved the encirclement, diminished the fury of their attack.

On the third night, Cavender, along with 422nd regimental commander Colonel George Descheneaux, received orders to attack along the Schönberg road and drive toward division headquarters at Saint Vith. To carry out the order, the 423rd would have to break out of the enemy encirclement. When Descheneaux read the orders, he bowed his head and mumbled, "My poor men. They'll be cut to pieces."

When night fell, Cavender took his beleaguered regiment northwest through the Alf Valley toward the Schönberg road and the Our River. The woods were thick, and it was very dark and muddy. The weapons carriers and command jeeps became bogged down, and his three battalions had difficulty staying in contact. German patrols weaved in and out of the area, preventing contact between the 423rd and 422nd, which was to be following but at what distance Cavender did not know. Due to enemy jamming and the weather, radio communication was erratic. He had lost contact with division after their last message.

As Cavender's lead elements emerged from the valley into a ravine, they were hit by a barrage of artillery and mortar fire. A patrol reported back that thirty German tanks and self-propelled guns were massed on their right flank and another column of armor was to their front, between their position and the Our River. They could go neither forward nor back.

Cavender set up a command post on a wooded hill and summoned his unit commanders; he asked them for their assessments. In the four days of fighting since the German offensive began, the 1st Battalion had suffered so many casualties it had ceased to exist as a fighting unit; the 2nd Battalion, apparently lost in the dark, had disappeared during the night; and the 3rd Battalion had been reduced to half strength. His infantrymen had no ammo remaining except for the few rounds each man carried. They had no artillery support or air cover. Food and medical supplies had run out, and some of the wounded were on the verge of dying unless they got proper attention soon.

Sensing the decision the colonel was weighing, one officer said, "I know it's no use fighting, but I still don't want to surrender."

"I was a GI in the First World War," Cavender said, "and I want to see things from a soldier's standpoint." He had seen too much bloodshed in the trenches of that war to sacrifice his men for a lost cause in this war.

He was silent for a moment, then looked at his watch.

"Gentlemen, we're surrendering at 1600 hours."

At that same hour and a mile away, Descheneaux of the 422nd, which was also outnumbered and ringed by enemy tanks, was reaching the same decision.

Cavender gave his men thirty minutes to smash their weapons and get rid of any German souvenirs. Then a staff officer stood atop a vehicle waving a white flag, yelling, "We surrender! We surrender!"

Before sunset, approximately three thousand U.S. soldiers from the two regiments assigned days earlier to a "very quiet" area in the Ardennes just across the German border became prisoners of war.* The next day, columns of U.S. prisoners trudged deeper into Germany, bound for POW camps. They were passed in the opposite direction by countless Panzer tanks, artillery batteries pulled by vehicles and horses, and nonstop columns of fresh Wehrmacht reinforcements.

That morning, a group of three hundred GIs from the 423rd, prisoners of the 2nd Battalion, 293rd Regiment, 18th Volksgrenadier, marched under armed guard down the Schönberg road toward Bleialf. Ritchie Boys Jacobs and Zappler were among them, along with the thirty Germans, also of the 2nd Battalion, whom they had interrogated after their capture in Bleialf on December 16. Now liberated, the ex-POWs walked in front of the group of Americans, heading back to rejoin their units.

Not far from the border and still more than a mile north of Bleialf, the group came to a customs house where for many years routine inspections of goods passing in and out of Germany had been conducted. Wehrmacht *Hauptmann* (captain) Curt Bruns, commander of the 2nd Battalion, had his command post there. A stocky twenty-nine-year-old redhead, Bruns was born on Juist, an island in the southern North Sea off the northern coast of Germany. He had commanded the battalion for nearly a year.

Spotting their battalion commander, two of the liberated German prisoners who had been interrogated by Jacobs and Zappler rushed over to Bruns and reported they had been interrogated by a pair of "Jews from Berlin." Bruns told them to bring the Jews to him.

Jacobs and Zappler were separated from the other Americans, who continued moving down the road toward Bleialf with their hands over their heads. When the interrogators were brought to

---

* Including the men of the 422nd and 423rd Infantry Regiments who surrendered on December 19, 1944, the 106th Infantry Division and its attached units lost within days 6,879 men captured, one of the largest mass surrenders in American military history.

Bruns, he stood them against the wall of the customs house as he questioned them. Had they interrogated his men in German? They confirmed they had. How was it possible they spoke such good German?

Jacobs explained that he had been a law student in Berlin.

Bruns asked a few more questions. Then, in front of his men, several of whom had been held captive by the Americans, Bruns said: *"Juden haben kein Recht, in Deutschland zu leben."* (The Jews have no right to live in Germany.)

Bruns huddled with one of his sergeants, Werner Hoffman, who commanded a platoon in the 2nd Battalion and was known among his men as an ardent Nazi. Then Hoffman went off to round up four other corporals and sergeants and brought them over to where the interrogators were still standing with their backs to the wall.

Jacobs now pleaded their case like the trial lawyer he had once hoped to be, beseeching that he and Zappler be treated as prisoners of war under the terms of the Geneva Conventions, as the captured German soldiers had been treated in Bleialf. The two Ritchie Boys were escorted down the road toward Bleialf, but any hope they may have had of being taken to rejoin the other American prisoners, who were now out of sight, was dashed. After two hundred yards they were directed to step off the road into an open field. They walked another thirty paces and were then told to halt.

Kurt Jacobs and Murray Zappler were ordered to keep their backs to the Germans now lining up abreast of one another. The two men stood facing a meandering stream a short distance in front of them, behind it a forest of evergreens that blanketed rolling hills covered in a fresh snowfall during the night.

They were then cut down by a thundering volley of rifle fire.

Werner Angress and the other paratroopers of the 82nd Airborne rested after the campaign in Holland and were reequipped at Camp Sissonne, a former French artillery base in northern France. They all waited expectantly for their promised Christmas leave, with most of them hoping they could enjoy themselves in Paris. A lucky few got leave in late November, but Werner was not one of them.

On the night of December 17, he was having a beer in the base canteen talking with buddies about what they were planning to do in Paris when a duty officer rushed in and said the division had been put on alert.

"Everyone report to your quarters immediately!"

Back at the barracks, they were told to pack for combat.

"Airborne?" someone asked.

"Not airborne. Infantry operation."

Anything not needed for combat, such as dress uniforms and shoes, went into duffel bags that were stored at the base. Ammunition and rations were distributed along with other supplies.

By dawn and minus a night's sleep, the men of the 82nd were ready, even if they were in no mood to return to action so soon. Big-rig tractor-trailers had pulled onto the base during the night, and the men, loaded down with weapons and equipment, climbed into the open trucks for a thirteen-hour ride to the Ardennes.

By December 18, the third day of the enemy offensive that would become known as the Battle of the Bulge, the entire center of VIII Corps had collapsed. Into this gap the Germans threw hundreds of thousands of fighting men and many hundreds of Panzer tanks to achieve a "bulge" sixty miles deep and forty-five miles wide that split the Allies' armies.

It was a freezing ride for the troopers of the 82nd. With no room to sit, they stood and swayed in the trucks like cattle going to the auction yard. They did not know exactly where they were going, having been told only that the Germans had broken through into Belgium. They also did not know until later that the last of their convoy cleared a crossroads in Belgium just minutes ahead of a fast-moving Panzer armored division. Suddenly they heard a rumbling, and the men in their rearguard jeep looked back to see Tiger and Panther tanks rolling through the intersection toward Bastogne, which had been the convoy's destination until it was changed en route to Werbomont, thirty miles farther north. Jammed shoulder to shoulder in the trucks, the paratroopers would have been in no position to fight enemy tanks.

The GIs didn't know this at the time, but U.S. infantry and armored divisions were hurrying to eastern Belgium to halt the German advance before it reached Antwerp. If they failed in this mission, it would delay the invasion of the German homeland and extend the war. As for the airborne divisions, the 101st had been sent to Bastogne to hold the southern shoulder against the enemy penetration, and the 82nd was to pinch in from the north.

Arriving at Werbomont, located at a vital junction along the Bastogne-Liège line, the 82nd fanned out in the dark to take up positions on high ground. The dull boom of artillery from the east was the only indication of the enemy's close proximity.

Werner hurried for the nearby headquarters of the 106th Infantry, the division the 82nd was reinforcing that had just relocated its headquarters from Wiltz after being pushed out of Luxembourg by the surprise German attack. He hoped that there he would be brought up to speed on the enemy forces and could mark their positions on a map for General Gavin and his staff. Along the way, Werner passed defensive positions that were being held by clerks, cooks, bakers, and others who clearly were not combat trained, manning antitank guns, mortars, and other weapons they did not know how to use. Some, he saw, were bent over trying to read instruction manuals.

Werner found the headquarters, a farmhouse, and stepped into the dimly lit room. In his nearly four years in the army, he had never witnessed such a wild scene. Officers who were supposed to stay calm and controlled were panicked and confused. There were fragmented reports about two Allied regiments on the other side of the German border having gone missing, amid countless sightings of German infantry and tanks that had pushed through Luxembourg and were advancing farther into Belgium. The air corps was adamant that the weather was still below minimums, thus keeping their aircraft grounded and the German attackers immune from air strikes.

Werner approached a colonel who seemed to be at the center of things, and said he was with the intelligence staff of the 82nd Airborne and had been sent to gather intelligence about enemy forces. Obviously shocked by his accent, the colonel stared wide-eyed at Werner, then bellowed: "He's a damn German! Arrest him!"

Werner pointed to the U.S. flag sewed onto the shoulder of his jumpsuit jacket, forgetting it had faded to white from so many washings.

"We're finding Germans in American uniforms," said the colonel, convinced that he had nabbed a spy.

Werner knew he was in a bind because the 82nd was not yet on the local communications net, so he couldn't have the colonel call his superiors. For half an hour, when they both should have been attending to more pressing matters, he tried reasoning with the officer, explaining his background and duties as a German-born U.S. Army interrogator of German prisoners of war.

"Colonel, if I was really the enemy, it would make very little sense for me to come in here asking for information *about* the enemy. And to brazenly walk into a divisional headquarters? Alone?"

Several junior officers seemed to be enjoying the confrontation, smiling and winking at Werner, indicating that the colonel was crazy and that Werner shouldn't be overly concerned. Still, it wasn't sorted out until Werner convinced the colonel to send someone to find the 82nd Airborne. Soon an airborne staff officer arrived to vouch for Werner.

Early the next morning, the enemy attacked the newly arrived paratroopers with armor thrusts by thirty to forty tanks supported by infantry. Over the next several days, the 82nd stalled the enemy assault, then began advancing eastward against the German front lines. They moved on foot, like infantrymen, dragging behind them in the foot-high snow sleds packed with extra ammunition and supplies.

When they came across a badly wounded paratrooper lying in the snow at the edge of a road, Werner saw that a medic was giving the man first aid. Just then, an artillery round whistled overhead. Like everyone around him, Werner hit the ground. When he stood up after the nearby explosion, which sent snow and dirt flying in all directions, Werner saw that the medic and his patient lay dead.

Such were the dangers around them; they spent most of the time in the open, subject to nearly constant enemy artillery fire. At night they dug foxholes in the frozen earth, unless they were lucky enough to find some previously dug by retreating Germans, which they used, giving thanks for the unintended hospitality. Fir tree branches served as mattresses.

The IPW teams often had the freedom to operate independently, and one night Werner decided to join one of the regiment's battalions in the hope that they would take some new prisoners he could interrogate. The 82nd was fighting units of the 6th Panzer Army, and General Gavin and his staff officers needed good, timely intelligence about the enemy's strength, weaponry, and capabilities.

When he found no new prisoners waiting at the battalion command post, Werner moved even closer to the front lines, where he knew it was often easier to get information from newly captured prisoners while they were still in shock. He also liked the camaraderie of being with smaller units that were closer to the front because there wasn't all the saluting and formality of headquarters. Many officers close to the action didn't want to be saluted for fear of being picked off by enemy snipers. He found the battalion's machine gun company dug in at the top of a hill. Locating an unoccupied foxhole, he settled in for the night. Shortly after midnight, Werner witnessed his first nighttime German infantry attack by the light of rocket-launched flares. Cheering and shouting encouragement to one another, SS soldiers charged uphill like zealots, straight into the machine gun fire of the paratroopers. Even as the German bodies began to stack up, the SS kept coming, trying frantically to crest the hill and overwhelm the U.S. company.

Suddenly, two Americans ran past Werner, headed to the rear. He recognized them as the captain, who was the company commander, and his top sergeant. They were fleeing to safety! This meant the machine gunners were now leaderless. Werner, who was firing his own weapon at the shadowy figures charging up the hill, knew he had no business taking over the company. But who else would do it? Just then, he heard a young Jewish lieutenant he knew, a platoon leader in the company who was in the foxhole next to him, yell in an authoritative voice: "I have command!"

In the face of the enemy's fanatical charge, the lieutenant issued all the right commands. Under his steady hand, none of the Americans broke from their positions and the attack was thwarted. At dawn, Werner climbed from the foxhole and crept from one dead German to the next, searching their pockets for documents that might contain important information. While dead enemy soldiers were less valuable than live ones, they served a purpose, too.

Werner never again saw the company commander or the sergeant who had deserted their men. He later learned they had both been court-martialed and convicted of cowardice under enemy fire.

New Year's found Werner and his IPW team in an abandoned farmhouse in Haute-Bodeux, a village thirty miles south of Liège. Together with the regimental intelligence section, they spent several days there, enjoying the heat from a wood-burning stove.

One day, a tough-looking German sergeant was brought in for questioning. He was no longer youthful looking, and the numerous decorations on his tunic showed that he had fought in many battles. He acknowledged Werner curtly, then started telling his young interrogator that he knew his rights under the Geneva Conventions and would provide only his name, rank, and serial number. As Werner began to question him, the prisoner kept his word.

Werner had found that few prisoners invoked the international treaties when facing an interrogator's questions. In most cases, they talked freely, either out of plain fear or in the hope that if they coop-

erated they would somehow be rewarded. But this veteran warrior
was having none of that.

Werner shrugged and sat back. Addressing the prisoner as *Spiess*
(First Sergeant), he inquired in German just how such an experienced old bird like him was taken prisoner by a bunch of young
Yankees. Offended, the prisoner began to stutter in response, then
exploded in indignation. As the sergeant spewed an angry torrent of
words, Werner interrupted with brief tactical questions, all of which
were promptly answered before the sergeant continued his diatribe.
In this way, Werner soon knew the identity and strength of the sergeant's unit, the names of his commanders, and other information.

All the while, Werner looked terribly bored, even yawning occasionally. He always wanted a prisoner to think the information he
was providing was routine and unimportant and that it was nothing
the Americans didn't already know. For the same reason, Werner
never took notes during an interrogation. He had found that these
techniques tended to put prisoners at ease and keep them talking.

Finally, Werner had another stroke of insight and he challenged
the sergeant again, saying he no doubt was unable to read a U.S.
military map.

"Natürlich kann ich das!" the prisoner shouted. (Of course I can!)

Werner pulled out a map, and soon he knew where the sergeant's
regimental headquarters was located, where their machine guns
were placed, and even where the German soldiers lined up to get
their chow.

Once Werner had run out of questions, he stood, wished the
sergeant well, gave him a few cigarettes, and they shook hands. As
soon as the prisoner was taken away by an MP, Werner grabbed a
notebook and wrote down everything the sergeant had told him.
Then he typed up his report, which provided valuable new targeting information for the regiment's artillery batteries, and sent it
straight to headquarters.

At Camp Ritchie, Werner had been graded down for interrogations because he refused to scream and act abusively, which the pig-headed examiner insisted was the only way to treat prisoners of war. Without being boastful, Werner felt as though his own approach had been validated, and he knew he had become a good interrogator. His efforts in the field had earned him two promotions in three months, the final one that winter in the Ardennes, when he sewed on master sergeant stripes. However, there was one interrogation during the Battle of the Bulge of which he was not proud.

In early January, Werner was with the First Battalion of the 508th as they advanced slowly eastward in ice and snow against stiff German resistance. After one very long day, they had stopped late at night, and Werner was trying to find a dry place to sleep when he was summoned to the command post in a farmhouse. The intelligence officer said they were surrounded by Germans and had lost contact with the rest of the regiment. Being surrounded was nothing new to an airborne unit, because they regularly parachuted behind enemy lines, but the officer said it was vital they find out which enemy units had them encircled. Some recently captured prisoners were being brought in, he told Werner, and they needed to quickly extract from them any valuable intelligence they had about the strength and ca-pabilities of the German forces that had them surrounded.

Shortly, Werner was facing three German enlisted men. From their *Soldbücher*—pay books—he saw they had previously served in the Luftwaffe as ground troops. But their pay records didn't indicate to which infantry unit the men had been transferred, so that's where Werner started. To speed things up, he decided to interrogate them all at once, which was not something he or other interrogators nor-mally did because it could give them a sense of solidarity and safety, and they could support one another in refusing to say anything.

He started asking his questions, but none of them said a word. He tried everything that had worked in the past for him, but they remained silent. A few troopers who had brought in the prisoners were crowded into the kitchen where Werner was conducting the interrogations. Seeing the trouble he was having, they offered to beat up the prisoners. Werner said no to that, but in a sudden moment of recklessness, he turned to the prisoners and said the GIs would shoot them if they didn't talk. Still nothing. When Werner told the troopers what he had threatened to do, they grinned. One said he would gladly take care of that for Werner.

By now, Werner was feeling uneasy at how things were proceeding. The battalion had been constantly on the move, fighting much of the time, and most of the men hadn't slept or eaten properly for days. Everyone's nerves were shot, his included. Now the battalion was surrounded by Germans, of unknown strength and capabilities, and Werner urgently needed to get accurate information.

Werner again demanded that the prisoners answer his questions, but no one said anything. Finally, he told them he would count to ten. If he reached ten, and they continued to refuse, they would be shot.

He started counting out loud.

"Eins. Zwei. Drei. Vier . . ."

When Werner reached nine, the senior noncom spoke up, giving the number of the unit to which they had recently been transferred.

As it turned out, they were stragglers who hadn't found their new unit, so they knew nothing about its strength or fighting capability. In other words, their information was useless. The entire scene, Werner realized, had turned into a terrible farce. He was exhausted, frustrated, and had felt pressured to get results in order to save American lives. But how close had he really come to letting one of his prisoners be shot only to force the other two into revealing nothing of importance?

There was so much killing on both sides, and Werner had seen and done his share. Was there a difference between shooting an enemy soldier charging up a hill or throwing a hand grenade at enemy machine gunners, and killing prisoners of war in order to gain valuable information to save American lives? He believed there was. You killed someone who was trying to kill you or your buddies, but not someone who was unarmed and at your mercy, such as a prisoner of war. As drained as he had been that night, mentally and physically, and as much pressure as he had been under in that farmhouse, he refused to rationalize it later. He never forgave himself or forgot what he might have caused that wintry night of war.

Werner did not hate the enemy prisoners he interrogated, although some—especially the SS soldiers and their haughty officers—were difficult to take when they flashed their Master Race arrogance. But most of the prisoners he interrogated were conscripts, and some of them had been forced to serve in the German army from conquered territories. Now, as prisoners of war, they were defenseless and scared, much as he had been when he was taken prisoner in Normandy. He knew how it felt.

He never told any of the thousands of Germans he interrogated that he was a German Jew, although he thought some guessed it. Whenever he was asked why he spoke such good German, his standard reply, "I am an American of German descent," was correct as well as incomplete.

Often he was asked by prisoners—usually in whispers—whether they would be tortured or shot. No doubt they had seen, if not taken part in, such acts by their own forces. To this question, he also had a standard response.

"No," Werner Angress always said. "After all, we're not Nazis."

10

RETURN TO DEUTSCHLAND

After the breakout of Allied forces from Normandy in July 1944, Guy Stern's team joined with three other IPW teams assigned to the First Army's cage. For these twenty-four German-speaking interrogators, being assigned to the headquarters of a large army of more than a dozen divisions and some three hundred thousand soldiers meant their job was to concentrate less on gathering tactical intelligence—the location of local defenses and the strength of nearby enemy forces—and more on obtaining big-picture strategic intelligence for the generals to use in planning the next major battle or campaign of the war.

The cage never stayed in one place for long but moved to wherever headquarters relocated. For security reasons, it was never closer than a mile or so from where First Army commanding general Courtney Hodges met with his staff, but it was also near enough for the interrogators to easily access it day or night. Both during and after the Battle of the Bulge in December 1944, and into early 1945, German prisoners of war were locked up in the First Army's cage by the thousands.

The setup of the cage had not changed since it went up at Foucarville near the invasion beaches a week after D-Day. It was made of high, barbed-wire fences and had sectioned-off common areas, some the size of city blocks, as well as smaller holding pens. On sites chosen by the provost marshal, army engineers had become adept at disassembling and raising the interlocking pieces of the cage, like traveling circus workers rapidly putting up their big top in what had been an empty field. The prisoners were guarded by a company-sized MP unit, which prevented them from escaping, escorted them back and forth to interrogations, and assisted in their eventual transfer to more permanent POW camps.

Since Guy's promotion in Normandy to head Survey, he had been collating and evaluating intelligence in response to specific requests from higher-ups. Guy loved the big-picture lens his new job gave him. Much as he had done in high school as a star reporter for the school paper, whether it was interviewing Thomas Mann or Benny Goodman, he researched his subjects thoroughly, then wrote about them in engaging detail; only now, his work wasn't for a student body readership but for Allied commanders and war planners. His regular "Special Reports" were distributed to more than forty higher commands, including Eisenhower's Supreme Headquarters Allied Expeditionary Force (SHAEF), then based in Versailles. One of Guy's projects, urgently requested by SHAEF, was to prepare a report on the German railroad system. He had been given a list of questions, and to answer them, he and other interrogators questioned a total of 150 prisoners who had formerly worked for the German railroad. They selected only prisoners who had worked on the railroad as recently as September 1944 to ensure their information was current. Guy's report—dated January 9, 1945—found that due to Allied air strikes and German retreats, there was a growing shortage of locomotives and rolling stock, and he was able to paint a vivid picture of the German railroad workers. Guy described them as "dutiful but tired men and women, 95 percent of them [Nazi] Party members," a requirement for getting the job. However, he believed their "devotion to duty may be attributed more to a fear of consequences than their 'patriotic effort.'" Allied bomb-damage experts were perplexed by how the Germans were able to get the trains running so quickly after their tracks were destroyed by bombs. Guy discovered that the Germans had perfected prefabricated rail sections; when one was destroyed, they simply removed it at night and replaced it with a new section, and by morning the trains were running again. In conclusion, Guy wrote: "At present the German RR system is still in a surprisingly healthy condition. However, it appears as if manpower, material and lubricants are steadily getting worse. This, coupled with Allied air attacks, might in the near future bring about a serious disruption of the German RR system and therewith topple an already shaky overall transportation system." As a result of Guy's findings about prefabricated replacement tracks, Allied planners adjusted the schedule of their bombing missions; instead of hitting a railroad line or switching yard only once and assuming it would be out of commission for a long while, the bombers were assigned to go back in a day or two for another strike, and to keep returning.

The next week, Guy produced another report, "German Preparations for Chemical Warfare," which the staff of XXI Corps had requested. Germany had introduced poison gas in World War I in 1915, and the subsequent deployment of more than one hundred thousand tons of chemical weapons by both sides during that war had killed thirty thousand soldiers, including two thousand Americans. The terms of the Geneva Conventions prohibited the use of poison gas, but the Germans had already violated other terms of the treaties, so there was a growing concern that they might use it anyway, especially as the war turned against them. In researching this critical report, Guy drew up questions for interrogators to ask prisoners about the possibility of gas warfare. Some prisoners reported receiving training with gas masks, having to pass through a gas chamber and practice firing a rifle and machine gun while wearing one. Guy learned that German soldiers were told that gas would likely be distributed by airplanes, gas hand grenades, mines, artillery, and gas-filled metal flasks. He quoted one German company commander as telling his men that they should be very attentive to their chemical warfare training because "all indications point to the future use of gas." The soldiers were told that if anyone would use gas, it would probably be the Russians. Several divisions had compelled their troops to wear gas masks on the way to the front. But Guy estimated that at least 25 percent of German officers and soldiers did not believe in the probability of gas warfare, and demonstrated this by throwing away their unwieldly gas masks once they reached the front.

For Guy, the major takeaway of this study was that Germany had been preparing its soldiers to *defend* themselves from gas attacks, but had not trained them to use chemical warfare against others. The Germans were not, in his opinion, preparing to initiate gas warfare against Allied troops.

In conclusion, Guy wrote: "The German High Command keeps its soldiers, as well as German civilians, well aware of the possibility of gas warfare. The reaction of both, the civilians and soldiers, is one of great anxiety and foreboding. They believe that Germany would be the loser in every respect in case this kind of warfare is initiated."

When the First Army was ordered to retreat westward during the opening days of the Germans' Ardennes offensive in mid-December, its headquarters, along with the cage, was relocated from Herbesthal in northern Belgium to the town of Huy, thirty miles away. Prisoners awaiting interrogation were placed in the cells of a former Gestapo prison in the Citadel of Huy, on a cliff high above the town, overlooking the Meuse River. The large barbed-wire enclosures went up next to the Citadel. Just as the GIs were moving in, a wave of German V-1 rockets dropped on Huy, likely aiming for the town's main bridge over the Meuse. But the bombs hit everything except the bridge, setting some houses ablaze and blowing out the windows of others. One V-1 landed just outside the Citadel, sticking nose-first in the mud without exploding.

The fortresslike Citadel had withstood centuries of wars and occupations, and Guy was safely tucked inside during the attack, busily preparing a new report on the precise routing of German supplies such as fuel, ammunition, and food from the home front to the front lines. He looked up from his work and in sauntered a tall, square-shouldered replacement sergeant named Fred Howard, who would promote some exciting if often radical ideas that would help the First Army's interrogation teams spread out in new directions.

He had been born Manfred Ehrlich in Berlin, which he and his Jewish parents—his father owned a shoe store—fled in 1939 due to Nazi persecution. With the assistance of relatives who signed affidavits for them, they settled in New York City. When he entered the U.S. Army in early 1943 and became a U.S. citizen three months later, Manfred exchanged his German name for the all-American "Fred Howard." The surname owed to his fascination with the movie *The Scarlet Pimpernel,* starring Leslie Howard. After completing basic training, Fred was selected for the ASTP program and attended the City College of New York and Georgetown University before arriving at Camp Ritchie in February 1944. He graduated three months later, and was sent overseas in fall 1944. His first assignment had been to examine a cache of German documents at the former Gestapo headquarters in Paris before his transfer to First Army headquarters.

When the new man walked in, Guy immediately had a job for him. "Can you draw worth a damn?" he asked. The information Guy had collected for his latest report was solid, but he knew some graphics would help make the network of supply routes and transfer locations more comprehensible. His own artistic abilities were limited to rudimentary stick figures.

Guy was in luck, because Fred had worked as a designer in New York. His drawings to scale perfectly illustrated Guy's report, and a new partnership was forged. Over time, the two men realized how well they complemented each other, not just in skills but also in temperament: Fred, the wildly creative one with an abundance of chutzpah; and Guy, more disciplined and intellectual, providing both the anchor and counterpoint to Fred's free-flowing and at times outlandish ideas.

When Captain Rust, who in Normandy had put Guy in charge of Survey, decided to initiate a second special section called Targets, he tabbed Fred to head it. The mission was to provide bomber crews with the location of enemy industrial targets. The requests were straightforward enough, such as: "Supply map coordinates for new ball-bearing factory outside Schweinfurt." But what that meant was that Fred had to acquire accurate targeting information from German soldiers who had grown up in Schweinfurt and who probably had friends and relatives working in the factory. Fred had learned all the interrogation methods taught at Camp Ritchie, but

German-born Ritchie Boy Fred Howard served with Guy Stern at First Army headquarters. *(Family photograph)*

there was nothing routine about this kind of interrogation. Even the slowest-witted German knew that the information would be used to bomb his hometown, and many who had been cooperative and talkative up to that point began to clam up.

"How do I break these guys to get targeting information?" Fred asked Guy after another fruitless interrogation.

Guy started ticking off the four basic techniques of interrogation they had been taught at Camp Ritchie. To the first three, Fred said he'd tried them all. Impressing prisoners with what he knew to get them talking ("superior knowledge"), or offering them a cigarette or candy bar as a reward ("bribery"), or talking about a nonthreatening subject that interested them, like soccer ("find common interests")— none of them worked, Fred said, when it came to Targets. Then Guy got to number four: "Use of fear."

"Fear," Fred parroted. "Okay, Guy, you've been out here doing this longer than I have. What scares these SOBs the most?"

"That's easy," Guy answered. *"Sieg oder Sibirien."*

"Victory or Siberia?"

"To be taken prisoner by the Soviets is a fate worse than death."

Fred jumped up, excited. "Let's import a Ruskie!"

Guy shot down Fred's idea as impractical. While SHAEF had Soviet liaison officers at its headquarters, he pointed out, there were none assigned to the First Army.

In no more than a few seconds, Fred had another idea.

"How about one of us turning into a Russian?" he asked.

They took the idea to Captain Edgar Kann, formerly their second-ranking officer, who had just taken over the team when Captain Rust was given a new assignment. Kann was also a German Jewish immigrant, and he was younger and more adventurous than his predecessor.

"Hell, why not try it?" said a grinning Kann, and that's how they created Commissar Krukov.

Fred and Guy worked out the details. Guy would play the irascible Russian, even though he didn't know a word of the language and had to practice a fake Russian accent. His model was the "Mad Russian" character on Eddie Cantor's radio show, which he had listened to on Sunday evenings at his aunt and uncle's in St. Louis. Within a few days, everyone around headquarters agreed that Guy could do a decent German impersonation of a demented Russian. Then Guy and Fred set out to assemble a proper wardrobe.

The MPs were told to confiscate any Russian medals and other Soviet souvenirs they had found while searching German POWs. When a handful of Russian soldiers were liberated from the Wehrmacht, some clothing exchanges were made, trading U.S. uniform blouses and jackets for Russian equivalents. Soon, Guy had a complete, if irregular, Russian uniform festooned with colorful medals and ribbons. They furnished a tent as a mock liaison office, hanging up a sign that said, COMMISSAR KRUKOV, LIAISON OFFICER. The final touch: above where Guy would be seated was a framed photograph of Stalin that was signed to his "good friend, Comrade Krukov."

It didn't take long for them to get their first customer. When the next targeting questionnaire landed at First Army headquarters, one of Fred's first prisoners refused to answer questions about his hometown's military factories. After he failed to get the German to open up, Fred put on his most sorrowful expression.

"I understand your position, but please understand mine. Last month we received orders that we must turn uncooperative prisoners over to our Russian allies. I don't like it, but I must ask you to please come with me now."

Fred took the prisoner under escort to the tent where Commissar Krukov, in full attire, awaited his cue. Fred announced that he had a prisoner to hand over, and instantly, the Mad Russian had an attack of apoplexy. Their well-rehearsed dialogue was delivered in German.

> GUY: You imbecile, what kind of sorry specimen are you bringing me? That Nazi won't even survive the transport to our Siberian salt mines!

FRED: Commissar, I must ask you to calm down and respect my uniform and not shout at me, or I will take this prisoner back to my office.

GUY: You will not do that! This room is Russian soil!

Fred walked his shocked prisoner back, telling the German he hated to leave him at the mercy of Commissar Krukov.

But even after that scare, the prisoner was still reluctant to spill the beans about his hometown factories, knowing full well he would be giving information that would likely result in them being bombed.

"I feel sorry for you," Fred said. "You are still so young and probably throwing your life away. But we will have to go back, because I have my orders."

All it took was a second visit to the crazed Russian for the prisoner to decide to tell Fred everything he knew about his town's factories.

Guy and Fred were impressed with themselves and began to add new wrinkles to their good cop/bad cop routine. For example, Fred would suggest that a defiant prisoner write his "last letter" to his family before he was turned over to the Russians, who "do not recognize such humanitarian gestures." This role-playing broke most of the difficult prisoners and gave Fred the kind of information he needed. But not every German was taken in by the charade. A few of the smarter and more experienced ones figured out how difficult it would be to transport prisoners across half a war-torn continent to reach the Soviets on the eastern front. But many of the Germans were too afraid to think that through, and for them the threat of being turned over to a crazed Russian and sent to Siberia worked so well that the air corps issued a unit citation to the First Army's Ritchie Boys for providing such reliable targeting intelligence.

Guy's new partnership with Fred had taught him that imagination could be an interrogator's most important asset. While their training at Camp Ritchie served as a solid foundation, there were times in the field when it was best to throw away the book, and this went beyond their creation of Commissar Krukov. For instance, after difficulties with German officers who were flat-out unwilling to be questioned by any enlisted men, Guy, Fred, and the other interrogators—the majority of them sergeants or a lower enlisted rank—simply reached into their collection of donated officer insignias and snapped the appropriate one onto their collar to make themselves at least equal to the *Offizier* they were about to face. Elsewhere in the army, an enlisted man impersonating an officer would be subject to a court-martial, but for the interrogators, such a ploy that worked to get information was considered fair game.

Some interrogators served as screeners, their role being to quickly determine which prisoners might possess worthwhile information. One morning, a screener brought Guy a diminutive twenty-four-year-old German prisoner named Karl Laun. He was an Austrian draftee who had served in a Wehrmacht antiaircraft artillery unit until deserting to U.S. troops near the Rhine River. Laun was carrying a diary of his last months on the front lines. It was one hundred pages long, and he had written it in shorthand. Laun and his diary were brought to Guy because he was the only interrogator around who could read German shorthand. While Laun said he was willing to read the diary aloud, no one at headquarters was comfortable using such information without someone confirming the entries. As soon as he opened it and began reading, Guy knew they had stumbled upon a bounty of classified information, including assessments of German morale, equipment, personnel, and armaments. The diary had details on troop, artillery, and armor movements, and other tactical insights. Laun also complained in the diary about Nazi ideology, which he said he had long disavowed for religious reasons. And he wrote unsparingly about evidence he had seen of an atrocity committed by Germans in the Ardennes during the Battle of the Bulge:

20 Dec 1944

*With dawn I return to our positions. Our bivouac area is
punctured by artillery craters. Without warning a monstrous,
abhorrent picture presents itself to me. Its horror slaps me in
the face. Corpses of murdered soldiers. Soldiers who after an
honest fight had surrendered to our paratroopers. They were
then turned over to the SS, who organized them for the
purpose of the slaughter. Who of these SS bastards has even
the slightest inkling of international law, or, for that matter,
of humanity? Nothing, absolutely nothing, is sacred to them.
There they lie, those U.S. soldiers, without weapons or
helmets, evidently shot from behind, mute witnesses against a
system of murder. They are the witnesses, but where is the
prosecutor and the judge? I know up above there is a higher
tribunal, and I'm certain if we down here don't punish them
that a just Lord will do it unfailingly.*

Guy worked with Laun to translate into English the complete
diary, with Laun explaining abbreviations and other cryptic ref-
erences. They turned it into a twenty-four-part series, "From the
Bulge to the Rhine: Diary of an Austrian Anti-Nazi." Each install-
ment was attached to Guy's daily intelligence report that went to
various commands, where the serialization acquired a loyal readership. In fact, after the last segment was distributed, one senior
officer asked for more. "But isn't there any sex?" Guy mentioned the
request to Laun, who had a wife and child at home in Vienna, where
he had been a university student before the war. Laun confirmed
there hadn't been much of that to write about, but he could make up
some juicy parts for the brass. He and Guy dashed out an erotic se-
quel that became a must-read at headquarters and other commands.

Karl Laun soon began doing valuable work inside the cage, listening to what the new prisoners said among themselves. He and

several other prisoners became the interrogators' "trusties," all of them proven anti-fascists. They would spend time in the cage, then tip off the interrogators as to which prisoners were worthy of further questioning. A prisoner who returned from his initial screening boasting of having fooled the Americans, for example, would be targeted for more intense interrogation. The trusties did so at great personal risk, as prisoners were beaten up inside the cage by other prisoners—usually devoted Nazis—for far less, such as speaking ill of Hitler. Eventually, when it became too risky to keep putting Laun back inside the cage, he was assigned to Guy as a stenographer. Laun sat in with Guy during interrogations, taking notes in shorthand, which Guy later referred to when writing his reports. The two men became close, and Guy came to appreciate Laun for his enthusiasm and sense of humor. One day, Guy was addressing a group of newly arrived prisoners, telling them their war was over and ordering them to fall in line for questioning. One tough German sergeant refused to do so. He spun around and barked to the others that the war was not over, and to keep quiet and remember that they were still proud German fighting men. From where he had been standing by Guy's side, Laun went over to the sergeant, who towered about a foot over him, reached up, and yanked down the visor on the sergeant's field cap so it half obscured his face. "Look at the big clown who thinks he's still fighting the war!" Laun announced in German. All the prisoners laughed. His resistance broken by that public act of disrespect, the sergeant stepped meekly back and the Germans all fell into line.

Guy came to appreciate that although there were many fanatic Nazis fighting for Hitler—he estimated about half of those he interrogated were fervent Nazis and 20 percent were willing followers who had bought into the Nazi ideology until they started losing—there were also decent men like Karl Laun in the Wehrmacht.

One morning in February 1945, a message came down from headquarters. Fred saw it first and hurried to Guy with the news:

Marlene Dietrich was performing her USO show the next day, twenty miles from Huy. Fred already had a plan. "Let's get over there, Guy!"

Dietrich had left Germany in the early 1930s for Hollywood, where she made six films over the next five years as Paramount Pictures presented her as a German answer to MGM's Swedish sensation, Greta Garbo. In 1937, when she was performing in London, several Nazi Party officials approached her offering lucrative contracts if she returned home as the Third Reich's leading film star. Even though her mother and sister still lived in Berlin, Dietrich, a staunch anti-Nazi and strongly opposed to Hitler, refused their offer and that year applied for U.S. citizenship, which she received in 1939. She had started a fund with several other Germans working in Hollywood to help Jews and dissidents escape from Nazi Germany. When the U.S. entered the war in December 1941, she became one of the first celebrities to go on a war bond tour, and was reported to have sold more than any other Hollywood star. Since then, she had gone on several USO tours, performing for Allied troops in Algeria, Italy, Britain, France, and Belgium.

Taking a jeep the next morning, Fred and Guy drove to the rural inn where she was scheduled to appear. The inn's large catering hall was already packed with soldiers when they arrived. There were no chairs, only hundreds of GIs on the floor sitting atop their steel helmets. Guy and Fred squeezed into the middle and perched on their helmets like everyone else. The stage, only a few feet above floor level, was bare except for a wooden chair in the middle and off to one side an upright piano with a stool. Everyone waited expectantly. After about fifteen minutes, a man came out and sat at the piano. Then the room hushed completely when the Berlin-born blonde strolled out, smiling and waving at the troops. What were often billed as the "loveliest legs in Hollywood" were covered in GI fatigues just like the ones the soldiers wore. She cracked a few jokes critical of the chow and accommodations, which drew boisterous

Movie star Marlene Dietrich having chow with GIs during a USO tour. *(U.S. Army Signal Corps)*

laughs from the GIs. She then told the men she had once had her heart set on becoming a classical musician but her cabaret and film career had left her with little time to practice. So she had taken up a different kind of instrument.

"Would you like to hear me play my musical saw, boys?"

Marlene's saw was famous, and the men cheered their approval. She plopped in the chair and grabbed a wood saw and violin bow. Gripping the saw's handle between her knees, she bent the blade from the top down with one hand, and began strumming the bow on the jagged teeth to create a high-pitched tune they all knew: "Lili Marleen."

She next sang a song that raised a thunderous cheer because they all would have loved to order a round of drinks: "Go See What the Boys in the Back Room Will Have," from her role as a saloon girl in the 1939 Western-comedy in which she costarred with James Stewart, *Destry Rides Again.*

When she finished her set, the whistles and applause were deafening. She returned for three encores, then blew kisses and waved farewell.

"Let's go backstage and meet her," hollered Fred. He jumped up and pushed his way through the crowd, with a dubious Guy following, wondering what they could possibly say that would be of interest to this movie star.

Behind the stage, they predictably found Dietrich ringed by all ranks of army personnel. Fred cut through the torrent of plaudits by addressing her in German as Frau Dietrich. He said his mother, Frau Ehrlich, had been Dietrich's masseuse on several occasions when she visited New York. She remembered Paula Ehrlich, said the movie star, who was clearly surprised to find a GI speaking flawless German. Now Fred had his opening. He introduced himself and Guy as interrogators at the First Army's POW cage and asked if she had ever seen such an enclosure. She had not, and her curiosity was piqued. So Fred invited her to take a ride with them twenty miles back to Huy. After a quick word to her pianist and escorts— "I'll be back in a couple of hours"—she followed Fred and Guy outside, leaving scores of disappointed and envious GIs in their wake, and piled into their jeep.

When they reached the Citadel, they drove right up the ramp to the cage. German officers were confined on one side of a narrow walkway, with enlisted men on the opposite side. As they walked down the center aisle, whatever curiosity Marlene had about seeing German POWs paled compared to their excitement at seeing her. The word spread rapidly in the cage: *"Marlene Dietrich ist hier!"* Hundreds of them pressed against the wire enclosures on both sides, trying to see her, speak to her, touch her. Dietrich initially waved to the men, but she was clearly taken aback by their sheer numbers. Although it was a friendly mob, it was still a mob of German soldiers rushing the fences and pressing against them all the way up the line, sticking their hands and arms through the wire.

"What the hell is going on?" said the MP captain of the unit in charge of guarding the prisoners. Before Fred or Guy could explain, the captain recognized Dietrich and said, "Get her out of here! Now! Or I'll have a riot on my hands!"

Marlene seemed relieved to get away from the mass of prisoners, many of whom were still whistling and cheering as they drove off. Safely back in the jeep, Marlene told Fred and Guy that she wasn't surprised the prisoners had taken such an interest in her because something similar had happened when she visited the border town of Stolberg, the first German city taken by the Americans. She had gone there with her U.S. Army escorts to gauge the reaction of her former countrymen to her voluntary exile.

"After all, I left Germany and came over to the American side," she explained to Guy and Fred. "I thought there might be some very strong resentments."

Nazi propaganda had termed her a traitor, but she had still gotten a warm reception in Stolberg. There were practically no men left in the town, parts of which had been leveled by American bombing and artillery fire. Walking down the street in her USO uniform with army escorts, she was immediately recognized by a Stolberg house-wife and soon was surrounded by a crowd of admiring women and children. Some of the women went house to house collecting baking ingredients that were in short supply and made a simple cake, which they presented to her as she departed.

In telling the story to Fred and Guy, Marlene was moved to tears. She said that simple Stolberg pastry was more memorable than the gourmet petits fours served to her in the salons of Paris. It had made her believe that many Germans accepted and even supported her for what she had done in trading Nazi tyranny for freedom in America.

As they parted at the entrance to the catering hall, where her escorts, responsible for her safety, were relieved to see her again, Marlene thanked Fred and Guy for the adventure. She told them how meaningful the USO tours were for her, that they helped her feel she was doing her part in the war effort. She added with a wide smile, "There is no audience I have been more in tune with than you boys in the U.S. Army."

The relief everyone was now feeling after the defeat of the Germans' last major offensive of the war in the Ardennes led to another caper for Guy and Fred, suggested to them by Captain Kann. Showing them a "funny paper" put out by the headquarters of a Canadian command, he said, "Get up something funny like this for us so we can send it out attached to our daily intel report." It was, Guy mused, humor on command, no easy task. They left the captain's tent clueless as to how to amuse him, let alone the forty-odd headquarters who received their daily intelligence reports.

Approaching his interrogation tent, Guy found a Wehrmacht corporal dancing from one foot to the other waiting to be interrogated. He was a skinny "Sad Sack" type who could have posed for George Baker's popular GI cartoon character. It turned out Obergefreiter (Corporal) Joachimstaler had been a company clerk, and after only a few questions, it became clear he was a paper-pusher who knew nothing of any importance. When he urgently asked to be excused "in order to answer nature's call"—a quaint saying compared to how soldiers normally spoke of bodily functions—Guy had a stroke of brilliance.

Hurrying to Fred's tent, he said, "I've got it! We'll make out that this guy Joachimstaler was Hitler's latrine orderly."

Questions tumbled out of Guy and Fred. Where had he served Hitler in such a capacity? How did he find himself at the front lines and liable to capture despite holding such an exhalted position? Answers to such questions, whether based on what they knew of the German army or just dressed up to sound good, came easily for the experienced interrogators. But they were left with one final one to figure out: What secrets had they been able to extract from Hitler's privy?

Guy came up with the answer: "Corporal Joachimstaler frequently observed that the Führer has a shriveled scrotum."

Their faux interrogation report, rapidly fleshed out by howlers from others on the IPW teams, was approved with delight by Kann and appended to their main intelligence report for distribution that day, with a subtle warning at the bottom: "Contents may already be compromised."

The report drew rave reviews. Within hours, calls of approval came in from headquarters up and down the line, along with abundant chortles, guffaws, and back-slapping. But shortly after midnight, the field telephone rang in the command tent, where Guy, by a stroke of luck, was on night duty.

He answered the phone, "Sergeant Stern."

"Guy, this is Billy," said Bill Galanis, a communications clerk at army headquarters whom Guy had known as a fellow student at Saint Louis University. "Listen, that funny report of yours? The fat is in the fire. A liaison officer with the OSS in Paris read it and phoned Washington. He's asked for a Hitler expert to fly over and question your latrine orderly."

Certain that a wild-goose chase across the Atlantic by a high-ranking officer as a result of their hoax would unleash a court-martial for everyone involved, Guy rushed into the captain's sleeping quarters and awakened him with the news. Kann was no less concerned. He got on the phone and woke up his immediate superior, a colonel at army headquarters, and explained what had happened. Luckily, the colonel had enjoyed the latrine orderly report and said he would take care of it. Within hours, the OSS liaison officer withdrew his request for a Hitler expert.

The mild-mannered little clerk, Obergefreiter Joachimstaler, was sent on to a POW camp not realizing that he had suddenly become a celebrity, and all because he had to make an urgent trip to the latrine.

On the night of January 18, 1945, a newly captured German soldier was brought to Guy, who was told that the prisoner wanted to report a war crime. Corporal Heinrich Kauter was a former communist who had been interned at Landsberg concentration camp as "unworthy to bear arms" prior to being drafted in 1942, when Germany was desperate for manpower. Guy knew the prison, fifty miles west of Munich, as the place where Hitler had been incarcerated after a failed coup attempt in 1924 and where he wrote his autobiographical manifesto, *Mein Kampf*.

Kauter told Guy that he had been a member of the 293rd Regiment of the 18th Volksgrenadier Division and had taken part in the attack on Bleialf on December 16, 1944. Kauter was one of thirty Germans the Americans captured that day. He recalled being questioned that night by two German-speaking interrogators who divulged to their prisoners that they were "Jews from Berlin." Kauter noted that with Bleialf surrounded, the Americans were unable to evacuate their POWs to the rear and instead kept them under guard in a farmhouse west of the town. When the Americans surrendered a few days later, the prisoners were freed, and German soldiers then took some three hundred American prisoners.

Kauter told Guy how when they reached the customs house near the Belgian-German border, some of these repatriated German prisoners pointed out the two Berlin Jews to an officer, who had them separated from the other Americans who were being evacuated to stalags deep inside Germany. He then ordered a detail of his men to take them down the road, where they were shot.

Guy was stunned by what he heard and probed for more details.

"Who was the officer who ordered the execution?"

"Hauptmann Bruns. I don't know his first name."

"What is his position?"

"Commanding officer of 2nd Battalion, 293rd Regiment."

"Who carried out the orders?"

"Feldwebel Hoffman," Kauter said. "A platoon sergeant in my company, 6th Company. And other corporals and sergeants from the 5th and 6th Companies."

Guy prepared a report naming "Capt. BRUNS (2 Bn 293 Regt)" as a suspect in the execution of the two U.S. soldiers. This ensured that if or when Bruns fell into Allied hands he would be held for questioning. He listed Kauter as a "highly reliable" witness. He put a hold on Kauter so he would be kept in isolation at the cage, where he could be interviewed by an investigator from the army's Office of the Inspector General (IG), which was beginning to document war crimes for legal prosecutions.

The next day, Kauter was questioned under oath by Lieutenant Colonel Hermann Meyer, an assistant IG. Kauter repeated what he had told Guy but added more details about the execution. He said Hauptmann Bruns spoke briefly to the two Americans and then announced, "The Jews have no right to live in Germany." Before they were shot, Kauter continued, the two Americans protested and asked to be treated as captured soldiers.

Q: *How were they standing? With their hands in the air?*
A: No, at attention with their backs to the firing squad.

Q: *Where were they shot?*
A: Shot in the back.

The army investigators were limited in how far they could take the investigation. U.S. forces had not yet secured the Bleialf area, where heavy fighting was still taking place, which meant that a search for the bodies and any further evidence would have to wait.

Guy knew that the 106th Division had lost the two entire regiments in that area in the opening days of the Battle of the Bulge. He was certain that the two dead American interrogators must have been members of a regimental IPW team assigned to the 106th. It tragically illustrated why so many Ritchie Boys had changed their German or Jewish names before shipping overseas, and why they destroyed clues to their past such as addresses, photographs, and letters, which could not be found on them should they become POWs. They never even spoke to one another in their native tongue. Although they had been trained not to reveal anything about themselves—they all had cover stories to explain their language skills to prisoners—some interrogators broke this rule, taking a perverse pride in telling an arrogant or impertinent Nazi that they were Jewish. But even those who made such revelations usually refrained, wisely so in event of their own capture, from telling POWs they were from Germany or anywhere in Europe.

For Guy, the reported execution of two U.S. interrogators was his worst fear come to life. It was why he had not dreaded a quick battlefield death as much as he did being captured by the Nazis and having them discover that he was a German Jew. This was the nightmare of everyone on his team and every Ritchie Boy he knew.

Less than three weeks later, on February 7, "Capt. BRUNS" of the 2nd Battalion, 293rd Regiment, 18th Volksgrenadier, was captured by units of the U.S. Third Army in a bunker at Schwarzer Mann, ten miles northeast of Bleialf. Interrogators at Third Army headquarters had read Guy's report on Bruns's alleged role in the executions of two American soldiers, and they sent their prisoner immediately under heavily armed escort to First Army headquarters. Because of the seriousness of the crimes being investigated, Bruns was put in his own cell.

Curt Bruns was twenty-nine years old, with blue eyes and thinning red hair. He had been a grocery clerk in Stuttgart before entering the army in fall 1936, by which time Hitler's military buildup was well under way. He advanced steadily through the ranks of the German army, becoming a Wehrmacht officer on September 1, 1939—the day Germany invaded Poland—and a battalion commander in January 1944. He had a wife and young child who lived in Bad Kissingen, a Bavarian spa town.

During his initial interrogation, Bruns recalled the two American prisoners who spoke German and acknowledged that he had ordered them separated from the other American POWs, though he claimed he did not know they were Jews. He confirmed that he had spoken to them in German, and one of the GIs had told him he had studied law in Berlin. As to what happened to them after his men marched them away, Bruns said he was only later told they had been shot on orders of his regimental commander, Lieutenant Colonel Witte. He admitted Witte was not at the customs house at the time and arrived a few hours later. And he said that he and Witte did not discuss the two prisoners because they had more pressing matters to deal with. According to Bruns, Witte was recalled to Berlin a short time later and court-martialed for disobeying orders during the fighting at Saint Vith. The interrogators suspected Bruns was fingering his senior officer in ordering the killing of the two Americans because he had reason to believe that Witte was dead.

A German prisoner named Anton Korn was placed in a cell next to Bruns and told to get him talking about the Jacobs and Zappler case. Korn, a former political prisoner in Germany because of his membership in the Communist Party, had been inducted into the army and captured in Normandy. In the months since, he had been made a trusty at First Army headquarters, where he had been used by Guy, Fred Howard, and other interrogators to help them get information from and about other prisoners. At five foot ten, with a muscular build, Korn could have passed for a middleweight boxer, and he was capable of taking care of himself in the cage. Korn's communist affiliation reassured the Americans, as everyone would have been badly embarrassed if he turned out to be a Nazi in disguise feeding them bogus information. But all the interrogators who worked with Korn agreed he was reliable, accurate, and trustworthy.

Korn spent two days in the cell next to Bruns, pretending to be a tough German paratrooper sergeant who had killed a number of Belgian civilians and was being investigated by U.S. authorities for war crimes. Bruns believed the story, and that got him to open up about his own case. He told Korn about his battalion taking hundreds of U.S. prisoners on December 20, 1944, among them two German Jews who had interrogated his own men days earlier. Bruns said he had ordered that the two Jews be "mowed down," explaining that he had solemnly sworn "regardless of whether Germany will win the war or not, to devote my life to the destruction of Jews." Bruns stated he was unafraid of incriminating witnesses as he was "mentally superior to these men." He bragged to Korn about outsmarting the interrogators by giving the name of his regimental commander because he knew they would never be able to find him. Bruns admitted to other heinous deeds, including killing some of his own men with a machine pistol when they said they wanted to surrender rather than fight several days before his own capture.

Less than a week later, the bodies of two dead Americans were found in the field near the customs house, just across the German border north of Bleialf. Just days earlier, the 4th Infantry Division had cleared out all enemy opposition in the area. U.S. forces had taken that long—nearly two months—to return to the positions across the Our River that had once been held by the 106th Infantry when the Germans launched their surprise Ardennes offensive.

That same afternoon, Technician Fourth Grade John Swanson and another member of the graves registration section were led to the scene by members of their division's MP platoon. The area had been covered by snow that had recently started melting. They found the dead GIs on their backs, about eight inches apart in a trench that was only two and a half feet deep. The arms of one man were down at his side; the other man's arms were frozen in the thrust position, as if he had tried to catch himself from falling forward. Their bodies and faces were intact, not torn up like artillery shell and shrapnel casualties. From the front, no major wounds were visible, only small amounts of red liquid clotted around the eyes, ears, mouth, and nose. It looked like blood, but more than likely it was the purge fluid seen in decomposing bodies, the result of decayed tissues leaking from the lungs and brain. Neither dead man was wearing shoes or a helmet. One had on a field jacket as an outer garment and the other a wool army overcoat. Both men had dark hair. The younger was of average build, the older stocky. There were no weapons, ammunition, canteens, or other military gear on or near their bodies.

One body was identified by a set of dog tags and the other by a driver's license and Social Security card. Before being slipped into body bags, the corpses were tagged: KURT JACOBS and MURRAY ZAPPLER.

The next day, Hauptmann Curt Bruns was questioned by Lieutenant Colonel Meyer, the assistant inspector general (IG) who had earlier taken a sworn statement from the witness, Corporal Kauter.

Bruns denied that he had given the orders to shoot Jacobs and Zappler and claimed that he hadn't even heard about the killings until he was told by one of his soldiers. He admitted to ordering the two German-speaking interrogators separated from the other American POWs and escorted away by his men, but he again claimed his regimental commander must have ordered the killings.

"Who shot these men?" Meyer asked.

Bruns replied: "The prisoner escorts from my battalion."

When Meyer asked him why he wouldn't admit that he ordered his men to shoot the prisoners, Bruns said he stood by his statements.

Ten days later, Bruns was questioned by Lieutenant Colonel Jesse E. Bishop, the lead investigating officer. Bruns once again denied that the two Americans were shot on his orders or even that he knew about the killings firsthand, although he seemed to slip up when asked where the executions had taken place, replying, "About five hundred meters from the customs house, which can be marched in five minutes."

The U.S. investigators decided to take Bruns out to where the bodies had been found. While army lawyers were confident that Korn's testimony would be persuasive at trial, they hoped that taking Bruns to the scene of the crime would shake him up and get him talking. And if he was feeling at all guilty, perhaps he might even make a confession.

Karl Frucht, one of the German-born interrogators who worked at First Army headquarters with Guy, accompanied the suspect, along with two armed MPs. They drove past the customs house, parked, and walked into the meadow where the bodies had been discovered. Frucht reported that Hauptmann Curt Bruns not only had nothing to say, but as he stood over the shallow grave of the two Ritchie Boys, he "did not move an eyelid."

After the fall of Saint-Lô, Martin Selling's team moved south in an all-night convoy with the 35th Infantry Division of Patton's Third

Army. Near Falaise, they faced off with the Waffen-SS division Das Reich, an elite unit that had as its symbol a *Wolfsangel*, an early Nazi symbol inspired by an actual wolf trap. The division was already guilty of war crimes, and it had been rushed up from southern France to try to stop the Americans from breaking out at Saint-Lô. When that failed, they were ordered to act as rear guard for other German units escaping encirclement through the Falaise Gap to live and fight another day.

Martin saw these SS soldiers as brutal cowards with oversized egos. They were so accustomed to lording over French villagers and poorly armed Resistance fighters that being shot at by U.S. soldiers enraged them. They had been known to execute American POWs, including a captain from Martin's regiment and his driver, who had been captured after taking a wrong turn.

Summoned to his regiment's command post, Martin walked in to find an outraged American colonel and a glaring SS *Scharführer* clutching a white flag and the latest issue of *Stars and Stripes*. Standing between them was an unarmed GI. The two officers were shouting and gesticulating without understanding each other. When Martin appeared, the colonel and the German looked to him to straighten things out. It took some back and forth in both languages, but soon the situation became clear. The GI had been taken prisoner by SS troops. Before his capture, he had obtained an advance copy of *Stars and Stripes*, which had a picture of three blondes and the caption, "Three captured German nurses." The GI showed his captors the picture and convinced them he had come to negotiate the release of the nurses. The SS lieutenant had accompanied him over to U.S. lines under the white flag to facilitate an exchange of prisoners: one GI for the three nurses. The problem was that no one knew anything about any German nurses; the picture and caption seemed to be a joke. And at this moment not a funny one.

The regiment's command post was atop the western slope of a deep valley and the Waffen-SS forces were dug in on the eastern slope, with an open highway connecting the two across the

vineyard-covered valley. The German lieutenant had walked with
his American prisoner through the center of the U.S. lines without
being blindfolded, so he now knew their strength, the layout of their
defenses, and the location of the command post. The German officer was still angrily asking about the nurses, and the U.S. colonel
was livid because under the rules of war, the use of the white flag
meant he would have to allow the SS officer to return to his side.

Martin had the unpleasant task of explaining to the German that
there were no nurses to liberate and that he was now going to be
blindfolded for the walk back. The colonel then directed Martin to
take the German back to his lines.

On the long walk across the valley, with the German Jew leading the blindfolded SS officer by the crook of his arm and telling
him when to watch his step, the two began to talk. The officer
could tell that Martin was German, and he asked why Martin had
emigrated. Instead of answering, Martin asked about reports that
Das Reich had wiped out the entire population of the French village of Oradour-sur-Glane, some five hundred men, women, and
children. The German officer confirmed what Martin had heard,
but attempted to justify the killings by claiming they resulted from
somebody firing at them from the village. Martin, sickened by this
excuse for mass killings, asked no more questions.

As soon as Martin saw the German troops, he stopped and removed the lieutenant's blindfold. Without saying another word, he
turned and started the walk back. On his solitary return across the
exposed vineyards and road, he realized how stupid he had been
not to have brought a white flag for himself. He saw that soldiers on
both sides were watching him, crouched in half-hidden positions
behind the vines and bushes, and he suddenly felt naked and exposed. With every step, he expected to be shot in the back, perhaps
by the *Scharführer* himself, who had been so blasé about murder.
But the kill shot never rang out, and Martin finished the longest
walk of his life on shaky legs and drenched in sweat.

When he reached the other side, he found that the colonel had given orders to pack up his command post, which was already hurriedly being moved.

They remained locked in combat with the SS division for several more days, then suddenly the SS withdrew through the gap filled with other retreating Germans. Martin saw that these martinets were no longer the vaunted Nazi supermen of the past, although they could still put on a convincing show to frightened civilians and their own rear-echelon troops. Unlike typical Wehrmacht infantry units, they were well motorized, and they demanded the right-of-way even as they raced to the rear. The men of Das Reich, it seemed, were deathly afraid of being captured.

A week later, Martin was busily interrogating new prisoners when he was interrupted and told to report to the intelligence officer. When he walked into regimental headquarters, he found several stern-faced staff officers staring at a message from Third Army headquarters. They were being asked to explain why the regiment had not passed on information from a prisoner they had interrogated who was a member of a German tank unit operating nearby. Headquarters deemed it vital information that armored tanks were operating in the area in light of the regiment's plan for an upcoming attack. Martin thought back to his recent interrogations, and couldn't recall anyone being from a German tank unit or saying anything at all about Panzer tanks in the vicinity. A message was sent back to the Third Army stating there were no reports of enemy tanks in their sector.

An hour later, a command staff car pulled up with a major and two Counter Intelligence Corps (CIC) investigators looking to question Martin. They accused him of not including German tanks in his IPW reports, and it became clear that they were questioning not only his competency but his loyalty. They could not understand why he was so determined to deny the presence of armored forces in front of his regiment. They pushed him to admit *something;* as a mere sergeant, and one with a "heavy accent," he had perhaps misunderstood something? Or made an omission?

Overhearing the cross-examination, the regiment's assistant operation officer, Captain Orval Faubus, finally asked the investigators where *they* had gotten the information that a prisoner had reported tanks.* Their initial silence was nearly as bad as their explanation. An MP had been escorting some POWs back from interrogations, and—using his high school German—he had asked the prisoners why they wore blue-gray uniforms instead of the usual German army gray. They answered, *"Panzergrenadiere."* Hearing *panzer,* the guard excitedly told his MP battalion commander that there was German armor in the area, and that officer passed the word to higher-ups.

Unfortunately, it was bad information. Martin had interrogated some of the men in the blue-gray uniforms. *Panzergrenadiere* were formed earlier in the war to be motorized infantry units attached to armored divisions. Their units mainly operated on the Russian front and had suffered heavy losses. They had been hastily patched up, stripped of their remaining motorized equipment, and shipped to the western front to fight as regular infantry, while retaining their distinctive uniforms and unit designations. For several days, Martin had reported their presence in the regiment's sector and given their accurate strength and composition as an infantry-only force.

Somehow, this explanation was not enough for the major and the investigators from headquarters. Martin had an uneasy feeling they had come looking to unmask a German spy in the ranks. The investigators wanted the regiment's planned attack for the next day to be postponed due to the "conflicting reports" of armor. Faubus looked at Martin, who repeated that he had heard nothing at all about enemy tanks in the area. Faubus and the rest of the regimental staff

---

* Orval Faubus served as the thirty-sixth governor of Arkansas, from 1955 to 1967. He is best remembered for his 1957 stand against the desegregation of the Little Rock schools in which he defied a unanimous decision of the U.S. Supreme Court. He became less confrontational with the federal government during the administrations of Presidents John F. Kennedy and Lyndon B. Johnson, with each of whom he remained cordial and both of whom carried Arkansas.

accepted Martin's stand, sent the investigators packing, and carried off the attack the next morning as planned, without a single German tank being spotted.

Although he had controlled his emotions while standing up to the threats and pressure put on him by the investigators from headquarters, the encounter left Martin furious for a long while. Hadn't he and the other German-speaking interrogators proved their worth and loyalty yet? What did it take? He realized how easily the attack might have been called off for no good reason, and he knew it would only have resulted in his regiment losing the momentum gained by its recent advances. A delay would have given the enemy time to reorganize and strengthen their defenses, which could have meant more American casualties.

In mid-December, the 35th Infantry moved into position near Haguenau, in the Alsace-Lorraine region of northeast France, fifteen miles from the German border. A bundle of maps were distributed with their new objectives, including the German city of Karlsruhe. But just two hours later, the maps were recalled, and the men were given word that they were being redeployed due to a surprise enemy offensive. They pulled back ninety miles to Metz, where they were resupplied, then dispatched north to help stop the German offensive through the Ardennes.

It was snowing nonstop, and during a three-day drive on icy mountain roads in whiteout conditions, Martin's only point of reference was a heavily loaded kitchen truck in front of their jeep. Arriving at their destination on New Year's Day, the regiment was given the mission of clearing their sector of enemy troops, with little notion of how many troops there might be or where they were located. They immediately sent out the reconnaissance platoon to probe the area.

Regimental headquarters was set up at a farm and the IPW team found shelter in an empty henhouse. Later that day, the reconnaissance platoon returned with their catch: ten German prisoners of war, one officer and nine enlisted men. Martin decided to start with the officer. In strutted a smartly dressed young captain who demanded to be officially presented in surrender to an officer of equal or superior rank.

Martin explained that they had neither the time nor inclination to call out the regimental band to greet him, and considering that he was already a prisoner of war, *any* American soldier was his superior. Upon hearing Martin's impeccable German, the captain realized to his horror that this wasn't just an American who spoke German, but surely a native German who had immigrated to America. He castigated Martin as a traitor.

Martin now dropped the hammer on the Nazi. He said it had been made extremely clear to him during Kristallnacht that as a Jew he was not German. Stiffening his tone, he added ominously that the same message had been beaten into him during his time as an inmate at Dachau. *Can you imagine,* Martin asked the captain, *what would have happened to me at Dachau if I had confronted a concentration camp guard the way you are confronting me?*

The captain was livid with rage. It was a shame, he told Martin, that he had ever been released from Dachau.

From the documents the captain carried, it was clear he had spent most of his nascent military career on administrative duty and had only recently been assigned to the front lines, where he indicated he had made a commitment to help win the war or die on the battlefield. As his capture had deprived him of those glorious options, he was now attempting to make up for his loss of face by insulting his Jewish interrogator. Martin nearly lost his temper more than once and wanted to slap the German for his insolence. But he held back. Getting angry would do no good. Instead, Martin remained icily calm.

When the captain realized he had no choice but to deal with Martin, he supplied his name and rank. As a matter of pride he wanted to go on record that he had become separated from the rest of his unit and for three days had tried unsuccessfully to reestablish contact with them or other German troops. He and his men had only been captured because they had run out of food and ammunition.

Martin knew it was not unusual for German soldiers, when they became separated from their units, to hunker down in one place or even hide from their own troops until they had the opportunity to be captured by the Americans. Then, to save face, they often made up stories of how hard they tried to look for their comrades. But Martin figured this Nazi zealot could be trusted to have scoured the area looking for German troops as he claimed, which meant if he could not find any, they must actually be gone. The captain had volunteered exactly the information Martin was looking for. At some point, he guessed the captain would realize the blunder he had made in his self-righteous rage, but by then it would be too late.

To confirm what he had inferred from the captain's testimony, Martin spoke to the captain's men, who were not fans of their arrogant young leader. Sure enough, they talked freely about the days the captain had them marching aimlessly around the empty countryside looking for their own troops but finding none. Martin now had the confirmation he needed.

The regimental staff was relieved to learn from Martin's report that the immediate area was clear of German forces. They ordered units to extend their lines farther with greater speed and confidence. Martin's outfit was soon on its way back toward the border for the final push into Germany that had been delayed by the Ardennes offensive, and he was excited to be part of it.

Martin Selling could not wait for that day when he stepped on German soil as a U.S. Army soldier.

After the 6th Armored Division's swift advance across the Brittany peninsula, it pivoted eastward and cut across France. For Stephan Lewy and his OB team, it became an even faster-moving war. They were charged with keeping an updated operations map showing the location and strength of all enemy units in their immediate area. The division—part of Patton's Third Army—moved so rapidly their latest military maps covered areas they had already left behind, and out of necessity they were using Michelin tour guides picked up in towns along the way.

Additionally, Stephan constructed a large wall map using cardboard backing covered with sheets of acetate. He listened on the wireless to the nightly war news from England, France, and Germany in all three languages, then drew the reported positions of Allied and enemy forces so the command staff had a complete picture of the battle lines in Europe. General Grow often started his day with his nose up to the large map, and whenever Patton showed up he also stopped to ogle it, because he was interested in what lay hundreds of miles ahead.

Stretched supply lines caused shortages of fuel for U.S. tanks and other vehicles, so the advance halted for days at a time to await truck deliveries from the rear. In spite of the fits and starts, the 6th had worked its way across the Belgian border by mid-December. It was poised south of the Ardennes to strike into the Saar region of southwestern Germany. After the surprise German offensive into the Ardennes, the division was ordered north to help defend the besieged city of Bastogne, where the 101st Airborne was encircled. On December 22, Brigadier General Anthony McAuliffe, acting division commander of the 101st, answered a German request for his surrender with a terse message back: "Nuts!"

Four days later, the 6th, after making a ninety-degree turn to the north, entered the Battle of the Bulge. It rushed to the zone southeast of Bastogne, now under constant enemy artillery shelling. The Germans were massing a force estimated at six divisions to the east of Bastogne, but with the 6th suddenly at their flank, they were forced to reposition men, tanks, and artillery. On New Year's Day, the 6th, which Patton called one of his two best armored divisions—along with the 4th, the other "twin engine" of the Third Army—launched an attack along its entire front. On that day, living up to

Patton's credo to always attack first, it was the lone U.S. division attacking the enemy, not just defending.

Bastogne held, and by the second week of January 1945, it was clear that the Germans' gamble in the Ardennes had failed. Suddenly fighting a rearguard action, they tried desperately to get as much of their armor, equipment, and troops as possible back across the Our River and behind the Siegfried Line to blunt the expected Allied invasion of Germany.

Hordes of enemy prisoners were taken in the Ardennes. Stephan was assigned to accompany one, a German one-star general, back behind the lines. They transported him in a tank so he couldn't be identified during transit, to avoid a possible rescue attempt. After delivering him to the Third Army's sprawling POW cage, Stephan walked past where prisoners were devouring fresh eggs, fresh meat, and freshly baked bread. The men of the 6th had spent nearly two hundred consecutive days on the front lines, eating mostly cold K-rations. Stephan was disgusted that enemy prisoners were eating better than the GIs in the field who were doing the fighting. He was tempted, for a moment, to sit down and enjoy a hot

Stephan Lewy behind the wheel in northeastern France on the way to Bastogne, Belgium, October 1944. *(Family photograph)*

meal. But given who his tablemates would be, he decided it wasn't worth it.

Back with his division and in the crush of round-the-clock interrogations that often meant working forty-eight hours straight, Stephan found himself at a fold-up table in a large tent facing a German SS major who refused to say anything other than his name and rank.

He had seen during recent interrogations that some Third Reich soldiers, far from considering themselves defeated, were prepared to put up a last-ditch fight to defend the Fatherland. *We will throw them back into the ocean, the arrogant, big-mouthed apes from the New World,* promised one unfinished letter found on a prisoner. *They will not get into Germany. We will protect our wives and children from all enemy domination.*

But Stephan was exhausted. With no pretenses or niceties, he demanded to know the strength and location of the forces they faced. The officer, head held high, remained mute.

Finally, Stephan stood, reached for his trenching tool for digging foxholes, and told the prisoner to follow him outside. After a short walk, Stephan, as he aimed his .45 pistol at the prisoner, threw the shovel on the ground.

"Ein Loch graben," Stephan said.

The Nazi picked up the shovel and began digging as ordered.

After a while, Stephan told him to make it deeper and longer.

The prisoner did, without uttering a word.

Stephan then told him to lie down in it to make sure it fit him, and the officer did so. He then climbed out and dusted himself off.

Stephan handed him two wooden slats and told him to write his name and rank on one of them for the cross that would mark his grave.

That was when the German broke and started talking.

Later, Stephan thought about what he had done. Yes, he had secured tactical information about the enemy units they were fighting. But had the end justified the means? Probably not, he decided. He knew psychologically mistreating a prisoner was a court-martial offense. It was the only time he had done such a thing, and he never would again. He knew he had let his anger get the best of him, and he wasn't proud of it.

Like other Ritchie Boys, Stephan had been trained to detach himself from any personal and emotional aspects of interrogation. But as he faced the SS major that day, he could not shake the sense of haunting danger such men had instilled in him most of his life. Stephan realized that the closer he came to returning to Nazi Germany, the more pent-up resentment, and even rage, he was feeling.

PART
THREE

———◆———

We had heard rumors about the existence of camps. I didn't know what to expect. I was afraid I might find my mother or sister among the dead.

—MANFRED "MANNY" STEINFELD

11

THE CAMPS

Even in early April 1945, few American civilians, or for that matter soldiers fighting the war in Europe, knew the name Buchenwald. It stood in a forest of beech trees for which it was named—Konzentrationslager Buchenwald, which meant Concentration Camp Beech Forest—on the northern slopes of Ettersberg Mountain, five miles from the German city of Weimar, renowned for its culture heritage. Weimar had been the focal point of the German Enlightenment (1650–1800) and home to the country's most beloved author, Johann Wolfgang von Goethe, as well as composer Franz Liszt and artist Paul Klee.

But since the 1937 construction of Buchenwald, one of the largest Nazi concentration camps, the area had served a much darker purpose. The camp was surrounded by an electrified barbed-wire fence, watchtowers manned by SS guards, and posts with machine guns. Buchenwald also had its own crematorium. In seven years, a quarter of a million people from all over Europe had been sent to Buchenwald to perform slave labor in armament industries and limestone quarries, until they were worked to death under the Nazi policy *Vernichtung durch Arbeit* (extermination through labor) or they were weeded out as unfit to work and executed.

Deaths by hanging, shooting, and lethal injection, as well as starvation, illness, disease, and medical experiments, exceeded an estimated fifty-five thousand, not including the thousands more who
died after being shipped from Buchenwald to other concentration
camps.

   In April 1945, with Patton's Third Army rapidly approaching
from the west, the Nazis began to evacuate Buchenwald, fearing
its liberation. The small contingent of women prisoners, about five
hundred, was taken by train and on foot to the Theresienstadt concentration camp in German-occupied Czechoslovakia. On the first
day of the evacuations, five thousand male prisoners were force-
marched to Weimar, and hundreds of the sickest died en route or
were killed by guards. At the train station, they were packed into
sixty rail cars with little food or water, their destination the Dachau
concentration camp, 250 miles to the south.*

   On the afternoon of April 11, a forward element of the 6th Armored was approaching the village of Hottelstedt, about two miles
from Buchenwald, where they ran into some SS stragglers and engaged in a brief firefight before the Germans surrendered. As the
GIs were lining up fifteen prisoners to be taken to the rear, dozens
of unarmed men in gray-and-blue-striped prison uniforms suddenly
rushed out of the woods and began striking the Germans with their
bare fists. The stunned and confused Americans pulled the attackers off their prisoners. The inmates told the Americans that they
had been held at a nearby concentration camp where these SS men

---

* Detours along the way delayed what would become known as the Dachau
Death Train. Upon its arrival nineteen days later, only thirteen hundred inmates were able to walk the short distance from the rail spur into the Dachau
compound. Three days later, units of the Seventh Army's 42nd and 45th Infantry Division, after a brief battle with the camp's guards, liberated Dachau's
more than thirty thousand survivors. At the train yard, U.S. troops found thirty
rail cars filled with decomposing corpses. All told, from April 6 to 10, approximately 25,400 prisoners were evacuated from Buchenwald; many of them died
before or after reaching their final destinations.

had been guards. They frantically pointed down a road in the direction of the camp.

No one with the 6th Armored knew anything about a concentration camp in the area. The inmates had pointed south, but the advance unit and the 6th Armored's tank columns a few miles behind it were heading east. Disregarding his orders not to stop or slow down, the commander halted his unit's advance and dispatched a four-man reconnaissance team led by Captain Frederic Keffer, a battalion intelligence officer, in a six-wheeled armored vehicle. Two of the inmates from the camp climbed aboard to show the way, and they soon came to a twelve-foot-high barbed-wire fence. The soldiers could see that behind it were hordes of scrawny men in the same prison stripes.

Leaving two men with the vehicle, Captain Keffer and Sergeant Herbert Gottschalk, a Berlin-born Ritchie Boy, crawled through a hole the inmates had made in the wire fence after the camp was abandoned hours earlier by the SS commandant and his men. The GIs were swarmed by filthy, cheering inmates. They picked up the American captain and threw him into the air, caught him, and tossed him up again, as though he were the winning quarterback of a football game.

When Keffer returned a short time later and reported what he'd found, his commander sent an urgent radio message to 6th Armored headquarters seeking food, water, and medical help for thousands of survivors of a Nazi concentration camp named Buchenwald.

The next day, Stephan Lewy, assigned with the 6th Armored's other Ritchie Boys to serve as translators, arrived at Buchenwald. Stephan had long known that concentration camps existed in Germany, but this was the first one he had seen. He was shocked by the size of the camp, the thousands of prisoners it held, and the pitiful conditions under which the emaciated inmates were living. His father had been caught in an early Nazi roundup in 1933 and was sent to the newly opened Oranienburg concentration camp outside Berlin. He had been released two years later after suffering a heart attack. Stephan still remembered when his father returned from the camp and how gaunt he looked, with most of his teeth missing.

Still, when Stephan arrived at the Buchenwald camp, he was unprepared for the living skeletons he found there. In front of the first barracks, he came to a group of men who were just skin and bones sitting and lying, as if in a trance, next to a pile of decomposing bodies. Stephan was horrified to see an arm suddenly reach out from the midst of the corpses. The living, the dying, and the dead were all mixed together.

One of the first survivors Stephan spoke to was a German Jew. He explained that the prisoners were segregated by nationality and by the color of a triangular patch—called a *Winkel*—sewed on their striped jackets. Yellow was for Jews, red for communists, black for Gypsies, pink for homosexuals. The inmates told him that the various nationalities were assigned to their own barracks and blocks in the camp.*

The windowless, unheated barracks had been designed to house four hundred prisoners each, but many were crowded with up to two thousand. Inmates slept atop wooden planks stacked five levels high, usually four or five to a bed with only a single blanket to cover them even in winter. Coarse mattress covers filled with lice-infested straw were the only bedding allowed. Each morning they discovered that more of their fellow inmates had died during the night. They stripped them for any warm clothes, then dragged the bodies outside and deposited them atop growing mounds of corpses.

The liberated prisoners who could stand struggled to their feet to hug passing GIs. *We are free!* they shouted in a multitude of languages, and despite their weakened conditions and the horrors they had endured, gaiety echoed throughout the camp those first days

---

* A U.S. Army report of April 16, 1945, tallied approximately 20,000 surviving prisoners at Buchenwald on the day of its liberation. This number included 4,380 Russians, 3,800 Polish, 2,900 French, 2,100 Czechs, 1,800 Germans, and 1,200 Hungarians; about 4,000 were Jewish.

of freedom. Through his interactions with the survivors and seeing their relief and gratitude knowing their suffering was over and they had a chance to begin life anew, Stephan, amid the horror, felt his greatest satisfaction of the war.

As the soldiers distributed food, army medical personnel went around warning prisoners to start with only small amounts at first, as overeating can stress the digestive system, pancreas, and liver after a near-starvation diet. Unfortunately, not everyone showed such restraint, and some survivors died from overeating in the first few days.

Stephan took down the symptoms of the various illnesses and diseases that the inmates described to him—typhus, contracted from a lice-borne bacteria, was a major killer—which he relayed to army doctors so they would know what treatments and medications were needed.

The next day, Stephan and a group of soldiers took several empty 2.5-ton army trucks into the nearest town, Weimar, seven miles away. Finding the town's mayor, he told him they required a hundred men to come out with them immediately to start cleaning up the camp and burying the dead. Stephan said they would need another hundred civilians the next day and every day after that until the work was done. When the mayor started to object, Stephan cut him off.

He repeated, *"Hundert jeden Tag."* (One hundred every day.)

The first hundred townsmen were loaded into the army trucks and driven to the camp. When they arrived and stepped from the trucks, they stared with blank expressions at the surroundings and gaunt inmates. Then, as if they were a chorus demanding absolution, they began denying responsibility.

"Wir wussten nicht." (We didn't know.)

"Niemand sagte uns." (No one told us.)

Stephan had no patience for the denials. How could these people not know that such inhumanity was occurring in their own back-yard? How could they not have noticed the odor of the dead and

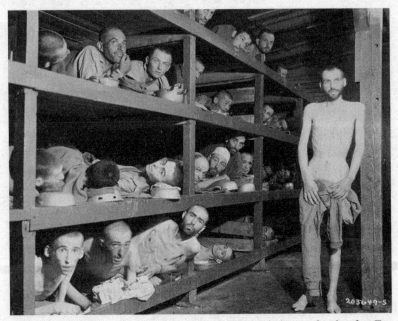

Liberated inmates at Buchenwald stare out from their wooden bunks. Future Nobel Peace Prize winner Elie Wiesel is pictured in the second row of bunks, seventh from the left, next to the vertical beam. *(United States Holocaust Memorial Museum)*

dying that filled the countryside and the dark smoke that spiraled from the towering chimney above the crematorium? How could they have lived so close and been oblivious for so long?

The one hundred locals continued to arrive each day, and they took their orders from Stephan and the other Ritchie Boys. For the most part, Stephan was able to control his feelings, although not always.

"Der Geruch ist schrecklich," said one man, complaining that the smell was awful as he helped drag corpses to a mass burial pit.

Breathe deep, you bastard! Stephan wanted to scream. *It is you with your blind obedience to authority that caused this.*

A few of the locals seemed genuinely moved by the pitiful scenes. One older man, wiping his tears as he spoke, told Stephan he knew there were prisoners being detained at Buchenwald, but that was all he knew and he had never imagined this. Stephan had been trained to look for the obvious signs of lying, and this old man did not have the darting eyes or twitchy expressions of a liar. Stephan believed what he was saying, even if he knew the man *should* have known what was happening so nearby.

On April 12, elements of the 80th Infantry Division arrived to take control of the camp and start evacuating the liberated prisoners. Several journalists arrived with them, including Edward R. Murrow. His live CBS radio broadcast from Buchenwald became one of his most famous: "I asked to see one of the barracks. It happened to be occupied by Czechoslovaks. When I entered, men crowded around, tried to lift me to their shoulders. They were too weak. Many of them could not get out of bed. I was told that this building had once stabled eighty horses. There were twelve hundred men in it, five to a bunk. The stink was beyond all description."

The 6th was soon back on the move eastward to capture more towns and bridges in their last battles and deepest thrust into Germany. As he left Buchenwald behind, Stephan was haunted by the reality that the end of the Third Reich was not coming soon enough for so many. He was also aware that it was a miracle his father had lived to make his way to America, and that he hadn't died in a camp like Buchenwald.

Stephan Lewy had a strong sense that his father's decision to send him out of Germany in the summer of 1939 and into the care of the Jewish Rescue Organization in France had likely saved him from a similar fate.

Guy Stern came to Buchenwald three days after its liberation. First Army headquarters was now at Bad Hersfeld, ninety miles to the west, and there was no military reason to make the trip, but Guy went with several members of his IPW team, including Captain Kann. He felt that he had to.

As they had advanced farther into Germany, they had been

interrogating more prisoners who had served as guards at different concentration camps. During his sessions with them, Guy had found individual Third Reich soldiers unwilling or unable to see the enormity of what they had done or accept any responsibility. They all claimed to have been lowly functionaries only following orders. In the aggregate, they had no conscience about what they had done. Now Guy was to see German barbarism with his own eyes.

They parked their jeep outside Buchenwald's main gate and walked right in. Guy was instantly struck by the faces of the inmates: loose-hanging skin and slack jaws not unlike the look he had seen on dead soldiers. Even though this is what he had expected to see, nothing could prepare him for the real thing. Many of the liberated prisoners appeared to be more dead than alive, and yet they were all welcoming and thankful and eager to hug anyone in a U.S. Army uniform.

Large containers of fresh drinking water had been set up around the camp. Inmates who were unaccustomed to abundant water clustered around them, drinking from tin cups that had been passed out. A short distance away, one man found old habits hard to break, and he bent over to drink from a muddy puddle, as he had surely done many times before. A GI placed a hand under the man's arm and brought him up, pointing to a container of fresh water. The inmate hobbled over to get a drink.

Guy noticed that many of the newly freed men still cowered and looked around furtively, as if they expected to see SS guards ready to pounce. When Guy stopped to speak to one group of survivors, another inmate standing nearby started loudly berating his fellow survivors for not coming to attention when speaking to the American soldier, as the Germans had required them to do or be viciously beaten. Being liberated did not mean sudden freedom from the habits enforced and traumas inflicted by their recent enslavers. Guy could see that some of those habits and traumas would fade slowly, if at all.

Guy saw a U.S. Army doctor he had met when he was interrogating wounded German soldiers at a field hospital in France. Guy was struck by how clean and pressed the doctor's uniform was, even in the middle of Buchenwald. The doctor spoke a little German, and he was cautioning one of the concentration camp survivors who couldn't stop himself from eating too much too quickly. He was telling the man that overeating right now was dangerous.

Small bites, he counseled. *You can come back for more later.*

The doctor placed his arm around the man, who still wore his filthy prison clothes, and gently led him away from the food. When Guy saw the doctor a short time later, he asked the question he had been mulling over in his mind since they arrived: What were these men's chances of regaining their health?

"Well, Sergeant, I can't give you statistics," said the doctor, "but a good many won't make it. Even with the food, water, and medicine we've brought in, it's already too late for some. I'm afraid they'll be joining the ranks of the dead, and there's not a damn thing we can do for them."

Guy saw groups of German civilians carting remains and placing them on the mounds of naked bodies so decomposed they were falling apart. Overwrought, he could not hold back tears.

Next to him, the master sergeant of the First Army's MP company was taking in the same macabre scene. They had been together since Omaha Beach. Master Sergeant Hadley was a beefy, corn-fed Midwestern Protestant from Steubenville, Ohio; he was a disciplinarian with his men and never gave quarter to them or the prisoners in the cage.

Guy started to step back, not wanting Hadley to see him crying. But then he saw that the tough MP sergeant had turned away and raised a forearm to cover his eyes. Sergeant Hadley was bawling like a baby.

The camp was crowded with U.S. Army personnel, and more medicine, food, clothing, and other supplies were arriving hourly.

Later that day, Guy and the other interrogators left to return to their duties at headquarters. They sat mostly silent during the drive back, all stuck in their own thoughts and feelings.

For Guy, seeing Buchenwald, the first and last concentration camp he would ever set foot inside, was traumatizing. When his parents saw him off on the SS *Hamburg* to America in 1937, he believed in his heart that he would see them again, along with his brother and sister. The plan had been for him to settle in St. Louis and find someone to sign their affidavits so they could join him in the United States. For Guy, that expectation had tempered the sadness of saying good-bye. Of course, nothing had gone as they had planned, and yet in the years since his mother's last letter in 1942 from the Warsaw ghetto, he kept alive the hope that his family would find a way to survive, and that once the war was over they would all be reunited.

But what he saw at Buchenwald ripped at his heart and took away what hope remained.

On April 28, 1945, the night before his twenty-first birthday, Manny Steinfeld left 82nd Airborne headquarters to join a late-night patrol across the Elbe River in northern Germany. The mission was to capture some enemy prisoners to interrogate before the division crossed the Elbe in force. On the way to meet the patrol, Manny's jeep got a flat tire, and he was delayed by an hour while changing it. The flat tire turned out to be an early birthday present for him.

By the time Manny arrived, the patrol, consisting of eight troopers and a lieutenant, had already pushed off at 10 P.M. as planned, paddling flat-bottomed assault boats across more than four hundred yards of open water. Everything was quiet until they were within fifteen yards of the opposite shore, when they were hit by heavy enemy machine gun fire. The canvas boats were ripped apart and only two survivors were able to swim back to safety.

At a time like this, these were the worst kind of losses for a veteran outfit like the 82nd, as everyone knew the war was winding down and no one wanted to be counted among its final casualties. The men who had been with the division the longest had made four combat jumps and fought in five campaigns. So far, they had bucked the law of averages, but they knew the longer they were exposed to fighting, the more likely it was that the odds would catch up with them. After everything they had been through, getting killed or maimed now just didn't seem fair.

On April 30, the same day Hitler committed suicide in his underground bunker as Soviet forces approached the outskirts of Berlin, the 82nd Airborne crossed the Elbe at four places near Bleckede and established a bridgehead against moderate resistance. Under orders from General Eisenhower to make a fast and furious advance toward the Soviets in order to keep them from advancing too far to the west and gobbling up too much territory by war's end, the paratroopers pushed thirty-six miles the first day. Along the way, they took six hundred German prisoners, many of whom by this time were no longer interested in fighting or dying for Hitler or the Fatherland.

By the afternoon of May 2, division headquarters was located in the charming town of Ludwigslust, fifty miles east of the Elbe. Standing outside the eighteenth-century Palace of Ludwigslust, which would serve as his last and most opulent command post of the war, General Gavin, in a parachute jumpsuit faded from three years of war and carrying his omnipresent M1 rifle over his shoulder, looked like any other GI but for the two stars on his collar.

That afternoon, a trooper reported to him that a German officer under a white flag was looking for the U.S. general in charge. Escorted over to Gavin, the Wehrmacht staff officer said he represented General Kurt von Tippelskirch, commander of the 21st German Army Group, who was ready to surrender. A meeting was set for that evening at the palace, located in the middle of a vast garden and English-style park with canals, fountains, and artificial cascades.

For the rest of the day, large numbers of German soldiers came out of the woods and milled about on the roads. As the hours passed, their numbers increased. Ordered by the Americans to throw away their weapons and start walking to the rear, a long procession of defeated Germans moved westward, heading back toward the Elbe.

Manny was summoned for the surrender meeting.

When the appointed hour came, the scene could not have been a starker contrast from the devastation of the war across all of Europe. The formal surrender was carried out in a high-ceilinged room that had quilted silk wall coverings, sparkling chandeliers, and life-sized oil paintings of former residents hung on the walls. General von Tippelskirch was resplendent in a full-length leather coat, belted at the waist. With a cool and proper manner, he offered to surrender if he could keep his army where it now stood and if Gavin would tell the Soviets to cease their attacks from the east. Gavin replied that he had no control over what the Russians would do. Either von Tippelskirch would surrender unconditionally so his men could walk unarmed toward the rear through U.S. forces to the west—or the 82nd Airborne would continue to fight his army and push them eastward, thereby cornering von Tippelskirch's remaining forces, some of whom would surely fall to the Soviets. Clear that he would rather surrender to the Americans than the Soviets, the German general agreed to the terms. Gavin dictated a surrender document, which was typed up while everyone waited. In an adjacent room, Manny worked on the German translation, which he added to the document underneath the paragraph in English, which read:

LUDWIGSLUST, GERMANY
2 MAY 1945

I, Lieutenant General von Tippelskirch, Commanding General of 21st German Army, hereby unconditionally surrender the 21st German Army, and all of its attachments and equipment and appurtenances thereto, to the Commanding General of the 82nd Airborne Division, United States Army.

On that day—one "without precedent in American military history," Gavin later observed—an army group comprising 150,000 troops with all its tanks, vehicles, artillery, assorted equipment, and small arms, surrendered to a single division less than one-tenth its strength.

Since Manny knew some Russian—he had been required to study it when the army sent him to college in 1943—Gavin had him go with the division's recon platoon the next morning as it headed east to make contact with the Soviet army. It was a hair-raising ride in a few vehicles that sped past German troops who the Americans hoped had gotten word of their army's surrender. If they hadn't, the U.S. vehicles would be easy targets. When they drove into an abandoned area that appeared to be no-man's-land between the retreating Germans and the advancing Russians, the only evidence of war was piles of discarded German weapons left in the ditches next to the road.

At approximately 10:25 A.M. on May 3, the forward units of the two great Allied armies that had defeated the German army on the eastern and western fronts met in the town of Grabow. It was the deepest penetration into northern and central Germany by any U.S. division during the war. There were at least thirty Soviet tanks of the 8th Brigade of the 8th Russian Mechanized Corps parked in the streets, and soldiers from both sides came together, laughing and hugging, because they knew the war was over. Manny climbed atop a Soviet tank, wrapped an arm around the main gun barrel, and joined other smiling GIs and Russians as pictures were snapped. It was a memorable few hours, as the soldiers from the two Allied armies relaxed, shook hands, took pictures of one another, and shed some of the weight of the long war.

But when the Americans returned to Ludwigslust at about 3 P.M., Manny's mood abruptly plummeted when he learned that he was being dispatched to a concentration camp that had been discovered outside of town. During the war, he had heard many rumors about the existence of Nazi death camps, and he had recently read an

Manny Steinfeld (*right*) greeting Russian soldiers in Grabow, Germany, on May 3, 1945. *(Family photograph)*

article in *Stars and Stripes* about Buchenwald's liberation. As he drove to the camp outside of Ludwigslust, Manny knew that he was about to see the human toll for himself.

The main gate of Wöbbelin concentration camp was wide open when he arrived, and the guard towers were deserted. Manny had noticed the stench of death before the camp even came into view. Army medical personnel wearing Red Cross armbands were ministering to living skeletons who wore filthy prison-striped uniforms. A flatbed truck parked just inside the barbed-wire enclosure was stacked with bodies that had turned bluish-black. Manny stepped from the jeep and stopped. He could go no farther.

The last time he had heard from his mother was a letter in 1941. She said rumors were circulating in their hometown of Josbach that the six Jewish families faced deportation to Poland. Manny had no idea if she and his sister, Irma, had been transported to the east or if they were still in Germany. It now occurred to Manny that Poland was twice as far away from Josbach as Ludwigslust—in fact, some 250 miles farther. Was it possible they had ended up being sent here instead?

For the longest time, Manny Steinfeld was unable to enter Wöbbelin. He was overwhelmed with fear that he would find his mother and sister among the dead.

For Werner Angress, watching the German army collapse in April 1945 was almost surreal. He had been born and raised in Berlin, had experienced firsthand the Nazis' seizure of power in 1933, and for years after had felt humiliated, threatened, and fearful until he immigrated to America. Now, the end of the war against Hitler and the Nazis felt almost personal.

On April 30, Werner was standing by a country road crowded with Germans—soldiers and civilians alike—fleeing the Russians and heading west toward the Elbe River, when a passing GI in a jeep called out the news: Hitler had killed himself.

Behind Werner was a truck loaded with crates of German food, Hungarian salamis, boxes of cigars, and cases of alcohol that had been seized that morning from passing German soldiers. Werner grabbed a bottle of Aquavit, a flavored Norwegian vodka, uncorked it, and made a toast to the dead Führer: "Long may he rot!" As he and his fellow 82nd Airborne paratroopers passed the bottle around, they all lit cigars.

It was later that same day that Werner heard of his division's discovery of Wöbbelin concentration camp. As news spread that U.S. forces had crossed the Elbe, the camp's SS guards ran off to avoid capture, leaving behind the starving prisoners, most of them too sick or weak to leave. But the next day three inmates did make it the few miles into Ludwigslust, smashing the window of a closed store to acquire civilian clothes. Several 82nd paratroopers spotted the men in prison stripes breaking into the store, questioned them, and alerted their superiors to reports of the concentration camp.

That same day, Werner drove to the camp with two intelligence

Wöbbelin concentration camp. *(United States Holocaust Memorial Museum)*

officers as passengers. At the time, he had never heard of Hitler's Final Solution, or of Auschwitz or the other Nazi death camps in Poland that had been constructed for only one purpose: to kill quickly and efficiently human beings by the thousands every day. Although he had known since the 1930s that concentration camps such as Dachau and Buchenwald existed in Germany, he had never seen one until he entered Wöbbelin. Inside the main gate, half-starved-to-death human beings lay on ground littered with excrement and rotten remains of food. It was all so appalling and the smell so foul that the officers with him rushed to the fence and vomited.

Wöbbelin had opened three months earlier as a transit camp for inmates evacuated from other concentration camps in the path of the Soviets as the Nazis sought to cover up evidence of the mass killings. Forced on long death marches from the east, the majority of prisoners arriving at Wöbbelin were men, but there was an adjacent, smaller camp with women inmates. All had been left behind barbed-wire fences without adequate food or medical care under catastrophic sanitary conditions.

In a washhouse, Werner found dead bodies stacked one atop the other. Some were in a state of putrefaction, with limbs, thin as sticks, falling off. Outside was a pit filled with water and a powdery chemical that looked like quicklime.

Inside one of the tarpaper shacks that served as barracks, one survivor was sitting in a shaft of light picking off lice. His legs were covered with open sores festering with flies and maggots. He twisted around to show Werner his back, lacerated with old and new scars and welts, reminders of beatings by the guards.

Back in the open courtyard, everywhere Werner turned were dead bodies and shrunken prisoners who seemed to be barely hanging on to life. Their faces, no matter their age, were old. For some, he knew their chances of survival were low despite the best efforts of doctors and medics from the division's medical company that

Gavin had rushed to the camp. Trucks were arriving to evacuate the sickest and most undernourished to an American field hospital that had been set up in Ludwigslust, where they would be given medical treatment and proper nourishment. Another one of Gavin's early orders: German soldiers caught in the area were being brought into the camp to pull bodies that hadn't yet completely decomposed out of the bubbling chemical pit.

Evacuation of freed survivors from Wöbbelin to an American field hospital. *(United States Holocaust Memorial Museum)*

Werner spent time speaking with the inmates, many of whom showed him the numbers tattooed on their forearms. Most came from European countries conquered by the armies of the Third Reich, and had been used— some for years—as forced laborers. About a quarter of Wöbbelin's nearly four thousand liberated inmates were Jews who had survived other camps before arriving here, where there had been no systematic exterminations. Rather, the estimated one thousand deaths in three months came from starvation, disease, and maltreatment.

Werner drove the two badly shaken officers back to Ludwigslust, then returned to the houses closest to the camp to find out from the residents what they knew about it. One man said he preferred to take a detour rather than to pass by it. Another said he hadn't been concerned about what was going on there because he had enough worries. Werner insisted on entering their homes and looking in their kitchens, where he found nearly full larders. Perhaps there had been some rationing, but they were not suffering, living in nice houses where even the dogs and cats were well-fed. Yet the residents seemed unconcerned by the poor starving souls a few miles away. What had happened to the Germany he had once known and loved? It was a nation that would have to pay for its crimes for years to come.

In accordance with a policy mandated by Eisenhower that ordered "all atrocity victims to be buried in a public place," along with a stone monument to commemorate the dead, Gavin issued his own orders.

Residents of Ludwigslust, especially those who during the past twelve years of Nazi rule had held some official position or had been members of the Nazi Party, were required to dig two hundred graves in the manicured gardens of the opulent Palace of Ludwigslust. Furthermore, Gavin mandated that the town's entire adult population be at the mass funeral service, after which they were to walk between the rows of graves, paying their respects to the victims. Each of the deceased lay next to his or her grave, their bodies wrapped in white sheets locals were required to provide from home, with their faces uncovered. Dozens of captured German officers, including five generals, were made to attend.

Werner and the 82nd's other Ritchie Boys were assigned to watch over the German officers, who stood with them behind one row of graves. When Ludwigslust's new mayor—the former one, doubtless a loyal Nazi, had committed suicide after murdering his wife and daughter when he heard the Americans were approaching—started speaking into a microphone, several German officers behind Werner turned their backs and lit up cigarettes.

Werner whirled around and demanded they drop the cigarettes. One tall German captain looked at him with daggers in his eyes. He told Werner he had no right to give an order to an officer, as he was merely a sergeant. Werner repeated his order, but the Germans kept smoking.

Werner drew his .45 pistol and pointed it at the captain's head.

"You have a choice," Werner said in German. "Either I shoot you

At left, German civilians forced to pay respects to two hundred victims from Wöbbelin concentration camp during burial ceremonies in Ludwigslust on May 7, 1945. (*U.S. Army Signal Corps*)

for disobeying my order or you extinguish your cigarette and face the funeral."

The captain gave him a hateful look but threw down the cigarette. The other Germans followed suit and turned back toward the services.

Only later did it fully sink in for Werner Angress that his finger had been on the trigger and his threat to shoot had been real.

Manny Steinfeld was also there that day. He had helped make the funeral arrangements for the two hundred Wöbbelin victims, and at the service, he was shocked by the locals' demeanor. They obviously did not want to be there and seemed to feel that an injustice had been done by making them attend. They watched the proceedings without showing any sympathy or remorse. Manny had never seen a funeral with so few tears. While the victims were at least getting proper burials, they were going to their final resting places as unidentified victims of the Nazis, with no loved ones to grieve their deaths. Indeed, many of their loved ones had themselves been victims. About one-fourth of the survivors were Jewish, so it was decided that an equal percentage of the graves would have a painted Star of David over them, and the rest had wooden crosses.

None of the locals Manny spoke to accepted blame or admitted to having any knowledge of the horrors that had taken place three miles away. In occupied Germany, the refrain "We didn't know" was becoming as common as *"Ich bin kein Nazi"* (I am no Nazi). The Germany Manny had left when his mother put him on a train as a fourteen-year-old to join other Jewish refugee children on a ship to America had *lots* of flag-waving Nazis. Now that the Thousand-Year Reich had fallen, where had they all gone?

The eulogy was delivered by the 82nd Airborne chaplain with whom Manny had crash-landed into Holland aboard a glider during Operation Market Garden. Now a major and a veteran of four parachute jumps into combat zones, George "Chappie" Wood spared none of the Germans in attendance.

"The world has been horrified at the crimes of the German nation; these crimes were never clearly brought to light until the armies of the united nations overran Germany. This is not war as conducted by international rules of warfare. This is murder such as is not even known among savages. Though you claim no knowledge of those acts, you are still individually and collectively responsible for these atrocities, for they were committed by a government elected to office by yourselves in 1933 and continued in office by your indifference to organized brutality. It should be the firm resolve of the German people that never again should any leader or party bring them to such moral degradation as is exhibited here."

When Manny had at last been able to walk into Wöbbelin concentration camp that first day, he passed mounds of skeletal remains. At one barracks, dead bodies were piled up four feet high at the entrance. Stepping into another barracks, he found emaciated men lying on straw in their own filth like farm animals.

Manny Steinfeld did not return to the concentration camp. He could not shake the fear that his mother and sister had ended up in such a place. If they had, he prayed that the end of the war had come in time for them.

12

DENAZIFICATION

On April 7, 1945, Hauptmann Curt Bruns was tried by a military commission at First Army headquarters in Duren, Germany. The charge against him for "ordering, directing or causing" the deaths of Ritchie Boys Kurt Jacobs and Murray Zappler after they became POWs was read aloud. Bruns pled not guilty through his U.S. Army lawyer appointed to defend him.

The case was one of several tried by a commission appointed by General Courtney Hodges, commanding general of the First Army, prior to the end of the war. It was specifically authorized by Supreme Headquarters Allied Expeditionary Force, which provided for trying under military law "those war criminals who are accused of such violations of the laws and customs of war that threaten the security or impair the efficiency of our forces." The commission that would decide Bruns's fate consisted of five army colonels, a major, and a lieutenant. Conviction required the votes of at least five of the seven members.

Called as a witness for the prosecution, First Lieutenant Fred P. Drexel, of the 106th Infantry Division, who had been attached to Jacobs's and Zappler's IPW team until a month before their deaths, testified that both men were German-born Jews who became naturalized U.S. citizens.

In a pretrial memo, an Inspector General investigator pointed out that if Jacobs and Zappler had been citizens of Germany at the time they were captured and shot, the defense might claim their execution as spies was justified under "privileges of lawful belligerents," even though under the laws of war they would first have had to be convicted by a military tribunal. When the trial began, the defense attorney followed exactly this strategy, asking on cross-examination if Drexel had "any direct personal knowledge" they were "actually citizens of the United States."

"No, sir, I do not."

On redirect, the prosecutor drew out from Drexel that he and Jacobs and Zappler had all been trained at the Military Intelligence Training Center at Camp Ritchie, then asked: "Was it compulsory in the school you attended for nationals of countries or nations other than the United States to be naturalized before they were assigned to IPW teams?"

"To the best of my knowledge, it was, sir."

Next to take the stand was the German corporal from Bruns's battalion who had first reported the executions to Guy Stern. Heinrich Kauter testified to being captured along with other Germans on December 16 and being interrogated by Jacobs and Zappler. He explained how he and the other Germans were liberated by their own forces on December 20, and while they were passing the customs house some of them reported to Hauptmann Bruns about being interrogated by two German Jews.

"What did Captain Bruns say about the two American Jewish soldiers?" asked the prosecutor.

"He said, 'The Jews have no right to live in Germany.'"

After the two interrogators were pulled from the group, Kauter said, they were lined up with their backs to the wall of the customs house and spoken to by Bruns, who then called over Sergeant Hoffman.

"What orders did Captain Bruns give to Sergeant Hoffman?"

"I didn't hear," Kauter said.

Kauter did, however, hear one of the Americans say to Bruns and Hoffman in German that they wanted to be treated as American POWs under the Geneva Conventions.

Q: *What did Captain Bruns say?*
A: He didn't say anything.

Q: *What happened next?*
A: They were taken away by Sergeant Hoffman and four men.

Q: *Were those men armed with weapons?*
A: Yes.

Q: *What happened after they marched them off?*
A: They took them away from the customs house, not far away from the corner of the forest, and shot them.

Q: *Did you see these two Americans shot?*
A: Yes.

Q: *Did you hear the shots fired by these German soldiers that hit these two American soldiers?*
A: Twice it was fired, yes.

Q: *You speak of hearing fire twice. Did you mean single shots or shots in volley?*
A: Volley.

Q: *Did you see the American soldiers fall?*
A: Yes, they fell.

Q: *Where was Captain Bruns at the time these shots were fired and the Americans fell?*
A: He was on the street.

The next witness called was First Army trusty Anton Korn, who testified to his two days spent in a cell adjacent to Curt Bruns, during which time Bruns told him of his hatred for Jews and admitted to ordering the two American interrogators to be separated from the other POWs and shot.

After briefly cross-examining Korn, the defense called its one and only witness, Curt Bruns. Under questioning by his attorney, Bruns admitted for the first time that he knew "maybe one" of the German-speaking Americans was Jewish. He told how he had them separated from the other POWs so he could question them, but claimed, also for the first time, that he put them back at the "end of the column" of hundreds of American POWs as they marched away.

"Do you know what, if anything, happened to those two German-speaking soldiers later?" asked his attorney.

"Yes. At ten o'clock the group of prisoners went away, including the two German-speaking soldiers. At two o'clock I heard what happened. My commander . . . must have given the order to shoot [them]."

Under cross-examination, Bruns stuck to his story that he had heard about the shootings only after the fact. He identified Korn as being in the cell next to his for two days and admitted to talking to him "about a case," but denied making the admissions of guilt Korn attributed to him.

The prosecutor next asked Bruns if he had made the statement "Jews cannot live in Germany."

"No," answered Bruns.

The sworn statement of Margarethe Meiters, a nineteen-year-old German woman who lived in the customs house, was placed into evidence. She had told army investigators she knew who Hauptmann Bruns was, but she never talked to him because he was "too cocky." She saw him on the morning of December 20 yelling to his men escorting the group of American POWs, "If they don't hold their hands up, I'll shoot them!" She then entered the customs house to do her chores and did not see the two Americans removed from the larger group. Later that day, Margarethe said that Lieutenant Oppermann, whom she knew was Bruns's adjunct, came into the customs house and told her, "In Germany there isn't room for captured Negroes or Jews. Today we shot two Jews. Didn't you hear it or see it?" She told him she had not. The lieutenant went on to describe the grisly details of the murders: that they had been shot in a meadow up the road and they were "still lying there . . . we didn't bury them," in case she wanted to go out and see them. She did not.

Then both attorneys gave short closing arguments.

Upon secret written ballot, the commission members concurred in a finding of guilty, and by a vote on a separate ballot, they sentenced Curt Bruns to death by firing squad.

At 9:30 A.M. on June 14, 1945—five weeks after the war in Europe ended with Germany's unconditional surrender—U.S. Army MPs came for Hauptmann Curt Bruns in the Braunschweig city prison west of Berlin. They drove him to a quarry outside of town that was being used by the army for executions. Placed before a tall wooden stake, he was asked by a colonel if he wanted to make a last statement. Bruns said only that he was dying an innocent man.

His feet were tied together and his hands tied behind the stake. He was offered a blindfold, which he accepted. The U.S. Army firing squad marched into position, a sergeant leading eight privates carrying locked and loaded rifles. One rifle contained a blank cartridge, so that no individual could know whether he had fired a fatal bullet.

They halted and formed a line facing the prisoner.

"Squad, ready!" commanded the colonel.

"Aim!"

All eight rifles were lifted into position.

"Fire!"

Hauptmann Curt Bruns was struck by a single volley.

Hauptmann Curt Bruns, convicted by a military tribunal of ordering the murders of Ritchie Boys Kurt Jacobs and Murray Zappler, arriving at the quarry where he was executed by a firing squad on June 14, 1945. *(U.S. Army Signal Corps)*

He slumped over at the stake, dead, dressed in the same German officer's uniform he had worn that day in front of the customs house.

In late April 1945, Stephan Lewy and the 6th Armored awaited the Russians near Chemnitz, some fifty miles from the German-Czech border. No one in the division was pleased when they withdrew west of the Mulde River to avoid any clashes with the Russians. After having spent the war moving forward, the 6th's commander, Major General Grow, hated to go backward and give up "any of our ground."

Contact was made on May 6 when two Soviet infantry divisions arrived in Chemnitz. Naturally, everyone in the 6th was eager to see the infamous hordes from the east, and they weren't disappointed by what they saw. The Red Army had utilized every possible kind of vehicle, including horse-drawn wagons, to transport troops and equipment. The parade included civilians mixed in with soldiers in myriad uniforms, everyone all scrambled into columns that seemed to have no order. Young and old, men and women, Mongolians and Caucasians, all marched together, completely out of step with one another, and looking less like an army and more like a band of misfits. Their weapons and equipment seemed so antiquated and unimpressive that some GIs openly questioned how this ragtag outfit had been able to so soundly defeat the Germans on the eastern front.

Two nights later, the generals of both armies and their staffs held a shindig that started off stiffly but loosened up after many shots of Russian vodka. One decorated U.S. airborne colonel and regimental commander, after going through the entire war without sustaining an injury, leapt from a second-story window to show the Russians how American paratroopers jumped from airplanes. He fractured his leg on landing.

There were east-meets-west parties for the lower ranks as well. At one of them that same evening, Stephan and another Ritchie Boy, speaking Yiddish, attempted to convince a Russian Jewish soldier to defect to the American side in order to have a better life. He listened to their pitch with evident interest, but demurred. *I can't,* he finally said. *My family is stuck in Russia. If I do anything like that, they will suffer.*

The next day, May 9, all active operations in the European Theater of Operations ended under terms of Germany's unconditional surrender. The 6th Armored, after a short period of rehabilitation and maintenance, was sent to Aschaffenburg for occupational duties that included maintaining public safety and setting up a military government.

General Eisenhower had ordered the arrest of all leaders of Nazi organizations. As the National Socialist Party was organized down to neighborhood blocks, in a city such as Aschaffenburg, with thirty thousand residents, that meant a significant number of Nazis to be rounded up. Stephan was quick to volunteer for the job.

The first thing he did was go to the local police station.

"I want the names of all the Nazi block leaders in the city," he told the clerk behind the counter, who himself was likely a Nazi. Germans kept good records, Stephan knew, and luckily the station hadn't been leveled in the weeklong battle that had ended in early April when the Germans defended the city with particular determination, resulting in house-to-house fighting and widespread urban destruction.

The clerk dutifully pulled bound records off the shelves from a bookcase against the wall. They contained names, addresses, and group affiliations. Stephan enlisted two husky MPs, and they set to work. Twice weekly—on Tuesdays and Thursdays—they left at 4 A.M. in a 2.5-ton truck and went block by block knocking on doors, just as the Nazis in Berlin had knocked on doors at all hours looking for his father and other Jewish men. When they found someone on the list, he was loaded in the back of the truck. When there was no more room, Stephan would drop off the newly captured Nazis at MP headquarters, where they were held in cells and prisoner cages for questioning. As word spread around town, Stephan often only had to knock once, and the man of the house, fully dressed and clutching a small suitcase, would instantly open the door, say good-bye to his wife, and climb into the truck.

Stephan wished his father could see these Nazi roundups.

Most of the men he brought in—about seventy-five each day— were interviewed and released. The official Allied policy of "de-Nazification" was to ferret out Nazi officials and remove them from whatever positions they held, but the impracticality of the program soon became apparent (it was officially ended in 1948). Nazis had been running the power plants, sanitation departments, railroads, and sundry other necessary functions for years, and their expertise was needed if the new Germany was to recover from the devastation of war. It bothered Stephan that so many Nazi Party followers were put back on the streets and into their old jobs, but there was nothing he could do about it. Besides, he knew it would be impossible to keep every Nazi block leader in jail because there weren't enough cells in the country. His mission had been to find them, bring them in, and lock them up. Regardless of how long they stayed behind bars, Stephan reveled in the satisfaction of this assignment. He knew he was scaring the Nazis by picking them up, and disrupting their lives by taking them from their families, however briefly, just the way they had scared him and his father and mother, split their family apart, and disrupted their lives. All in all, it was one of the more gratifying jobs of his time in the army.

One day, Stephan was walking down the street with another GI when a woman ran up, screaming in German to arrest a man.

"Verhaftet ihn! Verhaftet diesen Mann!"

She pointed to a well-dressed man on the sidewalk who was hurrying away. In perfect English, the man said over his shoulder, "That woman is demented." Stephan ordered the man to stop until he could get more information. The man protested but did as he was told.

The woman said she recognized him as a Nazi doctor who had done medical and chemical experiments on concentration camp inmates.

Stephan asked, *"Wie kannst du das wissen?"* (How do you know?) She lifted her skirt and showed her terribly scarred legs.

"Ich war eines seiner Opfer," she said. (I was one of his victims.)

Stephan turned to the man and told him he would have to come in for questioning.

In an interrogation room at MP headquarters, the man admitted he was a medical doctor but denied ever working in a concentration camp. His nervous, sweaty demeanor suggested otherwise.

The man's ID gave his home address. Stephan, while others continued to question the doctor, paid a visit to his home with one of his beefy MPs. A woman answered the door. Stephan told her he needed to speak to her about her husband.

She let them in, and they followed her into the kitchen. She was wringing her hands as she stood by the sink, acting every bit as nervous as the doctor. As she poured a glass of water, her hands trembled. Stephan sat at the kitchen table with the MP behind him.

"*Ja,*" she said warily.

Stephan asked if her husband had been a doctor in a concentration camp.

Oh, no.

Did he perform experiments on prisoners?

He didn't do that.

Stephan wanted the truth, and he knew he hadn't gotten it from the doctor or his wife up till now. He casually placed his .45 pistol on the table simply as a stage prop, but it was a very effective one.

Without changing his tone, he said if he couldn't get the information he required, he would wait for her husband to come home. Her eyes fixed on the gun, she began to backtrack.

I think he worked in a camp. Ja.

The doctor's claim of never working in a concentration camp was soon demolished by his wife, who handed over papers that gave the names of camps and the dates that he had been assigned there.

Back at headquarters, Stephan arranged for the Nazi doctor's transfer to another military prison facility, and for other agencies to take over the investigation and gather additional evidence for a war crime trial.

For Stephan Lewy, his return to Germany had turned personal.

After Manny Steinfeld's 82nd Airborne Order of Battle team was disbanded, he was assigned to the three-man military government office in the city of Boizenburg, some thirty miles west of Ludwigslust.

Until April 30, Boizenburg had its own concentration camp, one of eighty subcamps in the Neuengamme system that was responsible for at least fifty thousand deaths from forced labor, lack of food, improper sanitation, disease, and Nazi brutality. Wöbbelin, which

Manny would never forget after seeing its prisoners and assisting with the burial ceremony in Ludwigslust, had also been a Neuengamme subcamp.

In another one of those chance encounters taking place on the streets of Germany between newly freed survivors and their Nazi oppressors trying to meld back into society or escape to safer havens, a woman who had survived five years of imprisonment at Ravensbrück women's concentration camp was using a coupon to buy bread at a bakery in Boizenburg in May 1945 when she spotted a man in high boots. Although she only glimpsed him from the side, the sight of him made the blood rush to her heart. *Was it really him?* She felt she had no choice but to make sure.

The woman was Margarete Buber-Neumann, the forty-five-year-old widow of Heinz Neumann, once a leading German communist, with whom she had gone to Moscow in 1937. After her husband was arrested and shot in a Stalin purge, she spent two years in the gulag before being handed over to the Nazis with other German communists as part of the German-Soviet Nonaggression Pact of 1939. The Nazis sent her to Ravensbrück with other so-called undesirables. Since gaining her freedom in April, she had been on a tortuous journey to Bavaria by foot and bicycle. Malnourished, ill, and not even halfway there, she had stopped to rest for a few days in Boizenburg.

As she followed the man, the distance between them grew shorter. She looked for American soldiers to hail but saw none. If it was him, should she grab him by the arm to hold him? No, he would only knock her over with blows of his fists as he had done to so many defenseless women. At one point he stopped to look in a shop window, and she had to walk past him. Then, after she paused at a window farther down the sidewalk, he overtook her again, then turned into a side street. She knew it would soon be too late. He would get away and might never be seen again by anyone who knew who he was. She was now certain the man in the high boots was Ludwig Ramdohr.

For the past three years, Ramdohr had been the Gestapo chief at

Ravensbrück, the only Nazi concentration camp built for women. Between 1939 and 1945, 130,000 women from all over Europe were imprisoned there. The women were beaten, starved, tortured, forced into slave labor, and randomly executed by firing squad, by public hanging, or at outside gassing facilities. In early 1945, Ravensbrück became an extermination camp when the SS installed a gas chamber, and some five thousand to six thousand women were gassed in only a few months.* Even in such a murderous setting, Ramdohr was notorious for his bestial cruelty. He specially designed his own interrogation room for working over prisoners. His methods were crude and brutal. He would start off by making them stand with a strap pulled through ankle shackles and tied around their neck, forcing them to bend over at a painful angle. Or he would lash them with his leather whip or give them an injection of narcotics.

Ramdohr rarely wore a uniform, preferring a dark flannel suit. He didn't care what the SS commandant thought, because Ramdohr answered only to his Gestapo bosses in Berlin. He ran an elaborate spy network based on rewards and punishment, seeking incriminating evidence on prisoners as well as guards and administrators. To extort the information he wanted, he would force a woman to lie stomach down on a table; then, with her head hanging over one edge, he would grab her hair and submerge her face in a bucket of water until she nearly drowned. Another of his torture techniques was to have a woman fold her hands, then he inserted pencils between her fingers and pressed down on her hands until her fingers broke. A favorite device he designed was a coffin with ventilation holes that he could close and metal claws that penetrated the flesh. He also used his infamous "shower method," where a woman was brought into a special shower-bath and made to take off all her clothes. Ramdohr turned on cold water from all sides, including fire-hose strength sprays from the top and bottom. When

---

* The total death toll at Ravensbrück is unknown, but estimates put the figure at between thirty thousand and fifty thousand women.

she tried to move or use her hands to protect herself, she would have a bucket of water thrown into her face, or she would be set upon by an attack dog.

After a session with Ramdohr, most women couldn't walk and had to be dragged back to their cell unconscious. They were brought back another day for more of the same if Ramdohr was unhappy with the results of his interrogations, which often drew false confessions and groundless accusations to stop the agony. Hearing the name "Ramdohr" was enough to make women in Ravensbrück tremble, as Margarete did now when she saw him on the streets of Boizenburg.

At last, she spotted three American soldiers walking down the street and rushed to them, speaking German. *"Bitte verhaften Sie diesen Mann!"*

Manny Steinfeld was the only one who understood her, and he asked why she wanted a man arrested. She told him who Ramdohr was and gestured wildly toward where he had turned the corner. Manny saw that she still wore a striped camp shirt under her light jacket. He told her to stay where she was, and he and the other soldiers took off after the man in the high boots and caught up with him a few blocks away.

"Hände hoch!" Manny yelled.

Ramdohr put his hands up as ordered, and he was searched for weapons. They brought him back and stood him in front of Margarete.

He looked so different now with fear contorting *his* face, she thought. It was a look she had never seen on him before.

Are you Ramdohr? she asked tentatively.

Frau Buber, you do me wrong. I also once was against the Nazis.

Manny took them both to the military government office. Once there, Ramdohr confirmed to Manny he had been at Ravensbrück but denied being a member of the Gestapo or SS. He said he had only been a police detective investigating financial crimes there, and he should be allowed to go on his way immediately.

Manny moved to another interrogation room, where he asked Margarete to start at the beginning with all she knew about Ramdohr. She described in graphic detail how Ramdohr abused and tortured the women in camp. Manny tried to remain dispassionate as he took notes, but his hands shook and he tasted bile. He pictured his mother and sister suffering at the hands of such a monster. Margarete said that Ramdohr, after one brutal session with her, kept her in solitary confinement for fifteen weeks of "dark arrest" that nearly drove her mad.

Manny knew that in order to keep Ramdohr in custody, the first step was getting some proof that he was Gestapo or SS, as all former members of those Nazi organizations were subject to automatic arrest as possible war criminals. That ensured they would not be able to disappear inside Germany or to another country as army investigators found other victims and documented their alleged crimes prior to charges being filed.

"He claims to have been a police detective, not Gestapo," Manny said. "He also claims not to have been SS. Did you ever see him in uniform?"

In Margarete's recollection, Ramdohr had always worn a business suit. But then she remembered one day when she was still in solitary confinement that a ray of light had abruptly come in through a flap that opened in the door. She had gone up to it and stood blinking, meeting Ramdohr's glare, and he had been in an SS uniform. It was a chink in Ramdohr's own story of being only a policeman, and Margarete's signed statement along with her witness account gave Manny what he needed to hold Ramdohr and refer his case to Allied legal authorities for further investigation.

Ludwig Ramdohr never again walked the streets a free man. He was convicted twenty months later—after testimony by many of his victims, including Margarete Buber-Neumann—in the first of seven trials for war crimes committed by officials and staff at Ravensbrück. Along with nine of his codefendants, Ramdohr was sentenced to death. He went to the gallows on May 3, 1947.

By then, Manny was out of the service, and he read of the execution in the newspaper. Feeling neither joy nor remorse, he was only thankful that the U.S. Army and a twist of fate had allowed him to be in Boizenburg, Germany, that day when one brave camp survivor faced down her Nazi tormentor.

13

GOING HOME

After the German surrender, Martin Selling was sent to a central depot at Bad Schwalbach, Germany. It was to here that most of the IPW teams in Germany came to be given their new assignments. In addition, the depot was swamped with army officers who had spent the war at home but had arrived in its closing days to gain "combat experience" in furtherance of their careers.

Martin watched with disdain as these stateside warriors grabbed the choicest assignments in the new military government being established in postwar Germany, and freely discussed pleasure trips to Paris and elsewhere—all while throwing the calling card "Military Intelligence" around to get priority air transportation and hotel accommodations. As it appeared he would be at the depot for a while before getting his new assignment, Martin requested a few days off to search for family members he had lost contact with.

A newly arrived major denied his request. Martin stared at the breast of the major's blouse, barren of medals, theater-of-war ribbons, battle stars, or overseas stripes. Martin asked sarcastically whether his combat service counted against him. The indignant major demanded an apology. Martin, who was now a second lieutenant after receiving a battlefield commission, said he would sooner take a court-martial.

In no time, Martin became quite unpopular among the newly arriving officers who had sat out the war in the States with cushy jobs. And he chafed at the new rules laid down by the Johnny-come-latelies, which centered around lots of "spit and polish" and endless personnel inspections. His open contempt for them apparently served him well, as Martin's new team was the first to get new orders to another base.

Assigned three enlisted men and two jeeps, he arrived with his intelligence team at 1st Armored Division headquarters in Gerabronn, a small town in south-central Germany. The division staff was surprised to receive them and didn't know what to do with them. The division intelligence officer said he had no work for the team at present and would let them know when something came up. Martin decided not to show his face unnecessarily at division headquarters and told his men they were free to do as they pleased as long as he knew where they were and they did not get themselves or him into any trouble.

Now free to undertake his personal mission, Martin drove fifteen miles north to Niederstetten, a town of five thousand residents where his aunt Gitta—the widowed sister of his late father—had moved with her three children in 1938 after they were picked up by the Nazis during Kristallnacht on the same night as Martin, and released the next day. He had no idea what had happened to them after he left Germany in 1939. Growing up, Martin had been very close to his aunt and cousins, who had lived on a neighboring farm in Lehrberg.

Wearing his army officer's uniform and still packing the .45 sidearm he had carried throughout the war, Martin went to the town hall for information. The mayor was friendly and overflowing with helpfulness, although he said he knew nothing about the fate of the deported Jews beyond what was on an official list with the heading SHIPPED EAST. When Martin read the list, he found the names of his aunt Gitta, her daughter, Kaethe, and her sons, Bernhard and Ignatz. The mayor said none of the town's Jews had yet returned from "the east."

A few days later, Martin took another road trip, this time to Lehrberg, thirty miles away. He had not been back to his hometown since being arrested during Kristallnacht and sent to Dachau. Now he was returning as an American officer, riding in an army jeep driven by his sergeant. They stopped at the home of one of Martin's former neighbors, and soon the living room was filled with other neighbors as word spread of his return. Martin noticed there was not a Jew among them. They told him they didn't know what happened to his aunt and cousins after they had moved away, or any of the other local Jews after they were taken away in 1942.

One of Martin's father's closest friends was a butcher whom his father helped to become a cattle trader. The friend had become quite successful and brought in his two sons as partners. After the older man died, the sons had broken off all contact with Martin's family and became vocal, influential anti-Semites. Now, in the neighbor's living room, one of the sons approached Martin with his hand outstretched to the American officer if not the Jew. Martin refused to shake his hand, a rebuff that was noticed by everyone in the room. Before leaving town, Martin told some people where he was stationed in case any of his relatives showed up.

Three days later, his cousins Kaethe and Ignatz hopped off a slow-moving freight train as it rolled through Lehrberg. They were excited to learn that Martin had just been there and was stationed nearby. Ignatz, who was now eighteen, borrowed a bicycle and pedaled thirty miles to Martin's base. He was exhausted by the time he found Martin, and the cousins warmly embraced. Even before Martin could ask about the rest of the family, Ignatz started telling what had happened to his family.

He said they had all been transported to the Stutthof concentration camp in Poland in the summer of 1942. Upon arriving, everyone over thirty-five years of age, including their mother, was separated out, taken into a nearby wooded area, and shot. The younger ones had to strip the clothes off the dead and bury the naked bodies in a mass grave. Then they were put to hard labor. Bernhard's skills as an auto mechanic got him assigned to take care of the camp commandant's car, while Ignatz was put in a work gang. When the starving Ignatz was caught stealing bread a few months later, he was condemned to death. Bernhard was able to save him from the gas chamber by telling the commandant that if they killed Ignatz, they would have to kill him, too. Apparently Ignatz's mechanical abilities were highly valued by the commandant, because from then on, Ignatz had served as Bernhard's assistant.

Ignatz told Martin all of this dispassionately, seemingly unaware of the horror etched on Martin's face. But now Ignatz paused and took a deep breath before continuing. Bernhard was dead, he told Martin. He had succumbed to typhoid only a day before the guards abandoned the camp as the Russians approached. *"Eines Tages."* (One day.) *"Eines Tages,"* he repeated sadly.

Ignatz had walked out of the camp and wandered back to Germany, hopping one freight train after another. In the Berlin rail yard, he had found his sister sitting atop a flatbed car loaded with lumber on a train pulling out for Leipzig. He hoisted himself aboard, and they had been together since.

Martin had always known Ignatz as the young daredevil in his family, but he had grown from a tousle-haired boy pulling pranks into a serious young man responsible for watching out for his sister now that their mother and older brother were dead and they were all alone. Martin knew it was a miracle that Ignatz and Kaethe had survived the concentration camp and a second miracle that they had found each other, something that was eluding countless other families in the chaos of postwar Europe.

Martin drove Ignatz back to Niederstetten and made sure his cousins had extra food and clothing. Kaethe looked pale and unhealthy, so Martin took her to a local doctor for a checkup. Hanging around for a few days, he reintroduced himself to the mayor and made a point of flashing his uniform around town, hoping it would mean any survivors returning from the camps might be cared for a little better knowing that the U.S. Army took an interest in them. He also filed a legal claim that ultimately led to his cousins getting back their mother's house, which had been sold by the Nazis. Martin also contacted their older sister, Martha, who had immigrated to America in the 1930s as a domestic servant and now lived in New York. Eventually, Ignatz and Kaethe joined her in America.

Soon Martin was on a Victory ship heading to the United States.

Years later, when he wrote and privately published a memoir of his life before and during the war, the book's dedication read: "To Nemesis, the Goddess of Fate and Retribution, and to the United States Army, which enabled me to repay in a small way all the miscreants and their henchmen who unleashed the brutality and malevolence."

Guy Stern had had no strong feelings when he first set foot on German soil during the war; they emerged only after the war ended and

Ritchie Boys Guy Stern, Walter Sears, and Fred Howard (*left to right*) celebrating the end of the war on V-E Day (May 8, 1945) in the town of Bad Hersfeld, located in the heart of Germany. *(Family photograph)*

he returned to his hometown of Hildesheim, where he felt the agony of being awakened to a new reality.

For much of the war, Hildesheim, population sixty-five thousand, was overlooked by Allied bombers because the military potential of its industry had been underestimated. However, a metal works in town produced components that were used in aircraft, such as constant-speed propellers, landing gears, and engines, while other nearby plants made tank parts, torpedoes, and rubber products such as life jackets and inflatable dinghies. In the forest southwest of the city, an engineering company manufactured starters, generators, and other components for truck and tank engines.

The war caught up with Hildesheim late—six weeks before it ended—but, ironically, not because the Allies discovered it was an industrial hub, but rather because a new Allied bombing directive targeted the northern German city as part of a broad initiative to undermine the morale of the German people. At 2 A.M. on March 22, 1945, British and Canadian bombers commenced their attack, dropping a total of nearly five hundred tons of high explosives and more than six hundred incendiary bombs. Nearly two-thirds of the buildings in the city were destroyed or damaged, and the bombs leveled much of the historic district that had long retained its medieval character. Left in ruins was the Hildesheim Cathedral, on the outside of whose apse grew the world's oldest living rosebush, which local legend had long claimed ensured the town's prosperity. Fifteen hundred civilians were killed.

Guy arrived in Hildesheim a few weeks after the war ended. It was his first time back since he left at age fifteen nearly eight years ago. Now stationed in Koblenz, 250 miles to the south, he had gotten approval for the trip from the British command, since Hildesheim was in the British sector of a newly divided Germany.

As his jeep rolled into town, Guy was struck with an eerie sensation of knowing a place that held so many memories and yet barely recognizing it at all. Some buildings that he knew still stood, but they were standing alone in a ruined cityscape like a few teeth in an otherwise toothless mouth. There was the soccer stadium, now destroyed. There was the building that housed his youth gym club, flattened. Guy was required to report to the British commander of the city, and with trembling hands on the steering wheel, he found his way. A British major looked at Guy's papers, announced "all's in order," and assigned a city policeman to accompany Guy while he was in town. The cop was a young newcomer to the force, as many veteran policemen, loyal members of the Nazi Party, had fled or been fired.

They located the street where Guy had lived with his mother and father, his younger brother, Werner, and little sister, Eleonore, but when they reached the building where they had lived in a high-ceilinged third-floor apartment abutting his father's small fabric store, they saw that it was only rubble. Steel beams protruded from heaps of debris and everything else was flattened or incinerated. There had once been stores at street level, but they had been pancaked by the wrecked building. Former residents had chalk-marked their names and new addresses on girders in front of their ruined

Hildesheim in ruins, 1945. *(U.S. Army Signal Corps)*

residences. In front of the collapsed optical store, a message on a beam told customers that the optician Kleinschmidt was conducting business from his home outside the town and gave the address. He was one of the lucky ones, the policeman told Guy, because half the residents of the city were now homeless.

They drove down Lappenberg street, once the town's most scenic neighborhood, past the vacant lot that had once held the Moorish-style synagogue he had first visited at age six on a High Holiday. The lot was barren, as it had been since the Nazis burned down the synagogue in 1938 during Kristallnacht, one year after Guy left Hildesheim and Germany for America.

With the policeman's help, Guy found the temporary quarters of the Ebeling family. Gerhard Ebeling had been among Guy's few gentile classmates to remain friendly with him after the Nazis came to power. His father was the customs official who had done the Sterns a favor by coming to the house to seal with his official stamp Guy's trunk—without even glancing inside—for his trip to America.

When Mrs. Ebeling opened the door and saw Guy, she burst out crying. She threw her arms around him, holding him tightly.

Guy had brought coffee, canned foods, and chocolates, which were difficult to come by and much appreciated by Mrs. Ebeling. When Herr Ebeling appeared, he came over and shook Guy's hand warmly. A subdued and aloof man whom Guy did not know well, the older man was smiling, clearly glad to see his son's boyhood friend.

When Guy asked about Gerhard, they said he had been drafted into the Wehrmacht and had been captured by the British. Guy was relieved to hear that Gerhard had survived the war. He assured them their son was surely being processed along with the hundreds of thousands of former German soldiers and would be home soon.

After that, there was an uncomfortable silence because Guy couldn't find his voice to ask what had really brought him here. Herr Ebeling saw it on his face and stepped in, volunteering what he knew about Guy's family. He described how they, like all the

Jewish families in town, had been forced from their home and lived for a time in an overcrowded collective house, one of eight so-called "Jews' Houses" in town. This concentrated housing was mandated by the local Gestapo as a way to control the Jewish population and facilitate their deportation.

The Jews of Hildesheim were soon sent away in several group transports, he explained. Each family was allowed one hundred pounds of luggage, with men, women, and boys carrying suitcases and wearing backpacks. They were told to bring their cash, securities, savings books, and jewelry with them, but when they were strip-searched inside the old riding hall, the SS and other Nazi functionaries confiscated their valuables. From there they walked to tram line #11 to ride to Hanover.

Herr Ebeling said he heard that they had stayed for a few days in a fenced-in transit camp, then were put on a train to Warsaw, a journey which, according to documents that surfaced some years after the war, took place on March 31, 1942.

Guy told the Ebelings about his mother's letter in the summer of 1942 from Warsaw, where she'd told him they were living in a single room. This was the last he had heard from her, and he told the Ebelings how much he had hoped to find them when he joined the U.S. Army and returned to Europe. If not during the war, then after it was over.

Throughout the story Herr Ebeling was telling Guy, his wife, who had known Guy's mother quite well, had been unable to stop crying. Guy recalled his mother telling him that the Ebelings had long been appalled at the brutalities of the Third Reich, though Herr Ebeling had to be careful not to offend the Nazis in order to keep his job at the customs office.

Now Herr Ebeling shook his head sadly. *None have come back from Warsaw,* he said quietly. Then: *Günther, I fear your family will not return.*

There was much Guy still did not know about the Nazi extermination camps in Poland. He did not yet know that the Warsaw ghetto was the largest of all the Jewish ghettos in Nazi-occupied Europe, with more than four hundred thousand Jews from Poland, Germany, and Czechoslovakia forced into an area slightly larger than one square mile. Or that the first of more than a quarter million men, women, and children from the ghetto were transported by cattle cars to Treblinka the same summer he received his mother's last letter, in which she wrote, "We hope for better days."

He did not know that the first train carrying five thousand Jews from Warsaw arrived at Treblinka on July 23, 1942, with a daily train continuing to bring the same number. Or that upon arrival at Treblinka, which was built for the express purpose of killing all the innocent and defenseless human beings sent there by the Third Reich (more Jews were killed at Treblinka than at any other extermination camp other than Auschwitz), they were herded into dressing sheds and made to strip, supposedly to take showers. The men were usually killed first, inside three closed-off, interconnected barracks, each twenty-six by thirteen feet with double walls insulated with packed earth. The interior walls were covered with small orange terra-cotta tiles with metal faucets set into the ceiling, giving it the appearance of a regular shower room.

Unlike victims at Auschwitz and Majdanek, who were gassed by hydrogen cyanide in the form of Zyklon B, Treblinka's inmates were systematically killed using the exhaust fumes from the engine of a dismantled Soviet armored tank captured during Germany's invasion of Russia in 1941. The tank engine was housed in a room with a generator that supplied the camp with electricity. The engine's exhaust was pumped through inflow pipes that opened into all three death chambers, each of which held some four hundred people. For twenty minutes, the women and children waiting outside heard the men's sounds of suffering. Then the bodies of the men, who died from suffocation and carbon monoxide poisoning, were placed onto carts and wheeled away, and the women and children were herded inside, destined for the same fate.

Within a few months, a new building housing ten gas chambers was constructed, equipped with more fume-producing engines, which made the extermination process more efficient. Soon a train transport of three thousand people could be killed in three hours; in a busy fourteen-hour workday, twelve thousand to fifteen thousand people were murdered.

Guy did not know the full extent of this horror as he drove away from Hildesheim the next day. But his journey home had erased whatever hope he had that he would be reunited with his family. The truth was inescapable.

As he left the town of his youth, Guy Stern had no intention of ever returning.

As soon as the war ended, Werner Angress asked General Gavin for a few days' leave and the use of a jeep to drive 350 miles to Amsterdam, where he hoped to find his family. Just a year ago he had personally asked the general for permission to jump on D-Day even though he'd had no parachute training. Gavin had said yes then, and he approved Werner's request again.

On Gavin's instructions, Werner was provided with an official pass that stated he was traveling to the Netherlands on 82nd Airborne business. There was no firm date for his return or any limitations listed for the trip, a sign of the general's generosity and trust. Once Werner's personal mission was concluded, he was to return to Ludwigslust, where the division was still stationed.

Before leaving, Werner asked his buddies for their latest issue of cigarettes, which everyone received weekly, as well as any extra K-rations. It was well known that the winter of 1944–45 had been a hungry one for the Dutch, and there were still severe food shortages. The cigarettes were used by smokers and nonsmokers alike as currency, and with enough of them, one could buy anything that was available.

In a jeep packed with food, coffee, and cartons of cigarettes, Werner left Ludwigslust on the morning of May 12 and drove west on the autobahns. Although slowed by detours around some destroyed bridges, he made the trip in a single day, arriving in Amsterdam that night. Exhausted, he decided to find a hotel and start his search in the daylight. He got a room for a carton of cigarettes at the elegant Amstel Hotel, which was packed with Canadian officers whose units had liberated Amsterdam a week earlier. There was still no hot water or electricity in the rooms, but the clean sheets, towels, mattress, and pillows were luxury enough after some of the holes in which Werner had spent his nights since parachuting into Normandy on D-Day.

Early the next morning, he drove to Cliostraat 39 in south Amsterdam, where his parents and brothers were living when he left for the United States in 1939. He had heard nothing from any of them since their last letters in December 1941, shortly before America entered the war against Germany, after which his letters to the address had gone unanswered. He parked, found the apartment, and pressed the bell. He waited, not knowing for what. Would the next face he saw be his dear mother's? Or his father's? One of his brothers'? Or the face of a stranger?

A sleepy-looking man in a dressing gown answered the door.

"Your name Angress?" the man asked.

Taken aback, Werner could only nod.

The man said that a woman named Henny Angress had come to the door the day before. "She said if her son from the United States showed up, I was to give you her new address."

Werner found the address a few blocks away. When his mother opened the door, she looked at him and nearly collapsed, shrieking and sobbing. He hugged and consoled her even as her appearance frightened him. In the six years since he had seen her, she had lost forty or fifty pounds, and she was so wobbly she could hardly walk. She introduced him to the people she was staying with, explaining that they had all just emerged from underground hiding places. They all looked as malnourished as his mother.

Werner hurried out to the jeep and bought in armfuls of K-rations, distributing them with the warning to eat slowly and in small doses. The family offered to share the salad they had been eating, which Werner declined. It looked to be grass they must have picked from the front yard.

Henny told Werner that his brothers were staying nearby, and she was expecting them any minute. She explained that the three of them, after avoiding earlier deportations, had gone underground in September 1943 after the Nazis had ordered that the Jews remaining in Amsterdam were to report the next day to the train yard. Henny and the two boys had survived with the aid of the well-organized Dutch resistance movement, whose members had risked arrest, and even execution, whenever the Nazis had discovered them harboring Jews.

When Werner asked about his father, his mother said he had not returned to Holland. In her last letter, she had written that Papa had been arrested for breaking currency laws and taken to Berlin, where he was tried and convicted for smuggling the family's life savings out of Germany. He had been sentenced to Brandenburg Prison. She told him that her sister, Margot, who had married an Aryan and had stayed in Berlin during the war, had written to her just before she and the boys went into hiding. Her letter said that Papa had been released from prison in late 1942, but that he had been sent directly to Auschwitz concentration camp. His mother said she hoped he would be returning to them soon.

Werner knew more about Auschwitz and the Nazi death camps than his mother, but he decided to keep this from her, for now. Still, he knew what this most likely meant for his gentle and upstanding father, and it hit Werner in the gut. He knew it would be too much for her to bear right now. Henny eventually turned to the Red Cross for help in locating her missing husband. After a lengthy delay, they informed her that he was no longer alive.

Henny Angress lived until age ninety-three, but not long enough to discover the full truth about her husband's fate. Werner took up the task, and in the 1990s a researcher found his father's file in the Berlin Landesarchiv (state archives). Documents revealed that after his release from Brandenburg and transport to Auschwitz, Ernst Angress died there on January 19, 1943. An attachment from the Auschwitz *Standesamt* (registry office) contained this note: "The Jew Angress died of heart failure." Heart failure and ordinary diseases were commonly listed as official causes of death at Auschwitz, where the SS camp administrators never reported that a single person was gassed to death.

When Werner's brothers showed up, the boys' reunion was tinged with the disappointment of not having their father with them, but they were joyous to have found each other. Fritz and Hans were amazed to see Werner in Amsterdam so soon after the end of the war and in the uniform of a U.S. Army paratrooper. Hans, sixteen, carried a crumpled bunch of just-picked wildflowers he handed to their mother on her special day.

It was Sunday, May 13. Mother's Day.

Werner Angress reunited with his brothers, Hans and Fritz, and his mother in Amsterdam on Mother's Day 1945. *(Family photograph)*

Dramatis Personae

Werner Angress, 82nd Airborne Division. Werner declined a commission in the U.S. Army so he could leave Germany and the war behind as soon as possible. He returned to the United States, where Wesleyan University, not bothered that he had quit school in Germany after eighth grade, accepted him as a student. He graduated Phi Beta Kappa with a B.A. in history and earned a Ph.D. at UC Berkeley. He taught modern European history at Wesleyan, Berkeley, and SUNY Stony Brook. The author of many articles and four books, including a memoir, *Witness to the Storm: A Jewish Journey from Nazi Berlin to the 82nd Airborne,* he served on the Board of the Leo Baeck Institute for the Study of History and Culture of German-Speaking Jewry for three decades.

After believing as a young soldier in 1945 that Germany had "forfeited its right to exist as a state," Werner retired to his hometown of Berlin in 1988. One of the few Ritchie Boys to return to live in Germany, he spent his remaining years in the country that had given him the best and worst of memories. He visited German schools and recounted for the students what it was like to grow up Jewish under the Third Reich, and the lessons he learned during the fight against fascism.

Werner died in Berlin, the city of his birth, in 2010 at age ninety.

Victor Brombert, 2nd Armored Division and 28th Infantry Division. After the war, Victor learned that his aunt Anya, who had gone missing after a roundup of foreign Jews in Nice, had died in Auschwitz. So had his summertime love, Dany Wolf, along with her young child.

He returned to the United States and studied at Yale, where he obtained his Ph.D. in Romance languages and literatures and was appointed to the faculty. He rose to become chairman of the Department of Romance Languages and Literatures. In 1975, he accepted an appointment at Princeton University as professor of comparative and romance literatures. The author of fifteen books of literary criticism, as well as a memoir, *Trains of Thought: Memories of a Stateless Youth,* he served as president of the Modern Language Association of America. In 2008, Victor was named a Knight of the Legion of Honor, France's highest award, for his role in the liberation of that country during World War II.

Together with his wife, Beth, an author of several historical biographies, Victor maintains a home in Princeton as well as a pied-à-terre in his beloved Paris and a summer residence in the Chianti region of Tuscany.

"Being a Ritchie Boy was important to us all," Victor recalls. "It gave us a sense of meaningful activity in a just war that in one way or another connected with our personal lives and experiences. The men on the teams were bright, available, not always expert warriors by a long shot, but certainly our hearts were in everything we did."

Victor retired in 1999 after fifty years of teaching. He continues to publish and lecture in the United States and Europe.

Stephan Lewy, 6th Armored Division. After his return from the war, Stephan went to night school to earn his high school diploma, then to Northeastern University for a business degree. He eventually became a CPA and spent most of his career working in finance for two large hotel chains. He and his wife, Frances, had two children.

Stephan learned only decades after the war that just months after he joined his parents in America in 1942, the OSE home at Chabannes in France was raided by pro-Nazi gendarmes, who arrived with a list of young Jews considered old enough for arrest and deportation. Stephan knew that his name was likely on that list. Among those taken were Marjan Sztrum, the eighteen-year-old banjo player in the Chabannes band and talented artist who had painted a fresco on the dining room wall depicting a farmer on a tractor. He was killed at Auschwitz.

Stephan didn't return to Germany until the 1990s, and then only with trepidation. In Berlin, he passed by the site of the Auerbach Orphanage, where he had spent half of his first fourteen years. The orphanage had been forcibly shut down by the Nazis in 1942. A sign in front memorialized the more than one hundred Jewish children, along with twelve teachers, who were deported and murdered that year.

Stephan retired in 1991 in Manchester, New Hamphire, and three years later saw the movie *Schindler's List,* which inspired him to begin talking for the first time about his experiences under the Nazis. Encouraged by a teacher friend to speak to her class, he found it therapeutic, even when answering one of the first questions asked by a young student: "Are you like a cat with nine lives?" He has since spoken to more than twenty-eight thousand schoolchildren. "When I look into their faces as they listen to my story," he says, "I have hope that I can make a difference. My story shows what can happen if people do not act. Perhaps if enough people hear these stories, history will not repeat itself. I only hope the world has learned a lesson."

A widower since his wife's death in 2010, Stephan lives in Williamville, New York.

Martin Selling, 35th Infantry Division. After the war, Martin studied engineering under the GI Bill. He graduated from Stevens Institute of Technology in New Jersey in 1949 with a degree in mechanical engineering, and received an M.S. in industrial management three years later. He married Hilde (Kaufmann), who had emigrated from Germany in 1938 with her parents. They had two children. Martin spent most of his career with AT&T Bell Laboratories. He stayed active in the U.S. Army Reserves, from which he retired in 1978 as a lieutenant colonel.

In 1965, he took his family to Germany to visit his hometown of Lehrberg, where he discovered that the name of his uncle Ignatz, his father's older brother who was killed in action in World War I, had been chiseled off the town's war memorial during the Nazi era along with other Jewish names. Then they stopped at the Dachau Concentration Camp Memorial Site. He had intended to show his children where he had been held, where so many Jews had died. But the camp looked sterile and deserted, and it was filled with too many ghosts for Martin, who became so overcome with emotion that they had to leave. "We Jews were undoubtedly the major victims of the Nazi regime," he told his family, "but there were others." He well remembered all those he had met in Dachau who had little or no chance of getting out.

Martin's memoir, *With Rancor and Compassion: The Memoirs of a Jew Who Thought He Was a German,* was published in 2003. About his days as a Ritchie Boy, he observed: "We immigrant newcomers were proud of the contribution we provided in the war effort, although it was not known about or greatly appreciated by many Americans. Even if we were only small pieces in an elaborate jigsaw puzzle that had to be assembled in order to win the war, we German-speaking refugees were like 'natural resources' in America's fight against Hitler and the Nazis."

Martin died in 2004 at age eighty-six.

Manny Steinfeld, 82nd Airborne Division. In May 1945, Manny returned to his hometown of Josbach to try to find out what had happened to his sister, Irma, and widowed mother, Paula, whose last letter in fall 1941 cited rumors of their pending deportation. When Manny arrived, none of Josbach's six Jewish families were left. A neighbor said his mother and sister had been "resettled" in late 1941 and knew nothing more.

In December 1945, after his return to the United States, he received a letter from Palestine telling him that his younger brother, Herbert, along with several other Jewish settlers, had been shot and killed by British soldiers who had received reports that they were harboring fighters against British rule. Manny was devastated. His mother had sent his brother to Palestine a few months after she had gotten Manny out of Germany. He wondered, *Was there no place on earth safe for Jews?*

It took years for Manny to learn where and how his mother and sister had died. After their deportation to the Riga ghetto in Latvia, he found out they had been sent to Stutthof concentration camp. In 2001, he visited the Stutthof Memorial Museum. The Nazis kept meticulous records of all the inmates, and Manny discovered in the camp archives that his mother and sister arrived from Riga on October 1, 1944; his mother died on December 30, 1944, and his sister died ten days later. The cause of death for both was listed as "heart failure," which was on nearly every death record. Even after extermination by gassing began at Stutthof in June 1944, the records never reported that as the cause of death.

On the same trip, he returned to Ludwigslust, where he saw that the wooden markers on the two hundred graves of the Wöbbelin concentration camp victims were gone. He was told they had been used as firewood during one frigid winter. The mayor said they had been raising money to replace them. Manny asked how much more they needed and wrote a check for the balance. He later went back for the rededication ceremony of the Ludwigslust cemetery.

Manny and his wife, Fern (Goldman), raised a family in Chicago, where he became a successful furniture manufacturer. Now retired in Florida, he says, "Sometimes I wonder if I should have been a Nazi hunter instead of a furniture manufacturer. I still have a difficult time whenever I think about how many people died. The Nazis tried to wipe out my family. I am the sole survivor. But I have thirteen descendants, and that's not too bad."

Guy Stern, First Army Headquarters. After the war, Guy moved to New York City. After receiving his B.A. degree at Hofstra University and his M.A. and Ph.D. at Columbia, he became a professor of German studies, intent on separating the "gold of German culture from the dirt and toxin of the Nazi years." He became a scholar of exile literature and the writings of those who perished in concentration camps. For the next fifty years, he taught at Columbia University, Denison University, the University of Cincinnati, and Wayne State University, where he remains a distinguished professor emeritus. Guy is currently director of the Henry and Wanda Zekelman International Institute of the Righteous at the Holocaust Memorial Center Zekelman Campus in Farmington Hills, Michigan. He was married to Judith, a schoolteacher, who died in 2003. He is now married to Susanna Piontek, a German short story writer and poet forty years his junior. They live in West Bloomfield, Michigan.

Guy returned to his hometown of Hildesheim in the 1960s to speak at the dedication of a new synagogue. He found the Thousand-Year Rose flourishing once again, climbing up the wall of a new cathedral that had replaced the one leveled by bombs in 1945. The parts of the world's oldest rosebush above ground had been destroyed, but the roots remained alive under the ruins.

In 2012, Guy was accorded the rights of an honorary citizen of Hildesheim in recognition of his "conciliatory efforts and for the dialogue between the religions and cultures." A plaque was placed in front of where his family had once lived, stating: "The Jewish family Stern lived here until its deportation in March 1942. Father Julius Stern, Mother Hedwig and the siblings Werner and Eleonore were murdered."

Guy stayed lifelong friends with Fred Howard, with whom he

acted in concert as "Commissar Krukov" to obtain valuable intelligence from German prisoners. Always a fount of new ideas, Fred became a pioneer of modern in-store merchandising, founding the largest point-of-purchase display company in the United States and becoming a multimillionaire. He died in 2008.

In 2017, Guy was named a Knight of the Legion of Honor for his role in the liberation of France during World War II. As for his years as a Ritchie Boy, Guy said, "Eisenhower called it a crusade in Europe. It was that. But for us, the German-Jewish refugee soldiers, it was a private crusade. We *had* to defeat the Nazis."

Gravesite of murdered Ritchie Boy Kurt Jacobs at Henri-Chapelle American Cemetery, located on a hill overlooking a bucolic valley in Belgium. *(Carl Wouters)*

Gravesite of murdered Ritchie Boy Murray Zappler at Henri-Chapelle American Cemetery. *(Carl Wouters)*

Murray Zappler and Kurt Jacobs

The two murdered Ritchie Boys were initially buried at a temporary U.S. military cemetery in Foy, Belgium. They were interred there on February 15, 1945, two days after their bodies were recovered in the field near the customs house just across the German border.

In the late 1940s, the army repatriated many of the Americans buried at Foy to the United States in accordance with their families' wishes. When the Foy cemetery closed, Jacobs and Zappler were brought for permanent burial, on January 9, 1949, to Henri-Chapelle American Cemetery, east of Liège, Belgium, where they remain at rest with nearly eight thousand other members of the U.S. military who died in World War II.

Acknowledgments

Narrative nonfiction starts and ends with rigorous research, which allows an author to be meticulously selective in using only the material that adds to the impact of the story. My two lead researchers, Steve Goodell and Dan Gross, both of the Washington, D.C., area, were extraordinarily helpful during the course of this two-year project. Steve is a superb archival and online researcher in all facets of World War II, and Dan has amassed a Ritchie Boys database with information from some twenty thousand personnel records. I was also assisted by Nadine Kaufmann in Berlin; Jamie Woodring in Michigan; Lori Miller of Redbird Research in St. Louis; Ruth Quinn and Lori Tagg at U.S. Army Intelligence Center, Fort Huachuca; Carl Wouters in Belgium; Karl Laun in Austria; Lea Bauer and Christiane Oechsner-Bauer in Germany; and Sabine Anton in New York.

Special thanks to the dedicated staff and volunteers at the Holocaust Memorial Center (HMC) in Farmington Hills, Michigan, especially Guy Stern, director of the HMC's Zekelman International Institute of the Righteous, who, in 2011, curated an exhibit, *The Secret Heroes,* the first in-depth exploration into the lives and achievements of the Ritchie Boys, as well as his assistant, Shirlee Wyman Harris, and former HMC director Steve Goldman. I am also grateful to the late German filmmaker Christian Bauer for his moving 2004 documentary, *The Ritchie Boys.*

Closer to home, thanks to my William Morrow editor, Henry Ferris, and his assistant, Nick Amphlett, for their enthusiasm and support; to my literary agent, Dan Conaway, for his sage advice; and to his Writers House colleague, Genevieve Gagne-Hawes, for her keen eye.

This book would not have been possible without the limitless patience and tireless contributions of Victor Brombert, Stephan Lewy, Manny Steinfeld, and Guy Stern, all of whom spent many hours, days, months—okay, *years*—answering my unending questions in person, on the phone, and via e-mail. To this list I also add Percy and Dan Angress, sons of the late Werner Angress, and Tom Selling, son of the late Martin Selling.

I interviewed many Ritchie Boys throughout the United States. They include Henry Bretton, Al Eisenkraft, Eric Gattmann, Ed Holton, Gunter Kosse, Maximilian Lerner, Richard Schifter, Charles Stein, and Rolf Valtin. I am grateful to them all for their time and recollections.

Sources

Complete book publication details are supplied in the bibliography. U.S. Army records such as unit histories, action reports, war diaries, field interrogations, Camp Ritchie historical files, and records and transcripts of war crime trials are at the National Archives II (NARA), College Park, Maryland. Military personnel records are at the National Personnel Records Centers, St. Louis, Missouri. Survivor testimonies are from the USC Shoah Foundation. Transcripts of interviews by Christian Bauer from his German documentary *The Ritchie Boys* were accessed at the Deutsche Kinemathek Film Museum in Berlin. Interviews for the Veterans History Project are available from the Library of Congress.

Prologue: Germany 1938

Martin Selling: Martin Selling survivor testimony (Shoah Foundation, 1996); Martin I. Selling, *With Rancor and Compassion: The Memoirs of a Jew Who Thought He Was a German;* "Kristallnacht: A Nationwide Pogrom" and "Dachau: Establishment of the Dachau Camp," United States Holocaust Memorial Museum (USHMM); Nikolaus Wachsmann, *KL: A History of the Nazi Concentration Camps;* Paul Berben, *Dachau: The Official History 1933–1945*.

PART ONE

1: Saving the Children

Günther Stern: Author's interviews with Guy Stern (2014–16); Guy Stern interviewed by Steven Remy, German-Jewish Émigré Oral History Project (May 14, 2005); Stern, "The Americanization of Günther," in Deborah Vietor-Englander, ed., *The Legacy of Exile: Lives, Letters, Literature;* "Jews in Prewar Germany," U.S. Holocaust Memorial Museum; Dr. Rudolf Zoder, *Die Hildesheimer Straßen;* Christiane Segers-Glocke, "Baudenkmale in Niedersachsen: Stadt Hildesheim"; William Grange, *Historical Dictionary of German Literature to 1945;* Arthur D. Morse, *While Six Million Died: A Chronicle of American Apathy;* Sommers Children's Bureau, letter to German-Jewish Children's Aid (Feb. 11, 1937).

Manfred Steinfeld: Author's interviews with Manfred Steinfeld (2015–16); Manfred Steinfeld, "Reflections of Josbach—Life in the 30s," in Philip K. Jason and Iris Posner, *Don't Wave Goodbye: The Children's Flight from Nazi Persecution to American Freedom;* Marcie Harrison, *A Life Complete: The Journey of Manfred Steinfeld; About Face,* a documentary film by Steve Karras; Manfred Steinfeld, "Josbach, Germany," in Steven Karras, *The Enemy I Knew: German Jews in the Allied Military in World War II;* Janice Petterchak, *A Legacy of Style: The Story of Shelby Williams Industries;* Richard Shifter, "Afterword," in *Don't Wave Goodbye;* Maurice R. Davie, *Refugees in America.*

Stephan Lewy: Author's interviews with Stephan Lewy (2015–16); Stephan Lewy survivor testimony (Shoah Foundation, 1997); Lillian Belinfante Herzberg, *Stephan's Journey: A Sojourn into Freedom;* Stephan Lewy, "From Refugee to GI," in David Scrase and Wolfgang Mieder, eds., *The Holocaust Personal Accounts*; Marion A. Kaplan, *Between Dignity and Despair;* Jonathan Kirsch, *The Short, Strange Life of Herschel Grynszpan;* Martin Gilbert, *Kristallnacht: Prelude to Destruction.*

2: Escaping the Nazis

Martin Selling: Martin I. Selling, *With Rancor and Compassion: The Memoirs of a Jew Who Thought He Was a German;* Martin Selling survivor testimony (Shoah Foundation, 1996); "Dachau: Establishment of the Dachau Camp," United States Holocaust Memorial Museum (USHMM); Paul Berben, *Dachau: The Official History 1933–1945.*

Werner Angress: Werner T. Angress, *Witness to the Storm;* Percy Angress's interviews with Werner Angress (1980–1986); Werner Angress, "Early Memoirs."

Stephan Lewy: Author's interviews with Lewy; Lewy testimony (Shoah Foundation); Herzberg, *Stephan's Journey: A Sojourn into Freedom;* Lewy, "From Refugee to GI," in *The Holocaust Personal Accounts;* Katy Hazan, *Rescuing Jewish Children*

During the Nazi Occupation: OSE Children's Homes, 1938–1945; The Children of Chabannes, documentary film by Lisa Gossel; Bernard Warschauer, "The Exodus"; speech by Stephan Lewy at Daniel Webster College, NH (2007); "Testimony of Stephan Lewy," filmed at Keene State College (2009).

3: A Place to Call Home

Günther "Guy" Stern: Author's interviews with Stern; Stern, "The Americanization of Günther"; Stern interviewed by Remy, the German-Jewish Émigré Oral History Project; "*Scrippage* Reporter Interviews Thomas Mann," Soldan High School newspaper (March 24, 1939); Guy Stern, "The Eminence and the Pupil: Meeting in St. Louis" (2003).

Manfred "Manny" Steinfeld: Author's interviews with Steinfeld; Harrison, *A Life Complete: The Journey of Manfred Steinfeld;* Petterchak, *A Legacy of Style: The Story of Shelby Williams Industries.*

Victor Brombert: Author's interviews with Victor Brombert (2015–16); Victor Brombert, *Trains of Thought: Memories of a Stateless Youth;* Victor Brombert, *Musings on Mortality;* Victor Brombert, "Return to Omaha Beach," *Princeton Alumni Weekly* (Jan. 26, 2005); Victor Brombert interviewed by Christian Bauer (2004); Herbert Agar, *The Saving Remnant: An Account of Jewish Survival.*

PART TWO
4: Camp Ritchie

Martin Selling: Selling, *With Rancor and Compassion;* Selling testimony (Shoah Foundation); Martin Selling interview, "Veterans History Project" (2003); Thomas D. McDermott, "Aliens of Enemy Nationality," INS Training Lecture (May 1943); George Bailey, *Germans: The Biography of an Obsession;* author's interviews with Thomas Selling and Hilde Selling (2016).

Werner Angress: Angress, *Witness to the Storm;* Percy Angress's interviews with Werner Angress; Angress, "Early Memoirs"; Werner Angress interviewed by Christian Bauer (circa 2004); Tom Angress, "Hyde Farmlands Diary"; Franklin D. Roosevelt, "Arsenal of Democracy," speech (Dec. 29, 1940); McDermott, "Aliens of Enemy Nationality"; Joshua Franklin, "Victim Soldiers: German-Jewish Refugees in the American Armed Forces During World War II"; George J. Le Blanc, *History of Military Intelligence Training at Camp Ritchie, Maryland;* Becky Dietrich, "Stories of the Summit Plateau and Beyond in the Valley" (1970); Bailey, *Germans: The Biography of an Obsession;* "Secret Heroes: The Ritchie Boys," an exhibit of the Holocaust Memorial Center, Farmington Hills, MI; Military Intelligence Division, War Department, *Order of Battle of the German Army, February 1944;* Max Oppenheimer Jr., "Camp Ritchie and American Military Combat Intelligence."

5: Going Back

Victor Brombert: Author's interviews with Brombert; Brombert, *Trains of Thought;* Angress, *Witness to the Storm.*

Guy Stern: Author's interviews with Stern; Guy Stern, memoir in progress, chapter 3; interview with Guy Stern, U.S. Holocaust Memorial Museum (1990); Guy Stern, *Oh What a Funny (?) War;* Stern interviewed by Remy, German-Jewish Émigré Oral History Project; Guy Stern interviewed by Christian Bauer (circa 2004).

Werner Angress: Angress, *Witness to the Storm;* Percy Angress's interviews with Werner Angress.

6: Normandy

Werner Angress: Angress, *Witness to the Storm;* Percy Angress's interviews with Werner Angress; Ward Smith, "I Saw Them Jump to Destiny," BBC News of the World (June 1944); Angress interviewed by Bauer; Werner Angress, "In Normandy, the World Looks Upside Down"; Werner Angress, "Normandy Diary, June 6–27, 1944."

Victor Brombert: Author's interviews with Brombert; Brombert, *Trains of Thought;* Brombert, *Musings on Mortality;* Brombert, "Return to Omaha Beach"; Brombert interviewed by Bauer; Donald E. Houston, *Hell on Wheels: The 2d Armored Division.*

Guy Stern: Author's interviews with Stern; interview with Stern, U.S. Holocaust Memorial Museum; Stern, *Oh What a Funny (?) War;* Stern interviewed by Bauer; Stern, memoir in progress, chapter 3; Virginia Irwin, "Only Prison Camps Are Lighted," *St. Louis Post-Dispatch* (July 24, 1944).

7: The Breakout

Martin Selling: Selling, *With Rancor and Compassion*; Selling testimony (Shoah Foundation, 1996); Richard Langworth, *Churchill by Himself.*

Stephan Lewy: Author's interviews with Lewy; Lewy testimony (Shoah Foundation); Herzberg, *Stephan's Journey: A Sojourn into Freedom*; George F. Hoffman, *The Super Sixth: History of the 6th Armored Division in World War II.*

Victor Brombert: Author's interviews with Brombert; Brombert, *Trains of Thought;* Brombert interviewed by Bauer.

8: Holland

Manfred "Manny" Steinfeld: Author's interviews with Steinfeld; Harrison, *A Life Complete: The Journey of Manfred Steinfeld;* Clay Blair, *Ridgway's Paratroopers: The American Airborne in World War II.*

Werner Angress: Angress, *Witness to the Storm;* Percy Angress's interviews with Werner Angress; Angress interviewed by Bauer; Forrest Dawson, *Saga of the All American (82nd Airborne Division);* www.ww2-airborne.us/units/508; Rick Atkinson, *The Guns at Last Light;* James A. Huston, *Out of the Blue;* David Bennett, *A Magnificent Disaster;* Martha Gellhorn, "Stand Up and Hook Up!," in Dawson, *Saga of the All American;* James Megellas, *All the Way to Berlin;* James Gavin, *On to Berlin;* Werner Angress's letters to Curt Bondy (Sept. 5, Oct. 5 and 10, 1944).

9: The Forests

Victor Brombert: Author's interviews with Brombert; Brombert, *Trains of Thought;* Brombert interviewed by Bauer; Paul Boesch, *Road to Huertgen: Forest in Hell;* Max Oppenheimer Jr., *An Innocent Yank at Home Abroad;* Thomas G. Bradbeer, "Major General Cota and the Battle of the Huertgen Forest: A Failure of Battle Command," U.S. Army Combined Arms Center; Edward B. Miller, *A Dark and Bloody Ground;* Atkinson, *The Guns at Last Light;* Hugh Cole, *The Ardennes: Battle of the Bulge.*

Kurt Jacobs and Murray Zappler: Author's interviews with Albert Eisenkraft (2015–16); Cole, *The Ardennes: Battle of the Bulge;* Atkinson, *The Guns at Last Light;* Charles B. MacDonald, *A Time for Trumpets;* Andy Rooney, *My War;* Alan W. Jones, "Defense of St. Vith: A History of the 106th," *The CUB,* February 1948; Benjamin S. Persons, *Relieved of Command;* Headquarters 12th Army Group, JAG, "Report of Investigation of Alleged War Crime"; Charles C. Cavender, "The 423 in the Bulge," *The CUB,* November 1946; R. Ernest Dupuy, *St. Vith: Lion in the Way;* Steven B. Wheeler, "Bleialf Is Overrun"; John Toland, *Battle: The Story of the Bulge;* Charles Cavender, *The Memoirs of an Old Soldier;* Alan W. Jones Jr., "The Operations of the 423rd Infantry," Advanced Infantry Officers Course (1949–1950); "Record of Trial by a Military Commission in the Case of *United States v. Curt Bruns,*" Case No. 6-56 (April 7, 1945).

Werner Angress: Angress, *Witness to the Storm;* Percy Angress's interviews with Werner Angress; Angress interviewed by Bauer; Werner Angress, "Belgium: In the Field"; Atkinson, *The Guns at Last Light;* 82nd Airborne Division: G-2 reports, action reports, interrogation reports (December 1944).

10: Return to Deutschland

Guy Stern: Author's interviews with Stern; Karl Frucht, "From the American Scene: We Were a PWI Team," *Commentary* (Jan. 1 1946); Stern, memoir in progress, chapter 3; interview with Stern, U.S. Holocaust Memorial Museum; First Army G-2 Periodic Report, "From the Bulge to the Rhine," 12/13 (March 1945); Guy Stern, *Marlene Dietrich: My Chance Encounter with a Movie Star;* Stern, *Oh What a Funny (?) War;* Stern interviewed by Remy, German-Jewish Émigré Oral History Project; Stern interviewed by Bauer; Guy Stern, "In the Service of American Intelligence: German-Jewish Exiles in the War Against Hitler"; "Record of Trial by a Military Commission in the Case of *United States v. Curt Bruns,*" Case No. 6-56; Headquarters 12th Army Group, JAG, "Report of Investigation of Alleged War Crime" (June 18, 1945); Karl Frucht, *A Statement of Loss: A Survival Report.*

Martin Selling: Selling, *With Rancor and Compassion*; Selling testimony (Shoah Foundation).

Stephan Lewy: Author's interviews with Lewy; Lewy testimony (Shoah Foundation); Herzberg, *Stephan's Journey: A Sojourn into Freedom;* "Testimony of Stephan Lewy," Keene State College; George F. Hoffman, *The Super Sixth: History of the 6th Armored Division in World War II.*

PART THREE
11: The Camps

Stephan Lewy: Author's interviews with Lewy; Lewy testimony (Shoah Foundation); Herzberg, *Stephan's Journey: A Sojourn into Freedom;* "Testimony of Stephan Lewy," Keene State College; George F. Hoffman, *The Super Sixth: History of the 6th Armored Division in World War II;* "Buchenwald" and "The 6th Armored Division," United States Holocaust Memorial Museum Website; Mark Abramson, "Buchenwald: Concentration Camp Stands as a Memorial to Thousands Who Perished There," *Stars and Stripes* (March 25, 2010); Wachsmann, *KL: A History of the Nazi Concentration Camps;* Flint Whitlock, *The Beasts of Buchenwald;* Robert Clary, *From the Holocaust to Hogan's Heroes;* Joseph F. Moser and Gerald R. Baron, *A Fighter Pilot in Buchenwald: The Joe Moser Story.*

Guy Stern: Author's interviews with Stern; interview with Stern, U.S. Holocaust Memorial Museum; Stern interviewed by Bauer; Stern interviewed by Remy, German-Jewish Émigré Oral History Project.

Manfred "Manny" Steinfeld: Author's interviews with Steinfeld; Harrison, *A Life Complete: The Journey of Manfred Steinfeld;* Gavin, *On to Berlin;* Steinfeld, "Josbach, Germany"; Manny Steinfeld, oral history, Holocaust Memorial Foundation of Illinois (circa 1989); Manfred Steinfeld, oral history, University of South Florida (2008); David Lewis, *Manfred Steinfeld: Victim and Victor.*

Werner Angress: Angress, *Witness to the Storm;* Percy Angress's interviews with Werner Angress; Angress, letter to Bondy (May 7, 1945), published in Richmond *Times-Dispatch* (June 4, 1945).

12: Denazification

Kurt Jacobs and Murray Zappler: Headquarters 12th Army Group, JAG, "Report of Investigation of Alleged War Crime"; "Record of Trial by a Military Commission in the Case of *United States v. Curt Bruns.*"

Stephan Lewy: Author's interviews with Lewy; Lewy testimony (Shoah Foundation); Herzberg, *Stephan's Journey: A Sojourn into Freedom;* Hoffman, *The Super Sixth.*

Manfred "Manny" Steinfeld: Author's interviews with Steinfeld; Harrison, *A Life Complete: The Journey of Manfred Steinfeld;* Steinfeld, "Josbach, Germany"; Steinfeld, oral history, Holocaust Memorial Foundation of Illinois; Lewis, *Manfred Steinfeld: Victim and Victor;* Margarete Buber-Neuman, *Under Two Dictators: Prisoner of Stalin and Hitler;* Sarah Helm, *Ravensbrück: Life and Death in Hitler's Concentration Camp for Women;* Judith Buber Agassi, "A True Story"; Judge Advocate General's Office: War Crimes Case Files, Ravensbrueck (Ludwig Ramdohr).

13: Going Home

Martin Selling: Selling, *With Rancor and Compassion*; Selling testimony (Shoah Foundation); Ignatz Selling, unpublished memoirs.

Guy Stern: Author's interviews with Stern; "The Bomber's Baedeker—Target Book for Strategic Bombing in the Economic Warfare Against German Towns," *GeoJournal* (Oct. 1994); Stern interviewed by Bauer; Stern interviewed by Remy, German-Jewish Émigré Oral History Project; Chris Webb and Michal Chocholaty, *The Treblinka Death Camp; Memorial Book: Victims of the Persecution of Jews 1933–1945,* National Archives of Germany.

Werner Angress: Angress, *Witness to the Storm;* Percy Angress's interviews with Werner Angress.

Appendix

THE RITCHIE BOYS

In a postwar study by the U.S. Army, "The Military Intelligence Service in the European Theater of Operations," the consensus among division intelligence officers was that 58 percent of all combat intelligence gathered by the U.S. Army in the European Theater of Operations was the product of Military Intelligence teams. The majority, 36 percent, came from German-language interrogations conducted by IPW teams.

Historical records indicate there were 1,985 German-born Ritchie Boys who served in World War II. A roster of those soldiers follows.

Aach, Jack
Abraham, Artie
Abraham, Henry J.
Abraham, Herbert A. H.
Abraham, Kurt
Abraham, Leo
Abraham, Peter F.
Abt, Karl W.
Ackerman, Bruno J.
Adler, Arthur
Adler, Bert J.
Adler, Frank L.

Adler, Fred J.
Adler, Fritz Anton
Adler, Hans
Adler, John H.
Adler, Kurt S.
Adler, Martin
Adler, Solomon Otto
Aehlig, Walter M.
Albiez, Fritz
Albrecht, Eric M.
Albrecht, Erich A.
Aldrich, Edward

Alefsen, Erich
Alexander, Ernest M.
Alexander, Herman
Allen, Herbert W.
Altman, Werner F.
Altroggen, Rudolph O.
Amdur, Harry
Amson, Gaston
Andreas, Kurt R.
Anger, Bert Walther
Angress, Werner T.
Ansbacher, Edgar A.

Appel, Max
Araten, Sal
Armer, Rolf Chase
Arnhold, Henry H.
Aron, Ralph
Arons, Ernest L.
Aronson, Francis A.
Ashton, Harry N.
Atcon, Rudolph
Auerbach, Frederick F.
August, Otto
Babin, Gary
Bach, Alfred J.
Bachenheimer, Walter L.
Baer, Ernest
Baer, John Herman
Baer, Kurt Armin
Baer, Leo
Baer, Manfred
Baer, Martin A.
Baer, Max
Baer, Ralph H.
Baermann, Heinz
Baigelman, Maurice G.
Ballin, Henry
Ballin, Lucien A.
Baltuch, Joseph Samuel
Bamberger, Charles E.
Bamberger, Gerald F.
Bamberth, Peter H.
Bardach, Henry G.
Baron, Walter Martin
Bartels, August H.
Bartenstein, Eugene
Barth, Werner H.
Bartman, Robert
Bauer, Albert
Bauer, Arthur
Bauer, Hans
Bauer, Helmut F.
Bauer, Henry Helmut
Bauer, Ralph A.
Bauerle, Fred H.
Bauknecht, William P.

Baum, Eric B.
Baum, Frederick
Baum, Gerhard
Baum, Martin
Baum, Ralph M.
Baum, Rudolf
Baum, Walter
Beauvais, Peter
Becher, Herbert G.
Beck, Robert
Becker, Ernst D.
Becker, Walter
Beer, Walter
Beerman, Paul Herman
Behling, Otto E.
Behrend, Wilfred G.
Behrendt, Gary
Behrens, Kurt C.
Behrens, Walter
Behrens, Walter R.
Beier, Ernst G.
Beissinger, Ernest W.
Beissinger, Henry
Beller, Johann R.
Benario, Ernest H.
Bender, Fred
Bender, Herbert
Bender, Herbert F.
Bendix, Gerhart
Bendorf, Lothar L.
Benedik, Frank P.
Bennewitz, Eckhard
Bennigson, Rudolph
Benson, Curtis H.
Benson, Eric Frank
Benton, Kirk
Bergen, Curtis F.
Berger, David
Berger, Harry
Berger, Henry
Berger, Max
Berger, Rudolf
Bergman, Herman W.
Bergman, John

Bergman, Rolf
Bergmann, Gerhard
Bergmann, Paul
Berlin, Teddy
Berliner, Kurt
Berman, Frank W.
Berman, Fred
Bernhardt, August E.
Bernhardt, John P.
Bernheim, Jacob L.
Bernheimer, Herman
Bernkof, Bernard R.
Berthold, Herbert K.
Berton, Walter H.
Betz, Siegmund A. E.
Biberfield, Ernest S.
Biel, Heinz Hermann
Biel, Ulrich E.
Bielefield, Gunther A.
Bienstock, Josef H.
Bierer, Walter
Bierig, Julius
Biermann, Franz J.
Biever, Curtis Henry
Bindczyck, Peter A.
Blackett, Gustav
Blackwell, John H.
Blake, Peter J.
Blank, Rolf David
Blatner, Manfred
Blau, Ernst
Bloch, Ernest
Bloch, Ernest H.
Bloch, Gustave
Bloch, Hans W.
Bloch, Henry W.
Bloch, Lothar
Blum, Harry
Blum, Julius F.
Blum, Peter W.
Blum, Walter H.
Blumenstein, Josef L.
Blumenthal, Fred
Bock, Adolph Carl

Bock, Helmuth
Bodenheimer, Fred S.
Bodlander, Walter V.
Boehm, Donald G.
Boehme, Werner
Boekhaus, William F.
Boemanns, Herman J.
Boettcher, Bernard P.
Boettingheimer, Ludwig
Boguch, Harry
Boksen, Herbert
Boll, John J.
Bondy, Eric Heinz
Bonne, Walter
Bonnitt, Thomas L.
Bornstein, David
Bornstein, Siegfried
Bowman, Howard C.
Brabbee, Ralph Albert
Brady, Hans A.
Brand, Paul Joachim
Branden, Kurt
Brandes, Konrad G.
Brandon, Lawrence D.
Brandt, Gerard M.
Braunthal, Gerard
Breisacher, Hans J.
Breit, Werner L.
Breitenbach, Paul
Breitfeller, Joseph C.
Bremler, Heiman Herbert
Brenner, Walter J.
Brenner, Walter S.
Brenton, Eric B.
Bretton, Henry L.
Brewer, Paul Walter
Brewster, Lee P.
Briefs, Henry W.
Brill, Klaus
Brinitzer, Peter H.
Brock, Carl M.
Brodersen, Hardy G.
Brohan, William Karl
Bromberg, Gerhard R. H.

Bromberg, Oswald H.
Brombert, Victor H.
Brotman, Gerald
Brotzen, Franz Richard
Bruck, Ferdinand F. A.
Bruer, Karl H.
Brull, Hans Frank
Brumme, Gunther A.
Brunswick, John H.
Bubel, Hans C.
Buchdahl, Julius
Buchholz, Ernest M.
Budwig, Ernest G.
Buettner, Adolph G.
Buhl, Max H.
Bunzell, Paul A.
Burchard, Henry H.
Burchard, William H.
Burg, Siegfried
Burian, Kurt
Burkhardt, Eric W.
Burmeister, Henry J.
Burmeister, Walter F.
Busch, Carl H.
Busch, Hans Peter
Buschen, Bernard J.
Butler, Henry
Bywater, John A.
Cahn, Herbert
Cahn, Walter W.
Caminer, Jack A.
Cappel, Henry
Carbe, Andre H.
Carey, William
Carroll, Roland
Carsch, Harry
Carsten, Ernest S.
Cassel, Henry W.
Cerf, Walter Hyman
Chase, Carl L.
Chwat, Norbert
Coby, Fred E.
Coenen, Bernard T.
Cohn, Ernest M.

Cohn, Frederic G.
Cohn, Gerald L.
Cohn, Herbert H.
Colbert, Joseph B.
Colbert, Servy M.
Collier, Ralph
Colmer, Hans J.
Colton, Ernest J.
Conrad, Henry C.
Cook, Henry H.
Corduan, Richard W.
Cornelius, Hans
Craig, Frank B.
Cramer, Ernest J.
Crane, Ernest J.
Czerner, Alfred
Czerner, Gerhard
Czygan, Wolfgang C.
Dabringhaus, Erhard
Danby, Warner
Daniel, Henry H.
Daniel, Werner
Danneman, Ernst
Dannhauser, Jacob
Danzig, Herbert
Darmstadter, Henry
David, Eric
David, Frank H.
David, Frederic Werner
David, Kurt Dietrich
David, Kurt S.
De Neufville, Robert
Deku, Henry
Delp, Horst G.
Denzer, Erich R.
Deppisch, Hans Curt
Dessauer, Henry T.
Dessauer, John S.
D'Etampes, Michel
Deull, John B.
Dexter, Henry C.
Didriksen, Alex P.
Diebold, Peter B.
Diehl, Karl Hugo

Diekmann, Walter H.
Dierks, Adelbert Gregor
Dietz, Otto
Dinkela, John H.
Dorner, Henry H.
Dorpalen, Thomas L.
Dower, Louis L.
Drechsler, Gerhard J.
Dreifus, Armin
Dreifuss, Ralph A.
Dreifuss, Walter
Drewello, Edward
Dreyer, Kenneth
Dreyfuss, Erich
Droeske, Fritz
Drucker, Walter
Dude, Ludwig
Duellman, Joseph W.
During, Theobald
Eaton, Joseph W.
Eben, Kurt J.
Ebert, Arthur O.
Ebert, Harry W.
Edgarr, Bernhard G.
Eggers, Jules H.
Eggert, Joachim
Ehlers, Kurt H.
Ehrlich, Arthur
Ehrlich, Carl Simon
Ehrlich, Max
Ehrman, John J.
Ehrmann, Ernest W.
Eich, Edwin K.
Eichenwald, Hans
Eilts, Hermann F.
Eimer, Leo
Eisenhauer, Adam J.
Eldodt, Joseph
Elfers, Hans
Elkan, Jurgen
Elle, Kurt D.
Elsner, Curt M.
Emanuel, Nick C.
Engel, Klaus H. C.

Engelmann, Hans B.
Engels, Gerd E.
Englander, John Louis
Epstein, Hans J.
Erbst, Otto C.
Erlanger, Gus
Erlanger, Herbert J.
Ermann, Henry H.
Essig, Erwin
Essig, Walter E.
Ettinger, Robert V.
Eulau, Herman
Ewald, Lux Henry
Ewald, William
Fabian, Hans J.
Fairbrook, Paul
Falck, Hans S.
Falk, Fred
Falk, George
Farkas, Murray
Fass, Julius
Feibel, Edgar L.
Feibelman, Leonard
Fein, Rolf A.
Feininger, Theodore
Feist, Herbert B.
Feitler, Ernest
Fendler, Rudolph
Fenger, Fred E.
Ferrell, Robert
Feuerstein, Raymond E.
Fiedler, Otto E.
Field, Harry B.
Fields, Fred D.
Finder, John Horst
Fink, Max G. L.
Finold, Irving Erwin
Fipp, Klemens Herman
Fischer, Franz
Fischer, Fritz
Fischer, Hans
Fischer, Harry
Fischer, John Hans
Fischer, Kurt Heinz

Fischer, Paul
Fish, George Harvey
Fisher, Werner S.
Fitschen, Kurt
Flatow, Max F.
Flatow, Walter
Flautz, Ronald G.
Fleck, Herbert
Fleck, Stephen
Fleisch, Harry M.
Fleischmann, Harry
Flentz, Herman J.
Fliess, Peter J.
Floersheim, Paul E.
Florsheim, George D.
Foerster, Walter A.
Forchheimer, Peter M.
Forrest, Gerald
Foss, Oliver U.
Foth, Albert E.
Fox, John W.
Fraenkel, George K.
Fraenkel, Herbert A.
Frank, Arnold F. W.
Frank, Benno D.
Frank, Eric L.
Frank, Harry
Frank, Herbert
Frank, John
Frank, Martin Hans
Frank, Otto
Frank, Peter R.
Frank, Walter
Frank, Werner K.
Frankel, Curt (Kurt)
Frankenberg, Hellmut J.
Frankenthaler, Felix
Frankl, Gunther
Frankl, Wolfe J.
Franklin, Harry Hans
Franks, Harry O.
Franzen, Ulrich J.
Frauendorfer, Joseph
Frazier, Thomas Lamb

Frederix, Arthur C.

Freedlander, Frederick O.

Freedman, Paul W.

Freedman, Ralph W. B.

Freier, Rudolf C.

Frenkel, George L.

Freudenberg, Walter

Freudenberger, Herman

Freudenthal, Curt

Freund, Walter Lothar

Frey, Helmuth F. W.

Frey, Otto

Fridberg, Charles

Fried, Paul G.

Friede, Dittmar H.

Friedlaender, Hermann

Friedman, Leo

Friedman, Rudolph E.

Friedner, Martin

Froehlich, Max

Frohlich, Walter M.

Frohman, Warner B.

Frohmayer, Albert

Fromm, John

Fromme, Ludwig H.

Fronauer, Henry J.

Frowenfeld, Charles E.

Fruendt, Roderick H.

Fuld, Arthur Jacob

Fuld, Berthold

Fuld, Jacob

Fuld, Louis

Fuld, Siegmund

Furst, Erwin

Furst, Robert A.

Furst, Walter G.

Gaertner, Bernard

Galewski, Ernst Jacob

Gallee, Carl F.

Gann, Frederick H.

Gans, Werner J.

Ganz, Walter H.

Gartner, Frank

Gartner, Walter

Gary, Hugh S.

Gattel, Gerhard J.

Gattmann, Eric

Gatzert, Ernest H.

Gatzke, Hans W.

Gebel, Kurt M.

Gedden, Joseph J.

Gehrels, Franz

Gellermann, Henry E.

Gellermann, Josef E.

Gellrich, Carlos

Georgi, Nephi

Gerard, Egon

Gerard, Fred S.

Gerber, Helmut E.

Gercke, Fred

Gerdes, Carl F.

Gerhardz, Vincenz

Gerlt, Karl H.

Gerould, Albert C.

Gerresheim, Paul

Gersman, John

Gerson, Edgar A.

Gerson, Kurt J.

Gerson, Walter

Gerst, Eric F.

Gersten, Herbert H.

Gert, Gerard M.

Gevers, Max E.

Giebel, Harry F.

Gleser, George F.

Goehner, Karl

Goeltzer, Wolf D.

Goettlich, Paul

Goetz, Eric Martin

Goetz, Henry

Goetz, John H.

Gold, George Helmut

Goldberg, Henry E.

Goldenberg, Paul H.

Goldenhar, Arnold

Goldmann, Egon

Goldmeier, Martin

Goldschmidt, Arnold A.

Goldschmidt, Erich I.

Goldschmidt, Ernest

Goldschmidt, Henry

Goldschmidt, Leo

Goldschmiedt, Martin

Goldsmith, Albert

Goldsmith, Gilbert V.

Goldsmith, Harry J.

Goldsmith, Herman

Goldstein, Frank Karl

Goldstein, Henry

Gontard, Herbert

Goodman, Hellmut M.

Goodwin, Alfred

Gottlieb, Fred

Gottschalck, Herbert M.

Gottschalk, Herbert

Gould, Robert G.

Gourley, Raymond S.

Graf, Ernst

Gragert, Philipp G.

Gramckow, Hans

Grass, Gary G.

Greene, Harold H.

Greenwald, Ernest

Gregor, Charles

Greif, Lucien R.

Greimel, Otto

Gress, Ulrich R.

Grey, Leo

Grieb, Gerhard R.

Griesman, Henry K.

Grimsehl, Georg H. C.

Grohman, Heinz G.

Grohs, Lothar

Grombacher, Gerd S.

Gross, Walter

Grueder, James E.

Gruen, Herman

Gruenebaum, Erwin J.

Grueninger, Gunther H.

Gruennel, Gottfried K.

Gruenthal, Peter

Grunbaum, Adolf

Guenther, Paul F.

Guerny, Eric H.

Guinsburg, Henry C.

Gumbel, Max

Gummers, Erwin

Gumpert, Milton

Gumpertz, Werner H.

Gunter, Herbert

Gunther, Eberhard

Gunther, Ernest J.

Gunther, Harry G.

Gunzburg, Ernest M.

Gutenberg, Arthur W.

Gutman, Fred J.

Gutman, Ralph J.

Gutmann, Hermann

Gutmann, Karl H.

Gutmann, Kurt E.

Gutmann, Theodore E.

Gutmann, Walter M.

Haac, Oscar A.

Haag, Helmut J.

Haarburger, Joachim M.

Haas, Herbert H.

Haas, Leo Louis

Haas, Robert

Haas, Walter A.

Haase, Walter William

Haberman, Josef

Habermann, Fred

Hable, Alfred H.

Haefner, Paul F.

Haeussler, Helmut H.

Hafel, Karl E.

Hagen, Gerard J.

Hagen, Holger E.

Hahn, Gerard John

Hahn, Herman

Haimann, Gunter

Haimoff, Charles

Hainebach, Hans J.

Hall, Joseph H.

Haller, Werner R.

Hallex, Helmut A.

Hallgarten, George W. F.

Halpern, Georges E.

Hamburger, Erwin

Hamersley, Walter

Hamilton, Fred Scott

Hamm, Eric

Hammel, Walter Max

Hammerschlag, Dieter K.

Hammerschlag, Max

Hanauer, Hugo

Hanauer, Walter

Hanf, Arthur H.

Hannes, Max R.

Hans, Theodor

Hansen, Frederick F.

Happe, Kurt G.

Harburger, Ralph D.

Harf, Arthur

Harlow, Ronney L.

Harriman, Edward E.

Hart, Hugh P.

Hart, Otto

Hartel, Gunther Ernest

Harter, Albert O.

Hartlieb, Kurt F.

Hartmann, Charles A.

Hartmann, Walter A.

Hartwich, Henry W.

Hartwig, Henry A.

Hasenclever, Walter Max

Hatry, Ralph S.

Haug, Fred

Haupt, Hans R.

Hauptman, Gerard G.

Hauschner, Ludwig

Hauser, Franz J.

Hauser, Jack H.

Hausman, Herbert

Haussmann, Richard E.

Hayes, Frank W.

Hayon, Norman Nissim

Hechinger, Fred M.

Hecht, Arnold H.

Hecht, Gerhard

Hecht, Henry R.

Hecht, Rolf G.

Heckscher, Helmut

Hecksher, Henry D.

Heesch, Peter

Heichelheim, Sigmund

Heid, Justin A.

Heidemann, Karl E.

Heidemann, Karl G.

Heilbron, Eric

Heilbrunn, Martin

Heiman, Peter

Heimann, Fred E.

Heimann, Jack H.

Heimann, Peter K.

Heine, Marc K.

Heineman, Charles E.

Heinig, John

Heinrich, Werner R.

Heinsheimer, Gerhard

Heitmueller, Rudolf

Heitzer, Joseph

Heldt, Herbert

Hellendall, Walter

Heller, Peter N.

Heller, Peter Niels

Helling, Curt

Hemer, Thomas H.

Hendricks, Klaus J.

Henning, Theodore W.

Henschel, Frederick W.

Henschel, Walter L.

Hentschel, Carl J.

Heppen, Curtis E.

Herbst, Ernest A.

Herbst, Henry

Herbst, Mac

Herman, Louis R.

Herrman, Kurt

Herrmann, Kurt J.

Herrmann, Thomas K.

Herrnstadt, Gerald E.

Hertz, Eric

Hertz, Eugene

Hertz, Walter P.
Herz, Frank Lewis
Herz, Harry H.
Herz, Leo S.
Herz, Walter J.
Herzberg, Ernst
Herzberg, Hans R.
Herzfeld, Herbert A.
Herzog, Harry
Hesekiel, Kurt
Hess, Albert G.
Hess, Eric
Hess, Ludwig
Hess, William W.
Hesse, Gottfried
Hesslein, Paul S.
Heuman, John
Heuman, Stephen
Heyden, Karl W.
Heym, Stefan
Heyman, Milton
Heyman, Vernon O.
Heymann, Gary M.
Heymann, Harry
Hilb, Eugene J.
Hilborn, Harold J.
Hill, Gerhard W.
Hiller, Hans A.
Hillringhouse, Fred G.
Hilston, Gerard G.
Hingst, Gunther F.
Hinrichs, Fred C.
Hinrichsen, Walter
Hippen, John A.
Hirsch, Ernest R.
Hirsch, Heinz S.
Hirsch, Herbert S.
Hirsch, Leo
Hirsch, Paul E.
Hirsch, Paul T.
Hirsch, Walter
Hirsch, Warner M.
Hirschberg, Max
Hirschberg, Walter

Hirschel, Fritz B.
Hirschmann, Fritz
Hirts, Ralph A.
Hobbing, Enno R.
Hochstadter, Walter H.
Hockley, Ralph M.
Hoehne, Harry K.
Hoelzl, Joseph F.
Hoerner, Emil
Hoffer, Wolfgang E. F.
Hoffman, Hans E.
Hohl, Robert W.
Hohner, Otto A.
Hollasch, Edward E.
Holsten, Herbert N.
Holterhoff, Hans A.
Holton, Edgar H.
Holzer, Ernest Jacob
Holzer, Frederick
Hons, Henry A.
Hopf, Fritz J.
Horn, George
Horn, John H.
Horn, Walter W.
Hornung, Godfrey J.
Horstmann, Harry
Horwitz, Ralph
Horwitz, Ralph E.
Howard, Fred
Hunger, Rolf
Hunter, John F.
Hurst, John W.
Ickert, Heinz
Iglauer, Hanns S.
Illfelder, Bernhard
Immerwahr, Henry R.
Intemann, Alfred W.
Irwig, Harry
Isenberg, Ernest S.
Isler, Herbert A.
Isler, Werner
Isserman, Manfred A.
Jacob, Bruno F.
Jacob, Ernest L.

Jacob, Hermann
Jacob, Norbert
Jacobi, Heinrich P.
Jacobi, Kurt E.
Jacobs, Harry A.
Jacobs, Henry
Jacobs, Kurt R.
Jacobsen, Henry B.
Jacobsohn, George P.
Jacobson, Henry
Jacoby, Arthur
Jacoby, Henry R.
Jacoby, Rolf
Jaeger, Erhard C.
Jaffray, Ernst A.
Jahnigen, Fredrick W.
Jansen, Henry J.
Jasen, Kurt F. Y.
Jasiek, Paul Hugo
Jastrow, Paul W.
Jellin, Curt
Jessel, Walter
Jochum, Carl P.
Joelson, David
Johnson, Hans V.
Jonas, James
Joost, Horst K.
Joseph, Ernest A.
Joseph, Ralph H.
Juelich, Henry H.
Jung, Richard H.
Jungnitsch, Roland E.
Kahn, Erich
Kahn, Ernest A.
Kahn, Ernest Otto
Kahn, Frank J.
Kahn, George Jacob
Kahn, Harry
Kahn, Harry I.
Kahn, Heinz M.
Kahn, Herbert
Kahn, Stephen M.
Kaiser, Ernest L.
Kalm, Ernest

Kann, Edgar W.
Kann, Jules
Kann, Walter
Kant, Hans G.
Kaplan, Harold N.
Kappel, Albert D.
Karlsruher, Gerhard
Karr, Howard H.
Karter, Alex
Kaskell, Peter H.
Katz, Albert C.
Katz, Gerald S.
Katz, Jack
Katz, Leo
Katz, Walter J.
Katz, Warner W. K.
Katz, William R.
Katzenstein, Alfred
Katzenstein, William B.
Kauffmann, Harry
Kauffmann, Siegmund
Kaufman, Ernest
Kaufman, Harry S.
Kaufman, Kurt W.
Kaufman, Rudolph
Kaufman, Walter
Kaufmann, Fred
Kaufmann, Fred D.
Kaufmann, Herbert
Kaufmann, Herbert O.
Kaufmann, Kurt
Kaufmann, Walter A.
Kaufmann, Walter C. H.
Kaufmann, Walter H.
Kaunitz, Jurgen
Kay, George Y.
Kay, Jean
Kay, John Lewis
Kayser, Ernest W.
Kehl, Fred G.
Kehrer, Henry P.
Kellen, Konrad
Kellerman, Rudolph N.
Kerman, Otto P.

Kessler, Gunther K.
Kessler, Hans T.
Kienle, Hans A.
Kirchberger, Fred A.
Kirchheimer, Erich
Kirk, Ernest H.
Kirschbaum, Alfred F.
Kirschberger, Joe Henry
Kittstein, Karl, Jr.
Kittstein, Nicholas C.
Klatte, Karl F.
Klauber, Roger J.
Klee, Henry D.
Kleikamp, Herman G.
Klein, Arthur
Klein, Herbert D.
Klein, Herbert H.
Klein, Kurt
Klein, Max L.
Kleinberger, Kurt
Kleinert, Carl J.
Kleinfeld, Immanuel
Klestadt, Helmut
Klotz, Herbert W.
Kluge, John W.
Knauth, Otto W.
Knisbacher, Max
Knoblauch, Herbert J.
Knoechel, Erwin J.
Knohl, Herbert
Knuepfer, Dieter C.
Kober, Werner D.
Kobrak, Helmut P.
Koch, Albert C.
Koch, Ewald
Koch, Herbert H.
Koch, Walter H.
Koehler, Herman R.
Koehnke, Hans F. W.
Kohlhagen, Werner S.
Kohlman, Herman
Kohn, Solly
Kohner, Willy
Kolb, Eugene J.

Kolb, Guenther
Koller, Henry W.
Kolmar, Hanns H.
Koopman, Jack
Koppel, Joseph
Koppel, Richard U.
Korf, Kurt F.
Kornfeld, Alfred H.
Korngold, Henry
Kosse, Gunter
Kosterich, Siegbert
Kostrich, Max
Kraemer, Fritz G. A.
Kramarsky, Bernhard
Kramer, Erich W.
Kramer, Siegfried M.
Kramer, William C.
Kraus, Herbert
Kraus, Max W.
Krause, Robert L.
Krause, William B.
Kreischer, Edmund W.
Kremnitzer, Ernest G.
Krempel, Jans A.
Krepper, Joseph R.
Krieger, Henry N.
Kriwer, Robert E.
Kroh, Herman H.
Kron, Walter V.
Krug, Walter W.
Kruszewski, Charles H.
Kuehn, John W.
Kugelmann, Kurt
Kuhn, Helmut A.
Kuhn, Ralph Erich
Kuhnis, Lothar P.
Kuhns, John P.
Kulkens, William B., Jr.
Kunreuther, William M.
Kunzel, Siegfried G.
Kupferschmidt, Alfred
Kurnik, Horst
Kurschner, Hans G.
Kurth, Hanns G.

Kurzman, Pincus
Kutter, Rudolph L.
Laarkamp, Bernard C.
Lamm, George L.
Land, Hans Alan
Landauer, Henry
Landauer, Ulrich E.
Landauer, Walter A.
Landis, John M.
Landman, Otto E.
Lane, Kenneth J.
Lane, Walter Werner
Lang, Herman L.
Lange, Jurgen C.
Lange, Rudolph C.
Lansing, Eric E.
Lanson, Gunther
Laredo, Joseph Arnold
Lau, Alfred A.
Laub, Lothar N.
Laudien, Kurt A.
Lauer, Peter H.
Laury, George H.
Lawson, Eric
Lea, Henry A.
Lebrecht, Curt M.
Lee, Sidney
Lee, Walter
Leeds, Harold
Leeds, Robert S.
Lehmann, Charles H.
Lehmann, Hans
Lehmann, Ludwig
Lehmann, Walter J.
Lehmann, Wolfgang J.
Lehnberg, Werner
Leikin, Paul
Leipzig, Walter
Leissner, Erwin
Leiter, Steven Max
Lekisch, Karl P.
Lemel, Henry W.
Lenard, Claude P.
Lenk, Walter E.

Lenovits, Nicholas
Lensen, George A.
Leonard, Walter
Leonberger, Karl
Leppek, Harry A.
Lert, Peter J.
Leser, Paul W.
Lesser, Kurt
Leven, Hans
Levi, Berthold
Levi, Heinz
Levi, Irving
Levi, Jack
Levi, Kurt
Levi, Peter
Levi, William
Levor, Henry
Levy, Edward
Levy, Fred
Levy, Jack
Levy, Kurt H.
Levy, Leo
Lewald, Werner
Lewenz, George F.
Lewkowicz, Martin Max
Lewy, Stephan Heinz
Liebenstein, Erick
Lieberman, Gerald
Lieberwirth, Alfred M.
Liebhold, Martin O.
Liebig, Gustav A.
Liebmann, Felix
Liedholz, Gerhard A.
Liepold, Walter
Light, Oscar P.
Linden, Walter M.
Lindner, John H.
Linn, Rolf N.
Lion, Curtis
Lion, Stephen C.
Lipman, Eric Marcus
Lipps, Henry A.
Lipton, Walter K.
Littman, Edward Hans

Lob, Erich M. W.
Lob, Werner
Loeb, Frederick M.
Loeb, Kurt
Loeb, Max
Loeb, Walter
Loebl, Willie
Loeffler, Erwin P.
Loeser, Hans F.
Loeser, Paul, Jr.
Loew, Ernest M.
Loewenbaum, George W.
Loewensberg, Joseph
Loewenstein, Ernest L.
Loewenstein, John A.
Loewenstein, John Hans
Loewenstein, Karl J.
Loewenstein, Walter
Loewenthal, John
Loewenthal, Kurt Jakob
Lohnberg, Fred M.
Loose, Gerhard
Lorch, Siegbert
Lord, Harry S.
Loring, Karl H.
Low, Ernest
Lowe, Walter J.
Lowell, John Howard
Lowen, Henry
Lowenstein, Dyno
Lowenstein, Harry
Lowenstein, Max S.
Lowenstein, Paul
Lowenstern, Henry
Lownds, John G.
Lublin, Jack
Lubow, Ralph
Lubran, Walter H.
Luchs, Alfred
Lucke, Herbert H.
Ludwig, Robert
Lunser, Herbert S.
Lustig, Peter
Lutz, Fred C.

Lychenheim, Heinz
Maas, Henry J.
Maas, Julius J.
Madauss, Hans
Madison, Gerald C.
Maebert, E. Walter
Magnus, Kurt
Mahler, Herbert
Mahler, Ludwig
Mahlgut, Erich P.
Maier, Manfred
Maier, Martin
Mainczyk, Steven
Malsh, Henry E.
Malsh, William R.
Malter, Henry
Malzer, Arnold
Mamsbach, Alfred H.
Mandel, Harold G.
Mandel, Siegfried
Mankiewicz, Don M.
Mankin, Paul A.
Mann, Frank F.
Mann, Harold O.
Mann, Klaus
Manne, Charles
Mannheimer, Ernst
Marck, Louis
Marcus, Fred W.
Marcus, Kurt Erwin
Marcus, Rudolf
Marcuse, Henry E.
Marechal, Hans H.
Mark, Henry
Mark, Joseph P.
Markheim, Jack J.
Markus, Heinz
Marshall, Fred
Martensen, John F.
Martin, Arthur
Martin, Charles A.
Martin, Richard
Marx, Ernest L.
Marx, Harry Guenter

Marx, Immanuel
Marx, Walter David
Marx, Walter Mathias
Mason, Henry L.
Masson, Harry J.
Mathews, Frank
Matlaw, Myron
Matrian, Herman L.
Maul, Alfred
May, Robert L.
Mayer, Bernhard A.
Mayer, Charles F.
Mayer, Claus
Mayer, Ernest D.
Mayer, Erwin S.
Mayer, Hans (32519748)
Mayer, Hans (32869111)
Mayer, Klaus
Mayer, Leon
Mayer, Louis
Mayer, Michael G.
Mayer, Paul A.
Mayer, Rolf J. F.
Mayer, William F.
Mayerhauser, Carl E.
Meier, Edgar
Meier, Hans J.
Meier, Leopold J.
Meier, Werner J.
Meinstein, Siegfried
Meissner, Hans
Melford, Walter R.
Melinger, Paul
Mendels, Herman
Mendelsohn, Paul
Mendheim, John M.
Menke, Walter E.
Menken, John J.
Mensching, Rolf
Menz, Frederick
Merel, Alfred
Merkin, Gerson I. H.
Merrill, John C.
Merritt, Wade H.

Mertens, Theodore
Merton, Richard G.
Merz, Robert H.
Messinger, Fred
Metzger, Eric J.
Meyer, Alfred G.
Meyer, Christian W.
Meyer, Fred A.
Meyer, Frederic G.
Meyer, Gerald
Meyer, Helmut W. J.
Meyer, Herbert
Meyer, Herbert H.
Meyer, Herbert R.
Meyer, Kurt
Meyer, Max
Meyer, Theodore O.
Meyerhoff, Erich
Meyerhoff, Hans
Meyersberg, Charles H.
Meyrose, William C.
Michael, Walter O.
Michaelis, Edgar
Michaels, Rudolf H.
Michau, Werner T.
Michel, Ernest J.
Michel, Frederick J.
Michel, Peter R.
Michel, Werner E.
Midener, Walter
Miller, Albert W.
Miller, Carl O.
Miller, Gerd
Miller, Lothar H.
Miller, Max
Mittelberger, Ernest G.
Moch, Franz
Moellerich, Harry
Mohr, Eric A.
Mohr, Henry A.
Monasch, Walter J.
Mond, Henry I.
Monroe, Earl K.
Moore, Ernest J.

Moos, Richard
Moosmann, Charles A.
Morgenstern, Werner H.
Moritz, Werner
Mosbacher, Stephen S.
Mosback, Frank T.
Mosblech, Arnold W.
Mosenthal, John W.
Moser, Herbert
Moser, Kurt
Moses, Hans
Moses, Jack
Mosler, Claude L.
Mosler, Rudolph L.
Moss, Warren P.
Motell, Curt
Motulsky, Claus
Mueller, Alfons
Mueller, Carl
Mueller, Frank H.
Mueller, John B.
Mueller, Robert H., Jr.
Muller, Henry
Munch, Helmuth G.
Mysior, Arnold L.
Nachman, Lothar E.
Nacke, Claus K.
Nagel, Walter
Nagel, Walter J.
Nahm, Albert
Nahrendorf, Richard O.
Namuth, Hans H.
Nash, Peter H.
Nash, Warner S.
Nathan, Eric
Nathan, Henry C.
Naumann, Manfred
Nellhaus, Richard E.
Nelson, Hans G. E.
Netter, K. Fred
Neu, Werner F.
Neuberger, Leo
Neuburger, Kurt
Neuhaus, Kurt

Neuman, Ernst
Neumann, Fred S.
Neumann, Joseph
Neumann, Kurt
Neuss, Henry
Neuwirth, David O.
New, Alfred
Newman, Ralph G.
Newton, Charles M.
Newton, Harvey P.
Niebergall, Fred
Nightingale, Alfred
Nilson, Nils C.
Nitka, Rolf Udo
Noether, Gottfried E.
Noller, Walter A.
Nordlinger, Walter
Norman, Henry J.
Norman, Werner H.
Norring, Fred S.
Norton, Henry
Nossbaum, John J.
Nothmann, Rudolf S.
Nova, Fritz
Noymer, Ernest A. A.
Nussbaum, Eric
Nussbaum, Fritz S.
Nussbaum, Norman
Nussbaum, Ralph
Oberhauser, Anton
Oberlaender, Bernhard
Oberlander, Henry J.
Odendahl, Ferdinand K.
Oechsle, Hans P.
Oelze, Carl W.
Ohlrogge, Frederick
Ohringer, Joachim
Olden, Edwin G.
Opel, Kaspar F. M.
Oppenheim, Felix
Oppenheim, Harold A.
Oppenheim, Larry L.
Oppenheim, Leopold
Oppenheim, Ludwig T.

Oppenheim, Rudolph
Oppenheimer, Alfred
Oppenheimer, Arnold F.
Oppenheimer, Fred M.
Oppenheimer, Gerard
Oppenheimer, Gideon H.
Oppenheimer, Jules O.
Oppenheimer, Max
Oppenheimer, Werner F.
Orbach, Henry
Ortmann, Erik J.
Oster, Harry
Oster, Joseph
Ostwald, Arnold
Ottenbacher, Rudolph
Otto, Frank P.
Otto, Herbert A.
Otto, Ingolf H. E.
Otto, John P.
Owen, William J.
Paepcke, Eric
Palm, Herbert L.
Papiermeister, Joseph
Pappenheimer, Claus
Parker, Victor
Patheiger, Frederick C.
Paul, Alfred
Pawlak, Hans A.
Pawlowski, Reinhold K.
Pecoroni, John M.
Peisak, Herbert A.
Peisker, Herbert E.
Penham, Daniel F.
Perls, Frank R.
Perratone, Pierre L.
Peters, Werner M.
Petsch, Rigoletto
Peuler, Heinz O.
Pfeifer, Robert D.
Picard, Claude M.
Pick, Gerard
Pilz, Walter P.
Pinner, Karl R.
Piper, Henry C. S.

Plaut, Albert S.
Plotke, Gunther Jerry
Podhorzer, Werner H.
Podolski, Gerald A.
Pokel, Ernest A.
Polia, John A.
Popper, Alfred
Portje, Paul R.
Pos, Edgar J.
Posen, Warner
Posner, Paul H.
Preminger, Alexander
Pressburger, Rudolf
Preuss, Peter P.
Pringsheim, Peter E.
Rabold, Karl H.
Racker, Wilfred H.
Rainier, Michael R.
Rall, Arthur
Randon, Claus P.
Ranis, Ludwig
Ranke, Hans O.
Rapp, Walter
Rapp, Walter H.
Rauner, Edgar L.
Rawson, Ralph
Rebhan, Salo
Reck, Max F.
Reed, Curt
Reed, Walter E.
Regensteiner, Max O.
Reher, Sven H.
Reiche, Ludwig P.
Reinach, Carl K.
Reinemund, Otto B.
Reinhardt, George
Reinhold, Herman
Reinsberg, Harry
Reitzes, Dietrich C.
Remak, John H.
Renberg, Guenther
Rentner, Gerhard A.
Reuther, John A.
Reynolds, Edgar M.

Rhee, Lawrence L.
Rheinstein, Ludwig
Rice, Hans Gustav
Rice, Harry H.
Richards, Robert W.
Richter, Ernest F.
Richter, Frank K.
Richter, Fred P.
Richter, Kurt M.
Riedel, Rudie
Riedle, Walter
Riemer, Hanns J.
Ries, Ernest M.
Ries, George
Riesenfeld, Ernest D.
Rieser, William H.
Ripp, Herbert
Rittmann, William
Robiczek, Henry A.
Robinow, Franz G. W.
Robinow, Wolfgang F.
Roche, Paul C.
Rockson, John George
Rodell, Fred
Rodell, Jerome W.
Roder, William E.
Rodes, John E.
Rodes, Toby E.
Roetter, Dietrich O. K.
Rogers, Theodore
Rogge, Herman
Rohlffs, Bruno O.
Rohrmann, Charles F.
Romeiss, Erwin J.
Ronald, William P.
Roos, Eric
Ropshaw, Fernando E.
Rose, Werner
Rosenberg, Albert G.
Rosenberg, Howard
Rosenberger, William R.
Rosenfeld, Herbert
Rosengart, Erwin
Rosenhaupt, Hans W.

Rosenow, Kurt
Rosenstern, Franz J.
Rosenstern, Klaus
Rosenthal, Ernest
Rosenthal, Felix R.
Rosenthal, Fred J.
Rosenthal, Rudy E.
Rosenwald, Eric
Rosenwald, Fred
Rosenwald, Henry M.
Rosenwald, Henry S.
Ross, Alfred
Ross, Eric F.
Ross, Gus M.
Ross, Harry A.
Rostock, Gunther H.
Roth, Herman
Roth, Joseph
Rothman, John
Rothschild, Adolf
Rothschild, Ernst L.
Rothschild, Fred
Rothschild, Richard
Rothschild, Robert G.
Rothschild, Walter
   (31052413)
Rothschild, Walter
   (33719491)
Rothschild, Walter H.
Rotszyld, Stephan S.
Rowe, Fred M.
Rowen, Fritz
Ruben, Ernest
Rudas, Hans J.
Rueggeberg, Werner
Ruelf, Fred
Ruhrold, Carl H.
Rundt, Stefan J.
Rusch, Peter J.
Sailer, William J.
Sakheim, George A.
Salm, Peter
Salman, Aron
Salomon, Ernest

Salomon, Martin
Salzmann, Raphael H.
Sampson, Alfred H.
Samuel, Henry A.
Sander, Kurt
Sander, Nicholas H.
Sanderman, Fred A.
Sanders, Eric A.
Sanders, Ernest H.
Sands, Edgar W.
Sarstedt, Frederick W.
Saunder, Jacques J.
Saur, Francis A.
Sawady, Herman
Schaal, Henry D.
Schacht, Joachim
Schaefer, Gerard
Schaefer, Howard
Schaefer, Jack H.
Schaefer, Robert G.
Schaeffer, Theodore W.
Schafer, Karl H.
Schafer, Mark S.
Schaper, Ernest
Schardt, Henry P.
Scharmer, Walter J.
Scheeper, Helmuth H.
Scheerschmidt, Gunter
Schefler, Theodore
Scheper, Walther
Scheuer, Paul J.
Scheuer, William S.
Scheuffle, Hans F.
Schick, Leonhard
Schieren, Kurt
Schiff, Thomas
Schild, Martin
Schildmann, Henry
Schilling, Falko M.
Schindler, Frederick N.
Schindler, Herbert
Schlanger, Alfred H.
Schlauersbach, Adam
Schleich, Henry G.

Schlesinger, Bernd G.
Schlesinger, Eric M.
Schlesinger, Gerald
Schlesinger, Herbert
Schlesinger, Manfred
Schlesinger, Thomas O.
Schlieper, Gerrit
Schloemp, Bruno G. W.
Schloss, Bert P.
Schluesselberg, Henry
Schmahl, Horace W.
Schmid, Hans W.
Schmidt, Bruno W.
Schmidt, George C.
Schmidt, Gerhardt R.
Schmidt, Gerlot W.
Schmidt, Walter L.
Schmitt, Hans A.
Schnaittacher, Fritz
Schneider, John F.
Schocken, Theodore
Schoeman, Walter G.
Schoeppler, Otto, Jr.
Schollmeyer, Kurt
Schonbach, Leonard
Schott, Werner S.
Schottenhamel, Max P.
Schrader, Guenther A.
Schrager, Howard
Schreier, William
Schrenzel, Eugene P.
Schroeder, Dietrich
Schuerlein, Karl B.
Schuessler, Fred
Schultze, Friedrich W.
Schulz, Thomas F.
Schulze, Henry
Schumann, Reinhold S.
Schurich, Felix C.
Schuster, Henry
Schutzman, Julius
Schwab, Alfred
Schwab, Helmut F.
Schwab, Henry

Schwabe, Erwin
Schwalbe, John
Schwalm, Horst R.
Schwartz, Frank
Schwartz, John
Schwarz, Albert B.
Schwarzer, William W.
Schwarzkopf, Bernhard
Schwarzkopf, Erich
Schwarzwaelder, Dietrich
Schwenk, Walter
Schwilling, Leo F.
Schwisow, George
Scolney, Walter J.
Seaback, Horace R.
Sears, Henry
Seckel, Paul B.
Seemann, Henry W.
Seewald, Walter J.
Seidel, Manfred F.
Seidlin, Oskar
Seidlitz, Walter K.
Seligmann, Hermann
Seligson, Walter R.
Sell, Carl M.
Selling, Martin I.
Selton, Walter J.
Semon, Gerard A.
Seymour, Earl F.
Sharon, Gerhard S.
Shaw, Gerald
Shearer, Paul S.
Sheeman, Herbert F.
Sheldon, Henry J.
Shellenberg, Robert N.
Sheridan, Fred
Sherman, Charles L. S.
Sherman, Howard
Shickman, Herman D.
Shotland, Alex E.
Shyburgh, John A.
Sichel, Kurt
Sichel, Rudolf D.
Siegel, Carl A.

Siegert, Henry G.

Siegmann, Heinz O.

Siegmann, Henry V.

Siemer, Heinrich B.

Sieradzki, Max

Siesel, Max

Siesel, Theodor

Sietas, Erich J.

Sievers, Henry

Silberberg, David D.

Sill, Waldemar R. H.

Silten, Max H.

Silton, Gerald G.

Simon, Ernest

Simon, Ernst

Simon, George A.

Simon, Helmut A.

Simon, Hermann E.

Simon, Martin S.

Simon, Walter M.

Simon, Werner T.

Simon, William

Sinauer, Ernst M.

Singer, Sidney

Sinzheimer, Hans S.

Sippel, Gerhardt J.

Skolnik, Harold T.

Skolnik, James I.

Skovron, Alfred

Slade, John H.

Smietana, Joel

Smith, Karl G.

Smith, William

Soberheim, Rudolf B.

Soldinger, Herman

Solmssen, Harold K.

Somers, Gerald

Somers, Hans P.

Somers, John R.

Sommer, Richard

Sondheim, Werner

Sorgatz, Gustav A.

Sowa, Otto

Spear, Hans N.

Speer, Klaus

Speiser, Theodore

Speyer, Gerard W.

Spiegel, Henry W.

Spiegel, Victor

Spiessmacher, Carl F.

Spindler, Fritz

Spiro, Herbert J.

Spitzer, Robert W.

Sponholz, Kuno A.

Spritzer, Hermann

Sproesser, Nils A.

Sprung, Albert

Stanton, Henry E.

Stark, Werner E.

Stave, Gunter R.

Stechert, Dietrich G.

Steen, Ernst

Steen, William J.

Stefen, William

Stein, Bert

Stein, Joseph

Stein, Kurt J.

Steinacher, Gerald F.

Steinberg, Bert Herbert

Steinberg, Gunther

Steiner, Adolf

Steiner, Carl T.

Steiner, Henry H.

Steinert, Carl E.

Steinfeld, Gerhard I.

Steinfeld, Manfred

Steinhardt, Walter

Steinhauer, Julius

Steinmann, Paul W.

Stern, Fred

Stern, Guy

Stern, Joe

Stern, Lothar

Stern, Otto

Stern, Richard Heinz

Stern, Siegfried

Stern, Walter

Stern, William R.

Sternberg, Frank

Sternberg, Frederick

Sternberg, Ralph

Sternberg, Robert H.

Sternweiler, Henry W.

Steude, Robert H.

Stevens (Stern), John M.

Stevens, Fred

Stevens, William Henry

Stiefel, Walter S.

Stiens, Carl H.

Stobe, Rudolph

Stoll, Charles

Stone, Frederick A.

Stone, Sidney

Stone, Walter

Storbeck, Herbert J.

Storbeck, Herman C.

Strange, Joseph L., Jr.

Strate, Paul H.

Straus, Irwin Y.

Straus, Wolf J.

Strauss, Alfred

Strauss, Artie

Strauss, Ernest N.

Strauss, Ernst S.

Strauss, Frederick L.

Strauss, Helmut

Strauss, Jack

Strauss, Jack L.

Strauss, Karl Henry

Strauss, Karl W.

Strauss, Max A.

Strauss, Walter

Strauss, Walter A.

Strauss, Walter Benno

Strauss, Walter L.

Strohmeier, Alfons J.

Strombach, Karl H.

Stromer, Adolf F.

Strutt, John

Sturm, Peter K.

Suda, Felix

Sudekum, Lothar

Suesser, Alfons
Suessmann, Emanuel
Sukey, Alfred G.
Sullivan, William M.
Sundheimer, Theodore
Swert, Alfred J.
Sylvester, Joseph E.
Taenzer, Erwin
Tannenberg, Richard J.
Tannhauser, John U.
Tarne, Eric P.
Tarsey (Tarschiisch),
    Alexandre R.
Taylor, Ransom T.
Tebrich, Harvey H.
Tebrich, John
Teichner, Hans H.
Teika, Ernest
Teitelbaum, Harry
Thalhammer, Joseph
Thees, Alfred N.
Theune, Herbert H.
Thiemecke, Gert
Thierfelder, Helmut E.
Thoma, August
Thomforde, Henry J.
Thompson, Sidney G.
Thormann, Gerard C.
Thormann, Wolfgang E.
Thron, Wolfgang J.
Tidemann, Karl W.
Tiemann, Arnold H.
Tislowitz, Ernst L. K.
Tobias, George
Toennies, Heinz A.
Traugott, Fritz J.
Trautmannsdorf, Francis
Trautwein, Willy C.
Trave, Horst B.
Travers, Frederick F.
Trefousse, Hans L.
Trepp, Samuel
Treumann, Walter
Trier, Edgar L.

Troendle, Ernest
Tross, Ralph G.
Trytell, Walter W.
Tuch, Hans N.
Tuteur, Fred Leon
Ubben, John Harms
Udelsman, Felix
Udhardt, Paul O.
Uhlig, Richard W.
Ulmer, Hans H.
Unger, Sam M.
Unterman, Israel
Urbach, Rudolf
Ury, Richard F.
Valic, Eugene V.
Valtin, Fred W.
Valtin, Ralph
Van Dyk, Fred
Van Eyck, Peter
Van Hollander, Adolph
Van Loon, Gerard Willem
Veitinger, Helmuth R.
Vendig, Alfred
Venohr, William A.
Vicas, George A.
Vodin, Ulrich G.
Voehl, Joseph
Vogel, Alfred J.
Vogel, Berthold
Vogel, Hans W.
Vogel, Harold H.
Vogel, Werner H.
Vogelstein, Wolfgang H.
Vogl, Adelbert
Vogt, William
Voigt, Erich G.
Vollert, Carl A. B.
Vollweiler, Henry V.
Von Bothmer, Bernhard
Von Eckardt, Wolfgang
Von Elbe, Joachim H. E.
Von Fritz, Peter K.
Von Klemperer, Franz
Von Klemperer, Klemens

Von Kohorn, Henry
Von Mach-Brandt,
    William
Von Schlieben, Hans G.
Voss, Ernest
Wachtel, Hans J.
Wagner, Edmund I.
Wagner, Erich R.
Wagner, John
Wagner, Walter W.
Wahl, John R.
Walber, John W.
Wald, Max
Wallace, Ingvar A.
Wallach, Ernest
    (35144719)
Wallach, Ernest
    (36850011)
Wallach, Frederick
Wallach, Kurt E.
Wallenberg, Hans
Wallenberg, Lesser H.
Waller, Herbert H.
Waller, Walter J.
Walter, Werner G.
Wanner, Maximilian
Ward, Curtis G.
Waring, Heaton M., Jr
Warner, Adolphe J.
Warner, Winston P.
Warnke, Uwe Jens C.
Wartenberg, George H.
Wartenberg, Rolf
Wassermann, Felix E.
Wassermann, Kurt
Watson, Conrad J.
Weber, Emil H.
Weber, George
Weber, John F.
Weber, Richard G. S.
Wege, Hans F.
Weidenreich, Peter H.
Weil, Eric L.
Weil, Ernest E.

Weil, Ernest L.
Weil, Joseph
Weil, Rolfe
Weiler, Albert G.
Weimersheimer, Samuel
Weinberg, Lothar L.
Weinberg, Mendel
Weinberger, Siegbert J.
Weingartner, Henry W.
Weinheimer, Herman
Weinschel, George
Weinstein, Charles G.
Weis, Anton
Weis, Arthur
Weiss, Arnold H.
Weiss, Edward A.
Weiss, Rudi
Weiss, William W.
Weissbart, Franz J.
Weitz, John H. W.
Weitzenkorn, Paul J.
Wells, Henry J.
Wenzel, George
Werder, Horst H.
Werner, Gunther A.
Werner, Hans
Werner, Victor E.
Wertheim, Alfred
Wertheim, Joseph H.
Wertheimer, Frederick
Wertheimer, Manfred
Werther, Erwin W.
Wesley, Fred
Wesley, Max G.
Wessely, Harold P.
Westermeier, Franz X.

Weston, Charles
Weyl, Peter K.
Wheeler, Frank M.
Wiederhold, Hermann
Wieners, Joseph F.
Wietepsky, Erwin
Wild, Ignatz
Wilkow, William
Willms, John H.
Willner, Philipp
Wilton, John H.
Winchester, Leonard J.
Windmoeller, Henry F.
Winkler, Richard E.
Winkler, Willi K.
Winn, Eric E.
Winter, Eric M.
Winter, Joseph A.
Winzen, John P.
Wirth, Otto
Wirth, Paul O.
Wirth, Werner K.
Witt, Fritz
Wittig, Werner R.
Wittkugel, Karl E.
Woerner, Eric A.
Wohl, Henry
Wohlfeiler, Max
Wolf, Frederick
Wolf, Gunther J. M.
Wolf, Harold H.
Wolf, Henry J.
Wolf, Ludwig
Wolf, Peter M.
Wolfe, Warner M.
Wolfes, Gerald H.

Wolff, Fred G.
Wolff, Hans M.
Wolff, Norbert
Wolff, Peter L.
Wolff, Walter C.
Wolff, Walter G.
Wolfson, Henry A.
Wormser, Stephen P.
Wortman, Lothar
Wunder, William O.
Wynder, Ernest L.
Yost, Henry John
Young, George
Young, Henry O.
Young, Martin
Zacharias, Heinz
Zahler, Max
Zander, Fred R.
Zanders, Herman
Zappler, Murray
Zatzkis, Joseph
Zeile, Robert C.
Zeyen, Otto G.
Ziegler, Gus
Ziegler, William
Ziegler, William F.
Zimmer, Bernard J.
Zimmer, William J.
Zimmerman, Kurt
Zinner, Philip
Zorek, John H.
Zucker, Adolph D.
Zumbroich, Herman, Jr.
Zuntz, Michael
Zweig, Gunter
Zweig, Michael H. W.

Fifty Ritchie Boys who died in World War II

Andersen, Peter H.
Andrae, Robert W.
Arsenault, Raymond A.
Balaber, Sidney
Bartal, Leslie
Baum, Gerhard
Benoit, John B.
Bentley, Robert D.
Collette, Jack Travis
Corneliussen, Axel E.
Demetriou, Fotios D.
Des Marets, Herbert N.
Dussaq, Reginald
Emanuel, Nick C.
Ermolieff, Nicholas
Foth, Albert E.
Friede, Dittmar H.

Gaertner, Bernard
Goeltzer, Wolf D.
Gottlieb, Fred
Gould, Robert G.
Gunther, Walter, Jr.
Hasto, Victor J.
Held, Abraham
Herring, Albert C., Jr.
Jacobs, Kurt R.
Kalamaras, Vassilios J.
Kiever, Philip M.
Knock, Edward D.
Kupferschmidt, Alfred
Lacour, John M.
Lando, Lewis L., III
Larick, Walter H., Jr.
Leveille, Charles

Maas, Henry J.
Mandelbaum, Walter
Mills, Benjamin W., Jr.
Mosbacher, Stephen S.
Peters, Peters Assad
Popper, Kurt
Robinow, Franz G. W.
Rogge, Herman
Rosenfeld, Edward L.
Rosenwald, Henry S.
Schlasinger, Larry S.
Siebert, Herbert A.
Sorbet, Reggie A.
Stippich, Walter P.
Zappler, Murray
Zumbroich, Herman, Jr.

Bibliography

Abt, Karl W. *A Few Who Made a Difference*. New York: Vantage Press, 2004.

Agar, Herbert. *The Saving Remnant: An Account of Jewish Survival*. New York: Viking Press, 1960.

Agassi, Judith Buber. *Jewish Women Prisoners of Ravensbrück: Who Were They?* Oxford, England: One World Publications, 2007.

Angress, Werner T. "Belgium: In the Field." Unpublished essay, 1945.

———. *Between Fear & Hope: Jewish Youth in the Third Reich*. New York: Columbia University Press, 1988.

———. "Early Memories." Unpublished essay, 1946.

———. *Witness to the Storm: A Jewish Journey from Nazi Berlin to the 82nd Airborne, 1920–1945*. Durnham, NC: CreateSpace, 2012.

Anzuoni, Robert P. *The All American: An Illustrated History of the 82nd Airborne Division*. Atglen, PA: Schiffer Military History, 2001.

Astor, Gerald. *A Blood-Dimmed Tide: The Battle of the Bulge by the Men Who Fought It*. New York: Donald I. Fine, 1992.

Atkinson, Rick. *The Guns at Last Light: The War in Western Europe, 1944–45*. New York: Henry Holt, 2013.

Bailey, George. *Germans: The Biography of an Obsession*. New York: Free Press, 1991.

Bard, Mitchell G. *Forgotten Victims: The Abandonment of Americans in Hitler's Camps*. Boulder, CO: Westview Press, 1994.

Bauer, Christian. *The Ritchie Boys: A Film by Christian Bauer*. Tangram Productions, 2005.

Bauer, Christian, and Rebekka Gopfert. *Die Ritchie Boys*. Hamburg, Germany: Hoffmann und Campe, 2005.

Beevor, Antony. *Ardennes 1944: The Battle of the Bulge*. New York: Viking, 2015.

——. *D-Day: The Battle for Normandy*. New York: Viking, 2009.

Bennett, David. *A Magnificent Disaster: The Failure of Market Garden, The Arnhem Operation September 1944*. Drexel Hill, PA: Casemate, 2008.

Berben, Paul. *Dachau: The Official History 1933–1945*. London: Norfolk Press, 1975.

Berenbaum, Michael. *The World Must Know: The History of the Holocaust as Told in the United States Holocaust Memorial Museum*. Boston: Little, Brown & Co., 1993.

Blair, Clay. *Ridgway's Paratroopers: The American Airborne in World War II*. New York: Harper and Row, 1985.

Blumenson, Martin. *The Patton Papers, 1940–1945*. New York: Da Capo Press, 1996.

Boesch, Paul. *Road to Huertgen Forest in Hell*. Houston, TX: Gulf Publishing, 1962.

Bradley, Omar. *A Soldier's Story*. New York: Henry Holt & Co., 1951.

Bradley, Omar, and Clair Blair. *A General's Life*. New York: Simon & Schuster, 1983.

Buber-Neuman, Margarete. *Under Two Dictators: Prisoner of Stalin and Hitler*. London: Pimlico, 2008.

Brombert, Victor. *Musings on Mortality*. Chicago: University of Chicago Press, 2013.

——. "Return to Omaha Beach." *Princeton Alumni Weekly*, Jan. 26, 2005.

——. *Trains of Thought: Memories of a Stateless Youth*. New York: W. W. Norton, 2002.

Caddick-Adams, Peter. *Snow & Steel: The Battle of the Bulge, 1944–45*. New York: Oxford University Press, 2015.

Cavender, Charles C. "The 423 in the Bulge." *The CUB*, November 1946.

——. *The Memoirs of an Old Soldier*. Unpublished.

Chamberlin, Brewster, and Marcia Feldman, eds. *The Liberation of the Nazi Concentration Camps 1945*. Washington, D.C.: U.S. Holocaust Memorial Council, 1987.

Clary, Robert. *From the Holocaust to Hogan's Heroes*. Lanham, MD: Taylor Trade Publishing, 2001.

Cohen, Roger. *Soldiers and Slaves: American POWs Trapped by the Nazis' Final Gamble*. New York: Alfred A. Knopf, 2005.

Cohn, Frederick G. *Signals: A Young Refugee's Flight from Germany in the Thirties*. Cornwall, UK: United Writers, 1990.

Cole, Hugh M. *The Ardennes: Battle of the Bulge*. Atlanta, GA: Whiteman Publishing, 2012.

Dabringhaus, Erhard. *Klaus Barbie: The Shocking Story of How the U.S. Used This Nazi War Criminal as an Intelligence Agent*. Washington, D.C.: Acropolis Books, 1984.

Davie, Maurice R. *Refugees in America: Report of the Committee for the Study of Recent Immigration from Europe*. New York: Harper & Brothers, 1947.

Dawidowicz, Lucy S. *The War Against the Jews 1933–1945*. New York: Holt, Rinehart and Winston, 1975.

Dawson, Forrest W. *Saga of the All American (82nd Airborne Division)*. Atlanta, GA: Albert Love Enterprises, 1946.

Delaforce, Patrick. *The Battle of the Bulge: Hitler's Final Gamble*. Barnsley, UK: Pen & Sword Military, 2014.

Diamant, Ann Redman, and Alfred Diamant. *Worlds Apart, Worlds United: A European-American Story—The Memoirs of Ann and Alfred Diamant*. Bloomington, IN: AuthorHouse, 2010.

Dimont, Max I. *Jews, God and History*. New York: Signet, 2004.

Dulles, Allen W. *The Craft of Intelligence: America's Legendary Spy Master on the Fundamentals of Intelligence Gathering for a Free World*. Guilford, CT: Lyons Press, 2006.

Dwork, Deborah, and Robert Jan van Pelt. *Holocaust: A History*. New York: W.W. Norton, 2002.

Edel, Leon. *The Visitable Past: A Wartime Memoir*. Honolulu: University of Hawaii Press, 2001.

Edwards, Donald A. *A Private's Diary*. Big Rapids, MI: D. A. Edwards, 1994.

Eidelman, Robert M., ed. *Ours to Fight For: American Jewish Voices from the Second World War*. New York: Museum of Jewish Heritage, 2003.

Ellis, John. *Brute Force: Allied Strategy and Tactics in the Second World War*. New York: Viking, 1990.

Farago, Ladislas. *Burn After Reading: The Espionage History of World War II*. New York: Walker and Co., 1961.

Faubus, Orval Eugene. *In This Faraway Land: A Personal Journal of Infantry Combat in World War II*. Conway, AR: River Road Press, 1971.

Feld, Nina Wolff. *Someday You Will Understand: My Father's Private World War II*. New York: Arcade Publishing, 2014.

Ferguson, Niall. *Kissinger: 1923–1968: The Idealist*. New York: Penguin Press, 2015.

Finnegan, John Patrick. *Military Intelligence*. Washington, D.C.: Center of Military History, 1998.

Fowle, Barry W., ed. *Builders and Fighters: U.S. Army Engineers in World War II*. Fort Belvoid, VA: U.S. Army Corps of Engineers, 1992.

Franklin, Joshua. "Victim Soldiers: German-Jewish Refugees in the American Armed Forces During World War II." Honors thesis, Clark University, 2006.

Frucht, Karl. *A Statement of Loss: A Survival Report*. Wien, Germany: Kremayr & Scheriau, 1992.

———. "From the American Scene: We Were a PWI Team." *Commentary*, Jan. 1, 1946.

Fry, Helen. *Churchill's German Army*. Stroud, Gloucestershire, UK: History Press, 2007.

Fry, Varian. *Surrender on Demand*. New York: Random House, 1945.

Fussell, Paul. *The Boys' Crusade: The American Infantry in Northwestern Europe, 1944–1945*. New York: Modern Library, 2003.

Gans, Manfred. *Life Gave Me a Chance*. Lulu, 2010.

Gavin, James M. *On to Berlin: Battles of an Airborne Commander 1943–46*. New York: Viking Press, 1978.

Gilbert, James L., and John P. Finnegan. *In the Shadow of the Sphinx: A History of Army Counterintelligence*. Washington, D.C.: Department of the Army, 2005.

Gilbert, Martin. *Auschwitz and the Allies: How the Allies Responded to the News of Hitler's Final Solution*. London: Michael Joseph Ltd., 1981.

———. *Kristallnacht: Prelude to Destruction*. New York: HarperCollins, 2006.

Goodwin, Doris Kearns. *No Ordinary Time: Franklin and Eleanor Roosevelt—The Home Front in World War II*. New York: Simon & Schuster, 1994.

Grange, William. *Historial Dictionary of German Literature to 1945*. Lanham, MD: Scarecrow Press, 2010.

Grossman, Atina. *Jews, Germans, and Allies: Close Encounters in Occupied Germany*. Princeton: Princeton University Press, 2007.

Habe, Hans. *A Thousand Shall Fall*. New York: Harcourt, Brace, 1941.

———. *All My Sins*. Sydney, Australia: Australasian Publishing, 1957.

Harran, Marilyn J., and John Roth. *The Holocaust Chronicle*. Lincolnwood, IL: Legacy Publishing, 2007.

Harrison, Marcie. *A Life Complete: The Journey of Manfred Steinfeld*. Privately published, 2013.

Hart, S., R. Hart, and M. Hughes. *The German Soldier in World War II*. Osceola, WI: MBI Publishing Co., 2000.

Hazan, Katy. *Rescuing Jewish Children During the Nazi Occupation: OSE Children's Homes, 1938–1945*. Paris: Somogy Editions D'Art, 2008.

Helm, Sarah. *Ravensbrück: Life and Death in Hitler's Concentration Camp for Women*. New York: Doubleday, 2014.

Heym, Stefan. *The Crusades*. Boston, MA: Little, Brown & Co., 1948.

Herzberg, Lillian Belinfante. *Stephan's Journey: A Sojourn into Freedom*. Baltimore, MD: PublishAmerica, 2003.

Hirsh, Michael. *The Liberators: America's Witnesses to the Holocaust*. New York: Bantam Books, 2010.

Hockley, Ralph M. *Freedom Is Not Free*. Houston, TX: Brockton Publishing Co., 2000.

Hodge, Deborah. *Rescuing the Children: The Story of the Kindertransport*. New York: Tundra Books, 2012.

Hofmann, George F. *The Super Sixth: History of the 6th Armored Division in World War II*. Nashville, TN: Battery Press, 2000.

Houston, Donald E. *Hell on Wheels: The 2d Armored Division*. New York: Ballantine Books, 1977.

Huston, James A. *Out of the Blue: U.S. Army Airborne Operations in World War II*. West Lafayette, IN: Purdue University Studies, 1972.

Hutt, David. *The Boy Who Wore White Stockings: From Hitler's Austria to Patton's Third Army*. Kibworth Beauchamp, UK: Matador, 2013.

Jason, Philip K., and Iris Posner. *Don't Wave Goodbye: The Children's Flight from Nazi Persecution to American Freedom.* Westport, CT: Praeger, 2004.

Jones, Alan W. "Defense of St. Vith: A History of the 106th." *The CUB,* Feb. 1948.

Jones, Alan W., Jr. "The Operations of the 423rd Infantry." Advanced Infantry Officers Course, Fort Benning, GA, 1949–1950.

Kaplan, Marion A. *Between Dignity and Despair: Jewish Life in Nazi Germany.* New York: Oxford University Press, 1998.

Karras, Steven. *The Enemy I Knew: German Jews in the Allied Military in World War II.* Minneapolis, MN: Zenith Press, 2009.

Kaufman, Isidor. *American Jews in World War II, Vols. I and II.* New York: Dial Press, 1947.

Kirsch, Jonathan. *The Short, Strange Life of Herschel Grynszpa: A Boy Avenger, a Nazi Diplomat, and a Murder in Paris.* New York: Liveright Publishing, 2013.

Klee, Ernst, Willi Dressen, and Volker Riess. *"The Good Old Days": The Holocaust as Seen by Its Perpetrators and Bystanders.* New York: Free Press, 1988.

Koestler, Arthur. *Scum of the Earth.* London: Eland, 1991.

Krammer, Arnold. *Nazi Prisoners of War in America.* New York: Stein and Day, 1979.

Koch, Oscar W., with Robert G. Hays. *G-2 Intelligence for Patton.* Philadelphia: Whitmore Publishing, 1971.

Kollander, Patricia, with John O'Sullivan. *"I Must Be Part of This War": A German American's Fight Against Hitler and Nazism.* New York: Fordham University Press, 2005.

Lagano, William J. *Ernst: Escaping the Horrors of the Nazi Occupation.* CreateSpace, 2010.

Laqueur, Walter. *Generation Exodus: The Fate of Young Jewish Refugees from Nazi Germany.* Hanover, NY: Brandeis University Press, 2001.

Lang-Slattery, Kathryn. *Immigrant Soldier: The Story of a Ritchie Boy.* Pacific Bookworks, 2014.

Langworth, Richard, ed. *Churchill by Himself: The Definitive Collection of Quotations.* New York: PublicAffairs, 2008.

Le Blanc, George J. *History of Military Intelligence Training at Camp Ritchie,* 4 vols. War Department General Staff, 1945.

Lerner, Maximilian. *Flight and Return: A Memoir of World War II.* CreateSpace, 2013.

Lewis, David, prod. and dir. *Manfred Steinfeld: Victim and Victor.* Documentary film, 2002.

Loeser, Hans F. *Hans's Story.* Lincoln, NE: iUniverse, 2007.

MacDonald, Charles B. *A Time for Trumpets: The Untold Story of the Battle of the Bulge.* New York: William Morrow, 1985.

Mandler, George. *Interesting Times: An Encounter with the 20th Century.* Mahwah, NJ: Lawrence Erlbaum Associates, 2002.

McManus, John C. *The Americans at Normandy: The Summer of 1944—The American War from the Normandy Beaches to Falaise.* New York: Forge, 2004.

McManus, John C. *The Dead and Those About to Die: The Big Red One at Omaha Beach*. New York: NAL Caliber, 2014.

Megellas, James. *All the Way to Berlin: A Paratrooper at War in Europe*. New York: Ballantine Books, 2003.

Melchior, Ib. *Case by Case: A U.S. Army Counterintelligence Agent in World War II*. Novato, CA: Presidio Press, 1993.

Military Intelligence Division, War Department. *Order of Battle of the German Army, February 1944*. Uckfield, UK: Naval and Military Press, 2009.

Miller, Edward G. *A Dark Bloody Ground: The Hürtgen Forest and the Roer River Dams, 1944–45*. College Station, TX: Texas A&M University Press, 1995.

Moore, Deborah Dash. *GI Jews: How World War II Changed a Generation*. Cambridge, MA: Harvard University Press, 2004.

Morse, Arthur D. *While Six Million Died: A Chronicle of American Apathy*. New York: Random House, 1968.

Nagorski, Andrew. *Hitlerland: American Eyewitnesses to the Nazi Rise to Power*. New York: Simon & Schuster, 2012.

Neitzel, Sonke, and Harald Welzer. *Soldaten: On Fighting, Killing and Dying*. New York: Alfred A. Knopf, 2012.

Neurath, Paul Martin. *The Society of Terror: Inside the Dachau and Buchenwald Concentration Camps*. Boulder, CO: Paradigm Publishers, 2005.

Nibley, Hugh, and Alex Nibley. *Sergeant Nibley: Memories of an Unlikely Screaming Eagle*. Salt Lake City, UT: Shadow Mountain, 2006.

Nordyke, Phil. *Put Us Down in Hell: The Combat History of the 508th Parachute Infantry Regiment in World War II*. Historical Ventures, 2012.

Oppenheimer, Max, Jr. "Camp Ritchie and American Military Combat Intelligence." U.S. Army Intelligence Center, Fort Huachuca, AZ, n.d.

———. *An Innocent Yank at Home Abroad: Footnotes to History 1922–1945*. Manhattan, KS: Sunflower University Press, 2000.

Parker, Danny S. *Battle of the Bulge: Hitler's Ardennes Offensive, 1944–45*. Philadelphia: Combined Books, 1991.

Penslar, Derek J. *Jews and the Military*. Princeton, NJ: Princeton University Press, 2013.

Perl, William R. *Operation Action: Rescue from the Holocaust*. New York: Frederick Ungar Publishing, 1979.

Persons, Benjamin S. *Relieved of Command*. Manhattan, KS: Sunflower University Press, 1997.

Petterchak, Janice. *A Legacy of Style: The Story of Shelby Williams Industries*. Rochester, IL: Legacy Press, 2000.

Pogue, Forrest C. *U.S. Army in World War II: European Theater of Operations*. Washington, D.C.: Department of the Army, 1954.

Pressman, Steven. *50 Children: One Ordinary American Couple's Extraordinary Rescue Mission into the Heart of Nazi Germany*. New York: Harper, 2014.

Render, Chuck, and Frank M. Brandstetter. *Brandy: Portrait of an Intelligence Officer*. Oakland, OR: Red Anvil Press, 2007.

Riva, Maria. *Marlene Dietrich*. New York: Alfred A. Knopf, 1992.

Rooney, Andy. *My War*. New York: Random House, 1995.

Rosbottom, Ronald C. *When Paris Went Dark: The City of Light Under German Occupation, 1940–1944*. New York: Little, Brown & Co., 2014.

Ryan, Cornelius. *A Bridge Too Far*. New York: Simon & Schuster, 1974.

———. *The Longest Day*. New York: Simon & Schuster, 1959.

Sayen, John. *Battle Orders: U.S. Army Infantry Divisions 1944–45*. New York: Osprey Publishing, 2007.

Sayer, Ian, and Douglas Botting. *America's Secret Army: The Untold Story of the Counter Intelligence Corps*. London: Grafton Books, 1989.

Schneider, Gertrude. *Journey into Terror: The Story of the Riga Ghetto*. New York: Ark House, 1979.

Schreiber, Gerhard, Bernd Stegemann, and Detlef Vogel. *Germany and the Second World War, Volume III*. Oxford: Clarendon Press, 1995.

Schwabe, Klaus. "American Occupation Experiences in Aachen before Germany's Surrender." Aachen (Germany) Historical Society: Special publication of the *Aachener Geschichtsvereins*, 2000.

Scrase, David, and Wolfgang Mieder, eds. *The Holocaust Personal Accounts*. University of Vermont Center for Holocaust Studies, 2001.

Selling, Martin I. *With Rancor and Compassion: The Memoirs of a Jew Who Thought He Was a German*. New York: Vantage Press, 2003.

Sevareid, Eric. *Not So Wild a Dream*. New York: Knopf, 1946.

Steinfeld, Manfred. *Awards & Memories 1938–2013*. Privately published, 2013.

Stern, Fritz. *Five Germanys I Have Known*. New York: Farrar, Straus and Giroux, 2006.

Stern, Guy. "Fifty Years Before the Class." Address given at Wayne State University, December 7, 2002.

———. Memoir in progress, unpublished (2016).

———. "The Americanisation of Günther," in *The Legacy of Exile*, ed. Deborah Vietor-Engländer. Oxford, England: Blackwell Publishers Ltd, 1998.

———. "His Eminence and the Pupil," in Michael Braun and Birgit H. Lermen, eds. *Man erzählt Geschichten, formt die Wahrheit: Thomas Mann—Deutscher, Europäer, Weltbürge*. Frankfurt am Main; New York: P. Lang, 2003.

———. "In the Service of American Intelligence: German-Jewish Exiles in the War Against Hitler," *Leo Baeck Institute Year Book XXXVII*. London: Secker & Warburg, 1992.

———. *Marlene Dietrich: My Chance Encounters with a Movie Star*. Cincinnati, OH: University of Cincinnati, 2002.

———. *Oh What a Funny (?) War*. Cincinnati, OH: University of Cincinnati, 2005.

Strong, Kenneth. *Intelligence at the Top: The Recollections of an Intelligence Officer*. New York: Doubleday, 1969.

Thomas, Shipley. *S-2 in Action*. Harrisburg, PA: Military Service Publishing, 1940.

Toland, John. *Battle: The Story of the Bulge*. New York: Random House, 1959.

Van Cleve, Thomas Curtis. *Observations and Experiences of a Military Intelligence Officer in Two World Wars*. Edited by John D. Davis. Potts Point Books, 2005.

Vietor-Englander, Deborah, ed. *The Legacy of Exile: Lives, Letters, Literature.* Oxford, UK: Blackwell Publishers, 1999.

von Elbe, Joachim. *Witness to History: A Refugee from the Third Reich Remembers.* Madison, WI: German-American Cultural Society, 1988.

von Klemperer, Klemens. *German Resistance Against Hitler.* Oxford: Oxford University Press, 1992.

Wachsmann, Nikolaus. *KL: A History of the Nazi Concentration Camps.* New York: Farrar, Straus and Giroux, 2015.

Walters, Vernon A. *Silent Missions.* New York: Doubleday, 1978.

Warschauer, Bernard. "The Exodus." Unpublished essay, 1940.

Webb, Chris, and Michal Chocholaty. *The Treblinka Death Camp: History, Biographies, Remembrance.* Stuttgart, Germany: Ibidem Press, 2014.

Weintraub, Stanley. *11 Days in December: Christmas at the Bulge, 1944.* New York: Free Press, 2006.

Wheeler, Steven B. "Bleialf Is Overun." www.battleofthebulgememories.be, 2012.

Whiting, Charles. *The March on London: Covert Operations in the Battle of the Bulge, December 1944.* London: Leo Cooper, 1992.

Whitlock, Flint. *The Beasts of Buchenwald: Karl & Ilse Koch, Human-Skin Lampshades, and the War-Crimes Trial of the Century.* Brule, WI: Cable Publishing, 2011.

Wiesel, Elie. *Night.* New York: Hill & Wang, 1960.

Winik, Jay. *1944: FDR and the Year That Changed History.* New York: Simon & Schuster, 2015.

Wyman, David S. *Paper Walls: America and the Refugee Crisis, 1938–1941.* Boston: University of Massachusetts Press, 1985.

Index

Page numbers in *italics* indicate illustrations.

BOOKS BY BRUCE HENDERSON

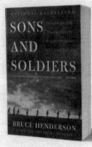

SONS AND SOLDIERS
The Untold Story of the Jews Who Escaped the Nazis and Returned with the U.S. Army to Fight Hitler

Joining the ranks of *Unbroken*, *Band of Brothers*, and *Boys in the Boat*, the little-known saga of young German Jews, dubbed The Ritchie Boys, who fled Nazi Germany in the 1930s, came of age in America, and returned to Europe at enormous personal risk as members of the U.S. Army to play a key role in the Allied victory. *Sons and Soldiers* is an epic story of heroism, courage, and patriotism that will not soon be forgotten.

RESCUE AT LOS BAÑOS
The Most Daring Prison Camp Raid of World War II

Rescue at Los Baños tells the story of a remarkable group of prisoners—whose courage and fortitude helped them overcome hardship, deprivation, and cruelty—and of the young American soldiers and Filipino guerrillas who risked their lives to save them. The Los Baños raid was hailed, years later, by General Colin Powell: "I doubt that any airborne unit in the world will ever be able to rival the Los Baños prison raid."

HERO FOUND
The Greatest POW Escape of the Vietnam War

In 1966, German-born POW Dieter Dengler proved to be no ordinary prisoner. With a heroic impulse to free not only himself but also other POWs—some of whom had been held for years—Dengler returned to his ship after six months of captivity—emaciated and ravaged with tropical maladies, but alive and free. Bruce Henderson, who served with Dengler aboard the USS *Ranger*, offers this riveting account of Dengler's story.

DOWN TO THE SEA
An Epic Story of Naval Disaster and Heroism in World War II

Beginning on December 7, 1941, Bruce Henderson follows four U.S. Navy ships and their crews in the Pacific until their day of reckoning three years later with a far different enemy: a deadly typhoon. Drawing on extensive interviews with nearly every living survivor, many of their rescuers, families of lost sailors, personal letters, and diaries, Henderson offers the most thorough account to date of one of the greatest naval dramas of World War II.